The Illusion of
Presidential Government

Also of Interest

† Available in hardcover and paperback.

The Illusion of Presidential Government

*edited by Hugh Heclo
and Lester M. Salamon*

*Westview Press / Boulder, Colorado
Published in Cooperation with the
National Academy of Public Administration*

Copyright © 1981 by the National Academy of Public Administration

Published in 1981 in the United States of America by
  Westview Press, Inc.
  5500 Central Avenue
  Boulder, Colorado 80301
  Frederick A. Praeger, Publisher

Library of Congress Cataloging in Publication Data
Main entry under title:
The illusion of presidential government.
  "Most of the chapters in this volume were originally prepared during the spring and summer of 1980 for use by a panel on presidential management convened by the National Academy of Public Administration"—Pref.
  Includes index.
  1. Presidents—United States—Addresses, essays, lectures. I. Heclo, Hugh. II. Salamon, Lester M. III. National Academy of Public Administration.
JK516.I43   353.03'1   81-10343
ISBN 0-86531-248-6   AACR2
ISBN 0-86531-249-4 (pbk.)

Printed and bound in the United States of America

Contents

Tables

Preface

Nothing about the presidency is as simple as it seems. How could it be? The office is more than a man but less than a fixed institution. It is a place where a never-ending stream of transient personalities are expected to perform vital, permanent functions for the rest of government, where an uncommon person is expected to act on the concerns of common people, to lead without being power-hungry, to manage without seeming manipulative, to speak for a nation that never expresses itself with one voice. The presidency is an altar erected by democratic opinion, sometimes for worship, sometimes for human sacrifice.

Amid this complex turmoil, the work of government goes on. Whatever one's likes or dislikes about a particular president, our system of government needs an effective presidency. But what does "effective presidency" mean? Can we really be expected to separate our understanding and appraisal of the office from our feelings about the "him" (and probably someday "her") who happens to be there? This book argues that we can. Each chapter addresses the problem of presidential effectiveness by looking at the major operations of the modern presidency—from struggles with Congress for control of administrative detail to problems of managing the economy and national security.

Work on this book began in the fall of 1979, before the Iranian hostage crisis and at a time of severe and widespread loss of confidence in the Carter presidency. It ended a month after the attempted assassination of Ronald Reagan amid an ebullient presidential honeymoon. No one is likely to discount the importance of such events. What *is* likely to be misperceived are the longer-term, underlying processes of government that constrain and shape the meaning of such dramatic events when it comes down to the day-to-day reality of governing. It is to this broader view that the chapters in this book are directed. If the authors and editors have succeeded, the analyses should have greater staying power than the presidential headaches and honeymoons of the last few years.

Most of the chapters in this volume were originally prepared during the spring and summer of 1980 for use by a panel on presidential management convened by the National Academy of Public Administration. They were then updated in March of 1981. For ourselves and on behalf of the other authors we would like to thank the members of the National Academy for their support in this work. Our special thanks go to George Esser, the president of the Academy, and his assistant, Jeff Jacobs, who made the entire project possible. Time and other pressures were never allowed to interfere with the Academy's initial directive that we should present and publish our own views, based on the most objective information available. We have tried to follow those standards throughout this volume.

At the end of this book we have included the final report of the National Academy of Public Administration's Panel on Presidential Management. As the views expressed in the body of the book are those of the individual contributors, so the report represents the views of the panel responsible for its preparation. Given the complexity of the subject, it is not surprising that different people at times come to different conclusions. But in a larger sense, the same viewpoint has animated the entire enterprise: to see the managerial role of the president steadily and as a whole, without illusions.

Hugh Heclo
Lester M. Salamon
Washington, D.C.

The Contributors

I. M. Destler is a senior associate at the Carnegie Endowment for International Peace, where he directs the research project on executive-congressional relations. He is the author of *Presidents, Bureaucrats, and Foreign Policy* (1972) and *Making Foreign Economic Policy* (1980). He earned his Ph.D. at the Woodrow Wilson School, Princeton University.

Louis Fisher joined the Congressional Research Service of the Library of Congress in 1970, after having taught for three years at Queens College. He holds a doctorate in political science from the New School for Social Research. His publications include *President and Congress* (1972), *Presidential Spending Power* (1975), *The Constitution Between Friends* (1978), and *The Politics of Shared Power* (1981).

Hugh Heclo is professor of government at Harvard University. A former senior fellow at the Brookings Institution, he earned his Ph.D. at Yale and is author of *A Government of Strangers: Executive Politics in Washington* (1977).

John Helmer was the former chief of the Urban and Community Impact Analysis unit of the Office of Management and Budget. He has served on President Carter's Reorganization Project and as an adviser to the World Bank and the United Nations, as well as to governments in Australia, Pakistan, and Sri Lanka. He received his Ph.D. from Harvard and is the author of several books, including *The Politics of Advice* (forthcoming).

G. Calvin Mackenzie is a professor of government at Colby College. He holds a Ph.D. in government from Harvard University, and he has worked for both houses of Congress and for the Department of Defense. He is author of *The Politics of Presidential Appointments* (1980) and editor of *The House at Work* (1981).

Anna Kasten Nelson has been a member of the George Washington University History Department since 1972 and is currently the director of the

History and Public Policy Program. A former staff member of the Public Documents Commission, she is the editor of *The Records of Federal Officials* (1977) and is the author of articles on nineteenth- and twentieth-century U.S. diplomacy and on recent problems surrounding access to public records.

Roger B. Porter is associate professor of public policy at the John F. Kennedy School of Government, Harvard University. A former Rhodes Scholar, he received his Ph.D. from Harvard University. He served as special assistant to the president and as executive secretary of the Economic Policy Board from 1974 to 1977. He is the author of *Presidential Decision Making: The Economic Policy Board* (1980) and of a forthcoming book on the U.S.-USSR grain agreement.

Lester M. Salamon directs the Public Management and Government Studies Program at the Urban Institute in Washington. From 1977 to 1979 he served as deputy associate director of the Office of Management and Budget and before that was an associate professor at Duke University. Dr. Salamon received his Ph.D. at Harvard and is the author of *Welfare: The Elusive Consensus* (1978). He is currently completing a book on policy management processes of the presidency.

Allen Schick is a senior specialist in American government at the Congressional Research Service. He received his Ph.D. from Yale University. He has taught at Tufts University and has served on the staff of the Brookings Institution. He is the author of *Congress and Money: Budgeting, Spending, and Taxing* (1980) and is the editor of *Public Budgeting and Finance*, a new quarterly journal.

Abbreviations

ABEGS   Advisory Board on Economic Growth and Stability

ACDA   Arms Control and Disarmament Agency

AID   Agency for International Development

BOB   Bureau of the Budget

CBO   Congressional Budget Office

CEA   Council of Economic Advisers

CEQ   Council on Environmental Quality

CIA   Central Intelligence Agency

CIEP   Council on International Economic Policy

COWPS   Council on Wage and Price Stability

CPI   Consumer price index

DPS   Domestic Policy Staff

EIS   Environmental impact statement

E.O.   Executive Order

EOP   Executive Office of the President

EPA   Environmental Protection Agency

EPG   Economic Policy Group

ERDA   Energy Research and Development Administration

FLRA   Federal Labor Relations Authority

GAO   General Accounting Office

GNP   Gross national product

GSA   General Services Administration

IIS   Inflation impact statement

JCS   Joint Chiefs of Staff

LMFBR   Liquid metal fast breeder reactor

MSPB   Merit Systems Protection Board

NAC   National Advisory Council on International Financial and
           Monetary Problems

NPS   National Policies Staffs

NSC   National Security Council

OCB   Operations Control Board

OMB   Office of Management and Budget

OPM   Office of Personnel Management

PACGO   Presidential Advisory Committee on Government Organiza-
           tion

PAD   Program Associate Director

PPS   Policy Planning Staff

PSB   Psychological Strategy Board

SALT   Strategic Arms Limitation Talks

SAODAP   Special Action Office for Drug Abuse Prevention

The Illusion of
Presidential Government

Introduction:
The Presidential Illusion

Hugh Heclo

Presidential government is an illusion – an illusion that misleads presidents no less than the media and the American public, an illusion that often brings about the destruction of the very men who hold the office.*

Presidential government is the idea that the president, backed by the people, is or can be in charge of governing the country. The President's national electoral mandate is translated into a superordinate responsibility over the machinery of government, and the president's job is defined as leading a followership. This is an "illusion" in the fullest sense of the word, for it is based on appearances that mislead and deceive. Each chapter in this volume probes a different facet of the image of presidential government, but the conclusions are the same. Far from being in charge or running the government, the president must struggle even to comprehend what is going on. When a president appoints a czar for energy or for the economy, when he convenes some top-level, super-secret meeting to solve a major national problem, it is not presidential government that is strengthened. It is the illusion.

But an illusion is not an outright lie. Illusions acquire their power over our thinking precisely because they contain some elements of truth. The two lines like these

that look unequal but that actually are not fool us because of the true perceptions of bounded space that we notice at the end of each line. So it is with the presidency. In truth the president *is* our only nationally elected officeholder, our sole chief executive (although the Constitution never uses that term). And there is nothing illusory about the structure deliberately

---

*A more sophisticated discussion of the term is in Richard E. Neustadt's article "Presidential Government," *International Encyclopedia of the Social Sciences*, vol. 12 (London: Collier-Macmillan, 1968), p. 451.

designed by the founders, which makes the presidency the only institution with a vested interest in bringing an executive-wide perspective to bear on problems facing the nation as a whole.[1]

But assigning the president a unique position is not the same as giving the president a mandate to govern. Even with the backing of a massive electoral majority, the president is not in charge. The president's job in the constitutional system is not to lead a followership; it is to elicit leadership from the other institutions of self-government and help make that leadership effective.

An illusion like that of presidential government also acquires the power of reality to the extent that we believe it. This circumstance is what makes the parable of the emperor's new clothes the central metaphor of political science. If the president is widely believed to be in charge, then he may gain real power to perform in accord with the illusion. This has happened periodically. But even when belief gives substance to the illusion, the effects are temporary.

Franklin Roosevelt is remembered as a man who was in charge, a president's president against whom all successors have been measured. Elected by a landslide in 1932, Roosevelt "passed" a flood of legislation in his first hundred days and put the stamp of his New Deal on government for decades. Generally forgotten now is the fact that F.D.R. was rarely clear about what he wanted, building inductively from what had already been proposed by others and which consequently had a good chance of being approved. In fact, he suffered serious setbacks in his first hundred days (e.g., having to accept as part of the emerging New Deal programs that he did not want, such as federal insurance of bank deposits) and succeeded in few major legislative initiatives after 1936.[2] F.D.R.'s real strength was that he was rarely deluded by all the talk about presidential government (his attempt to pack the Supreme Court after his 1936 reelection landslide was an exception).

Fresher memories—of Lyndon Johnson after 1964 or of Nixon after his 1972 victory—should be enough to indicate how fleeting is the "reality" created by belief in presidential government. Even believing cannot make it so, at least not for long. And yet the illusion endures. Why?

The Sources of Illusion

In essence, the illusion endures because many people need it. Taking a long-term view, the most remarkable thing about the presidency in our generation is not how it fell from grace after the Johnson and Nixon presidencies, but how, despite those men and those times, Americans faced with national problems continue to turn to the presidential office for help. If the presidency can survive the events of the Vietnam War and Watergate, there must be very powerful forces at work shoring up our expectations of the office.

The Structure of Our Situation

The first of these forces is the need of our other institutions of government for an active, involved presidency. This need has arisen quite irrespective of the popularity of given presidents or their programs. It is inherent in the logic of our modern governmental system. That fact was brought home to me vividly on the afternoon of that summer day in 1974 when President Nixon was to announce his resignation: I sat in the office of a top White House bureaucrat who continued to receive telephone calls from congressional staff asking whether or not pieces of relatively minor legislation were "in accord with the President's program"!

During much of the nineteenth century, other political institutions seemed to have little need for the presidency, except as a clearinghouse for patronage appointments. Since then those small needs have grown immensely, and they have done so because of the way the role of government itself has grown. Government has done "more" in at least three senses of that term, and each has generated its own kind of problems of complexity and coordination.

First, government has done more of any one thing, paying pensions not just to its own workers and war veterans but to almost everyone; not just delivering the mail but sponsoring and regulating a whole series of communications industries; and so on. This increase in scale creates *a first-order complexity-coordination problem*, in the sense that major effects of a given activity are felt by many more groups. Thus the federal government, which in the nineteenth century built a few hundred miles of national roads and canals, has in our own time created a complex system of interstate highways as well as airports and aviation routes. These affect mayors and governors, organizations of air traffic controllers and teamsters, and auto manufacturers and consumers of transportation. How can the claims of all these groups be coordinated?

Second, government has also done more things. Barely a hundred and twenty years ago, almost all federal activities could be grouped under five categories: postal services, customs work, diplomacy, opening up new lands, and Indian affairs.[3] Today it is difficult to think of any aspect of life in which government is not involved. Doing more things creates *a second-order complexity-coordination problem*: Many of the things government does are likely to interfere with each other. Highway programs that chop up neighborhoods interfere with housing and urban policies; policies to promote economic growth often seem to conflict with environmental objectives; the examples could go on and on. The more congested the government agenda becomes, the more policies and public agencies seem to bump into each other in confusing and unexpected ways. Who will bring order to this growing traffic jam?

Third, more government means not merely more things done more extensively; it implies a larger cumulative presence of the governmental sector vis-à-vis the rest of society. An analogy from natural history may help explain this phenomenon. As time went on, dinosaurs not only got bigger and competed increasingly with each other; they also carved out a larger place in the total ecosystem for themselves. Like the dinosaurs, government activity as an aggregate crowds in on the surrounding life of the nation—so much so that it becomes difficult to see where the private economy and our personal lives and individual designs for the future leave off and the public sector begins. Here then is *a third-order complexity-coordination problem*, namely the management of cumulative rather than just crosscutting impacts. Who is in a position to manage *that*?

The puzzles produced by the first, second, and third orders of complexity in modern government do not, in principle, require us to look to the presidency or even the national government for solution. As economists like to point out, coordination can occur through markets without any need to rely on central direction. And in fact many puzzles of who will get what, how contradictory actions are to be reconciled, and what it all adds up to are handled by marketlike behavior in government. That is to say, outcomes are often the inadvertent consequence of bargaining and other kinds of "to-ing and fro-ing" among many fairly autonomous participants. But few people are likely to believe that that is good enough. We expect governments, unlike markets, to address problems directly and make conscious choices. If we are faced with a conflict between speeding traffic flows and preserving neighborhoods or are annoyed by a mounting body of government regulation, we do not expect people in government to tell us that "things will work themselves out." We do not believe that benefits and costs should remain wherever they might happen to fall as a result of the play of supply and demand.

Where then in government shall we look for help with the triple complexity of modern government? The constitutional structure of a country has an enormous effect on the answer to that question. If a government is so constituted that a single party controls the institutions of government, one has little choice but to look to the ruling group or politburo of that party. If executive and legislative powers are commingled in a parliamentary system (where the party in power in parliament chooses the executive), then one looks to the Cabinet.

The United States has neither system. American attitudes are accordingly somewhat ambiguous as to how far they regard the president or the Con-

gress as responsible for dealing with major national problems. Both the executive and legislature seem to act independently of each other, and no
party is in a position to control both branches jointly. And yet the puzzles of
modern government will not go away. The claims of more and more groups
affected and mobilized by government activity demand concerted attention;
contradictions need to be reconciled; someone needs to see the "big picture"
of what is happening.

In meeting the challenge of coordination, Congress is at a disadvantage. It
has no single head to capture attention. Its committees and subcommittees
excel at pulling things apart, not putting them together. The messages it
sends are multiple and confusing. Given all this, it is not surprising that the
more one contemplates the problems, the more one's gaze turns from Congress to the presidency, even the post-Vietnam, post-Watergate presidency.
If ever there was a time to test this inclination, it was in November of 1979.
It was, some pundits liked to say, the era of the post-imperial presidency.
Moreover, President Carter's popular approval rating had by then sunk to a
point just below that of a disgraced Richard Nixon at the time of his resignation. The Iranian hostage situation had yet to rally the country (temporarily, as it turned out) around Jimmy Carter. That November Americans
were asked what they considered to be the nation's most important problem. The list of answers was predictable: inflation, energy, jobs, and foreign
threats. They were then asked, "How confident are you that (Congress)
(President Carter) (any president) can deal with this problem? The results
were as follows:[4]

	Very Confident	Fairly Confident	Not Confident	Don't Know	Total
Congress	7%	29%	57%	7%	100%
President Carter	6%	24%	64%	6%	100%
Any president	15%	44%	33%	8%	100%

They showed clearly that, even at this nadir of public support for the president, there was still a high level of faith that the presidential office could
somehow deal with the most pressing issues of the day.

These and similar opinion polls indicate that the general public feels a
strong need for a presidential office that can help cut through the complexity of modern public policy. Congress has developed a similar need. Thus, as
early as 1921, the presidency acquired powers to enforce a comprehensive,
executive branch budget, not simply because presidents demanded such
powers, but because an alliance could be formed with the congressional ap-

propriation committees that were newly empowered by the executive budget process. Likewise, presidential coordination of agency views on proposed or pending legislation (legislative clearance, as it is called) was initiated and developed at the request of Congress as an aid to its own committee work. Major advances in developing more comprehensive presidential programs were improvised, to a major degree, as a means of meeting congressional needs for information and helping Congress organize its work.[5]

The list could be extended for many pages, but the conclusion would be the same. Presidential capacities to coordinate the activities of the executive branch were created and countenanced because they met the needs of Congress. Any managerial device that fails to meet this test, however much the president might want it, is undoubtedly doomed to extinction. The congressional staffer who called on the afternoon of Nixon's resignation to inquire if a piece of legislation was "in accord with the President's program" (a term used in the president's legislative clearance process) was not trying to follow the president or be nice to him. He wanted to use the presidency—possibly to move the bill forward or backward on the legislative agenda, possibly to avoid having to study the details or possibly to shift the blame for inaction on a bill that some group favored from the shoulders of his congressman to those of the president.

The modern bureaucratic structure of government also needs the presidency. It is simply very useful to the agencies to have someone at the end of the line who, after otherwise interminable wrangling across bureaucratic boundaries, can at last make a decision. This does not mean that the agencies always appreciate the president's participation, nor that his decisions will necessarily be accepted as final as the debate shifts to the byways of Congress. It does mean that the presidency is a vital presence in helping all get on with their work.

This presence has become more useful as government has become more complex and coordination problems have increased. One recent study estimated that there are more than thirty independent agencies—that is, government units outside the structure of the regular thirteen departments of the executive branch. Casting a wider net, the General Accounting Office in 1978 listed some 120 federal regulatory agencies.[6] By another count there are no less than 200 different health offices, 190 environmental units, and 145 offices concerned with energy policy in the executive branch. No one really believes the president should be involved in the business of all these offices all the time. But when the need for an ultimate referee in their jurisdictional disputes arises, when no single lower participant can highlight the necessary priorities for Congress and the public, when bureaucrats sense that they are suffocating each other with endless committee papers and meetings, then the president becomes useful—indeed, essential—in their work.

Basically the same situation applies to parts of the political system beyond the Congress and bureaucracy. As our federal system has become more complex and interdependent, mayors and governors have found it useful to have a political focal point in the presidency for their problems. So, too, do groups interested in science policy and consumer and environmental issues, for example. It would be naive in the extreme to think that this attention to and need for the presidency is or must be based on any simple faith that "the president knows best." It is rooted instead in the structure of our situation.

Who will reconcile the claims of the many groups affected by the large scale of government activity? Cabinet departments and Congress, of course. But often the scale extends beyond the jurisdiction of any one department, and often the effects are too diffuse to be effectively represented by small congressional constituencies. The president can help.

Who will manage the contradictions that occur increasingly in government's activities? The bureaucracy cannot be absolved from responsibility for trying to do so, but if bureaucrats could coordinate themselves, the contradictions would not have arisen in the first place. Congress has a similar responsibility, but by definition there is no central authority in Congress to ensure the compatibility of its acts. Again, the president can help.

Who will watch over the cumulative thrust and direction of government? Certainly, as citizens in a democracy, we all must do so, but again the president is in an exceptionally good position to help us see things steadily and as a whole.

Basically the same answers apply whether we like or dislike a particular president, whether we wish to increase or trim the role of the federal government. Thus it seems no paradox at all to us that President Reagan, a fervent advocate of decentralization, should become the centralizing focus for a program of deregulation, budget-cutting, and devolution of federal powers.

The inherent structural need for the president in our modern policy system means that we cannot give up on the presidency when it seems to be working poorly. The office is essential to making our form of government work. But work how? The structural factor discussed in this section creates the potential for illusion, but it does not explain why the need for the president so readily becomes an illusion that he must be in charge. Here there are three other forces at work.

Media Requirements

The presidential office clearly needs the communication industry that has burgeoned in the last several decades. The media of print and pictures are the president's only means of communicating his message directly to the public. They allow him to gain the attention of bureaucrats and congressmen faster than any official presidential document within the government ever can. The media also serve the president by functioning as a surrogate representative of the public, allowing him to test ideas and positions. And not least, the media give the president a chance to build up a body of favorable response to his persona against the day when his specific messages prove unpopular.

These are powerful reasons for presidents to feed the media's demand for news. In our own generation, the White House has become ever more specialized and bureaucratically organized, devoting anything from 30 to 85 percent of its staff to massaging the media.[7] But the relationship is not one-sided. The president's need for the media *and* the media's need for the president—though they often fight over specifics—feed on each other. Their love-hate relationship contributes much to the apotheosis of the presidency.

The modern media industry has a vested interest in the illusion of presidential government. Its technology is far from neutral for our understanding of government. The media need simple "shots" and clean lines of conflict to communicate a "story." The most compelling image of a situation is a person, and the president is the most easily communicated person. Thus the media amplify what we know to be a predisposition in the general public: namely, an impulse to understand public affairs mainly through a prominent political actor's behavior and not in terms of more complex, situational factors.[8]

The nightly news broadcasts with the inevitable White House in the background do more than report a series of stories. They inure us to the view that government is what the president has done that day, what he has allowed "administration spokesmen" to say, or what he is working on if he has left for Camp David. To be sure, there have been more "shots" of Congress in recent years—the Capitol in the background or snatches of speeches on the House floor, where television coverage is now permitted. But such extended coverage is almost always used as a counterpoint to a White House story and is most easily communicated as a conflict between president and Congress.

Reporters, editors, newspaper chains, and television networks all compete for both what is scarce and what is marketable. "Exclusives" are more valued than other stories; access to the White House is more valued than contacts in departmental or congressional staffs; the president's time is more limited than anyone else's. Hence the massive media competition draws coverage toward the Oval Office like a magnet. But what is scarce is not necessarily what is valued. Personalities are more marketable than descriptions of situations; dramatic events and decisions sell better than complex processes; what can be visually encapsulated in an image penetrates a larger audience more easily than written thoughts that must be painfully pieced together to make a coherent picture. The search for a competitive edge drives the media toward the most scarce and marketable commodity, an exclusive, president-centered story. A single picture of the president bumping his head, collapsing after jogging, or falling off a horse must be worth fifty or one hundred in-depth reports on the development of a complex national policy.

The Requirements of a Presidential Party

What the media need helps to push the president into the forefront of our attention and to make the White House a backdrop to media requirements. And as noted at the outset, presidents and their staffs are willing partners in this enterprise. The presidential need for the media is, however, only a special case of a more general phenomenon: the need to build what might be called a presidential party, i.e., the president's "own" party, not the party—Republican or Democratic—to which he belongs. This need is the second major factor generating the illusion of presidential government.

Each president during the last twenty years has felt increasingly compelled to mobilize the White House to build the equivalent of a presidential party for governing. To some presidents, such as Lyndon Johnson and Richard Nixon, the inclination seems to have come naturally. Yet whatever their personalities, modern presidents have all been under pressure to move in that same direction. The reason can be found in a number of recent trends in American politics: a more politically volatile, less party-oriented public; a less manageable, more individualistic Congress; disappearing party hierarchies; and proliferating groups of single-minded policy activists.[9] All of these add up to a sandy, shifting political base of support for presidents.

These trends do not, as some have said, mean political "atomization"—breaking down of our political life into tiny elemental particles.[10] They imply rampant pluralism, with multiple groups crosscutting the political landscape into incoherent patterns. Atomization would produce anomie and a sense of anarchy, but there is little evidence of loss of faith in the political system.[11] Rampant pluralism produces what we in fact have: multiple, conflicting demands, frequent policy stalemates, and a sense of stagnation.

Presidents and their aides have had little choice but to try to cope with these trends by organizing the president's base of political support, not only through the media but with mayors, governors, interest groups, citizens' lobbies, local editors, and others. Consider some of the specialized staffing subdivisions that existed in the Carter White House *before* the active start of the 1980 presidential campaign. Equivalent units (and others) can be found in the Reagan White House, even if the titles are not always the same:

- Assistant to the president (women's affairs)
- Assistant to the president (organizational liaison)
- Special assistant for Hispanic affairs

- Special assistant for ethnic affairs
- Special assistant for civil rights
- Counselor to the president on aging
- Assistant for intergovernmental affairs
- Assistant for congressional liaison

Taken as a whole, the list indicates something more important than the desire of particular groups to have their representatives at the president's elbow. What these and similar operatives for other presidents suggest is an effort to reach out from the White House and build at least some lines of reliable political support for presidents. If one were inventing a political party, these are exactly the types of offices at branch headquarters that one would want to create. The list lacks only the local, grassroots units that would give such a quasi-party organization feet and hands. Some of President Carter's efforts at town meetings and convocations with local publishers were attempts to do just that, and for the second term there were plans on the White House drawing board to take the next logical step—systematic White House liaison with neighborhood groups. To organize support for the new president's budget- and tax-cutting program, the Reagan White House has done many of the same things and, if anything, has gone farther in trying to mobilize directly grassroots citizen coalitions in support of the president's program.

Given the success record of recent presidents, no one could claim that great victories have resulted from such efforts at presidential party-building. But the point is that the six post-Eisenhower presidents have felt it increasingly necessary to try to create the embryo of a political party for themselves. And that effort in turn draws attention and problems toward the White House as the apparent center of all government. The reality of pluralist government feeds the illusion of presidential government.

There is nothing very esoteric about the forces at work. If mayors and governors have trouble with Washington's administrative strictures, it is not enough for the president to refer their calls to some departmental appointee or bureaucrat. Doing that will not build the relations with these people that a president needs if his policies are to have influence. Hence someone in the White House is tapped to keep an eye on "intergovernmental relations." A small staff develops. The mayors' and governors' phone calls are returned from the White House, their entrée to the bureaucracy is smoothed a little. Likewise, phone calls from the White House help head off troublesome reactions from these officials when the president has a proposal to make. By helping them, the president also helps himself. In the longer run, however, the president also acquires a staff with an interest in continuing to process such casework and policy development. And this helps confirm the larger expectation that the president is somehow responsible for seeing to it that a fiendishly complex federal system works to the satisfaction of all concerned.

There is no need to belabor the point. The same dynamic applies in one area of presidential activity after another. Will the president work exclusively through a few senior congressional leaders, none of whom really seem able to guide the actions of the modern legislature? Or will he try to string together the many pieces of Congress that are in business for themselves? All the pressures of the moment dictate the latter course. Accordingly the president acquires an extensive congressional liaison staff, which does favors and attracts demands for more. Can a president rest content with channeling the relations he needs with all the proliferating interest groups in our society through a few top interest group leaders or an executive department, much less the Republican or Democratic Party National Committees? Not if the president wishes to be in touch with the people who can really deliver the support he needs. Hence a veritable political technocracy of White House aides has developed, helping the president in the short run and in the long run entangling the presidency in extensive networks of policy activists interested in particular issues.

Presidential party-building obviously contributes directly to the appearance of the regnant presidency. But notice, too, that there is an indirect effect in the same direction. What presidents do to meet their immediate needs is likely to undercut the already weak leadership of other political institutions that could counteract the image of presidential government. By trying to put the pieces together themselves—the pieces in Congress, in interest groups, in professional associations, in state and local government—White House people make it less necessary that anyone else should have to work through the ostensible top leadership of these groups.

Of course a president could choose to confine his bargaining to the speaker of the House and a few committee chairmen rather than subcommittees and their staffs. He could work mainly through the head of the AFL-CIO rather than individual unions and local labor bigwigs. Eventually that would strengthen the hands of these leaders as responsible participants with the president in coordinating the modern policy system. But in the here and now, it would mean counting on people who cannot deliver their memberships. Worse than that, it would mean negotiating compromises at the top when in fact the president could get more of what he wants by picking and choosing among subgroups that are already favorably disposed. Since presidents and their aides live in the political present, why should they bother to build up companion institutions of government? By and large they do not bother, and so contribute to the illusion.

The Constraints of Presidential Scholarship

Anyone who suggested that honest academic work may have a pernicious effect would be skating on thin ice. This suggestion promotes the wistful idea that writing on the presidency might actually have some impact on government. Worse than that, it is likely to annoy colleagues who write book reviews and comment on grant applications. Still, there is some evidence that ideas matter, especially when it comes to generating illusions.

One line of influence runs from many years of writings directed toward reform of the presidency. Deliberately or not, every group offering advice about presidential management during this century has based its recommendations on certain sets of beliefs concerning executive management. A recent study by Michael McGeary[12] identified three such "doctrines"; all of these have seemed to contribute to our expectations of presidential government. The study has summarized as follows the ideas that have been current at different times:

> The idea that the Constitution gave the President the role of chief administrator, limiting Congress to general policy-making and oversight, was first conceptualized by President Taft's Commission on Economy and Efficiency, 1910–13. . . . The Commission drew upon recent developments in municipal reform and business administration to conceive of the government as a great public corporation whose business was to provide certain functions or services to its citizens-shareholders. The democratically elected board of directors, the Congress, was responsible for making policy, but only a strong chief executive—the President as *Business Manager*—could ensure efficient and economical administration. . . .
>
> Imbued with the Business Manager doctrine, [the President's Committee on Administrative Management, 1936–37, led by Louis Brownlow] transcended the doctrine by assuming a strictly Presidential rather than a comprehensive, governmentwide perspective. They began to look for ways to help the Presidency in general and President Roosevelt in particular. . . . The President's Committee borrowed the doctrinal language of efficiency . . . but it made changes and additions which transformed the image of the Presidency from Business Manager to *Administrative Leader*. The managerial role under the first doctrine was a technical one of using scientific management methods to perform the government's business with economy and efficiency; under the new doctrine of Administrative Leadership, the President's role as manager was a creative one which encompassed the ends as well as the means of administration.
>
> The two doctrines, while perhaps only subtly different, led to quite distinct ways of organizing the Presidency. According to the first, the President immersed himself in day-to-day operations, continuously monitoring every facet of departmental activities through hierarchically centralized control systems—accounting, reporting, and budgeting. The Administrative Leadership doctrine sought to free the President from routine so as to devote his major personal attention to the future shape and direction of government programs. Institutional staff agencies [in the new Executive Office of the President] would manage the routine central business, permitting the President to inter-

vene selectively in operational problems that concerned him. . . .

The Brownlow Committee's doctrine soon became dogma for administrative reformers, gaining strength in 1949 when the report of the Hoover Commission . . . signalled bipartisan acceptance of the idea of Presidential leadership and Executive Office flexibility. . . . During the rest of the 1950s and most of the 1960s, studies of Presidential management focussed on reconciling Presidential flexibility with administrative control through improved Executive Office organization. . . .

The groundwork for a third doctrine was developed gradually during the Johnson and Nixon administrations by the Heineman Task Force (1966–67), Ash Council (1969–71) and reorganization efforts of 1970, 1971, and 1973. The hierarchical control structure of the Business Manager doctrine was, in effect, merged with the presidential policymaking role of the Administrative Leadership doctrine to create an image of the President as *Policy Manager*. Administration had been conceived as separate from and superior to politics under the Business Manager model, while administration and politics were interdependent but equally important in the Administrative Leadership doctrine. With the advent of the Policy Manager doctrine, however, politics permeated administration, since both jointly were seen to determine policy. In its final, if briefly implemented form in early 1973, presidential flexibility was reconciled with centralized control of the bureaucracy by the delegation of Presidential authority to staff assistants who were to become the operational program managers, subjecting even Cabinet Secretaries to authoritative "coordination."[13]

It should come as no surprise that all of these models are ideal types rarely realized in practice. Yet these concepts have surely colored the way in which seasoned observers have looked at and advocated changes in the presidency. By and large, it has been easier to gain support for reform and reorganization plans by invoking the president's general constitutional role as chief executive than to analyze in detail what that role actually is. To assume that the presidency is a simple office, that we all know what we want from the office—this has been a more politic course for reform than raising troublesome questions about the role of Congress or the machinations of the president's own complex bureaucracy.

The second source of intellectual influence in presidential scholarship comes from the mini-industry of presidential literature in more academic circles. To be sure, the naive version of presidential government—what is sometimes called the "textbook presidency"—has by now been largely abandoned. Few books still describe the presidential office as the chief source of government initiative or sole representative of the nation's interests. A more widely circulated and sophisticated view now emphasizes the constraints on presidential power, the abuses to which it is subject, and the exercise of that power as a matter of persuasion rather than command.[14]

And yet as useful as these correctives are, they too can easily mislead. It is only a short step from saying that the power of the president is the power to persuade to thinking that national policies are or should be a function of the president's power to persuade. The illusion lies in the assumption that it is the president who knows what others should be persuaded to do. We find it difficult to believe that beneath the veneer of top-level meetings, briefing books, polished decision memorandums and White House statements there is deep and abiding uncertainty, not to say ignorance. The best cure for such simple faith would no doubt be to sit in on private presidential conversations. Failing access to the Oval Office, the second-best cure would be to visit a presidential library and, shielding our eyes from the heroic museum displays, to read some of a president's own office papers with the admitted advantage of hindsight. Presidents try hard, but they do not have all the answers; often they and their aides do not even ask the right questions.

Having retreated from overblown descriptions of the textbook presidency to the discovery of constraints and the concept of power as persuasion, president-watching as such reaches an intellectual dead end. Knowing more and more about presidents tells us less and less about what is happening to the presidency. Watching presidents promotes the illusion that it is only what they do that matters. The perspective needs to be broadened. Academics, like the media, find it difficult to communicate the reality of complex interactions involving many people, but academics have a duty to try harder. To understand the office and how it might function more effectively as part of constitutional, rather than presidential, government, we need to look at what has been going on around and beyond presidents, often without their knowledge, comprehension, or interest.

The Dilemmas of Reality

The chapters in this volume try to move toward a broader perspective on the presidency. Part 1 examines two aspects of what is termed the "unwritten" constitution: the administrative activities of Congress and the organizational dynamics of the president's own bureaucracy. These are not without a basis in the written Constitution, but they involve bodies of practice about which the Constitution says little, yet which are now central to the workings of the national government.

Part 2 focuses on what is termed "process management." It examines two of the traditional tools—budgeting and personnel—and one newer development—the explosion of government regulation—that are central to the general problem of the president's role. The management of overall processes within government, as opposed to the substance of particular policy decisions and programs, is a little understood and yet vital dimension of governing in Washington.

The three major arenas of substantive policymaking—domestic, economic, and national security affairs—are dealt with in Part 3. Obviously, no neat line can be drawn to demarcate these arenas. That, as we shall see, is one of the chief problems bedeviling the organization of the modern presidency and national government.

The conclusion draws together some of the major insights that emerge throughout the book and spells out their implications for the future role of the presidency. In fact, these are really propositions for debate more than ultimate answers, for there is nothing simple about the modern presidency. At the very least, the chapters in this book show that what has happened to the presidency is more intricate—and interesting—than a simple increase or decrease in presidential power. Neither is it merely a set-piece competition between the presidency and the Congress.

What is really taking place is a remarkable experiment in self-government. By first one means and then another, we are searching for ways to make our inherited constitutional system, the oldest of existing democracies, cope with modern policy problems that the Founding Fathers could not have envisioned. Summoning up the illusion of presidential government is not much help.

Consider a few examples from the chapters in this book. Whatever we might expect from the president as chief executive, the vast bulk of ultimate administrative power rests with the Congress, not the president. The legislature is zealous in exercising and protecting that power for reasons that will never disappear under our existing political constitution. Administrative problems in the Washington bureaucracy are a responsibility of the leadership in the two branches, but how can the president and Congress take joint rather than mutually canceling actions to deal with them? That is not an abstract question. It underlies a mass of specific complaints by citizens and local officials about irrelevant, insensitive, and expensive government demands.

The president's own office is an organizational jumble, often generating the illusion of power but the reality of bureaucratic confinement. When we like what the president is doing, we would like him to be able to do more than flex a velvet fist in an iron glove. When we do not think the president is doing what is right, the strictures do not seem taut enough.

And so the dilemmas of reality add up. The budget process has increasingly escaped from the president's control. But to do very much about this would seem to require denying presidents a chance to escape from a narrow budgetary preoccupation. When it comes to the personnel process, we would like to help the president-as-executive manage but stop the president-as-politician from interfering with good government. Economic and domestic affairs strain any pretense that the president as an individual is "in charge," and they seem to require unfamiliar experiments in collaboration.

Yet the national security management process, which was invented at the end of the Second World War to institutionalize such collaboration, has tended to develop in just the opposite direction. What should be done?

The report printed at the end of this volume indicates what one group of highly experienced people suggest. Not everyone will agree, and the serious student should have little difficulty in discovering discrepancies as well as congruence between what this panel of prominent citizens recommended and what the authors of the preceding chapters have to say. It would seem that these or any alternative recommendations must address at least four pairs of crosscutting requirements.

1. The Presidency must be a political as well as a national office, sufficiently flexible to meet the personal needs of a democratic politician and sufficiently structured to protect the institutional integrity of the office and the impartiality of government administration.

2. The needs for managing long-term government processes and for making short-term policy decisions must be reconciled.

3. Central capabilities to deal with the triple complexity of modern policy must be balanced against the dangers of central power.

4. The accountability that comes from concentrating political authority must be weighed against the wider participation, responsiveness, and consent of the governed that come from dispersing political power.

These are not just interesting intellectual puzzles. They are deadly earnest tests of our capacity for self-government as the United States moves toward a twenty-first century rich in threat and opportunity. More important than what any elite panel decides is what large numbers of ordinary and, let us hope, well-informed citizens think about their national political institutions—at least that is the way it should be in a nation committed to grasping the reality and not just the illusion of democratic government.

Notes

1. See especially *The Federalist Papers*, numbers 70, 72, and 76; and Arthur Taylor Prescott, *Drafting the Federal Constitution* (Baton Rouge: Louisiana State University Press, 1941), pp. 544–646.

2. Frank Friedel, *Franklin D. Roosevelt: Launching the New Deal* (Boston: Little, Brown, 1973).

3. Very interesting analytic treatments of this history are contained in Samuel H. Beer, "The Modernization of American Federalism," *Publius*, Vol. 3, no. 2, Fall 1973 pp. 49–96; and in James Q. Wilson, "The Rise of the Bureaucratic State," *Public Interest*, Vol. 10, 1975.

4. See "Attitudes Toward the Presidency, A National Opinion Survey," conducted for station WHYY on behalf of the PBS production "Every Four Years," the Gallup

Organization, Princeton, New Jersey, October 1979.

5. Richard E. Neustadt, "Presidency and Legislation: The Growth of Central Clearance," *American Political Science Review*, Vol. 48, September 1954, pp. 644, 660–62; and Richard E. Neustadt, "Presidency and Legislation: Planning the President's Program," *American Political Science Review*, Vol. 49, December 1955, pp. 1014–1015.

6. U.S., Senate, Committee on Governmental Affairs, *The Federal Executive Establishment: Evolution and Trends*, 96th Congress, 2nd session, *Committee Print*, May 1980, Washington, D.C.

7. For these estimates and other generalizations about the changing relationship between the president and the media, see Michael B. Grossman and Martha J. Kumar, "White House Press Operations and the News Media," paper presented to the 1977 Annual Meeting of the American Political Science Association, September 1–4, 1977, Washington, D.C.

8. R. E. Nisbett and L. Ross, *Human Inference: Strategies and Shortcomings in Social Judgment* (Englewood Cliffs, N.J.: Prentice-Hall, 1980), Chapter 3; and Donald R. Kinder, Susan T. Fiske, and Randolph G. Wagner, "Presidents in the Public Mind," unpublished paper, Yale University, July 1980.

9. For example, Anthony King, ed., *The New American Political System* (Washington, D.C.: American Enterprise Institute, 1978), Chapters 3, 4, 6, 7, and 8.

10. Ibid., Chapter 10.

11. The debate on the evidence is contained in Patrick Caddell, "Crisis of Confidence I—Trapped in a Downward Spiral," *Public Opinion*, vol. 2, no. 5, October-November 1979, pp. 2–8; and Warren E. Miller, "Crisis of Confidence II—Misreading the Public Pulse," *Public Opinion*, vol. 2, no. 5, October-November 1979, pp. 9–15.

12. Michael McGeary, "Doctrines of Presidential Management," paper prepared for the National Academy of Public Administration Panel on Presidential Management, Fall 1979, Washington, D.C.

13. Ibid. The basic documents expressing these doctrines are (Taft Commission), *Report of the Commission on Economy and Efficiency*, House Document 854, 62nd Congress, 2nd session, 1912; (Brownlow Committee) *President's Committee on Administrative Management, Report with Special Studies* (Washington, D.C.: Government Printing Office, 1937); (Hoover Commission) Commission on the Organization of the Executive Branch of Government, *General Management of the Executive Branch*, (Washington, D.C.: Government Printing Office, 1949); aspects of the Heineman Task Force and the Ash Council are discussed in Larry Berman, "The Office of Management and Budget that Almost Wasn't," *Political Science Quarterly*, vol. 92, no. 2, Summer 1977, pp. 281–304.

14. These trends are well displayed in the first and second editions of Thomas C. Cronin, *The State of the Presidency* (Boston: Little, Brown, 1975 and 1980).

PART ONE
The Unwritten Constitution

Civics courses teach that the United States, unlike such countries as Britain, has a written constitution. In fact, it has both the written Constitution and an unwritten constitution. The legal document obviously shapes our political institutions, but so too do bodies of practice that have become established over time. Indeed, it is difficult to see how the written Constitution could work at all if such practical understandings did not allow us to "fill in between the lines" and to adapt to changing circumstances.

Two of the most important ambiguities in the written Constitution concern the working relations between the legislative and executive branches and the organizational content and operations of the president's own office. As Louis Fisher points out in Chapter 1, the designers of the Constitution at one time considered and then very wisely dropped the idea of spelling out in a constitutional amendment the separation of power among the branches of government. He goes on to show the justifications and means Congress uses to involve itself in government administration.

Fifty years ago the president's office consisted of little more than the president himself, two or three personal secretaries, and a small clerical staff. In Chapter 2 John Helmer outlines how far we have come since those days. A collection of presidential staffs now covers all areas of national policy. This presidential bureaucracy, which has grown with little overall intention or design, helps the presidency play an active part in hundreds of major and minor issues. By discussing a case study of a recent presidential decision, however, Helmer shows how easily this same bureaucracy can confuse, overextend, and complicate the president's leadership.

To understand how our unwritten constitution encompasses an active congressional role in administration and a growing problem for the president in managing his own bureaucracy is to begin to penetrate the illusion of presidential government.

1

Congress and the President in the Administrative Process: The Uneasy Alliance

Louis Fisher

The public administration school has been a steadfast opponent of congressional involvement in administrative matters. Part of the resistance is constitutional. Congress enacts the laws; it should let the executive carry them out. It is also argued, on a more practical level, that waste, confusion, and loss of accountability result when administration is divided between two branches of government. Both themes find expression in a veto message delivered by Woodrow Wilson in 1920.

> The Congress and the Executive should function within their respective spheres. Otherwise, efficient and responsible management will be impossible and progress impeded by wasteful forces of disorganization and obstruction. The Congress has the power and the right to grant or deny an appropriation, or to enact or refuse to enact a law, but once an appropriation is made or a law is passed the appropriation should be administered or the law executed by the executive branch of the Government.[1]

Wilson invoked a dream that no one has been able to transform into reality. At no point in our history have we with any precision, success, or permanence separated the functions of government into legislative and executive. This ideal model eludes our grasp at every turn. It creates attitudes and expectations that infect the relationships between the branches, producing a steady stream of recriminations and countercharges. Underneath the Wilsonian legislative/administrative dichotomy we often find "a concealed but deep distrust of democratic government and of democratic processes."[2]

The question is not whether Congress will or should participate in administrative matters. Both the formal structure of government and the informal dynamics of politics necessitate the active involvement of Congress. The undecided issue is whether legislative involvement will take place in an atmosphere of cooperation and mutual respect or in a climate of ill will and acrimony.

The Framers' Search for Efficient Management

The record of the Continental Congress from 1774 to 1787 contains a vast number of poignant stories about administrative experiments and managerial failures. Members of the Congress tried to handle the full range of government business—administrative and adjudicative as well as legislative. Not surprisingly, vital issues were neglected or mismanaged. Under pressure to make operations more efficient and reliable, Congress farmed out administrative duties first to committees, then to boards staffed by men recruited from outside Congress, and finally, in 1781, to single executives. "It is positively pathetic," wrote one scholar, "to follow Congress through its aimless wanderings in search of a system for the satisfactory management of its executive departments."[3]

Complaints about administrative deficiencies run like a connecting thread throughout these years. James Madison's interest in three branches of government was drawn more from the administrative record of the Continental Congress than from the theoretical writings of Montesquieu. Prior to the Philadelphia convention he confided to his friend and close associate, Thomas Jefferson, that Congress had mismanaged its powers under the Articles of Confederation and that even more demanding duties would be thrust upon the new national government. Administrative details, he said, would be best left to a separate executive. Alexander Hamilton voiced a widely held sentiment in 1780 when he said that Congress had "meddled too much with details of every sort." Congress was properly a "deliberative corps and it forgets itself when it attempts to play the executive." While proceedings were under way at the Philadelphia convention, Jefferson remarked that nothing was "so embarrassing nor so mischievous in a great assembly as the details of execution."[4]

These statements suggest that the framers could distinguish "executive" from "legislative," allocating these two functions to separate branches. In fact, the framers decided on an intermixture of powers. In No. 47 of the *Federalist Papers*, Madison argued that the theory of separated powers had been totally misconceived. It did not mean that the departments "ought to have no *partial agency* in, or no *control* over, the acts of the other." Paradoxically, the powers created by the Constitution had to overlap to keep the departments separate and independent. Madison drove the point home in Federalist 48: "Unless these departments be so far connected and blended as to give each a constitutional control over the others, the degree of separation which the maxim requires, as essential to a free government, can never in practice be duly maintained." The pure theory of separated powers gave way to the system of checks and balances we know today.

Some of the delegates at the state ratifying conventions were shocked by the extent to which the Constitution had mingled the branches. "How is the executive?" cried one delegate at the Virginia ratifying convention. "Contrary to the opinion of all the best writers, blended with the legislative. We have asked for bread, and they have given us a stone."[5]

Virginia joined North Carolina and Pennsylvania in demanding that a separation clause be added to the national bill of rights. Because of their efforts, Congress considered the following language: "The powers delegated by this constitution are appropriated to the departments to which they are respectively distributed: so that the legislative department shall never exercise the powers vested in the executive or judicial[,] nor the executive exercise the powers vested in the legislative or judicial, nor the judicial exercise the powers vested in the legislative or executive departments." The House and the Senate later agreed to delete this amendment from the list of twelve sent to the states for ratification.[6]

Had this language been adopted, it could have served only a hortatory function, warning each branch not to encroach upon the other. It could not have prevented Congress from delegating legislative powers to the president, from investigating corruption and waste within the agencies, or from exercising its specific constitutional powers to control and direct the executive branch. This supervisory power is derived from the power of the purse, Senate confirmation of appointees, statutory specifications for agency personnel, periodic hearings by congressional committees, audits by the General Accounting Office, informal contacts, and the general power under Article I to make all laws necessary and proper for carrying into execution not only the enumerated powers of Congress but all other powers vested in the government or in any department or officer. Newer techniques have been added to oversee administrative action, including the various forms of legislative vetoes and nonstatutory controls.

Conditions for Legislative Participation

The public administration school adopts the following model of the Constitution: The president functions as the chief administrative officer of a unified and hierarchical executive branch, capable of issuing authoritative commands to his subordinates in the agencies and departments. To preserve the principles of unity and responsibility, the president relies on his removal power to dismiss ineffective or disloyal employees. A competing model begins with the premise that Congress creates the departments and may specify the conditions under which laws are to be carried out. Executive departments serve more as the agent of Congress than of the president.

Both models have a legitimate place in our governmental system. One cannot override the other; efforts must be made to reconcile them. Presidents and their assistants need to appreciate that Congress is entitled to intervene in many administrative matters and is constitutionally empowered to direct a broad range of decisions by departments and agencies. Congress invites suggestions from administrators on pending legislation without raising questions of separation of powers. The record is equally clear that administrators can benefit from legislative input. The political process must accommodate traffic in both directions. If the congressional effort is discredited by using such epithets as "meddling" and "interference," members of Congress will brace themselves for an uphill battle and employ obstructive techniques of their own. An incoming president and his staff need to understand the conditions that motivate members of Congress to intervene in administrative matters. Many of the conditions relate to deficiencies within the executive branch and are therefore susceptible to presidential control or influence. Other interventions are reasonably drawn from the constitutional responsibilities of Congress. Keeping a sharp eye on these factors is more productive and enlightening than issuing broadsides about congressional "encroachments" or "usurpations." Rarely does Congress intervene for idle or frivolous purposes. Some members do act on short-term, cynical, and irresponsible impulses, permitting the politics of the moment to take precedence over managerial effectiveness, but it is unfair to apply this characterization to Congress as a whole. The bulk of congressional activity in questions of administration is legitimate and defensible.

Constitutional Stakes

The Brownlow Committee found that the effectiveness of the president in 1937 was "limited and restricted, in spite of the clear intent of the Constitution to the contrary." In recommending that administrative duties be centered under the president to restore accountability, and in trying to subject the independent commissions to presidential control, the committee constructed an inaccurate and unrealistic model of executive-legislative relationships. The committee's report reflects a Wilsonian dichotomy between legislation and administration: "We hold that once the Congress has made an appropriation, an appropriation which it is free to withhold, the responsibility for the administration of the expenditures under that appropriation is and should be solely upon the Executive."[7]

This doctrine of presidential autonomy has never prevailed, especially in the realm of appropriations. Congress is at liberty to appropriate in whatever detail it thinks advisable and has done so throughout its history. Through statutory language Congress may remove from administrators the flexibility that might be granted in more trusting times.

On many occasions executive officials act as agents of Congress, not the president. Congress creates the agencies and prescribes the duties of departmental heads. Leaving aside the anomalous position of the independent regulatory commissions, situations arise in which departmental workers are totally immune from presidential direction. "Ministerial duties," for example, require an official to perform a statutory function without the exercise of judgment or discretion. Neither the president nor a departmental head possesses any authority to deny or control a ministerial act. It would be an "alarming doctrine," said the Supreme Court in one case, that Congress could not impose upon any executive officer any duty it thinks proper, "which is not repugnant to any rights secured and protected by the constitution; and in such cases, the duty and responsibility grow out of and are subject to the control of the law, and not to the direction of the president."[8]

Attorneys general have agreed with this proposition. When laws define "what is to be done by a given head of department, and how he is to do it, there the President's discretion stops."[9] On many occasions the Justice Department has recognized that Congress may mandate administrative duties. Although the Constitution directs the president to "take Care that the Laws be faithfully executed," attorneys general have advised presidents that there are substantial political and legal constraints on their ability to intervene in departmental matters. These opinions, appearing as early as the 1820s, notified presidents that they had no legal right to interfere with a number of administrative responsibilities that Congress had assigned to the agencies.[10]

The Nixon Administration ignored these precedents when it embarked upon its large-scale impoundment of funds. White House officials repeatedly intervened to prevent agencies from carrying out their statutory missions. In 1973 and 1974, dozens of federal court decisions forced the administration to release the funds. These decisions typically reviewed the statutes and legislative history to find that Congress had imposed upon an administrative officer a duty that was ministerial in character, permitting no judgment or discretion by the officer and no interference by the White House.[11]

An incident during the Carter Administration illustrates the pervasive, ineradicable influence of Congress in administration. After John Gilligan had been named to head the Agency for International Development (AID), he was told by the chairman of a Senate appropriations subcommittee that agency-legislative relationships had deteriorated in the past because AID would divert economic aid to military purposes without consulting Congress. The senator told Gilligan that whenever AID decided to expend funds for purposes not previously justified to Congress, it had to seek the approval of the appropriations subcommittees that had jurisdiction over foreign assistance. Gilligan agreed to this clearance process as a way to improve congressional relations, and when the senator wanted the agreement reduced to writing he consented to that as well.

The letter was typed up and, as part of the standard procedure within an agency, routed through the general counsel's office. Questions were raised there about the legality of allowing congressional committees to participate in administrative decisions, and when the matter was referred to the Justice Department for an opinion, the suspicion of the general counsel's office was confirmed. Congress had overstepped its boundaries.

Upon learning that Gilligan could not send the letter, the senator raised the ante by inserting the agreement into public law. The foreign assistance appropriations bill for fiscal 1978 contained this language in section 115: "None of the funds made available by this Act may be obligated under an appropriation account to which they were not appropriated without the written prior approval of the Appropriations Committees of both Houses of the Congress." Carter signed the bill into law without indicating any constitutional misgivings about the clearance procedure, but on that same day he wrote to Secretary of State Vance, stating that the attorney general had challenged the constitutionality of section 115. Consequently, Vance was to treat the section not as a legally binding requirement for prior approval but rather as a request by the appropriations committees to be notified, after which Vance and AID could spend the funds as they thought best.

These events suggest a major collision between the branches, with the president finally repelling a congressional effort to intervene in administrative details. So it was, on the surface. On the operating level, however, far below the constitutional principles argued by the White House and the Justice Department, things went on unchanged. The AID administrator sought the prior approval of the appropriations subcommittees before diverting funds. Everyone seemed satisfied. The president had defended his prerogatives, the administrator maintained good relationships with Congress, and the review committees continued to exercise their controls.

Delegated Powers

As a result of broad grants of legislative authority, agencies necessarily make policy when they issue regulations, spend money, enter into arms sales, and take other actions that determine national priorities and commitments. It is unlikely that Congress will ever legislate in sufficient detail to substantially narrow this discretion. For reasons both good and bad, Congress will pursue its two-pronged strategy: making broad grants of power and insisting on a share in overseeing programs and activities. As Arthur Macmahon remarked in a 1943 study, the need for legislative oversight of administration "increases with executive initiative in policy and the delegation of discretion under the broad terms of statutes."[12]

This kind of trade-off explains the growth of committee vetoes during World War II. Because of the volume of wartime construction, Congress found it impracticable to authorize in a public law each defense installation or public works project. It delegated power broadly, but not without legislative controls. Beginning with an informal system in 1942, all proposals for acquisition of land and leases were submitted in advance to the naval affairs committees for their approval. Relying on that understanding, Congress passed a general authorization in a lump sum without specifying individual projects. Two years later, Congress converted the nonstatutory understanding into public law. Additional "coming into agreement" provisions were added in 1949 and 1951, requiring the approval of the armed services committees for acquisition of land and real estate transactions. Presidents Roosevelt and Truman did not like the committee-approval system, but they did not want Congress to return to itemized statutes. The compromise was basically satisfactory to both branches.

A similar pattern appears with congressional controls on defense reprogramming (shifts of funds within an appropriation account). Under pressure of having to prosecute World War II, Congress consented to lump-sum appropriations. But as a technique for retaining a semblance of legislative control, a "gentlemen's agreement" required the War Department to notify the military appropriations subcommittees and to obtain their approval before effecting significant shifts of funds. The opportunity for executive discretion increased still further when Congress, in response to recommendations by the Hoover Commission in 1949, began to consolidate appropriation accounts. In the case of defense, the number of accounts dropped from about one hundred to fifty. As the size of the accounts grew, so did the opportunity for administrative flexibility.

Congress took several steps to reestablish its control. The appropriations committees added restrictive language to their reports, gradually insisting on regular reports on defense reprogramming and, in some cases, prior approval by those committees. With the introduction of annual authorizations in 1959, the Armed Services Committees participated in these notification and prior-approval procedures. Although the controls are nonstatutory (included in committee reports rather than in public laws), the Defense Department elevated the controls to a more formal level by incorporating them in departmental directives and instructions.[13] However uncomfortable the executive branch may be with this degree of congressional involvement in administrative decisions, the prospect of reverting to a great number of appropriation accounts is even more disagreeable. Each increase in congressional delegation brings with it a commensurate increase in congressional participation in agency decisions. Presidents and their agency heads seek additional flexibility and are willing to accept the legislative conditions attached to the authority.

Consider the type of calculation that entered into reorganization authority. In 1938, President Roosevelt asked Congress for authority to reorganize the executive branch. Congress insisted on the right to disapprove a reorganization by a concurrent resolution (a two-house veto). Roosevelt argued that disapproval would have to take the form of a joint resolution, to be presented to him for his signature or veto. Passage of a concurrent resolution, he said, would be "only an expression of congressional sentiment. Such a resolution cannot repeal Executive action taken in pursuance of a law."[14] Roosevelt abandoned this constitutional doctrine a few days later after concluding that the House of Representatives would never consent to the delegation of authority without retaining for itself the check of a two-house veto. Action by joint resolution, with the possibility of a veto, would require both houses to achieve a two-thirds majority to override the veto, instead of acting by simple majority through a concurrent resolution.

The growth of legislative vetoes, regularly objected to by presidents as a legislative encroachment on administrative duties, is part of the accommodation by chief executives who sought greater delegated power. A recent example is the authority to impound funds. Prior to the Nixon administration, placing funds in budgetary reserve was a standard administrative function carried out by the Bureau of the Budget. The authority to make routine impoundments—setting aside funds for savings and contingencies—had been granted by Congress in 1950 with the Antideficiency Act amendments. But the Nixon administration decided to use impoundment for policy reasons to curtail or terminate programs it did not want. To protect its prerogatives, Congress rushed into the administrative arena, eventually passing legislation in 1974 that limits the president's power to impound funds. Congress may exercise a one-house veto over "deferrals" (temporary withholdings). For "rescissions," which are presidential proposals to terminate spending authority, both houses of Congress must vote their approval within forty-five days of continuous session. The president accepted this measure of congressional participation in administrative decisions in return for receiving a broad delegation of power to make policy impoundments.

If a future administration decided to oppose the use of one-house or two-house vetoes, that would not put an end to legislative involvement. Congress has other options available to it. In the case of agency regulations, Congress may use its power of the purse to prevent a regulation from taking effect. In 1978 and 1979, Congress attached to an appropriation bill a prohibition on the use of any funds by the Bureau of Alcohol, Tobacco, and Firearms to implement a proposed regulation that members feared would lead to gun control. In 1980, after the Carter administration announced that legislative vetoes over four regulations issued by the Department of Education were unconstitutional and nonbinding, members of Congress inserted language in appropriation bills to neutralize the administration's position, not only in education but in other areas as well. For example, the fiscal 1981 appropriation bill for the Transportation Department contains this language in section 325: "None of the funds in this Act shall be used to implement, administer, or enforce any regulation which has been disapproved pursuant to a resolution of disapproval duly adopted in accordance with the applicable law of the United States."

Constituency Interests

The First Amendment provides that Congress shall make no law abridging the right of the people "to petition the Government for a redress of grievances." Often these petitions go directly to members of Congress, who act as intermediaries between citizens and the administrative agencies.

Agency decisions on public buildings, local projects, social security checks, military installations, and other questions have a direct impact on a member's district or state. With the growth of bureaucratic complexity, legislators must assist constituents in locating the responsible agency and ensuring adequate attention. These are bread-and-butter issues for members of Congress. To wish away a system that is permanently in place would be a game of make-believe.

In fact, agencies are structured to deal with the inquiries that come from members of Congress. Departmental liaison officers have been established to handle calls from members of Congress who are interested in grants, contracts, projects, loans, benefits, and favors. These official channels of communication are standing invitations for members to ask about administrative actions and decisions. Recent studies, in which authors openly adopt a cynical attitude about Congress, charge that legislators have deliberately constructed a system that thrives on congressional intervention in administrative matters as part of a reelection strategy. Even these studies, however, admit that there is a legitimate need for congressmen to function as ombudsmen in our bureaucratic state.[15] As a caveat against such studies, it is important to note that members of Congress have been active in creating an administrative system that does *not* require legislative intervention. Instead of legislators dabbling in each administrative decision, we find a system of automatic formulas, entitlements, "uncontrollables," indexing, and other computations that are basically mechanical and clerical.

In his book *When Americans Complain* (Cambridge: Harvard University Press, 1966), Walter Gellhorn estimated that the casework sent to agencies by members of Congress resulted in only about 10 percent of the agency's previous decisions or actions being changed. He was critical of members who became preoccupied with petty and trivial requests from constituents, but 10 percent, or even half that, is significant leverage. Moreover, Gellhorn admitted that inquiries from citizens are often "unimaginatively overlooked by civil servants apparently more intent upon mass production than on subsurface exploration." Even when no change results from legislative inquiry, the member and the constituent have the satisfaction of knowing that the matter has been attended to.

Congressional intervention is often a healthy stimulus to producing needed changes in administrative procedures or corrective legislation. As one study concluded:

> An individual complaint or a request for a favor may itself be trivial, except to the aggrieved or hopeful citizen and his family. Responding to it may tax the energy and ingenuity of an overworked member of Congress and his staff. No single request left unheeded is likely to rock the Republic. But the provision of millions of such miniscule services, in their totality, amount to a major function of modern American government. How well these services are performed goes a long way in determining the confidence of citizens in their representatives.[16]

Casework is crucial for legislators unable to depend on the national or local party for reelection. American constituents have a reputation for being more outspoken in their demands than citizens from other countries. They have a strong sense of their rights and insist on being heard. The words of Edward Shils, describing this environment three decades ago, have a contemporary ring: "Unable to depend on the national party for re-election, [the American legislator] must cultivate and nurture his constituency more than legislators in other democratic countries where constituents are less clamorous and parties are stronger at the center."[17]

Constituents bring to the attention of members of Congress contradictory, conflicting agency regulations. One agency may not be aware that a regulation it issued, though faithful enough to its own legislative mandate, is inconsistent with another regulation promulgated by a different agency. This incoherence, unknown at the agency level, will become common knowledge to the constituent or businessman faced with contradictory commands from the federal government. A member, receiving this feedback, can press for administrative relief or changes in the statutory framework.

Congressional intervention is sometimes necessary to protect the constitutional rights of citizens. In the early 1970s Congress brought to light the military's surveillance of domestic political activities by American citizens. The army had been collecting reports on political events throughout the country, preserving the information in computers at Fort Holabird, Maryland. Although senior army officials initially denied the charges, Congress was able to demonstrate the existence of a widespread, systematic effort by the military to monitor activities of citizens and public officials. Legislative scrutiny and persistence brought the army's program to a halt. During the Nixon years, the Internal Revenue Service, the Federal Bureau of Investigation, and the Central Intelligence Agency were all active in using their resources and personnel to violate the constitutional rights of citizens. Congressional investigations represent an indispensable check on such illegal and intrusive agency operations.

Administrative Inattention and Indecision

Conditions may fester for such a long time in federal agencies that members of Congress, excited by lurid newspaper exposés, rush in to fill the vacuum. The furniture scandal of the General Services Administration (GSA) is a case in point. An article in the August 1955 issue of *Fortune* magazine issued this plea: "If better days are to come, they will come only when the White House decides to clean up GSA." The entreaty fell on deaf ears. Despite the responsibility of the Budget Bureau for examining agency operations and periodic reports from the General Accounting Office (GAO) revealing major deficiencies within GSA, the agency continued to do business as usual. Government warehouses bulged with furniture while GSA acquired vast quantities of new desks, chairs, files, and other equipment, much of it shoddy and defective. GSA Administrator Joel Solomon told the Senate Committee on Environmental and Public Works in 1979 that "the mess has drifted along to the point that I came on as Administrator."

It is an unfortunate fact that some federal administrators display little or no interest in administration. They excel at advocacy and self-promotion, not management. It is not unusual for top agency officials to ignore the findings and recommendations of audits, even though they formally sign off on such studies and promise to take corrective action. Recently the GAO offered this explanation:

> We believe that the reason internal control systems are in a state of disrepair is that top management has devoted most of its concern and emphasis to delivering funds and services and that effective controls over tasks and functions which lead to the delivery of these funds and services has had a low priority. Because of top management's insufficient concern for internal controls, middle

management reflects this same indifference. That sentiment is passed down to internal audit staffs which have spent little time evaluating the adequacy of internal controls over all agency functions.[18]

Responding to these weaknesses in agency management, Congress passed legislation in 1978 to create inspectors general in twelve agencies. The purpose of the statute is to keep Congress informed about "problems and deficiencies relating to the administration of such programs and operations and the necessity for and progress of corrective action." Citizens and agency employees are encouraged to contact the inspectors general to report specific examples of fraud and abuse in federal agencies. The legislative history of the statute revealed chronic deficiencies within the agencies: inadequate staff resources, ineffective organizational structures and reporting procedures, and a preoccupation with program operation at the expense of program review. These failures obviously resulted from congressional as well as agency negligence. Congress contributed to the problem; it has a responsibility to assist with the solution.

Spokesmen for the executive departments opposed the legislation for inspectors general. They argued that the provision for direct reporting to Congress without the clearance or the approval of the secretary represented a violation of the separation of powers doctrine. The procedure could indeed create an adversary relationship between the secretary and the Office of Inspector General, with the secretary placed on the defensive before a congressional committee because of information supplied by an inspector general. However, the experience of an inspector general in the Department of Health, Education, and Welfare (now the Department of Health and Human Services) shows that cooperation is possible between an inspector general and a secretary. In any event, Congress insisted on the reporting procedure as an essential ingredient to strengthen the capacity of legislators to oversee departmental operations.

Accounting procedures within the agencies have been so lax that administrators cannot even ensure that amounts owed to the government are properly recorded as accounts receivable. Overdue accounts are neither identified nor collected. Reacting to this deficiency, Senators Percy and Sasser introduced the Debt Collection Act of 1980. The Treasury Department estimated that, without remedial action by Congress and the agencies, billions will be lost to the government in delinquent debts.

Agency officials admit that the bureaucracy needs prodding from the outside. Congress, through its multiple access points, can expose agency defects that might otherwise go undetected. In a conference at the Brookings Institution in June 1979, one official acknowledged that GAO reports "frequently made it possible to energize an agency to do something they just couldn't get the inertia of the agency to address until that report hit the public press."[19] Intervention by Congress is imperative because of what James Sundquist has called the politicization or amateurization of the civil service: "At the top levels of the U.S. government, administrative capability has been allowed to decline, over a long period, with a resulting loss of capacity throughout the executive branch."[20] Some of this decline can be attributed to excessive suspicion on the part of presidents toward the bureaucracy, causing them to rely on political appointees rather than agency professionals. Congress has contributed to the decline by failing to lift statutory ceilings on federal salaries, a failure that has produced a demoralizing pay compression in the upper ranks of the bureaucracy.

Other administrative problems are a combination of legislative and managerial neglect. Wasteful spending in the closing months of a fiscal year is generally blamed on bureaucrats, but members help create the climate for waste by delaying action on regular appropriation bills, relying on continuing resolutions as stop-gap funding authority, passing huge supplementals late in the fiscal year, and simply appropriating more than agencies can sensibly spend. Agencies, for their part, abuse their spending discretion by committing large sums of money to low-priority items in the final weeks of a fiscal year, rather than letting the funds lapse. Millions of dollars are unnecessarily awarded to contractors on a noncompetitive basis in the last few days of a fiscal year. Contracts awarded under rushed purchasing procedures are often inflated in cost, both in the amount of the award and of administrative expenses needed for overtime work and temporary personnel.

These disclosures of waste inevitably bring Congress into the picture. Both houses of Congress were active in 1980 in placing new restrictions on year-end agency obligations. Basically this consisted of arbitrary percentages of obligations to be allowed in the final quarter (or months) of a fiscal year, combined with the granting of authority to the Office of Management and Budget (OMB) to make necessary waivers. These are patchwork solutions, however, and cannot fully compensate for the failure of Congress to make program reductions earlier at the legislative stage.

Congress has recently turned its attention to wasteful spending on consultants. This too is a joint legislative-executive product. Despite efforts by OMB to tighten the system, GAO has discovered that little or no consideration is given to in-house capability before awarding contracts; extensive sole-source awards preclude effective price competition; awards are made to former agency employees; and significant spending for consulting services in the final quarter of the fiscal year raises doubts as to the need for the services in the first place. Much of this spending has a "use it or lose it" flavor.

Predictably, Congress enters the fray with new legislative remedies. OMB resists statutory controls on consultants, warning that "you cannot legislate good management." But members of Congress are unwilling to pin their hopes on administrative controls that have proven themselves ineffective for decades. Senator David Pryor wondered if good management could be achieved solely through agency regulations. He advised the OMB witness: "You say regulation is the best way. I'm saying regulation has failed, and the GAO seems to agree."[21] Administrative inadequacies are, in fact, intertwined with a legislative scheme that pits one statute against another. Congress speaks with a forked tongue, mandating new programs for agencies while restricting the growth of agency personnel. Something has to give, and the obvious remedy up to now has been to contract out to the private sector.

Administrative Invitations

In some cases executive officials, aware of a problem but incapable of resolving it, extend an invitation to Congress to intervene to settle a dispute. The Armed Services Committees became involved in the selection of a weapons system in the 1950s after the military services demonstrated their inability to resolve their differences over air defense. In effect, Secretary of Defense McElroy asked Congress to step in and decide the question:

> SENATOR STENNIS. I am beginning to think that the Department of Defense would welcome a congressional decision on this matter and then you could move on into a more positive program.
> SECRETARY McELROY. You have certainly touched us in a place that I would call vulnerable.
> SENATOR STENNIS. I do not want to embarrass you.
> SECRETARY McELROY. You are not embarrassing us. This is one area where we have not done very well in making a decision.
> As far as I am concerned, it would not bother me if you held our feet to the fire and forced us in connection with this budget.[22]

The upshot of this encounter, was that the Armed Services Committees insisted that they authorize procurement programs each year. It was not long before the committees extended the requirement for annual authorization to research and development by the Pentagon. More recently the committees have become concerned that cost overruns in weapons systems are being financed by cuts in operation and maintenance, creating serious problems of military readiness. As a result, in 1980 Congress decided to add the requirement for annual authorization to the operation and maintenance accounts.

Many of the details in statutes and committee reports come at the request of agencies. Without specific directions from Congress, bureau chiefs can be besieged by various interests that want funds channeled in their direction and laws bent in their favor. To protect themselves from being whipsawed by these competing interests, program managers and budget officials may ask a member or committee staffer to add restrictive language to a committee report or public law.

Even when restrictive language is not included at an agency's request, executive officials may discover that life is more comfortable and manageable with such language. Statutory and nonstatutory restrictions allow administrators to say no to a foreign country or to a domestic interest seeking assistance from the federal government.

Administrative Abuses

Statutes and the U.S. Code are filled with hundreds of legislative restrictions that are a direct consequence of the use of discretionary authority for purposes never intended by Congress and often at cross-purposes with what Congress did intend. This kind of congressional "meddling" in administration is a response to deliberate abuse on the part of agencies and White House officials.

Angered by executive officials who exploit broad grants of legislative power to nullify congressional objectives, members of Congress retaliate by placing limitations in public laws. When flexibility in a statute is used by agencies to thwart congressional policy, the message to legislators is to write statutes with less flexibility and less discretion. Senator Muskie lectured one official in 1973, after discovering that a broad grant of discretionary authority had been used to cut in half a legislative commitment:

> Having in mind the devious motives that you pursued to undercut the purposes of Congress, I could now write better language and believe me, I will.
>
> The clear language and debate was what we were giving you, is what we understood to be legitimate administrative discretion to spend the money, not defeat the purposes. Then to have you twist it as you have, is a temptation to this Senator to really handcuff you the next time.[23]

In its 1976 study, "The President and Executive Management," the National Academy of Public Administration concluded that presidential accountability had been undermined by "excessive and detailed Congressional intervention in agency management." At the same time, the academy admitted that many of these legislative initiatives were a response to presidential abuse of power or to agency efforts to circumvent and ignore the intent of Congress. During the Nixon years, the administration reprimanded bureaucrats for "disloyalty"—not to the Constitution, or to statutory objectives, but to the goals of the White House.

A few examples will illustrate this linkage between congressional intervention and agency abuse. It had been the practice of the Pentagon, if a request to Congress for money for a program was denied, to channel other monies to the rejected program. The House Appropriations Committee said that to concur in such actions "would place committees in the position of undoing the work of the Congress. The Committee believes that this is an untenable position and notifies the Department of Defense that henceforth no such requests will be entertained."[24] Beginning in 1974, Congress prohibited by law the Pentagon from presenting a request to the appropriations committees to reprogram funds to an item that had been previously denied by Congress. This language appears each year in the defense appropriation bill.

Similar language has been used to curb abuses of contingency funds. Members of Congress discovered that these funds were being used not to cover emergencies or unexpected expenses but rather to restore funds that Congress had deliberately cut from agency requests. In the case of foreign assistance in 1960, Congress enacted language stating that no part of the contingency funds "shall be used for any project or activity for which an estimate has been submitted to Congress and which estimate has been rejected."[25]

Congress adopted statutory language in 1974 to exercise control over presidential impoundment. Within a short time it was confronted by "quasi-impoundments"—a variety of administrative actions to slow down a program opposed by the White House. One technique is OMB's imposition of personnel ceilings. Agencies receive the funds appropriated by Congress but lack the staff needed to spend the money. Members of Congress noted a recurring pattern: OMB restrictions invariably applied to programs that Congress had increased beyond the president's budget. In short, personnel ceilings were being administered to discriminate against congressional additions. To protect legislative priorities, members of Congress found it necessary to monitor personnel levels. Nonstatutory directives in committee reports were usually sufficient to check the administration, but in the case of the agriculture appropriation bill for fiscal 1978 Congress resorted to statutory language: "None of the funds provided in this Act may be used to reduce programs by establishing an end-of-year employment ceiling on permanent positions below the level set herein for the following agencies: Farmers Home Administration, 7,440; Agricultural Stabilization and Conservation Service, 2,473; and Soil Conservation Service, 13,995."

When the executive branch excludes members of Congress from the formulation of a policy, the administrative process is the last remaining stage for legislative participation. A recent study, after concluding that Congress was too deeply involved in policy *execution*, admitted that "this has come about largely because of the hangover of frustration over not having been adequately consulted on policy *formulation*, from Vietnam on."[26] Policy execution became the last train out of the station. Congressmen Clement Zablocki and Paul Findley, after waiting literally decades for the executive branch to include Congress in genuine consultation, finally turned to legislative vetoes and other extraordinary remedies in an effort to control administrative actions.[27]

Improper and Illegal Interventions

Congressional participation in administrative operations is, for the most part, legitimate, necessary, and beneficial. In some cases, however, what begins as a representative function becomes "influence-peddling," leading to indictments in the courts of members of Congress for using their legislative and oversight positions for personal gain.

The bribery statute (18 U.S.C. 201) is directed against public officials—including members of Congress—who seek or accept anything of value in return for an official act. The conflict-of-interest statute (18 U.S.C. 203) makes it a criminal offense for congressmen to receive or seek compensation for any services relating to any proceeding, contract, claim, or other activities of the federal government. Depending on the circumstances, members may seek immunity under the speech or debate clause of the Constitution, which prohibits questioning a senator or representative for any legislative act.

In numerous decisions, the Supreme Court has held that members of Congress may not use the speech or debate clause as a shield for contacts with the executive branch. Congressman Thomas Johnson (D–Md., 1959–1963) tried to influence the Justice Department to drop a pending investigation of a savings and loan institution. He was accused of receiving more than $20,000 for his efforts. In 1966 the Supreme Court decided that his contacts with the department were not protected by the speech or debate clause. Although a conspiracy count was dismissed, he was found guilty of violating the conflict-of-interest statute.

Congressman Bertram Podell (D–N.Y., 1968–1975) pleaded guilty in 1974 to conspiracy and conflict-of-interest charges after he had intervened in several federal agencies to help an airline company obtain a route between Florida and the Bahamas. His family law firm in Manhattan had been collecting monthly legal fees from the airline's parent company. In another action marking the limits of legislative intervention in agency activities, Congressman Frank Brasco (D–N.Y., 1967–1975) was found guilty of bribery and conspiracy in a scheme to obtain Post Office contracts for a trucking firm. More recently, Congressman Joshua Eilberg (D–Pa., 1967–1979) was indicted for receiving compensation for helping a Philadelphia hospital win a $14.5 million federal grant. After a federal court held in 1979 that his contacts with the executive branch were not protected by the speech or debate clause, he pleaded guilty to a conflict-of-interest charge.

This lack of immunity for legislator-to-executive contacts has been detailed in many decisions. In 1972, in *Gravel* v. *United States*, the Court noted that members of Congress are "constantly in touch with the Executive Branch of the Government and with administrative agencies—they may cajole, and exhort with respect to the administration of a federal statute—but such conduct, though generally done, is not protected legislative activity." This distinction between "legislation" and "administration" is easier to draw in court decisions than in actual agency operations. Often a legislative act is intertwined with a member's intervention in an agency. For example, Congressman John Dowdy (D–Tex., 1952–1973) was indicted for bribery, conspiracy, and perjury stemming from his intervention as a subcommittee chairman into a Justice Department investigation. He was charged with accepting $25,000 in return for assisting a home-improvement firm threatened by prosecution. The charges of bribery and conspiracy were eventually dropped because of the speech of debate immunity, particularly because of his status as subcommittee chairman, but after a new trial he was found guilty of perjury.

Aside from criminal prosecution, there are other limits on members who interfere with agency proceedings. Members immune under the speech or debate clause may face disciplinary action by the House or the Senate. In 1970 the House Committee on Standards of Official Conduct issued this guideline: "Direct or implied suggestion of either favoritism or reprisal in advance of, or subsequent to, action taken by the agency contacted is unwarranted abuse of the representative role." This principle puts legislators who serve on oversight committees in an awkward position. Intervention on behalf of constituents can create serious misinterpretations. An agency may wonder, if it fails to comply with a legislator's request, will the member vote to reduce the agency's budget or insert restrictive language in a bill? On the other hand, if the agency cooperates, will this put pressure on the member to support future agency activities that might normally have been questioned? Senator Paul Douglas adopted the following standard:

> Before I became a member of the subcommittee dealing with the affairs of the Reconstruction Finance Corporation, I felt it proper to communicate with that agency about loans which some of my constituents were seeking. While I tried at all times not to put any undue pressure on the directors of that body, as soon as I became a member of the subcommittee I stopped making any representations whatever to them. I was then engaged with Senator Fulbright in investigating the RFC and I knew that if I made even the barest inquiry, it might receive undue attention from the Board. I was also fearful that if the Board favored constituents in whom I took an interest, I would feel obligated to the members personally and could not impartially carry out my investigative work. I was in a sense a watch-dog for the public, and dogs who are liberally fed by visitors are seldom watchful.[28]

For agency proceedings that require a public record, members may not make off-the-record (ex parte) contacts that might jeopardize the fairness of the decision. Members may ask for status reports, but letters or contacts addressing the *merits* of a proceeding are prohibited from the time an on-the-record proceeding is publicly announced for oral hearing. Ex parte communications are not shown to agency decision makers. Communications received after the record is closed are answered by the agency's congressional relations office.

Similarly, there are restrictions on White House contacts with agencies conducting an adjudicatory proceeding or engaged in formal rule making. In 1937, when the Brownlow Committee recommended that the independent commissions be reassigned to the executive departments, it recognized that the judicial functions of the commissions would have to be set aside as wholly independent of the departments and the president. Even for informal rule making of existing executive agencies, there was considerable controversy and litigation during the Carter administration over limiting ex parte contacts by presidential advisers.[29]

In these questions of rule making and adjudication, the judiciary is available to protect the integrity and fairness of agency proceedings. Senate hearings in 1955 were so probing that the chairman of the Federal Trade Commission decided to disqualify himself from a pending case; the courts agreed that there are limits on the extent to which Congress may inquire into an agency's decision-making process.[30] Courts have also ordered an agency head to make new determinations after congressional pressures had invalidated an initial agency decision.[31]

On December 22, 1980, the U.S. Court of Appeals for the Ninth Circuit handed down a decision that President Carter praised as having "perhaps the most profound significance constitutionally of anything that's happened in my four years." The decision struck down a legislative veto that Congress had relied on for years to overturn executive determinations on deportation cases. Although the opinion ranges far and wide, speaking generally about legislative intrusion upon the executive and judicial branches, the decision is most supportable when confined to agency adjudications of individual rights where procedural safeguards are essential. In fact, the decision specifically excludes agency actions in situations "in which the unforeseeability of future circumstances" (as in the sale of nuclear fuel to foreign countries) might justify a legislative veto. The decision also recognizes that a different test is required to judge the appropriateness of legislative vetoes over agency regulations that seek to carry out statutory missions of "broad scope and complexity."[32]

Agencies have resources of their own to resist improper and illegal interventions by members of Congress. Investigations by the Justice Department are a formidable threat. Short of that sanction, it is usually sufficient to advise a member of possible transgressions. If that tactic fails, agencies can always alert the media. Members are loath to press a point that can produce unfavorable stories in the press and supply ready ammunition to future opponents.

The Essential Partnership

For both constitutional and practical reasons, administration has become the province of all three branches of government. It serves no purpose for a president to tell Congress: "This is administration. Leave me alone." Congress will participate, with or without the president's permission. The president's choice—really his only choice—is to treat Congress either as an ally or as an antagonist. Congress has the capacity and the spirit to play either role. Presidential encouragement is a key ingredient in determining the direction that Congress will take.

When the Brownlow Committee said, "The President needs help," it neglected to point out that help can come from Congress. The president needs the assistance of legislators. He cannot run the bureaucracy by himself. Even by adding fresh layers of White House staff, or by positioning his lieutenants in the agencies, it is impossible for a president to maintain control. Administration is not an executive monopoly. It never was; it never can be. The constitutional and political responsibilities of Congress require its active and diligent participation in administrative matters.

This is not to argue that congressional involvement will always be attractive or defensible. Indeed, it can be indiscriminate and even counterproductive. Let there be evidence of abuse in a few agencies, and Congress is apt to apply arbitrary, across-the-board penalties to all agencies, regardless of their individual records. The congressional remedy is not a butterfly net; it is a dragnet, sweeping everything before it, good and bad. Exceptions or rewards are not made for the effective administrator. The blunt instrument of statutory control may cause extensive damage to the agencies and to the private sector, as demonstrated in recent years by the congressional response to mismanagement of furniture funds, travel allowances, end-of-year spending, and consultant expenses.

Congress is not alone in its power to impose across-the-board, indiscriminate remedies. Immediately upon taking office, President Reagan ordered a hiring freeze for all civilian employees in the executive branch, back-dating his order to November 5, 1980. He cut travel by 15 percent; and consultant costs by 5 percent. And he hired fourteen inspectors general in the departments and agencies, with a total disregard for their individual achievements or the evaluations submitted by the Reagan transition teams. Not much here in the way of finesse or subtlety.

Reagan's performance as governor suggests that he knows how to forge an effective and cooperative relationship with the legislature. He selected advisers knowledgeable about the legislative process and pragmatic in seeking legislative solutions. His staffing of the White House conveys a similar spirit, as do his initial overtures to Congress. This augurs well for executive-legislative contacts. Once legislative attention has been piqued by agency scandals and embarrassing press reports, defensive reactions by an administration can only make matters worse. Presidential or White House obstruction will merely force Congress to operate independently in its search for a remedy. The costs of this exercise can be minimized if the president accepts the situation as it presents itself and acknowledges that serious deficiencies exist within the agencies.

Acknowledgement does not require ignominy or self-reproach. Such admissions come more easily if it is recognized that administrative defects are the product of many years of agency negligence that predate the present administration, exacerbated all the while by inadequacies, inconsistencies, and incoherence in the statutory framework erected by Congress. Agency failures result from a convoluted system of disincentives, executive as well as legislative. Both branches contribute to the problems of mismanagement. It is in the interest of the public that both branches work cooperatively in the search for solutions.

Notes

1. James D. Richardson, ed., *A Compilation of the Messages and Papers of the Presidents*, 20 vols. (New York: Bureau of National Literature, 1897–1925), Vol. 19, p. 405.

2. Paul H. Douglas, *Ethics in Government* (Cambridge, Mass.: Harvard University Press, 1952), p. 86.

3. Jay Caesar Guggenheimer, "The Development of the Executive Departments, 1775–1789," in J. Franklin Jameson, ed., *Essays in the Constitutional History of the United States* (Boston: Houghton Mifflin, 1889), p. 148.

4. Gaillard Hunt, ed., *The Writings of James Madison* (New York: G. P. Putnam's, 1900–1910), Vol. 2, p. 328; Harold C. Syrett, ed., *The Papers of Alexander Hamilton* (New York: Columbia University Press, 1961–), Vol. 2, p. 404; and Julian P. Boyd, ed., *The Papers of Thomas Jefferson* (Princeton, N.J.: Princeton University Press, 1950–), Vol. 11, p. 679.

5. Jonathan Elliot, ed., *The Debates in the Several State Conventions, on the Adoption of the Federal Constitution* (Washington, D.C., 1836–1845), Vol. 3, p. 280.

6. *Annals* of Congress, Vol. 1, p. 453 (June 8, 1789).

7. President's Committee on Administrative Management, *Administrative Management in the Government of the United States* (Washington, D.C.: Government Printing Office, 1937), pp. 3, 43.

8. *Kendall* v. *United States*, 37 U.S. (12 Pet.) 522, 610 (1838).

9. 6 Opinions of the Attorney General 326, 341 (1854).

10. There are several dozen such opinions. For some groundbreakers, see 1 Ops. Att'y Gen. 624 (1823), 1 Ops. Att'y Gen. 636 (1824), 1 Ops. Att'y Gen. 678 (1824), 1 Ops. Att'y Gen. 705 (1825), and 1 Ops. Att'y Gen. 706 (1825).

11. Louis Fisher, *Presidential Spending Power* (Princeton, N.J.: Princeton University Press, 1975), pp. 147–201.

12. Arthur W. Macmahon, "Congressional Oversight of Administration: The Power of the Purse I," *Political Science Quarterly* 58 (1943):161.

13. Fisher, *Presidential Spending Power*, pp. 75–98.

14. 83 Congressional Record 4487 (1938).

15. Morris P. Fiorina, *Congress: Keystone of the Washington Establishment* (New Haven, Conn.: Yale University Press, 1977), p. 76. See also R. Douglas Arnold, *Congress and the Bureaucracy* (New Haven, Conn.: Yale University Press, 1979).

16. Kenneth G. Olson, "The Service Function of the United States Congress," in Alfred de Grazia, ed., *Congress: The First Branch of Government* (New York: Anchor, 1967), p. 324.

17. Edward A. Shils, "The Legislator and His Environment," *University of Chicago Law Review* 18 (1951):572.

18. U.S., Congress, Senate, Committee on Appropriations, *Hearings on Fraud, Abuse, Waste, and Error in Government, Fiscal Year 1981*, 96th Cong., 2d Sess. 47–48, 1980.

19. Round Table Conference held at the Brookings Institution, June 1979, cited by James L. Sundquist, "The Decline and Resurgence of Congress" (unpublished manuscript, April 1980), p. 35 of Chapter 11.

20. James L. Sundquist, "The Crisis of Competence in Government," in Joseph A. Pechman, ed., *Setting National Priorities: Agenda for the 1980's* (Washington, D.C.: Brookings Institution, 1980), p. 554.

21. *Washington Post*, August 20, 1980, p. A2:2.

22. Raymond H. Dawson, "Congressional Innovation and Intervention in Defense Policy: Legislative Authorization of Weapons Systems," *American Political Science Review* 56 (1962):52.

23. U.S., Congress, Senate, Committee on Government Operations and Committee on the Judiciary, *Joint Hearings on Impoundment of Appropriated Funds by the President*, 93d Cong., 1st Sess., 1973, p. 411. The witness was William D. Ruckelshaus, administrator of the Environmental Protection Agency.

24. House Report No. 662, 93d Cong., 1st Sess. (1973), p. 16.

25. 74 Stat. 777 (1960).

26. Lee H. Hamilton and Michael H. Van Dusen, "Making the Separation of Powers Work," *Foreign Affairs* 57 (1978):27.

27. Louis Fisher, *The Constitution Between Friends: Congress, the President, and the Law* (New York, St. Martin's, 1978), p. 249.

28. Douglas, *Ethics in Government*, p. 91. For a comparable position by Congressman John Moss, see "How Hill Pressures Federal Agencies on Hiring," *Washington Star*, June 21, 1976, p. A1.

29. Paul R. Verkuil, "Jawboning Administrative Agencies: Ex Parte Contacts by

the White House," *Columbia Law Review* 80 (1980):943.

   30. *Pillsbury Company* v. *F.T.C.*, 354 F.2d 952, 954–956, 963–964 (5th Cir. 1966).

   31. *D.C. Federation of Civil Associations* v. *Volpe*, 459 F.2d 1231, 1245–1248 (D.C. Cir. 1971), cert. denied, 405 U.S. 1030 (1971).

   32. *Chadha* v. *Immigration and Naturalization Service*, 634 F.2d 408 (9th Cir. 1980).

2

The Presidential Office: Velvet Fist in an Iron Glove

John Helmer

A View of the White House

Across the small park in front of the White House in Washington, there is a well-known hotel, whose rooms have two prices. For those rooms that overlook St. John's Church, the daily charge is $114. But for those with a view of the White House, the charge is $134. Why is a view of Caesar worth $20 more than a view of God?

In Washington, even illusions are subject to the laws of the market, and while God has many houses, the president of the United States has only one. In this respect the White House is quite unlike the seats of power of the European states. It is not a palace like the Quirinale or the Élysée. Visitors are not kept at bay to watch a military parade but are invited to tramp through the front door in their tens of thousands every day but Monday. The accessibility of even the offices of the president is greater than that of almost any other head of government on earth.

To the agnostic, such symbols are illusory; the view of the terrestrial power worth no more than that of heavenly might and about as credible. But in Washington, the faithful are many, the illusion democratic, and the premium, even by hotel standards, cheap.

The illusion of the presidency is simply this: The institutional roles or powers of the president are government *limitations* on his authority and severe *restrictions* on the exercise of his personal policy. What in other countries would be regarded as sources of great political or administrative strength—direct popular election, party leadership, the power to appoint, direct, and remove a Cabinet of ministers and all senior echelons of the bureaucracy—are either nominal in character, conferring no substantial power, or they are shared by the president with Congress in a fashion that he cannot always anticipate or rely on. This illusion applies with special force to the bureaucracy of the president's own office.

The real workings of the presidency seem to defy analysis because the office is a moving target. This fluidity arises from several factors. First, there is the constitutional limit of four years to a presidential term and the increasing improbability in recent years of a president surviving to serve the legal maximum of two terms. Second, the office is the object of continual tinkering. During the Carter presidency, the White House was reorganized twice: The first occasion in 1977 resulted in a substantial cut in personnel and the reassignment of several staff units; and the second in mid-1979 led to new appointments, a rearrangement of functions and some titles, and several resignations. In addition, formal internal reorganizations were carried out in two of the most important staff units advising the president—the Office of Management and Budget and the National Security Council.[1]

This pattern of formal reorganization is quite distinct from the turnover of individual advisers, staff assistants, and other officials in the president's immediate entourage or his administration. It is uniquely characteristic of the American executive that its structure and functions are almost continuously subject to analysis, review, study, and restudy. The presidency never stands still, but neither do the major departments, bureaus, and agencies to which presidential power is formally and informally delegated.[2]

Among the most important of the long-term organizational changes is the transformation of the White House into the Executive Office. This change reflects much more, as we shall see, than bureaucratic proliferation and expansion. For it is the specific weaknesses of the presidency in commanding and controlling the government that have led individual presidents to the organizational improvisations that constitute the Executive Office. If the White House is the symbol of the president's power, the Executive Office—the continuously changing cluster of bureaus appointed by the president—represents incumbent presidents' efforts to give strength to the symbol, substance to the illusion.

The argument of this chapter takes three steps. The first briefly identifies the principal powers of the president. These powers represent a capability that is substantial in reserve but evaporates in action. In the second part, the development and dynamics of the Executive Office are analyzed to reveal a combination of internal and external forces that the president himself only partially controls. In the third and final step, I shall describe the process by which a recent major presidential decision was reached—a decision that was made, unmade, remade, and unmade all over again.

The conclusion of the argument is that the president's response to the illusory nature of his powers has produced an organization, the Executive Office, whose elements rarely serve their intended purpose for long (almost never outlasting the chief executive who created or inherited them), but which adapt, change, and for the most part, survive. In so doing, they operate beyond the coordination of the most conscientious head of government and beyond even the comprehension of the less conscientious.

The Illusion of the President's Powers

Party Leadership.

As the preeminent elected official of his party, the president is the acknowledged, although informal, head of the party. In practical terms, this does not mean very much. Except during presidential and congressional election periods, central party organizations are poor and small. Political partisanship, as measured by popular party registrations, is of declining interest to most Americans, few of whom subscribe financially to party organizations. Individual candidates, rather than party organs, attract the lion's share of private subscription, but even that has been declining in recent years, while financial support from political action committees (organizations formed to get around legal restrictions on corporate or union contributions) has been rising.

Up to 1968, perhaps, it could have been said that the main parties existed to wage election campaigns. Since then, largely as a result of changes in the party rules and federal and state laws for nominating, campaigning for, and electing candidates, even this function has been lost. As the number of states conducting presidential nominating elections (primaries, conventions) has steadily increased, a candidate faces a long, tortuous, and extremely unpredictable sequence of contests, each of which is influenced by local issues and local rules. Voter turnout in these preliminary elections is also so low—an average of 28.7 percent in the 1976 presidential primaries—that the tactics of winning them make party organization subsidiary or irrelevant to the techniques of mobilizing voter blocs that are identified by computer analysis of the electoral propensities of specific postal districts and telephone exchanges. The objective in this type of electioneering is to encourage only those likely to favor a candidate to go to the polls, while doing as little as possible to stir the opposition.

The upshot of the election process is that a president enters (or retains) office owing favors to many individuals, groups, states, and regions, but only nominal loyalty to his party. It is therefore appropriate that in President Carter's office, there were staff assistants with responsibilities for handling relations, involving requests, patronage, and complaints, with state and local governmental officials (assistant to the president for intergovernmental relations), with ethnic, racial, and religious groups (special assistants appointed to represent blacks, Hispanics, women, and Jews), and with major union and business groups. One assistant to the president in the Carter White House was formally responsible for liaison with the Democratic National Committee and other party organs, but this responsibility was subordinate to broad election strategy concerns. In the Carter White House, these "special interest" assistants competed with others in the process by which nominations for official positions were collected and decided. There was a separate director of the Presidential Personnel Office, which in Carter's case succeeded two almost independent streams of personnel recruitment that were set up after the election victory in November 1976. In that process, as in the others, institutionally, although not individually, partisanship was of little consequence.

Legislative Leadership

What the American president gains in freedom from party constraints, he loses to the independence of the legislature, unobligated to him and undisciplined by common party affiliation.

Formally, the president's power to legislate is very circumscribed. He may recommend draft legislation and request appropriations for government expenditures, but Congress may amend, revise, or reconstruct these measures as it sees fit. The president may veto legislation enacted by the Congress, although this may be overridden by a two-thirds majority vote of both chambers. The president may negotiate and make treaties with foreign powers, subject to Senate ratification.

In practice, the president has increasingly taken the initiative in sending draft legislation to Capitol Hill, and it has been customary for the congressional committees to respond to the initiative of the executive branch. But this is far from inevitable. In fact, support is not the appropriate term for the legislative relationship that exists between the president and Congress, and party affiliation is not a consistent predictor of either convergence or divergence of congressional votes and presidential policy.[3]

Presidential influence with Congress is conventionally assessed by measuring the proportion of bills passed or rejected in agreement with the president's position. The rate of presidential success—which peaked with 93 percent for Johnson in 1965—has dropped, although even Ford, in his best year, 1975, had a success rate of nearly 60 percent.

The figure is misleading, however, for the legislative process is long and complex. At every stage the president and his staff negotiate with the Congress and its staffs. This is true for policy formulation, legislative drafting, clearance of a bill for submission to Congress, committee hearings and markups, parliamentary debates, amendments, and votes. The process continues through the final stage when, after the congressional vote, the president must decide whether to veto the bill. This involves further rounds of consultations with and advice from White House staff, departmental officials, congressmen and senators, and representatives of private interest groups. At what point in a process that may take months or years can it be said that the form and detail of a legislative proposal is the president's initiative and position or the Congress's? Any simple answer is deceiving.

An alternative source of evidence for assessing presidential legislative leadership and power over the Congress is the budget and appropriations process. Constitutionally, the power to appropriate money for government expenditure is vested in the Congress. Until 1921, the secretary of the treasury played a greater role in collating the budget than the president, but the passage in that year of the Budget and Accounting Act removed much of the indepenence the departments had enjoyed vis-à-vis Congress in requesting their appropriations and eliminated the role of the Treasury in reviewing these requests. In their place, the Bureau of the Budget was created for the express purpose of coordinating, and where necessary, revising, reducing, or increasing the departmental requests before submitting them to the Hill. The establishment of this bureau is arguably the most important development in the evolution of the presidential office.

It must be emphasized, however, that the capability for budgetary coordination of cabinet departments and agencies increased merely the president's persuasiveness with Congress, not his authority over it. The Nixon presidency brought into focus a number of spending practices and financial powers that the Congress regarded as usurpations of its authority. Many of the abuses and most of the looseness of congressional budgetary supervision were eliminated by the Congressional Budget and Impoundment Control Act of 1974.

Since then, as Chapter 3 shows, the relationship between presidential and congressional spending powers has undergone considerable change. In President Ford's two budgets, the Congress appropriated more money than was requested. In President Carter's first two budgets, it provided less. In fiscal year 1980, this changed again, with Congress authorizing $13 billion more in spending authority than the president sought. In general, presidential budget making depends at least as much on what can be predicted about the Congress's likely response as on the departments' estimates of policy needs or the president's commitments. A head of government who can be embarrassed by making commitments his legislature may not grant him the resources to deliver is not in a position of distinctive budgetary authority, as is the case, for example, in Britain or Germany.

War Power

This is an element of presidential legislative leadership that deserves special mention. The United States has been engaged in military conflict almost constantly since 1945. Quite apart from the Korean War (1950–1953) or the Vietnam War (1964–1973) the president, as commander in chief of the armed forces, ordered the use of military force against foreign territory or interests, or on the high seas, a total of 215 times up to the end of 1975.[4] It is widely accepted that presidents have also authorized and directed intensive covert campaigns short of military force to financially isolate and economically destabilize unfriendly regimes (Chile, Vietnam since 1974, South Africa, Uganda, Rhodesia, and Iran in 1979), promote political factions, support internal coups d'etat, and so forth.[5]

Until 1973, war-making, particularly of the covert kind, was truly the sport of presidents. This was so for several reasons. Interventions, threats of force, and covert operations were free of many of the policy, political, and budgetary constraints that limited the president's will in domestic matters. Compared to his handling of interest rates, budget deficits, taxes, or tariffs, force seemed a more predictable, by far more reliable way to accomplish his ends than almost any other instrument of policy. But even if the effectiveness of force was more apparent in the first six months after a presidential move than twelve or thirty-six months later,[6] the immediate appearance could be counted on to boost the president's popularity polls. War-making also resolves, if only temporarily, the difficult problems of choice facing the president between defense and domestic expenditure allocations. Politically speaking, this is a choice that presidents can rarely gain credit for making, whatever they decide—except that a higher rate of growth for military than for domestic spending attracts less criticism when the public can see the dollars being spent in military action in some ostensibly hostile part of the world. So long as military moves are relatively inexpensive in American lives[7]—a vital qualification that President Johnson failed to take into account—they have been one of the few areas of discretion available to modern presidents.[8]

This discretion ended with the passage by Congress of the War Powers Resolution of 1973. The resolution substantially limits the uses presidents have been able to make of military force in situations not requiring a congressional declaration of war. It broadly defines these uses to include "the assignment of members of [the] Armed Forces to command, coordinate, participate in the movement of, or accompany the regular or irregular military forces of any foreign country or government when such military forces are engaged or there exists an imminent threat that such forces will become engaged in hostilities" (Section 8[c]). Hostilities are also broadly defined, and the president is required to make a report to the Congress whenever forces are moved from an alert status into areas where the threat of hostilities exists, either prior to or as a result of their presence. Congress is then empowered to disallow the president's action.

In addition to this resolution, legislation has been enacted to require the president to seek approval by the Congress of shipments of arms to foreign territories, unless he claims that shipment is in the urgent national security interest of the United States. Also, the charters of the domestic and foreign intelligence agencies have been revised to curtail covert operations.

There is no doubt that considerable scope for secret military operations still exists and that both the president and the Congress are agreed that this should remain so. However, the president's power in this area is now shared in a novel way, which in practice has inhibited the use of force in Angola,[9] Zaire,[10] Nicaragua,[11] El Salvador,[12] and other parts of the world.

The limit on the war power may not endure, but it has already produced significant pressure within the National Security Council, the cabinet subcommittee formally advising the president on national security policy, to find alternative means of international action than the resort to force or threats. The link, for instance, between the president and the Joint Chiefs of Staff was pointedly criticized by an internal 1979 reorganization study, which recommends the enhancement of the role of the State Department in the management of foreign policy crises and the coordination of presidential responses.[13] From the foreign perspective, the war power may be no less illusory than before, but from the presidential viewpoint, it has been considerably diminished.

Cabinet Leadership

The cabinet is one of the most misunderstood institutions of presidential government, and much breath has been wasted in asserting its nonexistence or its subservience to presidential will.

It is true that legally the cabinet does not exist as a collectivity. Presidential decisions are made (insofar as they are made at all, as will be seen shortly) on paper at the president's desk. But individually and collectively, presidential decisions are not possible without the cabinet members. The power of the cabinet in the American system is in fact vested—by the president's own authority to delegate his power, as well as by individual acts of Congress—in the individual cabinet officers and in the alliances they may make—with the congressional committees that oversee their legislative authorities, appropriations, and regulations; with the public interest groups, elites, and constituencies that the cabinet agencies deal with and generally represent;

and with other cabinet members, whose joint force in the subcommittee system can obligate the president at least as forcefully as he can bind them.

As in all governments, the president or a designate sits on formally and informally constituted subcommittees of the cabinet. The National Security Council is an example of a long-surviving, statutorily based subcommittee; it can appoint its own special coordinating committees as particular foreign or defense crises arise. The Domestic Council, a subcommittee made up of most of President Nixon's domestic department heads, was created legislatively in 1970 and abolished in 1977. It succeeded a brief Nixonian experiment with two smaller subcommittees, the Urban Affairs and Rural Affairs Councils, and it faded as a cabinet-level organ when President Ford established the Economic Policy Board. The titles largely explain the shift in function.

In addition, in economic policy, there are a variety of cabinet-level subcommittees on which presidential staff members are represented, and which may report to the president for his decision. These include the National Advisory Council on International Monetary and Financial Problems (established by legislation in 1945; superseded but still alive), the "Troika" and "Quadriad," the Trade Policy Committee, and (since 1977) the Economic Policy Group (see Chapter 7 for details). Membership in these groups varies; it may include both cabinet members and such noncabinet officers as the chairman of the Board of Governors of the Federal Reserve System and the chairman of the Council of Economic Advisors, both of whom are appointed to their posts by the president but whose agencies are formally established by statute. In the case of the former the law ensures virtually complete policy independence. Also included are such White House officials as the director of the Office of Management and Budget, the special representative on trade negotiations, and the president's assistant on domestic policy (Ford had an additional assistant on economic affairs).

The enumeration has only just begun, however, for the cabinet agencies are represented at the assistant secretary level on a vast and constantly changing number of interdepartmental committees. Few meet without including representation from several elements of the Executive Office. Nothing is decided unless subcommittee papers are first agreed to by Cabinet secretaries, and only then are the documents forwarded to the president for his review. In earlier times, these committees were called task forces; occasionally they have included nongovernment members, professional consultants, and scientific experts. Some of their work is published in the form of reports; most of it is compiled in decision memorandums, or more formally, in Carter administration parlance, in "Prims" (Presidential Review Memorandums, or PRMs).[14]

So far the interactions that have been identified are of formally titled officials at the secretary, deputy, assistant, or deputy assistant secretary levels.

It is instructive to look briefly at the way in which the president's domestic policy staff interacts with both officials and staff, within the Executive Office and beyond.

Table 2.1 reflects responses by presidential staff to questions about whom they met with or spoke to, directly or by telephone, on the day preceding formal interviews. It illustrates several networks of interaction—one, sideways, between domestic policy staff, the Office of Management and Budget, and staff of cabinet secretaries; a second, up a level in personnel terms, between domestic policy staff, ranking presidential assistants, and cabinet heads. The first network does the continuous daily business. It produces the draft documents of everything that counts in presidential government—legislative specifications, expenditure estimates, organizational charts, orders, choices, tactics, speeches, and announcements. The second network, meeting not quite so frequently, must read and approve the same flow of material before the president learns of it and before action can be taken in his name.

Table 2.1 also reveals the intense *crowding*, of individuals, of institutions, and of time, that characterizes presidential business. To use another metaphor, the business is often beset by traffic jams, occasions when too many functionally effective and institutionally authorized people converge on one location at the same level of the policymaking system. High-priority policy areas or crises—inflation, energy, Tehran—naturally multiply policy interactions inside and outside the Executive Office and overpopulate the networks. Observers frequently advise that in such circumstances the president would be better served with fewer staff, greater insulation, and more time to think. Since 1937, management experts have repeatedly been called upon to decide whether on these occasions, overlapping and competitive interaction represents valuable coordination of effort and comprehensive consideration of policy alternatives, or whether it is a tangle that has to be unsnarled.

The answers differ, simply because in presidential politics people dispute the value of everything the president does. One thing is indisputable, however. In the organizational complex for which the short appellation is the cabinet, there is nothing so simple as presidential leadership.

Other Instruments of Government

Thomas Jefferson once advised his successors to "take things always by the smooth handle." Insofar as he meant the institutions of American government, his advice is difficult to follow when even the oldest, most established institutions are so large, so differentiated, and so changeable that they are unfamiliar to most permanent bureaucrats, let alone to transient politicians.

What has happened is familiar to students of organizational pathology.

TABLE 2.1. Contacts of Ford Domestic Council Staff with White House Office, Cabinet, and Other Executive Office of the President[a]

	WHITE HOUSE OFFICE OR CABINET UNIT						
Frequency of Contact With[b]	President	Presidential Personnel Staff	Counsel's Office	Press Office	Congressional Liaison	Cabinet Secretaries	Secretaries' Staff
% Daily	0	69	25	0	13	6	38
% Weekly	13	19	6	13	19	31	38
% Monthly	44	13	0	0	13	31	6
% Infrequently	44	0	69	87	56	31	19

	EOP UNIT					
	Office of Management and Budget	Council of Economic Advisers	Energy Resources Council	Economic Policy Board	National Security Council	Council on International Economic Policy
% Daily	75	13	6	6	0	0
% Weekly	7	20	7	33	20	13
% Monthly	8	17	8	42	8	17
% Infrequently	6	35	48	19	49	45

[a]Data exclude director and deputy director of Domestic Council.

[b]Refers to face-to-face and telephone contacts.

Successive delegations of power by the president (or congressional mandates) to his cabinet officers and Executive Office staff stretch each official's span of control beyond the capability of any person (the president) or collectivity (the cabinet or its committees) to cope with the information and recommendations that are fed back or even to react quickly enough to the issues that their authority requires them to decide.

At the same time "overstretching" increases the difficulties of internal coordination. In these circumstances, the organization heads into a condition in which coping with purely internally generated work overtaxes its resources—a state of entropy in which the organization has difficulty even responding to dire emergencies on the outside.[15] The reputation of presidential power for prompt, if not exactly effective, action declines precipitously in such circumstances, particularly so if public opinion, fed by an ill-informed press, imagines that all the incumbent has to do is to reach for Jefferson's "smooth handle."

Complicating this problem considerably is the modern proliferation of instruments of policy that are legally under neither the president's nor the Congress's control and that cannot be coordinated by either. In a 1978 study of all 132 economic policymaking units of the executive branch (bureau level), it was found that the dozens of instruments (interest rates, tariffs, taxes, credits, loans, exchange rates, production controls, and so on) were apportioned among the units and among departments and agencies without formal or informal lines of operating authority or coordination.

The authority to fix interest rates, for example, was claimed as a sole prerogative by 2 units, while 5 others claimed to share responsibility. Fifteen different units claimed some authority for decisions affecting national commodity stockpiles. Nine units thought they had production control authorities, and in the area of greatest proliferation, 25 units responded that they exercised trade policy instruments. In some instances, one unit might claim to exercise sole authority over an instrument that another unit considered that it shared with the first. Among units sharing instruments, some said they coordinated explicitly with units at equivalent levels of other departments, while others responded that they coordinated only with the White House or the Congress. Exercise of the policy instruments required presidential approval in some cases; congressional approval in others; both in some cases; and none in others.

In the last category, there is the use by regular cabinet departments and the so-called independent agencies[16] of the power to make policy by *regulation*. Thousands of specific regulations, issued under very broadly defined authorities, constitute an enormously potent policy instrument, which can impose substantial costs on the economy, allocate resources from one economic sector to another, create eligibility for the receipt of government aid or take it away, license the commercial exploitation of new substances, save lives, clean the air, and ruin or rescue every imaginable class of enterprise. Only since 1974 would it be fair to say that the president has sought to intervene in the general regulatory process. But to exercise leadership in that realm is an improbable, if not impossible, task[17] (see Chapter 5).

The presidential system was designed with a mad monarch in clear view, so that the personality of the officeholder might not burst the institutional constraints. This has remained so. What the Founding Fathers cannot have anticipated is that in place of the monarch's arbitrariness, the system they created might be driven by the uncontrollable whimsy of the executive bureaucracy. What the novice president rarely grasps until too late is that it, not he, is the behemoth.

The President's Bureaucracy

It is important to distinguish between the White House as a place and the White House as an institution. There is, of course, only one building sitting in the middle of the block on Pennsylvania Avenue between 17th Street and East Executive Avenue. But in the same block there are three other buildings housing the staffs that institutionally make up the Executive Office of the President (EOP). A grey Victorian rococo structure is occupied by the offices of the president's junior assistants; his press and congressional liaison offices; staff of the secretary of the cabinet, of the president's assistant for domestic affairs and policy, and of the assistant for national security affairs; members and staff of the Council of Economic Advisors; and a variety of other high- and low-ranking officials and factotums. Across the street in one direction, in the capital's oldest office building and Lincoln's headquarters during the Civil War, are the former offices of the Council on Wage and Price Stability, which was abolished by President Reagan in 1981. Across the street in another direction is the New Executive Office Building, primarily the home of the Office of Management and Budget, the Office of Science and Technology Policy, the Council of Environmental Quality, and miscellaneous administrative and temporary offices.

Each of these buildings has its own symbols of identity, admission passes, cafeterias, menus, parking lots, security forces, and style. The world may imagine that the presidency is located in the well-known white mansion, but the work force of the presidency is scattered much more widely. Its members distinguish ferociously among themselves by their possession of the symbols of belonging to the White House and to the presidential office.

But if there once was a distinction between the White House and the Executive Office of the President—the former having existed since John

Adams's presidency, the latter legally only since 1939—this division can no longer usefully be made. For the president could not discharge the functions assigned to him by the Constitution, much less meet the obligations of tradition, political necessity, and new law, without the full range of units and bureaus that make up the Executive Office. Once the White House was adequate—indeed, early in this century presidents opened their own mail, wrote their own speeches, and answered their own telephones with little clerical, let alone analytical, assistance—but no longer.

The Growth of the Executive Office of the President

Were a president starting out anew he would be most unlikely to choose the particular configuration of EOP units that exists today (see Table 2.2). He would almost certainly insist on a large budget office. He would require a staff to manage his day-to-day decision process in foreign and domestic policy. He would need a White House office containing a number of senior aides close at hand, staffs for press and congressional relations, and a range of operational support. He would probably want an economic policy adviser, though not necessarily a council of them. Beyond these, his choices for institutionalized EOP staffing would reflect his own particular substantive and operational priorities as well as his organizational philosophy concerning what his Executive Office should or should not contain.

Of course, the president does not start with a clean slate. He inherits the EOP structure from his predecessors, and his immediate needs for staff support generally lead him to fill most senior EOP positions before he has the opportunity to review how much of the institutional structure he wishes to retain.

Analysis of the history of the EOP over the past three decades shows a consistent, although not widely understood, pattern of expansion. In budgetary terms the Executive Office has now grown to over eight times its size in 1950. The staff has grown in the same period from slightly more than 1,100 to more than 1,700—an increase of more than 50 percent. To put it yet another way, the number of units in the Executive Office went from five in 1939 to eighteen in 1977. This expansion has often been described as a system of runaway bureaucratic growth.

Commentators on the modern presidency have explained the phenomenon in many ways, emphasizing that since Truman the evolution of the EOP has been beyond the president's ability to control. Whereas the public has identified management of this type of growth as entirely within the president's power—and his political responsibility if he fails to stop it—experts and veterans alike have regarded the president as more the victim of the process than its beneficiary.

TABLE 2.2. Organizational Units of the Executive Office of the President, 1939-1981 (units in italics are currently in operation)

	Administration	Initiative	Duration
White House Office	Roosevelt	Public Law	1939-
Bureau of the Budget (name change, 1970)	Roosevelt	Public Law	1939-
National Resources Planning Board	Roosevelt	Public Law	1939-43
Office of Government Reports	Roosevelt	Executive Order	1939-48
Liaison Office for Personnel Management	Roosevelt	Executive Order	1939-53
Office of Emergency Management	Roosevelt	Executive Order	1940-43
War Agencies	Roosevelt	Executive Order	1943-46
Council of Economic Advisers	Truman	Public Law	1946-
National Security Council	Truman	Public Law	1949-
National Security Resources Board	Truman	Public Law	1949-53
Office of Defense Mobilization	Truman	Executive Order	1950-58
Office of the Director for Mutual Security	Truman	Public Law	1951-53
Telecommunications Adviser	Truman	Executive Order	1951-53
President's Advisory Committee on Government Organization	Truman	Executive Order	1953-61
National Aeronautics and Space Council	Eisenhower	Public Law	1958-73
Office of Civil and Defense Mobilization	Eisenhower	Public Law	1958-61
Office of Emergency Planning Preparedness	Kennedy	Public Law	1961-73
Office of Science and Technology	Kennedy	Public Law	1962-73
Office of the Special Representative for Trade Negotiations	Kennedy	Executive Order	1963-

TABLE 2.2. (Continued)

	Administration	Initiative	Duration
Office of Economic Opportunity	Johnson	Public Law	1964-75
President's Committee on Consumer Interests	Johnson	Executive Order	1964-66
Office of Special Assistant for Consumer Affairs			
National Council on Marine Resources and Engineering Development	Johnson	Public Law	1966-71
President's Council on Youth Opportunity	Johnson	Executive Order	1967-69
Office of Special Assistant for Youth			
Council for Urban Affairs	Nixon	Executive Order	1969-70
Office of Intergovernmental Relations	Nixon	Executive Order	1969-72
Council for Rural Affairs	Nixon	Executive Order	1969-70
President's Foreign Intelligence Advisory Board	Nixon	Executive Order	1969-77
Council on Environmental Quality	Nixon	Public Law	1969-
Office of Telecommunications Policy	Nixon	Public Law	1970-78
Domestic Council (name change, 1978)	Nixon	Public Law	1970-
Cost of Living Council	Nixon	Public Law	1971-74
Council on International Economic Policy	Nixon	Public Law	1971-77
Office of Consumer Affairs	Nixon	Executive Order	1971-73
Special Action Office for Drug Abuse Prevention	Nixon	Executive Order	1971-75
Federal Property Council	Nixon	Executive Order	1973-77
Energy Policy Office	Nixon	Executive Order	1973-74
Council on Wage and Price Stability	Nixon	Public Law	1974-81
Presidential Clemency Board	Ford	Executive Order	1974-75
Economic Policy Board	Ford	Executive Order	1974-77
Energy Resources Council	Ford	Executive Order	1974-77
Office of Drug Abuse Policy	Ford	Public Law	1976-78
Intelligence Oversight Board	Ford	Executive Order	1976-
Office of Science and Technology Policy	Ford	Public Law	1976-
Office of Administration	Carter	Executive Order	1977-

Detailed analysis of the facets of this growth reveal a somewhat different picture from either the popular or the expert view. The main sources of EOP growth have been:

- *Presidential initiative.* The first source of growth has been the president's desire to develop program initiatives using the EOP as a highly visible base for launching, coordinating, and implementing his objectives.
- *Congressional initiative.* Historically, many of the units of the Executive Office were put there despite rather than because of presidential initiative. They are there because Congress wanted and insisted on them, and they have remained there, whipsawed between presidential initiative and congressional resistance (or vice versa).
- *Presidential political strategy.* The third cause of growth has been the president's judgment of the resources needed to mobilize public opinion behind his policies as well as to wage campaigns for reelection.
- *The growth of the budget.* A final factor in the growth of the Executive Office reflects the fact that in both budget and manpower terms the largest single unit of the EOP has been the Bureau of the Budget/Office of Management and Budget. This in turn reflects aggregate growth in the federal budget, a trend that has been more rapid than the growth of the Office of Management and Budget (OMB) and has been beyond the ability of the chief executive to control.

Table 2.2 lists all major organizational units that have been included in the Executive Office since 1939. There has been some overlapping, particularly in the aftermath of the Second World War as the president's authority to operate special war management groups expired. The Office of Emergency Management, for instance, was absorbed by other war agencies, just as the National Security Resources Board was integrated into the Office of Defense Mobilization. This in turn was later folded into the Office of Civil and Defense Mobilization under Eisenhower. The post of Telecommunications Advisor, created by Truman, was abolished in 1953 and recreated by Nixon in 1970. Similarly, the Office of Science and Technology established by Kennedy had to be reinstated by Ford in 1976 after Nixon had allowed it to lapse. The Nixon drug policy unit expired in 1975, and a successor was appointed by Ford. It ended under Carter.

Despite the chopping and changing, six of the eighteen EOP units (counting the vice-president's office) with which the Carter administration began had their origins in or have been in continuous operation since the Truman administration; two others began in the Kennedy administration. Of the rest, six were the creation of the Nixon administration, and three of the Ford administration.

It is a common misconception to regard the current EOP as the legacy of the Nixon period. Congressional critics have frequently voiced this opinion, which reflects an understandable sensitivity to the widespread abuses of the Executive Office that were revealed during the Watergate period.[18] Notwithstanding the abuses, congressional analyses of the Nixon EOP have been inaccurate in a number of respects. It is true, as is evident in Table 2.2, that President Nixon created more EOP units than any other president (fourteen in eight years), but the picture of proliferation of units during this period overstates both the number of separate organizational initiatives issued in the president's name and the degree to which he rather than Congress initiated them.

The Councils of Urban and Rural Affairs, for example, along with the Office of Intergovernmental Relations, were small, cheap, and short-lived operations that were incorporated into the Domestic Council in 1970. The latter was not a new idea with Nixon, but had been specifically proposed by Vice-President Humphrey during the 1968 campaign and before that by Senator Muskie in Senate hearings in 1966.

Neither the Council on Environmental Quality, nor the Council on International Economic Policy, nor the Office of Consumer Affairs was the personal initiative of the president. One, Nixon actively resisted to the last minute; another was resisted and then accepted; still another was the result of complex negotiations between the White House and the Hill.

In general, it is difficult to say precisely on whose initiative units of the EOP have been established. Even when the president has proposed initiatives for his own office, Congress has been prepared to modify them substantially. Also, presidents have not been successful in resisting congressionally inspired reorganization plans for the EOP. To that extent Congress is as responsible as the chief executive for the aggregate gowth of the EOP. However, and more to the point if we look at this growth in budget and manpower terms, neither the congressional initiatives nor the proliferation of units under Nixon can together account for more than 13 percent of the total EOP budget or 9 percent of the total manpower strength since 1971; over the last quarter century only 7 percent of the EOP budget can be accounted for by identifiable congressional incentives. Congress may have caused much of the proliferation of small units in the EOP, but it has added little to the overall cost. This is so for the simple reason that aggregate budgets and manpower strengths for the EOP have been dominated from the very beginning by just two units, the White House Office and the Bureau of the Budget (BOB/OMB). Consequently, the reasons for the growth of these two units must account for a significant share of the overall growth of the Executive Office. During three of the last seven presidential election years, the budget for the White House Office, the EOP unit that we would expect to be the most sensitive to presidential campaign demands, has increased by a larger margin than its average rate of growth over the four- or five-year period surrounding each election year.

It is easier to suggest than to prove that presidential political fortunes have dictated expansion of the Executive Office. There are other reasons for the growth of the White House Office (WHO) and the EOP that cannot strictly be regarded as political in nature. For one, the expansion of the legislative business of Congress and the proliferation of congressional committees have increased severalfold the work load handled by the congressional liaison staff of the White House, and consequently both its size and cost. Growth of the Press Office and related functions is another major element in the growth of the WHO overall. Although it is broadly political in scope and objective and is regarded by critics as a type of permanent campaign staff, its growth reflects at least as much the demands of the nation's media as it does election tactics on the part of the incumbent.

A quarter of total EOP spending since 1950 has been on the budget agency. In the same period the federal government's budget has quadrupled in size. It is consequently reasonable to link the size of the budget to the size of BOB/OMB, and the growth of one to the growth of the other. The first inference is accurate, but the second is not. It is *not* the budget review functions that have driven the recent expansion of OMB. Indeed, throughout the period the ratio of examiners to budget dollars has been deteriorating. Since 1969, when the overall size of OMB began to increase, the number of these examiners has actually fallen. Internally then, the growth of OMB has flowed from the performance of nonbudgetary functions, in particular the expansion of the management divisions under President Nixon and subsequently in the Carter administration the implementation of the President's Reorganization Project.

It seems natural that the expansion of government services across the board should result in an expansion of the bureaucracy at the top to organize, provide, and monitor these services. And so it has in the case of the Executive Office of the President. Compared to the top managerial staff in a representative sample of government agencies, the total (constant dollar) outlays for the EOP have generally grown faster than some and slower than others. Overall, in the period from 1971 through 1978, the average real rate of increase in budgetary outlays was a moderate 26.2 percent for the EOP; only the Departments of Agriculture and the Interior, and the Office of Assistant Secretary of Health in the Department of Health, Education, and Welfare showed lower rates. The Departments of Transportation, Labor, and Commerce all indicated significantly higher average annual growth rates. By contrast, however, comparison of EOP outlays with those for the House of Representatives and the Senate, shows clearly that the legislative branch has far outstripped the executive branch in aggregate budgetary growth since 1971.

Thus it seems fair to say that a certain amount of the opposition in the press and in Congress to EOP growth reflects a misconception about the relative rates of bureaucratic growth government-wide. In most respects the evolution of the EOP has been modest by comparison with other executive agencies and with the growth of the legislative branch. To some extent also, critics of the presidency have been blind to these comparisons so that they may express opposition to the person or the programs of particular presidents more than to the bureaucratic structure of the EOP.

The Effect of Political Environment

In general, as an organization grows and becomes more complex, the process of maturation begins to insulate those inside the organization from what is happening in the outside world. Among "immature" organizations, however (i.e., organizations whose leadership has not had time to establish itself), a change of administration, a reorganization, or a new policy initiative can set off a chain reaction of personnel turnover and the displacement of responsibility at a faster rate than officials can cope with. In this situation, the organization loses its recognizable internal authority; the head office becomes a bottleneck for lower-level requests to approve action; and officials become dependent on outside groups rather than their nominal superiors for cues to act. For this reason, it is not surprising that the repeated reorganizations within the EOP (and the executive branch generally) have produced a high degree of responsiveness to the policy demands of the external environment.[19] Responsiveness, however, can breed dependency, in which case not only does the president lose control of the further reaches of his bureaucracy, but he discovers that he cannot activate the very core of the existing organization when he needs to. And so he improvises by adding new elements capable of rapid response.

In this perspective, EOP growth, with all of its unevenness in aggregate size over time and in the relative size and shape of the individual units, can be explained partly as a response to the unpredictable changes in the policy and political environment with which the president and the officials responsible to him have had to deal.

Consider these examples. The problem of continued budget deficits is one indication of an overload situation in government when the expectations that people (inside and outside government) have for policy exceed the capabilities of the economy and the machinery of government to deliver and pay for them. Scarcity of resources puts pressure on the president's staff to develop program and policy initiatives while balancing many competing interests in a rational and equitable manner. Success in this effort is related to the president's broader success in managing his legislative program in Congress and in restraining congressional spending in accord with the president's program. Crises in budgeting and in legislative relations have manifested themselves in the expansion of the congressional liaison (WHO) and budgeting (OMB) staffs. Likewise, there are broad movements in political response to the presidency and its programmatic successes and failures. The familiar seesawing of presidential popularity and the well-known crisis in popular confidence in both the federal government and the political parties have been a direct stimulus to the growth of the press and public liaison staffs employed in the WHO.

Bureaucratic responses to environmental pressure can be charted both as straight-line changes in budgetary outlays and manpower growth and in relative terms as uneven rates of development reflecting intense competition between units of the Executive Office for funds, manpower, and other resources.

Among the most stable of EOP units of the 1970s are also some of the oldest—the White House Office, OMB, the National Security Council, and the Council of Economic Advisors. These organizations have all remained relatively stable, at least as measured in budgetary terms, from year to year. An example of extreme instability in the 1970s was the Special Action Office for Drug Abuse Prevention (SAODAP) and President Nixon's commitment to initiatives in the drug policy field. The greater part of the SAODAP program was in the form of grants, both to other executive agencies and to agencies, contractors, and researchers outside the federal government. This was a program initiative that the president regarded as requiring the unique momentum that placement in the EOP alone could effect.

The rise and fall of individual EOP units is consistent with at least two different interpretations of the evolution of the presidential staff. In one view, the president is responsible for the rise and fall, himself stimulating the competition within the office between his staffs, rewarding units whose missions reflect his priorities and downgrading those whose missions no longer represent these priorities. In the other view, the EOP units compete among themselves for resources, court the president, OMB, and the congressional appropriations committees, and achieve ascendancy or failure, without regard to any reasoned design of the Executive Office or even a rough order of the president's priorities.

It is not possible to distinguish finally between the interpretations, particularly in the absence of any overall management or budgetary process guiding and balancing unit resources within the EOP. There is probably a degree of truth in both propositions. The key point is the underlying dynamic at work: The EOP has had perforce to adapt to the uncertain and unstable conditions of the policy environment. This necessity has in turn generated among White House officials greater self-consciousness in decision making and a demand on their part for reliable review and evaluation mechanisms to see that decisions, once made at one level, are implemented at the appropriate places and times at other levels; for forward planning to anticipate crises (especially in the prediction of resource scarcities); and finally, for coordinating mechanisms to ensure that both implementation and prediction serve the current decision-making process.

Public distrust and political alienation are also bound to set in train a sequence of bureaucratic responses that produce much the same characteristics in the EOP as do the other factors that have been identified. Such distrust tends to make the president's political future less predictable, and because crisis conditions make every executive move much more visible, risky, and questionable, political assessment in presidential decision making must reach down to the minutiae of policy. The development of analytical capability with a "presidential interest" has consequently grown quite significantly in both domestic and foreign areas; the methods of political analysis have become more sophisticated and more specialized, and the staff to provide it more numerous and more expensive.

In consequence, the need has grown on the part of elective officials to relate the detail of policy analysis to the exigencies of political survival. This in turn puts new and unusual pressure on the old distinction between "policy" and "politics" and between the two categories of people who used to serve different functions—between civil service and "neutral competence" on the one hand, and appointees, noncareer officials, and "political advisers" on the other.[20]

The Diffusion of Presidential Action

The framers of the Constitution left the finality of decision making where they put the greater part of popular sovereignty—in the Congress. Congress has delegated a great many powers to the executive, and in return required its legatees to report what they propose to do or what they have already done under their derived power. These requirements, as well as the modern exercise of presidential discretion and coordination, have a strong tendency to diffuse and obscure presidential leadership.

Required Decisions. Currently the president has hundreds of obligations to report to the Congress. Of the recurrent reports, there are forty-three annual obligations, which cover everything from the budget and the Economic Report (which are due on January 22 each year and usually accompany the presentation of the president's State of the Union message) to reports on foreign arms sales, the use of emergency powers, trade agreements, international drug control, energy conservation, exemptions from water quality and solid waste disposal standards, river basin development, and government employee salaries.

In the highly competitive bureaucratic environment of the Executive Office, these requirements are a boon to the units that must prepare them. For whether the president likes it or not, they force him to maintain the staffs necessary to meet his obligations. In addition, they are the teeth by which presidential staff tear the president's time away from other things. They compel him to decide what his staff, congressional committees, and special interest groups, though not necessarily he himself, want decided.

The competitiveness—by which presidents like Roosevelt and Truman sought to ensure that the advice they got was analytically rigorous and to multiply their options—took place in an Executive Office that was a fraction of its present size and leaner (less top-heavy) in shape. A single presidential counsel, like Clark Clifford under President Truman, had the responsibility for assembling the administration's proposals, coordinating the legislative drafting and budgetary processes, writing the president's messages and speeches, and guarding his political strategy. Reputations begun then seem more formidable today as the conditions in which staffs functioned no longer exist.

Were Truman and Clifford supermen? That depends on who is to be credited for the president's achievements and debited for his failures and on whether the former outweigh the latter. But that judgment presupposes an altogether different sort of evaluation. It is not an assessment of whether the smaller Executive Office was organizationally better equipped to execute its tasks than the current operation. The president's discretion *not* to decide many things has certainly been diminished in the past thirty years, but in other ways the scope of his discretion to decide has been enlarged. There is little the president can do about the burden of required decisions, but it is inconceivable that he would reduce the size of the Executive Office and thereby limit his capability for exercising that discretion.

Discretionary Decisions. In the larger and more complex Executive Office of today, the bigger units drive the smaller ones, not to mention the cabinet agencies, out of the market of presidential attention. They can do this by generating more issues for decision and a greater volume of paper than the president could fairly absorb if each staff unit had a nominally equal share of the president's time and stood in line for it. With advantages of size and resources, and using a variety of staffing tactics, some units can manipulate the rules of the game of executive decision making and exercise disproportionate influence over the process as a result.

There are several remedies for a president trying to reassert himself. One is to put a personal substitute in the line of paper flow, designate him as chief of staff, and refuse to attend to any but high-priority issues. Notwithstanding both personal and public qualms, the last four presidents have resorted to this device.

An alternative, on which President Carter relied before appointing his chief of staff in mid-1979, is to anticipate the principal items of government business each year and establish the priorities for presidential attention among them. From 1977 to 1979, the vice-president's staff was charged with drawing up a six-month list of policy issues that the Executive Office units and executive agencies expected to require presidential decision. The list was then reviewed by the president's senior policy advisers, and recommendations for ranking the items, deleting some, and bringing others forward were made for his approval. The resultant list became the agenda of the administration for the next half year—unless the president's mind was changed in the meantime.

In fact, the alternatives for mobilizing the president's discretion are limited only by the bureaucratic ingenuity of his staff. Table 2.3 illustrates a selection of the devices used to catch presidential attention and to develop recommendations for his decision in several high-priority policy areas within the last five years. It is by no means exhaustive.

Coordination Procedures. The table also draws attention to a technique of presidential decision making that is not well known, but that is becoming increasingly more potent as presidents grasp the limitations and liabilities of spawning special-purpose bureaucratic units. This technique relies on the issuance of an executive order, a directive from the president having statutory legal force in the executive branch, which lays down rules for analyzing issues and criteria of review that policy proposals must meet before being decided by the president. In the jargon of the trade, these are known as impact statements; essentially they are procedures for coordination.

Not all have originated with the president. In 1969, Congress wrote into the provisions of the National Environmental Policy Act the requirement that government agencies analyze their proposed projects to identify a wide range of environmental impacts and also to weigh the environmental benefits and costs of alternative proposals. This analytical procedure was also an attempt to coordinate federal government action with the environmental policy objectives enunciated in the act. For the most part, the reporting requirement, known as an Environmental Impact Statement (EIS), has been applied to agency projects whose impacts are limited to specific geographic localities. In 1975 alone, for example, federal agencies assessed more than 30,000 different projects for their environmental impacts, and although most of these assessments fell far short of a full-scale EIS, between 1970 and 1976 about 6,000 EISs were prepared. Substantial litigation has tested the analytical and procedural adequacies of these statements, and about 5 percent have been ruled inadequate and ordered to be repeated.

In a review of the EIS process in 1976, the Council on Environmental Quality (CEQ) urged agencies to focus their analysis more on program than project decisions. "The realization is growing," CEQ reported, "that many

TABLE 2.3. Mobilizing the President's Policymaking Discretion

	METHODS		
	Ad Hoc Interagency Group	New EOP Unit or Function	Procedure by Executive Order
Energy	Eizenstat Group (1979)	Energy Resources Council (1974-77)	---
	Cutler Group (1979)	White House Assistant (Schlesinger, 1977-78)	
		White House Coordinator (Cutler, 1979)	
		Energy Mobilization Board (1980-)	
Inflation	---	Adviser to the President on Inflation (1978-)	Inflation Impact Statement (1974-76) (Executive Order 11821)
Urban and regional affairs	White House Conference on Balanced Growth (1978)	Interagency Coordinating Council (1978-)	Urban and Community Impact Analysis (1978-) (Executive Order 12074)
	Urban and Regional Policy Group (1977-78)		
Regulatory reform	Regulatory Analysis Review Group (1978-)	Regulatory Council (1978-)	Regulatory Analyses (Executive Order 12044)

Federal actions can be grouped under program statements for more useful and systematic analysis. Repetitive actions or actions that affect a clearly delineated, meaningful geographic area are often defined as programs and are grouped into program EISs."[21] In 1975, thirty-eight analyses covering program proposals were submitted to CEQ.

The EIS procedure remains one instrument for both analytical review and policy coordination, but its scope is widely perceived as limited. Although, in fact, the wording of the statute defines environmental impacts very broadly, administratively speaking the EIS procedure has not resulted in the wide coverage of urban and regional policymaking that its framers perhaps intended. Instead, the focus as well as the impact of the statements has been largely at the level of individual projects and specific localities.

Other procedural approaches have also been tried, and although their purpose was not originally to focus on urban and regional policy, in time they have come to represent significant new tools for the president and the Executive Office to apply in that direction. For instance, in November 1974, President Ford issued Executive Order 11821 with the objective of improving agency decision making and coordinating agency initiatives with the president's concern for limiting the cost of government and the rate of inflation. The method adopted was called, somewhat inappropriately, the Inflation Impact Statement (IIS).

The IIS procedure marked a significant shift in analytical focus from the localized impacts identified in the EIS procedures. Threshold criteria for identifying proposals to be analyzed were $100 million in increased costs for the national economy as a whole in one year, or $50 million in one year for a single economic sector, industry, or level of government.

The executive order, along with OMB Circular A-107 that implemented it, required federal agencies to identify those legislative and regulatory proposals that were considered major by prevailing standards. Before these were sent to the Congress or (if regulations) published in the *Federal Register*, agencies were to prepare analyses of the proposals' costs and benefits, as well as the costs and benefits of alternatives. Two Executive Office units monitored compliance. OMB oversaw the analytical process as a whole and also evaluated IISs prepared for proposed legislation. The Council on Wage and Price Stability (COWPS) was responsible for evaluating IISs of proposed rules and regulations.

The weakness of the IIS process was largely the result of its short life; it expired on December 31, 1976, at the close of the Ford administration, after less than two years of operation. In so short a time, agencies were not able to regularize the role that IISs could play in the formulation of policy proposals. Rather, as a staff evaluation explained:

Typically an agency uses the IIS more as an input to the decisions that are
made *after* the proposal is published than to those made *before* such publication. To the extent that the analysis is performed outside the office which
develops the proposal (which is especially likely where an office has very
limited analytical capability), the analysis is not apt to be an important input
in the proposal's development. Furthermore, much of the work on an IIS is
completed just prior to the proposal's publication, which limits the effect of the
analysis in molding the initial proposal.[22]

Notwithstanding, the Executive Office had established a precedent for using analytical staff work, directed to cover particular kinds of policy impacts,
as a method for executive decision making, review, and coordination. To be
sure, OMB and the president's Domestic Policy Staff have traditionally had
the potential for undertaking this type of review, but conventional budet
review and legislative clearance processes have not attempted to do this
regularly for all major policy decisions. What was novel about the IIS process
was that it provided Executive Office policymakers with an overall perspective on agency initiatives, and by identifying conflicting goals, hidden costs,
and inadvertent impacts, it enhanced the central capability for coordination.

The Carter administration decided to revive the regulatory analyses that
the IISs had begun. Executive Order 12044, issued on March 23, 1978, provided, among other things, for a similar process of agency identification of
major regulations and the completion of regulatory analyses for those
regulations that "may have major economic consequences for the general
economy, for individual industries, geographical regions, or levels of government." The addition of a geographic or regional focus to the analyses was a
notable, if not widely appreciated, expansion of coverage. In addition, the
wording clearly indicates that both OMB and COWPS, which resumed
responibility for the new regulatory analyses as they had done with IISs,
were concerned to try to institutionalize the analytical process in time to
have a real influence over policy decisions themselves. The organizational
network was also expanded for review of the regulatory analyses. A
Regulatory Analysis Review Group (RARG) was established to comment
on, evaluate, and if necessary reject, agency submissions; this group included
the Office of Management and Budget, the Council on Wage and Price
Stability, the Council of Economic Advisors, the Domestic Policy Staff, the
Office of Science and Technology Policy, the Council on Environmental
Quality, and eleven cabinet-level agencies.

As with the IIS process, the emphasis of RARG review has been on assessing the costs and benefits of regulatory proposals in a conventional
macroeconomic or sectoral framework. By and large, despite the language of

Executive Order 12044, the tendency has not been to focus on the regional or urban area effects that were of primary concern to the Carter urban policy. It was to fill this gap that President Carter, on March 27, 1978, promised to create "a continuing mechanism" that would make the "analysis of the urban and regional impact of new programs . . . an integral and permanent part of all policy development throughout our government."[23] This was titled Urban and Community Impact Analysis. It is the first venture into a realm of central planning that is routine in European government but that has nevertheless not been carried on here since the Roosevelt Administration forty years ago.

The Anatomy of a Decision

Discovering the complexity of his decisions is an all too recent presidential experience, and not an inevitable one among incumbents who may not grasp just how complexity limits what the president can choose or determines whether he can decide at all.

Consider, for example, the decision to fund a new nuclear energy source, the liquid metal fast breeder reactor (LMFBR), which President Carter faced every year of his administration. The details of this particular program choice were unique, but the complexity of the decision facing the president is typical of any modern policy area that requires short-term decisions based on long-term guesses, that has both domestic and foreign policy implications (that compete with one another), and that raises alarms domestically among mutually hostile constituencies, to each of which the president may be indebted.

During the election campaign of 1976, Carter had expressed strong personal opposition to the development of commercial breeder reactors for the generation of nuclear power. Breeder reactors are fueled by enriched uranium, and the fuel cycle within the reactor "breeds" more plutonium than it consumes in fission. By the time the president was inaugurated on January 20, 1977, an expensive program to plan and construct a prototype breeder reactor had been under way for several years, and a site for construction of the reactor, at Clinch River, Tennessee, had been fixed. The Ford administration budget for fiscal year 1977 proposed further increases in expenditure to lead to testing of the reactor under experimental operating conditions. The results of those tests, it had been anticipated, would then lead to a government decision on whether and how to proceed to develop the technology for the new type of commercial nuclear plant.

It was clear at once to the new Executive Office staff and to the president himself that he had to make a quick decision. The new Domestic Policy Staff was determined to reconstruct the Ford budget proposals, but there was little time to do so and to give Congress, which is subject to its own strict budgeting schedule, time to assess the budgetary changes. At the same time, there were no shortcuts to developing alternative policies for the president to consider in an issue as complex as nuclear energy.

U.S. demand for electricity is expected to outstrip the supply of fossil fuels needed to produce it by the end of this century, and alternative sources of energy must be found and quickly put in development. An energy-generating technology like the LMFBR would provide a substantial energy benefit, even at fairly high levels of capital investment and operating cost, if we assume that the technology is safe from accident or sabotage; that its waste can be put out of harm's way for half a million years; that alternative energy sources would be less economical; that the economy will need as much electricity as is now thought; and that a world energized by thousands of plutonium reactors would be as comfortable as the present world of oil- and coal-fired stations.

But these were not the only issues. Indeed, the breeder reactor program directly or indirectly involved more elements of decision, and conceivably more jurisdictions and decision makers, than most problems that have faced past administrations.

There were, first of all, technical disputes. Every one of our assumptions was disputed by groups of professional scientists, engineers, and environmental planners. There were also conflicting reports from government agencies. On the economic cost-benefit side alone, there were detailed analyses from the Energy Research and Development Administration (ERDA), from the General Accounting Office, from the Joint Economic Committee of the Congress, and from the Congressional Budget Office, as well as numerous private and institutional studies. These did not agree.

Second, the technology of the components on which the Clinch River LMFBR project depended was in 1977 in varying stages of evolution. The various components were being researched, demonstrated, and tested in twenty-two different facilities scattered over sixteen states. The cost of this part of the project was more than $1 billion. Thus, any decision the president made was likely to affect employment and investment in several different regions, the state of Tennessee in particular. Concern about the regional and local implications of the decision was forcefully represented to the White House by Tennessee senators and representatives, among others.

Third, it was not at all easy for the president to assess the consequences of each decision that might be presented to him. The breeder reactor program had originally been designed in a series of steps, leading from basic components and process research, through the construction of a sequence of demonstration plants (each larger than the one before), to the full implementation of a commercial breeder system, which was to begin with one reactor in 1987 and to number 1,178 by the year 2011. Distinctions among research, demonstration, and phased commercial development are very difficult to draw. The average annual cost was estimated in 1976 to be $600 million (with a total cost to 1987 of at least $10 billion). Each new outlay had the effect of tying the project to a direction that limited the resources available to alternative paths, to alternative energy technologies, and to alternative goals. In 1977 the LMFBR program was the single largest commitment in the energy research and development budget, which in turn absorbed nearly 10 percent of all federal research and development. Ostensibly limited decisions affecting LMFBR would thus structure the entire range of research and development options available to the federal government. Also, as both federal government and private sector funds and management were involved (the private sector significantly less than was originally planned), the president's decisions on LMFBR affected long-term investment plans throughout the nuclear industry, which had actively resisted the nonplutonium options.

A fourth source of complexity in the decision reflected the president's strong public commitment to environmental safety. In this case, it just was not possible to gauge what the environmental impacts might be. Early environmental impact statements for the Clinch River project had been disputed, and it was the judgment of the Environmental Protection Agency that commercial development of the plant technology could not be reliably assessed. On the other hand, the ERDA program managers argued that the president did not have to make a decision on commercial implementation, and therefore take account of the environmental hazards, for at least another decade. To that, the environmentalists responded that as the president was committing himself to a very high level of spending, he was *ipso facto* going to preclude the development of alternative, and perhaps less environmentally risky, energy sources.

If the domestic issues were intractable, the difficulties of effective policy analysis became insuperable when the foreign policy consequences were introduced. For the president was actively canvassing the world for international commitments to limit nuclear weapons proliferation. This required strict controls on the diffusion of enriched uranium and plutonium. The administration felt that the international safeguards that existed at the time were inadequate. More reliable would be a commitment by Japan, Britain, several West European countries, and others to defer their development of breeder reactor and plutonium cycle systems and to cut off trade in both the technology and the fissionable fuels. The decision on the LMFBR was a test of the president's willingness to put off what he was simultaneously urging others to defer. If the United States believed the argument that it pressed on the Japanese and Europeans—that the world's supplies of uranium for conventional reactor systems were plentiful and that a new generation of breeder reactors would not be necessary for at least thirty years—then the president had to confirm it by putting an end to the Clinch River project.

The details of the decision-making process in this case remain classified. They were gathered together after the event in a report commissioned by the president. The purpose was to see how the process had been conducted and with what effect on the comprehensiveness of the information and policy options that were presented to him, the effectiveness of Executive Office coordination, and the capabilities of the president's staff to adhere to his priorities.[24]

In all, including the president himself, there were forty active participants in the decision-making process, representing eight different units of the Executive Office and another five cabinet-level agencies. Participants were counted if they interacted more than once on the issues involved with people outside their own EOP unit or agency. If those staffs were included that drafted agency positions and policy papers or participated in interagency negotiations on at least one occasion, the total would rise to almost one hundred. The cabinet made no recommendation on the issues, but the issues were referred to twice in the minutes. The president himself read at least five memorandums on the topic and had two scheduled meetings with staff to discuss it. One lasted for twenty minutes, the other for five. The principal medium of decision making was by memorandum. In addition, three senators from two states were directly involved, communicating informally with the president by telephone. Carter also communicated by letter with a congressman from a third state, who was chairman of a House committee with legislative jurisdiction over the breeder project.

The public record of what happened reveals that the president made a sequence of decisions over a ten-week period. In February 1977, the *New York Times* printed a leak claiming that Carter "urged cuts in [the] nuclear breeder device but his aides now propose an increase." On April 7, the president made a public statement suggesting that the Clinch River project would be cut back to "an experimental basis." In response, the Republican senator from Tennessee told the *New York Times* that he understood that work at Clinch River would be stopped. The newly elected Democratic senator from Tennessee told the paper that his understanding was different; he anticipated "no more than a reassessment of the Clinch River project." Also, the *Washington Post* reported from Japan that the president's statement had created uncertainty there about the future of Japan's breeder reactor program and about American attitudes toward supplying the reprocessed uranium that program would require. Finally, on April 20, the President announced his national energy policy, which included a statement that commercial reprocessing of uranium and recycling of plutonium for the breeder had been deferred. The word used to describe the decision on the future of Clinch River was "cancellation."

Dynamics of the Process. There were three, perhaps four stages in the process, depending on how the decision of April 20 is interpreted. What drove the staging of the process was this: Each decision reached was vague enough to be interpreted quite differently by major participants. This then required a further policy review to resolve the issue afresh. Staff work did not significantly reduce the issues or options for presidential decision at each stage, so that the president was confronted by roughly the same set of problems on each occasion.

These issues came up as a result of quite separate though parallel policy review processes (a foreign policy process, an energy policy development process, and a broad domestic policy review process). Neither the schedules nor the outputs of these processes were coordinated with one another. Consequently, it was inevitable that the president would be required to respond to each in turn and that each of his responses would be misunderstood by participants on the other tracks. The gloss put on these misunderstandings was that until the April 20 decision there had been a series of *temporary* decisions—holding actions pending a more detailed and coordinated review of the issues.

The first stage reflected the negotiations on the 1978 budget levels for the LMFBR program. The timing was dictated by the budget revision deadline, but neither the proliferation policy nor the energy policy could have been ready by then. On the other hand, the president was clearly on record as being opposed to the breeder reactor in one form or another. Campaign promises left a fairly wide margin for defining policy and program recommendations, which might have become the focus of the February discussions. The fact that they did not appears to have been the result of ambivalence on the part of the president's assistant on energy policy, James Schlesinger, about detailing the future of the program, and his unwillingness at that stage to engage the other participants in discussion of the options and contingent funding levels. His position in turn depended on the president's desire to limit internal debate on elements of the energy plan.

The National Security Council and the Domestic Council positions were in accord, insofar as both sought a budget option that would demonstrably reinforce the campaign commitment and indicate to foreign governments the administration's determination not to proceed with the plutonium cycle in commercial energy production.

The pressure of the clock appears to have driven the advisers away from detailed options analysis. Impending West German and Japanese decisions and related problems scheduled for international meetings in London, Persepolis, and Salzburg encouraged the national security adviser, Zbigniew

Brzezinski, to press the president for statements that could be taken into proliferation negotiations abroad. Without detailed planning of the LMFBR options, however, whatever statements the president might have been induced to issue ran the risk of reserving the options for the domestic program and appearing too vague, if not intentionally deceptive, to the foreign powers.

Alternatively, if the president sought to oppose clearly plutonium proliferation in the foreign arena, he ran an uncharted and untested course in Congress on the domestic issues. These problems were compounded by the unilateral tactics pursued in this early stage by both Brzezinski and Schlesinger, whose regular access to the president enabled each to act on his own priorities without informing or consulting the other.

The second stage ran from late February to April 7. In this period, the president decided to release a statement "to stop breeder reactors."[25] This decision did not in fact stop the LMFBR program. The decision was reached by two or three paths, depending on how they are counted. One path was taken by a review team, composed of nongovernment experts and public interest representatives. It was heavily weighted in favor of the breeder, so much so that at least one of the opponents of the breeder threatened to resign. Another interpretation of the review team was that it was the last chance the breeder proponents would have to make their case before the axe fell. The situation was quite unclear—the panel was stacked, but which side of the policy fight would get the coup de grace no one knew for sure.

The timing of the second stage was in fact determined by the National Security Council and the completion of its deliberations on nuclear proliferation issues. The visit of Japanese Prime Minister Fukuda, a West German–Brazilian agreement for reprocessing technology, last-minute negotiations with Japanese officials, and the State Department's preparations for a London conference of nuclear suppliers—these were the immediate pressures that drove longer-term policy planning out of the channels of presidential review. Time and access pressures, further stimulated by demands from Congress for a policy statement from the admnistration, so clogged the channels that on one occasion the president approved one recommendation without reading the policy analysis supporting it. However accidental this incident may have been, it is a common effect of uncontrolled timing on policy review—in a crisis situation the need to act absorbs whatever resources are available to consider the options. Thus, in crisis at the executive level, policy review as such can cease.

The April 7 statement produced an enormous amount of misinterpretation and confusion. Congressional doubts created demands for a clear delineation of administration intentions, but the terminology in which the options were publicly cast did not resolve the underlying ambiguities about the research status of the Clinch River breeder reactor, the level of funding of the component program supporting the reactor, the regional implications (especially for Ohio and Tennessee) of the first two items, and the alternative development paths for future nuclear energy research.

The final stage of decision ran from April 7 to April 20 and reflected the process by which the president accepted a range of options on the LMFBR, the plutonium cycle in general, and the Tennessee facility in particular. Deliberation on the options continued right up to the morning of the presidential speech on energy. But even at that point the participants remained unclear on the concrete implementation of the options. Additionally, a number of important policy considerations omitted in the earlier process now reemerged. These involved people who had not participated at all in the earlier stages – specifically, White House political advisers who entered at this point to negotiate with officials from the two states most immediately affected by the decision.

These negotiations went on for more than a month before the president issued a clarification of the budgetary implications of the April 20 decision for the Ohio and Tennessee locations of the reactor research effort. During this period too, there was intense congressional activity, with one House committee voting to restore the breeder reactor funds and a second committee voting to sustain the president's cut. Opposition was vocal in the Senate also. Six weeks after the final decision had been made on the LMFBR program, the president was still compelled to reiterate and refine the terms of that decision for those who felt that his position might still be shifted.

The Limits of Decision

What can be learned from this case? First, there was an important relationship between timing and staging. Without clearly marked stages of decision, deadlines, and finality of the decision itself, the timing of the process was both infinite as the stages were recapitulated and subject to sudden crisis. Insofar as all decisions appeared temporary and the time limits extendable, those participants who were dissatisfied with the outcome at one stage could hope to recover their initiative by launching a new round. Fostering a crisis atmosphere was, in this context, one tactic for outmaneuvering other players in the ongoing policy debate. Of course, the advantages so gained could be only temporary before the process began all over again.

Indeed, three years later, the Congress continued to argue over the issue without reaching final agreement with the administration. Proposals to legislate the ending of the Clinch River project failed to pass in both 1978 and 1979, and the president was compelled to strike a compromise, according to which the budgetary authority for the breeder reactor program would continue to remain high—at around the half billion dollar mark—while he sought to kill the Clinch River project and perhaps permit another reactor to be built in its place.

Second, it is especially difficult for the Executive Office, designed as it has been for many years with quasi-autonomous foreign and domestic policy staffs, to coordinate decision making on issues that cut across the two areas. To be sure, the case that has been described took place in the early days of the administration, and some of the difficulties of coordination reflected in the analysis were acknowledged at the time they occurred. As a result of the report the president received, a new set of procedures was established to attempt to remedy this problem. However, more recent analyses of national security staff work have confirmed that the problem has persisted.

The case may therefore suggest that as a general rule, to the extent that foreign policy problems are brought into the executive decision-making process with short lead times (typically involving large numbers of options and separate decisions that the president is required to address), they can capture a higher priority in the president's time and attention than can domestic policy issues.

The President's Time. In 1937, one of the earliest analyses of the administration of the president's business began with the dramatic advice: "The President needs help."[26] That conclusion seems less apposite today, as the case of the breeder reactor decision shows. The president has plenty of help in one sense, and yet in another he continues to need more. The presidential literature is replete with the same conclusion, phrased somewhat differently for new administrations, and applied to changing circumstances. But what sort of help?

With the Carter administration, it was perhaps clearer than before that adding new staff or new units to the existing apparatus of the Executive Office was not necessarily the sort of help that was wanted. Despite this, early reductions in both the number of EOP units and the overall number of presidential appointments were lost to the improvisation and growth that followed the traditional cyclical pattern to which I have already referred.

There has been considerable agreement among White House veterans that the president needs more time as much as he needs anything.[27] But the electoral cycle presses even more demandingly on the incumbent president now than it used to. Because his relationship with Congress is uncertain, he must be more sensitive than once might have been necessary to the consequences of his actions for the mid-term congressional election that takes place at the end of the president's second year. His own reelection campaign then commences quite early in the third year. By the fourth year, the campaign is at the forefront of his priorities. For only one year, the first for a one-term president, can it be said the he has time and some political incentive to consider longer-term problems and to make decisions and commitments whose results may not be immediately apparent. But for that period, he must either rely on his predecessor's budget estimates or compose his own budget request in little more than eight weeks after inauguration. That process can, as we have just seen, create enormous difficulties for deliberation. In the presidential environment, we might conclude, nothing is ever truly decided, acted upon, done. A decision, once taken, turns out to be a process of implementation, and that is nothing more than a skein of unraveling circumstance to be rewoven by the special interests, inside the government and out, who are shrewd or well-paid enough to keep watching. A president himself cannot hope to keep watch on all those whom he pays to keep watch, let alone take care of business.

Notes

1. Office of Management and Budget, *Staff Report,* 1979 (unreleased); Philip Odeen, *Staff Report on National Security Policymaking,* 1979 (unreleased).

2. Peri E. Arnold, "Reorganization and Politics: A Reflection on the Adequacy of Administrative Theory," *Public Administration Review* 34 (May-June 1974), pp. 205–211; Harold Seidman, *Politics, Position and Power: The Dynamics of Federal Organization* (New York: Oxford University Press, 1970). A 1978 survey of economic policy units, for example, found that one-half of the units reported having carried through an internal reorganization of some kind in the year before, one-third had altered major operating procedures, and one-seventh had reorganized their objectives, roles, and missions. John Helmer, *Findings of Economic Analysis and Policymaking Machinery Survey,* 1978 (President's Reorganization Project, unreleased).

3. John E. Jackson, *Constituents and Leaders in Congress* (Cambridge, Mass.: Harvard University Press, 1974); Paul Burstein, "Ending the Vietnam War: Components of Change in Senate Voting on Vietnam War Bills," *American Journal of Sociology* 82, 5 (March 1977), pp. 991–1006.

4. Barry M. Blechman and Stephen S. Kaplan, *Force Without War: U.S. Armed Forces as a Political Instrument* (Washington, D.C.: Brookings Institution, 1978).

5. Thomas Powers, *The Man Who Kept the Secrets: Richard Helms and the CIA* (New York: Knopf, 1979).

6. Blechman and Kaplan, *Force Without War,* pp. 86–89.

7. John E. Mueller, "Trends in Popular Support for the Wars in Korea and Vietnam," *American Political Science Review* 65 (August 1971), pp. 363–384; and John Helmer, *Bringing the War Home: The American Army in Vietnam and After* (New York: Free Press, 1974).

8. McGeorge Bundy, "Vietnam, Watergate, and Presidential Powers," *Foreign Affairs* (Winter 1979-1980), pp. 307–407.

9. Frank Snepp, *Decent Interval* (New York: Random House, 1977).

10. U.S., Congress, House, Committee on International Relations, Subcommittee

on International Security and Scientific Affairs, *Hearings on Congressional Oversight of War Powers Compliance: Zaire Airlift*, 95th Congress, 2nd session, August 10, 1978.

11. Claudia Wright, *New Statesman*, October 12, 1979.

12. *Nation*, special issue on intervention, July 15, 1979.

13. Odeen, *Staff Report on National Security Policymaking*.

14. John Helmer and Louis Maisel, "Analytical Problems in the Study of Presidential Advice: The Domestic Council Staff in Flux," *Presidential Studies Quarterly* (Winter 1978), pp. 45–67.

15. John Helmer, "The Dogmeat or the Sheep's Head: Is There a Socialist Method of Public Administration?" paper delivered at the 9th World Congress of Sociology, Uppsala, Sweden, 1978.

16. In the terminology of the U.S. government, the distinction is often made between cabinet and executive departments or agencies on the one hand and independent agencies on the other. The legal distinctions between the two elude precise identification. For practical purposes, both types of organizations are established by statute, and both are headed by appointees of the president. Heads of independent agencies are not designated members of the cabinet, but they may be invited to attend cabinet meetings regularly and sit as informal members of cabinet subcommittees. This is for the president to decide. Independent agencies themselves have different views on whether they report to the president and whether they are bound by his executive orders. Some agencies believe they have a legal power not to comply with executive orders, but this is disputed by the Department of Justice. The issue remains to be tested in the courts.

17. See Chapter 5 and Lester M. Salamon and John Helmer, "Urban and Community Impact Analysis: From Promise to Implementation," in N. Glickman, ed., *The Urban Impacts of Federal Policies* (Baltimore: Johns Hopkins University Press, 1979); U.S. Council on Environmental Quality, *Environmental Impact Statements: An Analysis of Six Years' Experience by Seventy Agencies* (Washington, D.C.: Government Printing Office, 1976).

18. U.S., Congress, House, Committee on Post Office and Civil Service, *A Report on the Growth of the Executive Office of the President, 1955–1973* (Washington, D.C.: Government Printing Office, 1972).

19. Randall B. Ripley and Grace A. Franklin, eds., *Policymaking in the Federal Executive Branch* (New York: Free Press, 1975).

20. Peri E. Arnold, "Reorganization and Politics: A Reflection on the Adequacy of Administrative Theory," *Public Administration Review* 34 (May-June 1974), pp. 205–211; and Hugh Heclo, "OMB and the Presidency – The Problem of Neutral Competence," *Public Interest* 10 (Winter 1975), p. 89.

21. U.S. Council on Environmental Quality, *Environmental Impact Statements*, p. 12.

22. Thomas D. Hopkins, *An Evaluation of the Inflation Impact Statement Program Prepared for the Economic Policy Board* (Washington, D.C.: Council on Wage and Price Stability, 1976), p. 4.

23. Presidential remarks quoted in Salamon and Helmer, "Urban and Community Impact Analysis." See also, *Forging America's Future: Strategies for National Growth and Development: Report of the Advisory Committee on National Growth Processes* (Wash-

ington, D.C.: Government Printing Office, 1976).

24. U.S. Office of Management and Budget, "Executive Office of the President Reorganization, Decision Analyses" (Final Report) (Classified, 1977).

25. *Washington Post*, April 8, 1977.

26. Larry Berman, *Office of Management and Budget and the Presidency 1921–1979* (Princeton, N.J.: Princeton University Press, 1979); Richard P. Nathan, *The Plot that Failed: Nixon and the Administrative Presidency* (New York: John Wiley, 1975); and Richard Rose, *Managing Presidential Objectives* (New York: Free Press, 1977).

27. Randall B. Ripley and Grace A. Franklin (eds.), *Policymaking in the Federal Executive Branch* (New York: Free Press, 1975).

PART TWO
Process Management

Dramatic events are the lifeblood of daily news coverage. Likewise, the most immediate problems and prominent decision issues are likely to preoccupy presidents and congressmen. No one doubts that questions of "substantive policy"—what to do about inflation, how to deal with an energy shortage, where to stand up to a foreign threat—are central to the activities of government.

There is, however, a second aspect of government that receives much less notice. This has to do more with how things get done, rather than simply what gets decided. Answers to this "how" question can, of course, take many forms. Accidents of personality, unique combinations of circumstance, and sheer mismanagement can impart a kind of random quality to any series of government actions. But the more regular and identifiable the type of decision, the more likely it is that there will be a distinctive *process* to help organize how things are done. The way people in government manage such general processes can often be at least as important in the long run as the way they manage particular substantive policy decisions.

Clearly there can be no neat separation between process management and policy management, which is analyzed in Part 3 of this volume. The difference is one of degree rather than of kind. Part 3 also analyzes how things get done, but the processes in question there lie in different arenas of substantive policy—domestic social policy, economic policy, and national security affairs.

In this part, the authors analyze developments in much more general processes of government. Basically, the government really has only three major resources at its disposal—money, people, and rules. These are also the three main tools that public administration experts have traditionally sought to strengthen to augment the role of the presidency in managing the executive branch. The three authors in this part take stock of the presidency in relation to the budgetary, personnel, and regulatory processes of government.

3

The Problem
of Presidential Budgeting

Allen Schick

The shocks administered to the federal budget by Ronald Reagan shortly after he took office in January 1981 were more than an attempt to reorder government priorities by spending more on defense and less on social programs. The president wanted to reestablish White House control over the budget; he wanted it to be a statement of his policies rather than a testament to presidential impotence. No longer would the budget be held hostage by the economy, David Stockman, the vigorous OMB director, announced. The president would cut taxes and spur economic growth, thereby ensuring a fiscal dividend in future years. The President's bold gamble will be examined later in this chapter, though it is now (March 1981) much too early to appraise the results.

The president makes the budget, but that does not mean that he controls it. For the chief executive, as for other budget makers, the federal budget can be a political burden—one of the things that has to be done—rather than an opportunity to shape the course of events. Although the executive budget still carries a presidential imprimatur (the media label it "Ford's budget" or "Carter's budget"), it is a less effective instrument of presidential power than it once was. The budget seems to be on "automatic pilot," with a direction and drive all its own, independent of the president's immediate objectives and priorities. Worse yet, some of the budget's key policies (such as the size of the deficit) and the economic conditions assumed in it (inflation and unemployment) often are at variance with the president's professed objectives.

Because the basic routines of budgeting are repeated year after year with little visible change, they mask the real decline in presidential budgeting. A succession of reforms (planning/programming/budgeting, management by objectives, and zero-base budgeting) has not significantly altered the manner in which federal budgets are prepared or the president's formal role in the process. But despite the continuities in procedure, budgeting is a troubled process. Major segments of the federal government are excluded from the budget, and a growing portion is "uncontrollable under existing law." Nowadays, the budget seems to be carried along by events more often than it shapes them. What was once treasured and has been diminished is the sense that policy is made in the budget. The budget appears, disappears, reappears; modifications made after the budget is issued often outweigh the decisions made in budget preparation. The budget is under constant scrutiny and challenge, like the White House itself. The president announces one policy, the economy delivers another; OMB issues its authoritative estimates, the Congressional Budget Office (CBO) comes back with more reliable ones.

The still incomplete and changing story of the fiscal 1981 budget illustrates the president's budget problem. Carter's first budget for the fiscal year (submitted to Congress in January 1980) recommended total expenditures of $616 billion and a $16 billion deficit. Just two months later, after intensive closed-door negotiations with congressional leaders, the president unveiled a balanced budget despite sizable increases in uncontrollable spending. The new budget proposed to reduce total expenditures through various program cutbacks. But deteriorating economic conditions and spiraling program costs forced Carter to abandon his hopes for a balanced budget. The president's third budget for the fiscal year (presented in July) carried a $30 billion deficit, along with $22 billion more spending than his previous plan contemplated. By January 1981, when Carter presented his budget for the next fiscal year along with revised estimates for fiscal 1981, the anticipated deficit had ballooned to $55 billion and total expenditures to $662 billion. During the year, automatic increases in uncontrollable accounts had done more to change the budget than had all the discretionary actions of the White House. The budget had become the destroyer of presidential dreams, compelling the chief executive to concede to forces beyond his control.

It is important to note, however, that the president's budget problem is more than a matter of numbers; it is rooted in the role and stature of the White House. After Watergate and Vietnam, the budget process was unavoidably tarnished by the president's loss of power and esteem. Once a spur to presidential vigor, the budget became an aspect of presidential decline. Presidential budgeting could not continue as an imperial and venerated process with the power and effectiveness of its principal client so reduced. The president's budget office was afflicted by the malaise that swept Washington. The Office of Management and Budget, once a bastion of presidential power, suffered through the 1970s a seemingly endless identity crisis, not quite sure of the role it was supposed to play or of the means for regaining control of federal finances.

The president's budget role was also challenged by a reassertion of congressional power. The Congressional Budget Act of 1974 established a rival budget process along with a legislative budget staff. Although Richard Nixon's overreaching impoundments triggered this congressional action, the Budget Act really was a response to presidential decline. Vesting the president with a budgetary role once heralded the growth of presidential power; in the 1970s, the congressional budget process signaled the retaking of political power by Congress.

The crisis in budgeting cannot be resolved without a new consensus on the role and purpose of the presidency. A president who is unsure of his job or his reach will not be able to effectively use the budget process. One possible way of reconstructing the president's budget role is to examine what it once was.

The Role of the Budget: A View from the Past

Before the Budget and Accounting Act of 1921, federal agencies went directly to Congress (and often to particular committees) with requests for money. The president was more than a passive bystander, but he was not decisively in charge of federal finances. The White House's role varied with the incumbent and the times, but the chief executive faced competition from other officials (principally the secretary of the treasury) for leadership of the nation's financial affairs.[1] Competition also came from Congress, which often used its power of the purse to intervene in what Woodrow Wilson termed the "details of administration."[2]

The 1921 act gave the president a budget staff (the Bureau of the Budget until 1970; the Office of Management and Budget since then) and empowered him to prepare an annual budget and submit it to Congress. This legislation is frequently cited as a turning point in the development of the modern presidency and in the transfer of political power from legislative to executive hands. Yet, at the start, the chief executive contributed more to the growth of the budget process than the process did to the augmentation of his power. The first budgetary presidents (Harding, Coolidge, and Hoover) did not use their new authority to significantly broaden the scope of their office. With limited program objectives, they were content to support the Bureau of the Budget's well-publicized economy drives. Charles Dawes, the first director of the budget, shrewdly recognized that by claiming to act in the name of the president, his new Budget Bureau would gain political independence from the Treasury Department, within which it was housed.³ Dawes and his successors were content to use the budget process for "routine business," which usually meant examining the estimates for possible cuts and guarding against agency efforts to expand their budgets. This narrow construction of its role allowed the Budget Bureau to practice parsimony in its own operations. For most of its first two decades, the bureau had only about forty staff people to handle all its responsibilities.

The budget process inherited by Franklin Roosevelt was inhospitable to his New Deal aspirations. FDR's efforts to revive the economy might have been hobbled if he had allowed the Budget Bureau to apply its routine methods to his legislative agenda. Roosevelt's solution was to bypass the Budget Bureau during his first term and to rely instead on his brain trust and other resources. Although this was a sensible short-term remedy, it did not equip the president with the institutional capability to manage the federal government, nor did it establish a permanent administrative framework suitable for his enlarged national objectives. By his second term, Roosevelt's principal concern was not to get his programs approved but to have them work in accordance with his policy objectives. Roosevelt entrusted the task of devising an appropriate administrative structure to his Committee on Administrative Management, chaired by Louis Brownlow.

The 1937 report of the Brownlow Committee proposed a Copernican change in the relationship between the president and the budget process. Rather than the president serving the purposes of budgeting, the budget was to become an instrument of presidential power. This revolutionary outlook clashed with the staff recommendation presented to the Brownlow Committee by A. E. Buck, the nation's foremost budget scholar. Buck defined the budget as a process for the orderly and efficient handling of the nation's money, and he therefore urged that its links with other financial activities in the Treasury Department be strengthened. "Both the preparation and the execution of the budget," Buck insisted, "are so closely entwined with Treasury operations that the Bureau of the Budget should be made an integral part of the Treasury Department."⁴ If this scheme had been implemented, the secretary of the treasury might have become first among equals in the cabinet and a political rival of the president.

This proposal violated the Brownlow Committee's main objective—to "give the President more effective managerial control."⁵ The committee summarily discarded its expert's advice and did not even mention Buck's proposal in its report.⁶ It opted instead for the Bureau of the Budget to become "the right arm of the President for the central fiscal management of the vast administration machine."⁷ It urged that through staff expansion the bureau "be developed into a serviceable tool for administrative management to aid the President in the exercise of overall control."⁸ It declared that because legislative clearance "is essential to the exercise of the authority and responsibility of the President, it should be applied to all legislation proposed by the executive departments and agencies and should not be limited to fiscal considerations."[9]

The prevailing verdict is that the Brownlow Committee succeeded in augmenting presidential power through the budget process. Within a few years, the Budget Bureau's size increased more than tenfold, and it became the principal staff agency in the new Executive Office of the President. Executive Order 8248 of September 8, 1939, gave the bureau a broad mandate to assist the president in superintending the administrative affairs of the federal government. By 1945, the bureau had become a different agency. It still reviewed agency estimates, but it had become the general staff for the president. The institutional presidency was in place, and the bureau's resources, skills, memory, and loyalty to the president could be passed on from one chief executive to the next.

Was this widely accepted assessment due to the Budget Bureau's deserved reputation as a pool of talented and resourceful public administrators or to its presidential service? One's evaluation of the Budget Bureau during the Roosevelt era seems to depend on whether the bureau is viewed from the perspective of the White House or from that provided by the budget process. The literature on budgeting definitely accords a prominent place to the Budget Bureau as a presidential agency.[10] Significantly, many Budget Bureau alumni were intellectual leaders of American public administration after World War II, and much of what we "know" about the bureau has been bequeathed to us by them.[11] The bureau and Harold D. Smith, its renowned director in the 1939–1945 growth years, are hardly mentioned in the numerous histories and studies of the Roosevelt era. When the bureau is discussed in these accounts, it often is shown to be on the losing end of arguments with other presidential agencies or actors, such as the Office of War Mobilization and James Byrnes, its politically astute director.[12] The broader literature (dealing with the president or the national government rather than with public administration or budgeting) leaves the impression that the bureau's status varied with the type of task it handled. On controversial matters or major policies, the bureau did not have a compelling advantage over other White House participants. On routine matters, such as helping federal agencies organize their work, it played a central role. Not surprisingly, many of the bureau's accolades were garnered by its administrative management division.

Yet the bureau did develop in those formative years a presidential mission and perspective. Smith's enduring accomplishment was to instill a sense of service to the president in bureau rank and file. For the first time, institutional service to the presidency became a career. The talented men and women who flocked to the bureau believed that making government efficient and making it responsive to the president were complementary tasks. For them, the reorganization of an agency's field offices or the coordination of statistical reports was presidential business, whether or not the particular matter actually came to the president's attention. Indeed, bureau staff saw their institutional responsibility as keeping these types of concerns off the president's desk. The bureau became the custodian of the president's institutional interests, a role it continued to play long after the lines between personal and institutional service were blurred.

As a permanent staff, the bureau made a vast pool of talent available to the president. With the bureau's staff enlarged to more than 500, the president could rely on it to handle everyday emergencies and follow through on White House decisions. The bureau had—or could put its hands on—information and advice needed by the president, and it became adept at assembling the relevant views and data on the issues facing the chief executive. The president could trust the bureau to see problems from his vantage point and to protect his interests when preparing the budget or performing its other responsibilities.

The Budget Bureau excelled as a presidential agency during the Truman and Eisenhower administrations, when the federal government settled into a more stable mode of operation than had been possible during the New Deal or the war. The successful transfer of resources and allegiance to Truman after Roosevelt's sudden death and to Eisenhower after the Republicans took command of the White House for the first time in a generation demonstrated the bureau's institutional strength and durability. The bureau's activities in the postwar years were quiet, unspectacular successes, but therein lay their importance. The bureau's performance—less than a decade after it had been recast into a presidential agency—was expected, taken for granted, already part of the routine of government. The bureau had a repertoire of procedures for its principal responsibilities, and it used them to serve presidential interests.

The Budget Routine

Routine, not in the sense of unimportant but of an established way of doing things, was a key to the bureau's success as a presidential agency. Neustadt's account of the legislative clearance process shows how the bureau routinized the very important task of formulating the president's legislative program. The bureau canvassed federal agencies for legislative proposals as part of its annual budget process. It had procedures for reviewing testimony and correspondence before they were forwarded to Congress and for soliciting comments on enrolled bills. These procedures were continued from year to year with little change. Neustadt reported that Eisenhower's first call for budget estimates incorporated the instructions for assembling legislative proposals devised by his Democratic predecessor. The use of these instructions, Neustadt concluded, represented "a bureaucratic continuum, an attempted restoration of routines, an action taken on the Budget's own initiative without advance assurance as to either agency response or ultimate White House reaction."[13] Far from regarding the bureau's move as an unwarranted trespass on presidential prerogatives, the White House welcomed it as a useful and orderly way of relating legislative proposals to current budget decisions.

The bureau's most routinized process was preparation of the president's budget. The call for estimates established a timetable within which budget decisions were made and gave the participants a renewed sense of the roles they were to play in the process. But participants also had substantive guidelines for preparing the budget. Eisenhower established budget targets early in the process and stuck with them throughout. "Budgetary processes under Eisenhower," Mowrey, Kamlet, and Crecine wrote, "were extremely orderly. . . . In many years, virtually all major budgetary issues were settled in the preview phase, and the review phase was one of relative inactivity."[14]

Routine was not just an incident of budgeting but a source of Budget Bureau power. Routines fixed the bureau's place in the presidential scheme of things, assuring it of a prominent role for which it did not have to fight year after year. By dint of routine, everyone knew that the bureau was in charge of budget preparation and that agency dealings with Congress had to be cleared through it. Routine meant that the presidency was institutionalized, not prey to the whims of those who happened to have the president's ear.

The absence of routine can be a tremendous disadvantage for the president's budgeters. Without a secure niche of their own, they may have to compete with personal staff who are closer to the president, are more directly attuned to his immediate interests, and are more likely to be adept at improvised strategies. When routines are inadequate, the boundaries between institutional and personal roles cannot be maintained, and careerists are impelled to prove their loyalty and skills by the same means as personal aides.

The Loss of Routine

Budgeting is the most comprehensive attempt to bring order and regularity to public decisions. It excels as an instrument of presidential power when the activities and interests of the president can be fitted into its procedures and timetable. But the president cannot always dictate his agenda or control his schedule. The presidents who have served since Kennedy generally have seemed to be less able – or less willing – to govern by routine than were their predecessors. Crisis drives out order and regularity, as overnight cables, morning headlines, the latest economic news, and other disruptions compel the White House to act. Overload of the presidency, whether in terms of work load or expectations, makes it difficult for the White House to work by the clock and the calendar. The in-box, "hot lines," unexpected floor amendments, and other daily alarms break the routine and debilitate the White House's ability to operate in an orderly, disciplined manner.

The calm, stable budget process managed by Eisenhower gave way to frenetic budgeting by later presidents who were forced to frequently adjust their spending and revenue targets in order to accommodate last-minute policy decisions and changing economic conditions. Since Kennedy, the president's "mark" or initial spending target (issued after OMB's spring preview) has been nothing more than a starting point and the levels actually recommended in the published budget have often diverged sharply from it. Computerization of the budget accounts and of the printing process has enabled OMB to delay the president's final decisions until a few days before the budget is released. Provisional budgeting, in which the numbers bounce up and down depending on the day's mood or news, has come to be regarded as a virtue, a means of keeping the president in charge of things. (At the suggestion of budget maker Charles Schultze, the Congressional Budget Act attached a "reconciliation procedure" to the second budget resolution, when final decisions are supposed to be made. Schultze pointed out to congressional leaders that this was how the president's budget was made, with the numbers changing until the last minute. However, after several years of experience with its own budget process, Congress, in 1980, shifted reconciliation to the first budget resolution, when initial decisions are made.)

Budgeting has become a process in which presidential decisions are but one set of possibilities to be reconsidered and subverted by later events and decisions. In this type of process, keeping the president's options open is regarded as sage politics, although it is destructive of budget routines. Budget decisions can be made at any time, in or out of season – in fact, as we shall see, inside or outside the budget process itself.

The destruction of routine has also reached the president's vital legislative work. Neustadt concluded his study of legislative planning in the Truman and Eisenhower presidencies with an expectation that the process would be continued in future administrations: "Clearly there is nothing transient about the venture as a whole, the compilation of an inclusive bill of particulars for presentation annually by President to Congress. This is now . . .

no less a matter of course in Eisenhower's time than formerly in Truman's; the practice which survives such a change of regime is likely to endure."[15]

It did not. When Kennedy began to rely on White House aides and task forces to develop his legislative program, he inevitably drained the routines established by his predecessors of relevance and content. Johnson further dismantled the legislative planning process by blanketing the White House with dozens of task forces, each one filing its own urgent report and demanding immediate action. The links between legislative development and budget preparation could not withstand the pressure for action, and the two processes drifted apart. The ad hoc report and the "for eyes only" memorandum (i.e., only the president was to see it) displaced the budget as the key decisional documents for the president.

Each president adjusts the budget process to his own style and interests. Nixon disengaged himself from budget making by giving the OMB director final say over most appeals; Ford (who had served for many years on the House Appropriations Committee) took a lively interest in the budget's details. My impression is that presidents tend to invest more time in budgeting when they enter office then when they have been in it for several years. Lyndon Johnson's crash drive to remake the budget after the Kennedy assassination was unmatched in terms of the time invested in his subsequent budgets. As a new president, Jimmy Carter carried to the White House the interest in budgeting he had demonstrated as governor of Georgia. But as his administration aged, Carter's attention to budgeting declined.

This pattern might be the result of fatigue. The budget recurs again and again, set in its own cycle. The routines that once patterned presidential decision making have turned into a grind, as improvisational processes preempt presidential attention and time. Contemporary presidents tend to seek out exceptional opportunities to put their stamp on policy or on public perceptions. The budget still forces action — nominally the president's — but it cannot compel his attention.

Presidents learn on the job. They take office determined to shape programs and policies their way; they then learn that the budget is mostly locked into its set course. They come to see the budget's routines as a constraint on their ability to act and as an obstacle to achieving their objectives. Understandably, therefore, they limit their involvement in budgeting. They keep the routines but change the president's role in the process.

Mowrey, Kamlet, and Crecine concluded their case studies of presidential budgeting with a plea for a more orderly process, but they doubt "that such a 'solution' is feasible in the face of the burdens, aspirations, and policy agenda of current and future presidents."[16] A workable solution cannot be confined to the budget process but must reach the other processes by which government decisions—including budget decisions—are made.

Making Budgets Without Budgeting

Budgeting is not an inherently powerful process. It generally does not command the same status in business firms that is attributed to it in the public sector. The budget's "action-forcing" capability partly explains its public prominence, but the manner in which the process is used determines its utility for the president and other government officials.

The test of a budget's power is the extent to which it is used to make financial decisions. In applying this test, it must be recognized that the budget is not a government's only process for making financial decisions. A pluralist political system could not abide by an arrangement in which all policies were decided through budget channels. The federal government makes budget decisions when Congress authorizes programs, when agencies implement them, when the president makes political comments or commitments, when agencies negotiate understandings with state and local officials, and in dozens of other ways. Sometimes the budget is deliberately bypassed when decisions are made; in other cases, decisions are put to a budget test before they are concluded.

The federal government (as well as other governments and private firms) might be said, therefore, to have two budget processes, structurally alike but quite different in the uses to which they are put. One is the process by which decisions are made; the other is the process by which decisions made elsewhere are recorded in financial statements. When an open-ended entitlement program is enacted without prior consideration of its cost or budgetary impact, the decision is made outside the budget process. Later, when the entitlement has to be paid, the budget will have to account for the program's cost, although the budget will not have been the arena in which either the program or its cost was decided.

Many major program decisions are made through the budget process, including most of the defense budget. If the federal government budgets for a particular weapon, funds will be available for it; if the weapon is excluded from the budget, it will not be acquired. However, social security checks will be mailed to beneficiaries regardless of whether the budget contains sufficient funds for this purpose.

Budgeting as a "decisional" process coexists with budgeting as an "accounting" process in each year's cycle. But the relative strengths of these processes fluctuate from year to year. In some years, policymakers knowingly circumvent the regular budget process in pursuit of their program objectives. During the "fat" years in the 1960s and early 1970s, many entitlement programs were greatly expanded with little regard for their budgetary impacts. Typically, the legislation establishing (or enlarging) these entitlements did not specify the cost, and when cost estimates were made, they often proved to be unreliable.

The "accounting" mode appears to predominate during periods of program expansion. When new programs are sought, it may be expedient to bypass the budget process rather than work through it. The budget can slow or subvert innovation by raising tough questions about cost and effectiveness and by directing attention to alternative means of achieving the program's objectives. It is a telling commentary on presidential attitudes toward budgeting that they seek to upgrade their budgetary capabilities after their main program objectives have been approved. Roosevelt, as noted above, bypassed the Budget Bureau during New Deal expansion; Johnson embraced planning/programming/budgeting only after his Great Society legislation had been enacted.

But when the White House (or Congress) wants to constrain government spending, it may insist that program decisions be made through the budget. A budget process can provide a forum for the consideration of cutbacks or program changes that might not get a hearing in other arenas. The current surge of interest in balanced budgets and spending limitations may strengthen the use of budgeting as a decisional process. But this is not the only possible outcome. Another possibility is to resort to "escapist" budgeting, in which federal officials delude themselves into believing that they are strengthening budget controls while they are actually subverting them.

In considering how and why budget processes are bypassed, it would be useful to distinguish among the various ways that governments make financial decisions independent of the budget. The three main routes are by nondecision, metadecision, and counter-decision. These categories overlap and they cannot be cleanly applied to every type of transaction, but they differentiate between advertent and active bypasses on the one hand, and inadvertent, passive ones on the other.

Nondecision making refers to instances in which policies in effect are continued without being reexamined and without new, explicit decisions being made.[17] Much of the federal budget is continued from year to year by nondecision. When programs funded in previous budgets are assumed to be worthwhile and the only task of budget preparation is to estimate their next year's cost, the budget process comes close to operating in a nondecision manner. But nondecision making can also affect a budget's increment. When spending for an entitlement program is automatically increased to accommodate a rise in the number of beneficiaries or in inflation, the budget grows by nondecisions.

Nondecision rules simplify the task of preparing a budget and reduce conflicts over public funds. A president who faced $600 billion worth of decisions in one year would find it difficult to get the budget to Congress on time or to resolve all the disagreements over how federal dollars should be spent. Though he might welcome nondecision making for part of the budget, a president would find his fiscal and program objectives seriously compromised if virtually all of the budget were allocated in this manner.

Metadecisions are instances in which policies established outside the budget determine how funds are spent. Unlike nondecisions, the government does not merely extend existing policies. But actions it takes independent of the budget govern the expenditure of funds. The enactment of an entitlement is a familiar form of metadecision. If Congress changes the eligibility rules for food stamps or entitles needy mothers to new benefits, its simple objective might be to improve the nutritional standards of Americans. At the time the decision is made, the budget might not even be an issue. But whether or not the president (or Congress) has the budget in mind, the new law's financial effects will have to be accommodated in the budget.

Clearly, it is easier to guard against metadecisions than nondecisions. In the latter, inaction assures continuation of a policy, along with its budgetary impact. In the former, budget guardians (such as OMB and CBO) can call attention to the budgetary implications. The government might still approve a metadecision, but at least it will have been informed of the relevant financial issues. Metadecisions, however, do not abide by the budget's routines. They can be made at any time during the year, and they need not compete explicitly against other claims on the budget. Not only do metadecisions have a substantive effect on budgetary outcomes, they also vitiate the budget process itself.

Metadecisions are made because budgetary values are not the only ones pursued by government. If all the White House wanted to do was to maintain a particular fiscal policy or uphold its budget decisions, it could shut off all metadecisions. Clearly, however, this would be unacceptable in the pluralist environment in which government decisions are made. In addition to managing its accounts, the federal government wants to ensure a stable income for farmers, nutritious meals for poor families, educational opportunities for youngsters, medical care for the elderly, and all the other social objectives paid for with federal dollars. When these conflict with budgetary objectives, the latter do not always prevail. In some circumstances, the government will be more sensitive to budgetary values than in others. But when nonbudgetary values are dominant, the government may make metadecisions even if it does not really want the budgetary results that ensue.

The third category, counter-decisions, actually is a form of metadecision. It represents instances in which the government knowingly and deliberately overrides a budgetary decision, unlike a standard metadecision, in which action is taken without cognizance of the budgetary impacts. If the president, for example, embarks on a balanced budget policy, but subsequently supports discretionary spending to stimulate employment or assist poor communities, his counter-decisions vitiate the earlier determination to balance the budget.

Metadecisions and counter-decisions expand presidential discretion. The president is not locked into a budget that prevents the realization of his other policy objectives, and he has a fuller range of options than if he single-mindedly stuck to his budget plan. The president's diverse policy agenda can be better attended to when he has a multiplicity of processes for making financial and program decisions.

But the bypassing and negation of the budget process force the president into an erratic budget policy, lacking constancy or direction. The zigzag budget course pursued by President Carter in fiscal 1981 was not due principally to presidential indecision but to Carter's inability to maintain a set course when competing objectives intruded. Moreover, whatever his other policy objectives, a president does have budgetary goals. These seem to be the ones that give way when the president resorts to metadecisions or counter-decisions. The budget becomes the receiver of the other decisions, not the process by which they are balanced against a comprehensive set of national objectives.

The Uncontrollable Budget

As a result of nondecisions, metadecisions, and counter-decisions, the federal budget has become more an accounting of decisions made by other means and less the process for making the decisions. The key indicator of this shift is the growth in "uncontrollable" spending, OMB's label for outlays required by existing law. Uncontrollables have climbed from 59 percent of total spending in fiscal 1967 to an estimated 76 percent in the fiscal 1981 budget. In dollar terms, fiscal 1981 uncontrollables exceeded $500 billion, more than total federal outlays just two years earlier. Even more critical than the absolute increase in uncontrollables is the extent to which they account for most of the year-to-year rise in federal spending. Fiscal 1981 spending in Carter's original budget was scheduled to rise $52 billion over the previous year's level. Approximately $10 billion of this increase was earmarked for defense, but key decisions in this area were made outside the budget process through White House bartering for Senate support of the SALT treaty. The other $42 billion was in the uncontrollable column. As a matter of fact, real spending for discretionary civilian programs was expected to decline.

Although the term "uncontrollable" is somewhat misleading, because Congress can change or repeal laws mandating expenditures, the concept offers a useful measure of the extent to which the budget has declined as the process for making financial decisions. Regardless of the amount provided for uncontrollables in the budget (or appropriations), the required funds will have to be made available. Spending can be averted only through non-budgetary actions such as legislative changes.

Presidential participation and effectiveness have been affected by the rise in uncontrollable spending. With more than 40 percent of the budget indexed to price levels, each percentage point increase in the consumer price index adds billions to total spending. It does not take the president long to realize that his budget is largely shaped by outside forces, not by White House decisions.

A sensible view of the president's involvement in budgeting is that he should concentrate on spending increments and pay little attention to the base. This strategy conserves the president's time, directs his attention to matters within his control, and enables him to avoid "no-win" budgetary conflicts. But as most of the year-to-year increase is predetermined, it is difficult for the president to use the budget to influence the rate or direction of the growth. A president facing this predicament has few satisfactory options. He can try to bring the increment under control, but only at the risk of stirring opposition from program beneficiaries and their legislative patrons. Significantly, Carter generally eschewed this course of action in 1980 at a time when pressure for spending cuts was unusually intense; one should not expect a president to embrace this option during ordinary times. It is too early to foretell what President Reagan might do, but some of his key economic and fiscal objectives may be unattainable unless he makes substantial reductions in uncontrollable programs.

The growth of uncontrollables weakens the president vis-à-vis Congress. As noted above, an uncontrollable expenditure can be averted only through legislative action. The president, however, has no assurance that Congress will go along with his efforts to curb mandatory programs. Few of the legislative savings requested in recent years (such as hospital cost containment, impact aid reform, and changes in cost-of-living adjustments for federal retirees) have been enacted into law.

A president can "escape" from his budgetary predicament by proposing unrealistic cuts in programs, by budgetary legerdemain that conceals the actual condition of the budget, or by producing low estimates of the costs of open-ended programs. Recent presidents have expanded their apparent budget discretion through these escape routes, but the increasingly vigilant and independent scrutiny of the budget by CBO makes this a more questionable approach than it once was.

Another option is for the president to divorce budgeting from other policymaking processes. Rather than resist the encroachments on the budget's decisional role, the president can join the forces beyond his control. A president can sidestep the budget through metadecisions or counterdecisions that are forwarded to Congress after the budget has been submitted and that take effect (or have their first major budget impact) in a later fiscal year. Caught between political pressures from program beneficiaries on the one hand and the budget's "bad news" on the other, recent presidents have increasingly resorted to various off-budget practices. Instead of financing costly initiatives in the budget, they have used loan guarantees, tax preferences, government-sponsored enterprises, and other transactions not accounted for in the regular budget process. Presidents have been willing to trade away control over future budgets in order to cope with current financial pressures. Of course, this convenient way out diminishes the utility of budgeting for contemporary presidents.

The Budget and the Economy

Nowhere has the breakdown in budget routines been more pronounced than in management of the economy. During the "New Economics" era of the early 1960s, the president's economic advisers were confident that they could fine-tune growth, prices, and jobs by increasing or withdrawing fiscal stimulus. They saw the budget as a means of keeping the economy on a stable course, supplying just the right amount of demand, without high unemployment or inflation.

Although it generated more budgetary turbulence than existed during the stable Eisenhower years, fine-tuning was compatible with existing budget routines. Policy changes were to be frequent, but they were also expected to be relatively small and manageable. The metaphor of fine-tuning suggested that someone would be in charge and that budget change would occur as an act of policy, not as a frantic or helpless reaction to conditions beyond control or comprehension.

Since the early 1970s, the expectation that the budget can master the economy has given way to the near-fatalistic notion that the economy dictates budget policy. In lieu of small, managed change, the federal government now muddles through stop-and-go swings, such as occurred during the 1981 fiscal year. In recent years, changes have been dramatic and unpredictable and have been followed by further policy gyrations before the original objectives were achieved. Richard Nixon lurched from a free-enterprise ideology to wage and price controls in 1971. Gerald Ford asked for a tax surcharge shortly after taking office in 1974; within months, however, he signed a steep tax cut into law. Jimmy Carter proposed a $50 tax rebate in 1977, but suddenly withdrew his proposal while Congress was preparing to act on the matter.

The economy does not stand still, and neither can the budget. Republicans and Democrats alike embrace the view that the federal government is responsible for the performance of the economy. It is only a short step from this view to the view that the government has an obligation to respond to every significant shift in the economy. When economic swings are small or gradual, it is possible for the government to keep its basic budget policy intact. But the shocks that buffeted the American economy in the 1970s made it difficult for any administration to set a policy and stick to it.

The combination of high inflation and persistent unemployment has weakened the capacity of the United States to control its economic fortunes. If the White House were to adopt a restrictive budget policy, it would get increased unemployment long before it succeeded in moderating inflation. Thus, when President Carter scrapped his deficit spending plan for 1981 in favor of a balanced budget, the Congressional Budget Office estimated that the inflation rate would drop by only 0.1 percent. But within months, when unemployment began to climb, the administration returned to a budget deficit. As the benefits are promised for the long run—the White House admits that it has "no quick fixes"—while the adverse effects come at once, it is not surprising that no administration has stuck sufficiently long to a single policy to ascertain whether it would work.

With stagflation (high inflation and high unemployment), the automatic stabilizers (progressive tax structure and unemployment benefits, for example) that soften the severity of economic decline have a destabilizing effect on the budget. Consider a situation in which both inflation and unemployment are rising. Each 1 percent rise in the unemployment rate adds more than $25 billion to the budget deficit. But with many entitlements indexed to the inflation rate, each 1 percent increase in the cost of living adds close to $2 billion to the deficit. The budget fuels inflation at the very time that the White House promises price stability.

As the economy deteriorates, pressure for government action escalates. Budget plans unravel and have to be changed frequently. This phenomenon is due not to inconstancy in the White House but to fiscal stress. More than a decade ago, Naomi Caiden and Aaron Wildavsky found that poor countries have "disappearing budgets"; they cannot adhere to a single fiscal plan for more than a few months.[18] The poorer a country is, the more budgets it has. Indeed, the "real" budget, that is, the one that actually conforms to transactions, is known only after the fiscal period is over. The budget is no longer a tool of planning or economic management but a record of what was. And the record is writ largely by forces beyond the government's control.

The United States is not a poor country, but it is (or is perceived to be) poorer than it once was. Poverty, from a budgetary standpoint, cannot be measured in terms of per capita gross national product (GNP) or other objective measures of economic wealth but represents a government's inability to satisfy all the politically legitimate claims presented to it. If the federal government seems less able to cope with its budgetary predicament, it is not because resources have dwindled—after all, federal revenues doubled between 1976 and 1981—but because demand for these resources has grown even more. To understand why and how demand has soared, we must look at the budget's political role.

The Political Budget

The federal budget has always been a political document, a means of distributing benefits to various interests and groups. Yet during the 1960s and 1970s, the budget has been politicized to an extent that greatly surpasses its traditional role as a distributor of benefits. It is not merely that federal spending is so much higher than it once was and that so much more is available for distribution. Arguably, the spending spiral has been both cause and effect of the budget's politicization. Higher spending escalates the stakes for beneficiaries who, in turn, campaign for increased outlays.

Politicization has transformed the federal budget from a means of financing public agencies into a conduit for the flow of funds to external (often private) interests. At one time (before World War II and probably for some years thereafter), virtually all of the budget went for the expenses and operations of federal agencies. The main purpose of budgets and appropriations was to supply funds for the continuation of government. If budgets were important, it was not because a 1921 law required their preparation, but because agencies would have to close their doors and cease operations if new funds were not forthcoming. The language of budgeting offered revealing clues to the purpose served by the process. It bears recalling that appropriations were once known as supply bills and that the Budget and Accounting Act provided for the president's budget to set forth "estimates of the expenditures and appropriations necessary . . . for the support of the Government."

Budgeting for the salaries and expenses of federal agencies was a relatively closed process involving agency and central budget staff and legislative appropriators. Few outsiders participated directly, although their interests might have been affected. This closure of the budget process was enforced in a number of ways, chiefly by restricting the flow of information. The budget was an obscure and, for most outsiders, unintelligible document. The "book of estimates" (as it was once called) offered column after column of numbers, with little or no explanatory text. Insiders knew what the line items meant; others were ignorant. Closure also prevailed in the appropriations process. Most hearings were limited to testimony from agency spokesmen, and appropriation bills were marked up (approved in detail) in executive session. Witnesses supported the president's recommendations, and information on how much their agencies really wanted was not usually volunteered. Especially in the House, appropriation bills were passed with few floor amendments, and attempts to authorize more funds than the president had requested were rare.

There were some exceptions to this pattern, predominantly in areas where the budget provided discrete benefits to outside interests. Rivers and harbors legislation was in this category, and it is not surprising that beneficiaries were attentive to the "pork" they were budgeted to receive. As a general rule, the more an agency's budget has been earmarked for distribution to outsiders, the more open has its budget process been to outside participants.

Over the years, the fraction of the budget going to outside interests has increased while the share spent on the operations of federal agencies has declined. Nowadays, most federal spending is ticketed for (1) state and local governments on the receiving end of federal assistance, (2) contractors supplying goods and services to government agencies, (3) persons entitled to transfer payments and other benefits, and (4) various nonfederal entities receiving grants from Washington. Frederick C. Mosher has estimated that only about 15 percent of total federal spending goes to activities that the federal government itself performs.[19]

Outside recipients have a direct stake in the amounts made available for their programs. By any political standard, they are parties to the budget and have as much (or more) of an interest than the agencies to which the funds are appropriated in the first instance. Inevitably, federal budget practices have adapted to the needs and interests of these outsiders. An early move was to include in the federal budget explanations of what the money was going for and statistical measures of the benefits being provided. Appropriations subcommittees began to invite more outside witnesses ("public" is the term they prefer) and in the 1970s their markups were opened to the public.

The federal budget is no longer a closed book. Its policies and impacts are analyzed in numerous publications. Interest groups invest heavily in the acquisition of timely budget information. High-priced newsletters proffer the latest budget news, and just about every major interest network has its own budget-watchers keeping track of developments in executive agencies and on Capitol Hill. Intelligence by outside interests has been perfected to the extent that many groups now issue accurate and detailed assessments of the budget within days after it has been released by the president.

The language of budgeting reflects its transformation from an internal financing device into a purveyor of benefits. Agency submissions usually are termed "requests," suggesting a more activist budget posture than merely estimating the cost of operations. The term "deficiency" appropriations has fallen into disuse, and all additional funds are appropriated as "supplementals." Power relationships among budgetary participants have also been altered. Authorizing committees have become active claimants on behalf of program beneficiaries, and many have converted from permanent to temporary authorizations in order to strengthen their influence over budgetary outcomes. The appropriations committees have become less effective guardians of the treasury, and they often act as claimants in pursuit of federal dollars for the programs favored by their members.[20]

The growth of uncontrollables is not an accident of federal budgeting but a response to its politicization. Uncontrollables vest beneficiaries with privileged claims on future budgets. As beneficiaries become more active, they seek protection against the vagaries of the annual budget and appropriations cycle: They lock in future benefits by making them uncontrollable.

Political budgets require different presidential styles than do budgets that supply funds to federal agencies. The latter operate through linkages between requesting agencies and presidential budget reviewers. The process can be orderly, with major decisions made through the cyclical routines of budgeting. Not so a political budget. It is made through all the channels and processes of politics, not through the budget alone. In particular, it is made in direct bargaining between the president (or his agents) and affected parties. The president makes budget decisions on the campaign trail, when he meets mayors and governors, when he speaks to a delegation of farmers or teachers. Presidential comments are convertible into budgetary commitments, whether or not the president is focusing on the budget when he makes them. The conventional routines of budgeting are too constricted and rigid for the making of political budgets. The techniques survive, but as explained earlier, they are increasingly used to account for decisions made through other processes.

OMB's Budget Process

As an agency serving the president, OMB has adapted to changes in the use of the budget process and in the president's role. It has become more an "accounting" and less a "decisional" agency than it once was. This change is reflected in the downgrading of its legislative clearance and budget review divisions. The former concentrates on routine matters (the thousands of items not sufficiently salient to warrant presidential attention) and to working with rival groups (such as the Domestic Policy Staff) that have easier access to the Oval Office. The budget review division is less involved in substantive budget policy than it once was, and its main role is to provide technical support for the process. This is a rational adaptation for an agency that makes nondecisional budgets.

The change in budgeting has also affected OMB's core—its examining divisions. OMB needs fewer examiners to "account" for the budget than to "decide" it. The number of examiners has declined since 1969, despite increases in total OMB staff and in the size of the federal budget. Holding down the number of examiners curbs OMB's capacity to get involved in many of the external decisions affecting the budget. OMB is not so much a bypassed agency as a neutralized one. Things still get cleared through it, and staff still attend an impressive array of meetings. But it is easier for other presidential officials to dismiss OMB views as the standard response of naysayers and to tune out when OMB representatives launch into their explanations as to why something will not work or should not be done.

Hardly anyone talks about OMB's loss of stature. It is to the president's advantage to convey the impression that he has a strong, effective budget agency, even when he takes actions that dilute OMB's role. Every year, the publicity mills grind out heroic stories about how the OMB director stood up to powerful department heads and interest groups and produced a tight, austere budget for the president. Maybe, but the evidence is less convincing with each year's zigzagging budget.

The politicization of the budget has impaired OMB in a number of ways. OMB is more exposed to outside influences but less knowledgeable about what is being done with federal dollars. It is no longer the sheltered agency that it once was, cloaked in presidential anonymity and working behind the scenes. Its leaders now make frequent appearances before congressional committees, defending the administration's policies and taking stands on controversial issues. OMB officials probably testify more often in a single month now than they did during a year in Eisenhower's administration. The budget director has become a public figure, quoted in the press and openly participating in policy debates.

OMB is no longer beyond the pale of lobbying; it is open to pressure from state and local governments and public interest groups. When a big city mayor takes a problem to the White House, he might be told to talk it over with OMB officials. The expectation is that the president's budget agents will be attentive to his political interests. Similar access is tendered to, or sought by, many other interests that do business with the federal government. The insertion of political assistant directors (formally designated as program associate directors, or PADs) in OMB's chain of command was a necessary change in a career agency that performed basic political work for the president.

The political budget is made not only by assessing agency needs and performance but also by responding to the demands of outside beneficiaries. However, OMB's information channels run to the agencies, and it has no comparative advantage over other participants in assessing external developments. It is not surprising, therefore, that the quality of OMB judgment is widely regarded as inferior to what it once was. This impression is fed by the availability of rival sources of information and by the exposure of OMB decisions to outside review. It is no longer difficult for interest groups to obtain raw agency estimates and to compare them to OMB recommendations. In the court of political opinion, OMB's views do not always appear as sound or defensible as they might in the privacy of presidential budget making.

In an age of political budgets, OMB has been politicized. This transformation has stretched over three decades; it certainly was not due solely to Nixon's "plot that failed." Over time, the once firm demarcation between institutional staffs serving the presidency and personal staffs serving the president has been eroded by pressure for OMB to be of greater utility to the president. Larry Berman related that James Webb, Truman's budget director, "decided that the Budget Bureau's institutional staff could help the President by dealing directly with Truman rather than through intermediaries."[21] Twenty years later, Lyndon Johnson was "badgering the Bureau Director to assign five of the best men" to White House duty.[22] Paradoxically, the growth of the president's White House staff actually increased demands on the budget agency to offer personal service. White House aides needed more backstopping; there were more meetings to attend, more memos to prepare, more presidential crises to resolve.

Once the line between institutional and personal service was breached, it was only a short step further to political service. OMB wanted to be useful to its only client, and as usefulness in the currency of Washington means being available and relevant, OMB responded accordingly. Without going into all the details of OMB's politicization[23] (and it still offers solid, objective service as well), two items suggest the current state of affairs. (1) On November 14, 1979, Budget Director McIntyre journeyed to New Hampshire to make an overtly political speech to that state's Business and Industry Association. At one time, OMB directors would not leave Washington during budget season; apparently, however, the calendar of presidential primaries was accorded primacy over OMB's budget review schedule. (2) The 1981 budget had a 120-page section on the "Major Accomplishments" of the Carter administration; this was the first time that the president's budget office incorporated a campaign tract into its budget documents.

Leveraging the Budget

Budgetary power is leveraged power. It involves much more than putting together the numbers and sending them to Congress. A budget process confined to this routine (as it was during the 1920s) can be effective only if the president is hell-bent on reducing expenditures and has few substantive program interests. The first budgetary presidents operated in this restricted manner, but since the 1930s, presidents have had other interests that have competed with budget cutting.

The scope of budgeting can be extended to other presidential functions for two rather different purposes: to extend its influence to other decisional processes, or to allow other functions to benefit from linkage to the budget process. Inasmuch as the budget is not the only means for making financial decisions, efforts have been made to coordinate it with some of the other decision-making processes. Legislative clearance is the leading illustration. It originated as a procedure for protecting the budget against circumvention, but grew into a process for formulating the president's legislative program. By tying the development of legislation to the budget cycle, it was possible to ensure that the president's budget and his legislative proposals were consistent and that budgetary issues were adequately considered when legislative proposals were made by federal agencies. Legislative clearance bolstered the position of federal budget makers by giving them a voice in the formulation of legislative policy.

A different set of considerations prevails when nonfinancial processes are linked to the budget in order to exploit its action-forcing capability. The processes drawn into the budget's ambit tend to be weak and incapable of commanding attention on their own. However, they are regarded in some quarters as important; proximity to the budget is sought as a means of overcoming their weakness. Various management activities have been organizationally conjoined with budgeting at one time or another. Coordination, planning, and evaluation have long been prime candidates. What these processes have in common is that they can be ignored without immediate or obvious peril. Perhaps a president ought to look ahead to the next generation's needs or back at past programs to see what they actually have accomplished. But the White House does not grind to a halt if it fails to plan or evaluate.

The notion that important but ignored activities ought to share in the budget's prominence is not limited to procedural matters. In March 1978, President Carter announced that federal agencies would be required to prepare urban and community impact analyses for major program initiatives. In August of that year, after failing to locate a satisfactory home for urban impact analysis, the administration tossed the responsibility to OMB, which issued guidelines (Circular A-116) synchronizing submission of the impact statements with agency budget requests. A year later, a campaign begun in the 1940s to lodge a civil rights office in OMB finally achieved success. OMB Director McIntyre announced that the placement of the civil rights unit in the president's budget office "gives the effort the clout it deserves."

Approximately two-thirds of OMB's staff is assigned to nonbudgetary functions. One might think, therefore, that the budget process is being productively leveraged to serve vital presidential functions. The ever-changing roster of management activities includes intergovernment coordination, information management and technology, reorganization, and regulatory reform. The sheer number of "additional" duties hitched to the budget process ensures that many of them will be neglected, no matter how assertive the rhetoric that accompanies their devolution to OMB. The peripheral activities compete against one another, and only the few that are perceived to have strong and current presidential interest are attended to.

The leveraged activities lodged in OMB fall into three catagories:

1. Central management functions that just about everybody assumes must be performed by OMB, whether or not it or the president has much interest in the work. Program evaluation and the management of information are of this sort. OMB's half-hearted attitude toward this type of work can be gauged by the small number of persons assigned to it.
2. Matters that a president gets off his back by dumping them in OMB's lap. Whatever lip service it gives the cause (civil rights, urban impact analysis, etc.), the White House has little interest in the work and OMB's own interest quickly fades. After only one cycle of reviewing budgets from a civil rights perspective, the drive ran out of steam. One can generalize that a weak, nongermane process will be disadvantaged by association with budgeting. It will be neglected by the agency charged with carrying it out.
3. Matters that the president is genuinely interested in but does not want to vest in a new agency. Regulatory reform was the best example during the Carter administration. It had some notable successes, but because of strong, sustained presidential support, not because it was housed with budgeting.

OMB struggled without success through the 1970s to establish an effective linkage of its budget and management sides. On most matters, the two proceeded on separate tracks, and examiners did not disrupt their routines to accommodate the new management activities. OMB's budget makers went about their main business without paying much attention to what the managers were doing. Rather than recognizing that the depreciation of their budgetary expertise and role means that they will need new functions if they are to regain presidential esteem, the budget examiners feel threatened by the managers. Insecure in their own standing, they do not see any long-term advantage in fusing budgeting and management into a more powerful process than either could be alone.

Looking back at decades of budgetary practice, one might conclude that administrative management rode the budget's coattails to success in the 1940s. But if this function was effectively joined to budgeting, it was because the budget staff benefited from the connection. Assisting agencies in upgrading their administrative processes went hand in hand with insisting that agencies do it the bureau's way. The old Budget Bureau also reaped dividends from the lines of communication forged with agency administrators. By getting involved in the internal management of federal agencies, the bureau was able to make informed and acceptable budget decisions.

If the president's budget office does not perceive any gain from linkage, the only recourse is for the president to insist that OMB create the linkages. But a distinction must be drawn between nominal support by the president and determination to further an important objective through the budget process. The latter is quite rare; when it occurs, it must be renewed by continuing infusions of presidential interest and support. This is rarer yet.

The President's Options

The president cannot have an all-purpose budget process and an all-purpose budget staff. He cannot get both institutional and personal-political service from the same group, nor can he deploy budgeting as both a means of making program policy and a tool of administrative management. The president has to decide whether to focus his budget process narrowly on the mainstream activities and agencies of government, allowing an increasing portion of financial transactions to occur outside the process, or to extend the budget's scope to the many off-budget items now excluded from it. The president thus has one option that would keep his political escape routes open and another that would constrain his budgetary freedom.

How the American political system adjusts to resource limitations, if this turns out to be a continuing condition, will influence the president's budget options. Political budgeting came of age in an era of almost uninterrupted economic growth, stretching from the New Deal to the 1970s. Incrementalism enabled the president and Congress to respond to budgetary pressures by allocating "growth shares" in the budget. Even though the level of uncontrollables increased, the president was able to take effective budget action by distributing increments to various programs.

One cannot know whether the current (real or perceived) economic adversity will prove to be an enduring or passing feature of American life. But budgeting will be a different process if one rather than the other possibility is realized. If economic buoyancy were to return, future presidents would be able to concentrate their budgetary attention on policy initiatives, just as past presidents did. But if scarcity proves to be a lasting condition, either tighter budgetary discipline or more budgetary escapism might ensue. There will be no easy rolling-back of the politicization of the budget. The trend toward spending on external interests has occurred in every Western democracy; once political pressures have been unloosed, it is hard to rein them in again.

The 1970s provided glimpses of both scenarios. The decade saw both increased budgetary control—the congressional budget process was the leading innovation—and increased escapism, as off-budget spending and credit programs proliferated. Faced with conflicting pressures, the political system has tightened and loosened controls at the same time. Future presidents might resort to similar tactics.

Reagan's Budget Gamble

A president who wants to shape the budget according to his preferences faces political and economic constraints. As the budget has grown, those advantaged by it have become more vigilant and active in protecting their benefits. They secure legal rights to payments from the treasury, sometimes in the form of indexed entitlements that automatically rise as the cost of living climbs. Entitlements and other uncontrollables have effectively barred recent presidents from achieving their budget objectives. So, too, have economic conditions. High inflation and high unemployment have defeated all recent efforts to curb federal spending and balance the budget. Because the budget is highly sensitive to the performance of the economy, failure to stabilize prices and produce economic growth has forced repeated changes in budget policy.

In view of these constraints, one might have expected a president determined to restore budget control to war against uncontrollables and seek balanced budgets. These objectives would have been in accord with conservative policy and, if successful, would have resulted in lower spending and smaller deficits. Ronald Reagan took exactly the opposite tack in his 1981 budget cuts. The president erected a *cordon sanitaire* around the most uncontrollable portions of the federal budget, protecting social security, medicare, and veterans benefits against budget cuts. He deftly targeted his budget reductions against weak political interests, especially low-income groups. The White House strategy was to recapture control of the budget by defeating the weak interests. This posture was based on the premise that it would be possible to surrender control over most expenditures and still shape the totals according to the president's wishes.

This policy entailed two assumptions. First, that weak interests would not be able to marshal support in Congress for their programs; second, that continuing inflation would not compel further steep increases in spending for the protected programs. Thus, the White House was gambling that a cooperative economy would moderate the growth in future claims on the budget by beneficiaries of protected programs.

This economic expectation was anchored in a proposal for steep, recurring reductions in marginal tax rates to encourage savings and investment. The president's plan was popularly characterized as an abandonment of demand management in favor of supply-side incentives. But this simplistic supply-versus-demand characterization masks the administration's radical departure from conservative precepts. The president proposed a $45 billion budget deficit, not the balanced budget that Mr. Reagan insisted on during the campaign. He was not cynically walking away from a campaign promise; rather, he was convinced that a traditional attack on inflation would, for the reasons discussed earlier, be counterproductive. Long before inflation was mitigated, unemployment would worsen, the deficit would rise, and the president (and Congress) would be compelled to finance an expansive policy. In order to break free of the economy's stranglehold on the budget, Reagan took a chance in the belief that tax cuts would spur growth without fueling inflation.

In sum, President Reagan gambled that by accommodating to strong interests, he could vanquish weak ones, and that by cutting both spending and taxes, he could bring inflation under control. March 1981 is obviously much too early for us to know whether this strategy will have the intended effects. But it can be said that if the president succeeds, the budget will once again be a potent instrument of the presidency; if he fails, the budget's impotence will be even more starkly revealed than before.

Notes

1. For a survey of the president's budget role prior to 1921, see Louis C. Fisher, *Presidential Spending Power* (Princeton, N.J.: Princeton University Press, 1975), pp. 9–35.

2. For a discussion of congressional exercise of its power of the purse in the nineteenth century, see Lucius Wilmerding, *The Spending Power* (New Haven, Conn.: Yale University Press, 1943).

3. Pursuant to a compromise between the House and Senate versions, the Budget and Accounting Act of 1921 placed the Bureau of the Budget in the Treasury Department but made it responsible to the president.

4. A. E. Buck, "Financial Control and Accountability," in President's Committee on Administrative Management, *Report with Special Studies* (Washington, D.C.: Government Printing Office, 1937) p. 142.

5. Quoted in Richard Polenberg, *Reorganizing Roosevelt's Government, 1936–1939* (Cambridge, Mass.: Harvard University Press, 1966), p. 17.

6. According to Polenberg, one of the three members of the committee, Charles Merriam habitually referred to the staff reports as "non-supporting documents." Ibid.

7. President's Committee on Administrative Management, *Report*, p. 16.

8. Ibid., p. 17.

9. Ibid., p. 20.

10. See, for example, Fritz Morstein Marx, "The Bureau of the Budget: Its Evolution and Present Role," *American Political Science Review* 39 (1945): 653–684.

11. Half of the fourteen contributors to *Elements of Public Administration*, the postwar textbook edited by Fritz Morstein Marx, had served in the Bureau of the Budget during its growth years.

12. Herman Somers, in his study of the Office of War Mobilization, noted its "growing tendency to disregard the Bureau and act independently." Quoted in Larry Berman, *The Office of Management and Budget and the Presidency* (Princeton, N.J.: Princeton University Press, 1979), p. 30.

13. Richard E. Neustadt, "Presidency and Legislation: Planning the President's Program", *American Political Science Review*, 49(1955):985.

14. David C. Mowrey, Mark S. Kamlet, and John P. Crecine, "Presidential Management of Budgetary and Fiscal Policymaking," *Political Science Quarterly*, 95(1980):405.

15. Neustadt, "Presidency and Legislation," p. 996.

16. Mowrey et al., "Presidential Management," p. 424.

17. On the concept of "nondecision," see Matthew A. Crenson, *The Un-Politics of Air Pollution* (Baltimore, Md.: Johns Hopkins University Press, 1971), Chapter 1.

18. Naomi Caiden and Aaron Wildavsky, *Planning and Budgeting in Poor Countries* (New York: John Wiley & Sons, 1974).

19. Frederick C. Mosher, "The Changing Responsibilities and Tactics of the Federal Government," *Public Administration Review* 40, 6 (November-December 1980), pp. 541–547.

20. For a discussion of the changing role of the appropriations committees, see Allen Schick, *Congress and Money: Budgeting, Spending, and Taxing* (Washington, D.C.: Urban Institute, 1980), Chapters 10 and 11.

21. Berman, *Office of Management and Budget*, pp. 39, 41–44.

22. William Carey, "Presidential Staffing in the Sixties and Seventies," *Public Administration Review*, 30(1970):454.

23. See Hugh Heclo, "OMB and the Presidency: The Problem of Neutral Competence," *Public Interest* 38 (Winter 1975):80–98.

4

The Paradox of Presidential Personnel Management

G. Calvin Mackenzie

Personnel administration lies at the very core of administrative management. The effective conduct of the work of the Government depends upon the men and women who serve it. Improved plans for governmental organization and management are of little value unless simultaneous recognition is given to the need for attracting, retaining, and developing human capacity in the public service.

> —from the report of the President's Committee on Administrative Management (1937)

Nothing so strikes the student of presidential management activities in the years following the 1937 report of the Brownlow Committee as a compelling sense of frustrated activism. The period is one of constant tinkering, of thrust and counter-thrust, of an unending search for administrative procedures and techniques that would make the most of the ample resources of the federal government. But when one peels away the layers of practice and proposal that have accumulated since 1939—through PERT and PODSCORB and PPBS and MBO and ZBB—there emerges a single constant: people. The complex maze of structures, procedures, and processes that meets the first glance of the casual observer distracts attention from the simple fact that the federal government is, in essence, an organization of *people* with tasks to accomplish and problems to solve.

As people are the government's fundamental resource, so are they the president's. Because the president's responsibilities are vast, the quality of his leadership is directly affected—and constrained—by the calibre of the personnel who work in the executive branch and the soundness of the system of personnel management.

Contemporary presidents have thought that the success of their administrations depended upon effective personnel management and have often vigorously and directly concerned themselves with this challenge. But for most of them this has not been an easy or a pleasant experience. They have found the problems of central personnel management enormous and unyielding and the solutions ephemeral or elusive.

In dealing with this concern, all presidents have been forced to confront one of the critical paradoxes of the modern presidency: Although the president is called the chief executive and is widely expected to manage the executive branch, he does not possess the effective control over personnel policy that such a task requires. His authority does not match his responsibility—nor does it match his needs.

To lead the country, the president must first be able to lead the executive branch of the government. And leading the executive branch requires that the president be able in a significant way to shape the composition and manage the utilization of principal executive branch employees. But for almost a century, presidents have frequently found themselves without the power or the instruments necessary to accomplish this task. There are a number of reasons for this dilemma, but the historical record suggests that the following are the most compelling.

First, personnel management in the federal government is an incredibly complex task. Today, the executive branch is composed of 3 million civilian employees and includes almost every known profession and vocation. Federal employees serve in every state, in every major city, and in almost every country in the world. The management of this work force is an enormous administrative enterprise. No other organization in the free world, public or private, has a work force as large or diverse. Hence the task of personnel management in the federal government is complicated simply because it is sui generis: There are few precedents or models for its managers to copy.

Second, those most responsible for personnel management in the federal government, the president and his appointees, bear the burden of being transients in office. Their lease runs for only four years, and that is rarely enough time to allow them to learn all they need to know about the federal personnel system. Skepticism, uncertainty, and confusion are the normal greetings a new administration receives from the federal service. It takes time for the permanent and the transient governments to get comfortable with one another, if they ever do at all. The longer that time, the more the opportunities lost for presidential leadership in policy development. A president who moves immediately to institutionalize his own personnel management preferences will find, as Jimmy Carter did, that even the steady exertion of presidential support can rarely bring this process to fruition until most of a presidential term has elapsed. Inevitably this means that most presidents will be stuck with inherited organizations and procedures for managing the government's personnel resources, management tools that may be ill-fitted to the task of personnel administration as they define it.

Third, the president must share personnel management authority with a potent and aggressive legislature. The Congress determines the shape of the federal personnel system. The Congress sets pay and benefit levels. The Congress establishes personnel ceilings for individual agencies, and one house of the Congress must consent to presidential appointments. Wherever he turns, the president's personnel management authority is constrained by the actions or the intervention of the Congress. The Congress places much the same value on its personnel controls that it does on its budgetary controls. These are important sources of legislative leverage in shaping administrative operations and policy directions; they are jealously guarded. This leaves the president with a significantly circumscribed latitude for personnel management. His own efforts to improve the quality of federal personnel management must always be adjusted to the preferences of congressional majorities.

Fourth, the president's role in managing the personnel resources of the government is further complicated by the peculiar interweaving of politics and administration that is characteristic of our political system. Personnel decisions are important political decisions. It matters who gets important federal jobs. It matters because they remain one of the principal rewards for successful political activity and because the selection of political appointees has no small bearing on the policy decisions of the federal government. The proposition that Herbert Kaufman offered fifteen years ago, "The type of man who holds high office often determines the type of policy the government pursues,"[1] is still fundamental to the dynamic of federal personnel decisions.

In the efforts of his administration to direct and manage the federal personnel system, the president is subject to unrelenting political pressures. They may come from a congressional committee chairman on a policy question, from an interest group over the selection of an appointee, or from federal employees' unions over the size of a cost-of-living pay increase, but whatever the source a president soon finds that most of his personnel decisions have important and complicated political ramifications. Hence he often finds himself on the horns of a painful dilemma. Personnel policy decisions that make good administrative sense often make no political sense, and vice versa. The safe and sound course between the Scylla of good administration and the Charybdis of good politics, both essential to effective leadership, is hard to plot and harder still to navigate.

These encumbrances weigh heavily on the president's efforts to bring about effective personnel management. They make even more imposing this already difficult component of his executive management responsibilities by ensuring the permanent absence of simple answers. It is starkly clear that in directing the management of the federal personnel system, nothing comes easily to an American president. He has to struggle to impose his policy views and his management concepts on the federal work force. To do so, he must learn to cope with an inheritance of disparate managerial tools and structures, with a jealous Congress, with a naturally skeptical bureaucracy, and with no small amount of systemic inertia.

The most important of the personnel management tasks confronting a contemporary president are these:

- The identification, recruitment, and wise deployment of noncareer, "political" executives.
- The development of mutually supportive relationships with the senior people in the career service.
- The establishment and maintenance of federal personnel policies that enhance responsiveness, dedication, and creativity throughout the federal bureaucracy.

Federal personnel management involves more than the performance of just these functions, but these are the three principal areas in which a president's interests intersect with the operations of the federal personnel system. As I shall suggest, the intelligent management of these responsibilities is critical to the quality of central personnel management in the executive branch, and beyond that, to the successful pursuit of any administration's policy goals. For that reason, they are the topic of this chapter.

The Recruitment of Political Executives

At almost every turning point in recent American history, one can identify key decisions made or shaped by people who were never elected to political office. Among those who participated in the deliberations of the Executive Committee of the National Security Council during the Cuban missile crisis, for instance, only one—the president himself—had gotten there through the electoral process. All the rest were presidential appointees. Much the same was true of those groups of officials responsible for military readiness at Pearl Harbor, and of those who developed the Marshall Plan, decided to invade the Bay of Pigs, conducted the war in Vietnam, or negotiated the SALT treaties. The quality of presidential performance, indeed the quality of government performance, is very much a reflection of the kinds of people who serve in appointive positions in the White House Office and at the top levels of the executive branch.

The attraction and retention of talented people is the sine qua non of good personnel management. "Ours is a difficult and exhilarating form of government," John Gardner has noted, "not for the faint of heart, not for the tidy-minded, and in these days of complexity not for the stupid. We need men and women who can bring to government the highest order of intellect, social motivations sturdy enough to pursue good purposes despite setbacks, and a resilience of spirit equal to the frustrations of public life."[2]

In recent decades, the task of recruiting political executives has tended to divide into two distinct phases. One occurs at the very beginning of each administration, the other phase after the transition is over. Each confronts a president with a different set of problems and a different array of possibilities.

The personnel choices a president makes during the transition period are perhaps as important collectively as any other set of decisions he will make during his time in office. Yet these choices are often made with inadequate preparation and often in a state of near-ignorance of the kinds of jobs being filled and the real abilities of the people selected to fill them. So many matters of consequence press upon a president-elect during the transition that he never has adequate time to give to the direct examination of candidates and their qualifications, or even to the establishment of a set of procedures to permit his staff to carry out that function effectively in his stead. The typical result is a helter-skelter process with personnel choices made by a variety of individuals, each interpreting the president's priorities in his own way, each coping with a different set of political realities.

But personnel difficulties in the transition period have served as a kind of early warning system for our recent presidents, alerting them and their staffs to the need for better organization and more sophisticated procedures for the selection of political appointees. The transition period marks only the beginning of personnel selection responsibilities that continue through a president's entire term in office. It normally takes a half year or more after the election to complete the initial selection of presidential appointees, and shortly afterward there begins the normal and constant task of filling the vacancies that regularly occur in the agencies and departments, in the regulatory commissions, and in diplomatic posts overseas. The substantial number of the positions for which a president has some appointment responsibility and the high levels of executive turnover that have long plagued our system of government have made personnel and recruitment an ongoing responsibility for a modern president.

Each recent administration has responded to this particular management imperative in its own way, but these responses have become increasingly similar. Indeed, if one takes the end of World War II as a starting point, it is possible to trace a developmental trend in the way contemporary administrations have managed the task of selecting important political appointees. Prior to that time, even through the administration of Franklin Roosevelt, the selection of political executives was treated primarily as a political, and only secondarily as a management, function. Reliance on personal acquaintances, on congressional recommendations, and on names that bubbled up through the party structure was the norm. National searches for qualified candidates rarely took place, scrutiny of candidates' backgrounds and abilities was uneven and often superficial, and concerns about a nominee's substantive competence and administrative abilities often took a back seat to the issue of his political pedigree and the strength of his political sponsors. Such was the state of the art in the selection of federal political executives.

Modernization of this process came slowly, but the first inklings of it began to emerge in the Truman administration. Truman's White House staff was not very formally organized. Selection of political executives was supervised for most of the Truman administration by Donald Dawson, an assistant to the president. Dawson had a staff of three or four people, mostly clerical, who helped in the routine handling of nominations, clearances, endorsements, and so on. It was still largely a one-man show, although Martin Friedman, a special assistant to the president, began to play a larger role in personnel selection after Truman's reelection. Harry Truman himself took a personal interest in his appointments, often suggesting candidates from his own acquaintance and making a point of interviewing individually each final candidate for a nomination before offering the job.[3]

The Truman selection effort began to bog down in 1950. A great many executives were leaving the government after long service in Democratic administrations, concerns over loyalty and security were making public service a less pleasant enterprise, and embarrassing scandals were beginning to pop up in places close to the White House. For these reasons and because there appeared little likelihood of a Democratic victory in 1952, it became harder and harder for the Truman administration to recruit qualified replacements for the growing numbers of executives who were leaving the government.

Necessity became the mother of invention, and in mid-1950 Martin Friedman and John Mee (the dean of the Business School at Indiana University on temporary duty at the White House) developed what came to be known as the "little cabinet" plan to improve executive selection procedures. It took its name from a group composed of subcabinet officers, mostly young, up-and-coming assistant secretaries, who developed the program and then supervised its implementation. The group's efforts had a dual thrust. It sought first to build a catalog of "qualified persons without reference to specific jobs on the theory that highly qualified executive personnel would be available for and qualified for a great number of top level positions."[4] That is, it wanted to create what in later years would come to be known as a talent bank. But it also sought to get a better handle on the kinds of jobs that were subject to presidential appointment and on the formal and practical qualifications they demanded. So the group also set about the task of building a master list of appointive positions with an appropriate job description for each.

This was a step of some significance in the development of the personnel management function in the White House. For the first time, an administration was attempting to build an outreach mechanism, a set of procedures, and an organizational structure that would permit it to search for appointees beyond the limited acquaintance of the president and his immediate staff.

The second aspect of the little cabinet plan was also significant. It recognized that effective personnel management had to start with a crystallized sense of the president's management needs. In earlier administrations, a political appointment usually was the result of an effort to find the right job for a particular individual. The little cabinet plan sought to reverse the thrust, emphasizing that sound personnel management should rather be an effort to find the right person for a particular job. That did not immediately become the norm, by any means, but the little cabinet effort marked the first evidence of a new direction in personnel selection. By expanding the opportunities for a personnel search and by providing specific job profiles to guide that search, the little cabinet plan aimed to bring more consistency and sophistication to executive selection procedures in the White House. It recognized a problem and a management need that would become increasingly apparent to Truman's successors.

Indeed, it did become apparent to Dwight Eisenhower and his staff very soon after the 1952 election. Cabinet and subcabinet selections in the Eisenhower transition period were the result of a very informal process, one in which neither search procedures nor evaluations of candidates were very systematic. But the new administration soon recognized that it could not govern effectively without a more sophisticated set of personnel selection procedures. Eisenhower and his staff felt the need for this because they recognized that routine turnover in noncareer positions would create a constant need for qualified appointees, and because they soon came to believe that only through the skillful utilization of presidential appointment powers could they begin to reimpose Republican control on a government that had been in Democratic hands for two decades.

The president himself was aware of and deeply concerned about this problem, and he delegated responsibility to Sherman Adams and Philip Young to develop a solution to it. They recommended, and Eisenhower agreed, that Charles F. Willis, Jr., be appointed to the new position of special assistant for executive appointments to supervise this effort and other matters dealing with noncareer executive appointments.

Willis devised a very elaborate plan to identify noncareer positions held by Democrats and to coordinate with the agencies and with Republican leaders the replacement of those Democrats with loyal Republicans. The plan itself was a failure. When leaked to the public, it was immediately criticized as a bare-faced Republican patronage operation. Its real and important objectives were lost in the public brouhaha, and to avoid further embarrassment, it was quickly abandoned. Willis left the administration soon thereafter.

But the position of special assistant for executive appointments survived for the remainder of the Eisenhower presidency and was subsequently held by Edward Tait, Robert Gray, and Robert Hampton. The special assistant served mainly to coordinate the selection process for noncareer executives at all but the very highest levels. He served as the White House contact with the Republican National Committee (which then had its own personnel office), with Republican senators and congressmen, and with the personnel officers in the departments and agencies. This was not a decision-making position in any significant sense; final selections were usually made by the president's chief of staff, giving heavy weight to the recommendations of important party leaders. The special assistant's principal responsibilities were to facilitate communication among the interested parties in each selection decision, to reduce the chief of staff's burden of choice by weeding out candidates who were substantively unqualified or politically unacceptable, and to manage the ample flow of paper that accumulates in the appointment process.

Creation of the Office of Special Assistant for Executive Appointments was the first glimmer of an institutionalized personnel function in the White House. The people who held that office during the Eisenhower years implemented information management techniques that made the executive selection process more efficient. But tidying up this process had little significant impact on the substantive components and the array of influences in appointment decisions. Heavy reliance continued to be placed on traditional political sources for the names of potential candidates. Little effort was made—or thought necessary—to expand the scope of personnel searches beyond these sources, to develop more sophisticated reference checks on recommended candidates, or to ensure that subcabinet appointments in the agencies and departments were congruent with the president's administrative needs and policy objectives.

The first real effort to break with this tradition of an agency-centered, partisan executive selection process came with the Kennedy administration.

Efforts in the Kennedy transition period to use a systematic approach in making cabinet and subcabinet selections, although vigorously pursued, had not been a notable success and, after his inauguration, Kennedy delegated responsibility for supervision of noncareer executive selection to Ralph Dungan, a member of his staff. To help him reorganize and upgrade the personnel selection operation, Dungan hired Dan H. Fenn, Jr., then a faculty member at the Harvard Business School.

Both Fenn and Dungan were troubled by the reactive nature of traditional methods of executive search. Historically, the pool of candidates had been made up of people known personally to the president or his staff or recommended by the national committee of the president's party, leaders of his party in Congress, special interest groups, or people in the relevant agencies. Although qualified candidates often emerged from these sources, they rarely provided a very broad spectrum of possibilities. The same names kept cropping up from the same narrow circles of acquaintances. The White House had always lacked a genuine outreach capacity, an ability to conduct an active nationwide search for qualified but unknown candidates for executive appointments, and this was a major source of concern to the new Kennedy personnel team.

One of the ways in which Fenn and his staff dealt with this problem was by creating what came to be known as the "contact network."[5] This was composed of lists of leaders in a variety of professions and occupations all across the country upon whom the White House could call to solicit candidate suggestions and references when an executive vacancy occurred. The contact network provided the president's staff with a source of independent, reasonably objective information that freed the White House from its traditional reliance on influential groups and individuals in Washington. The latter almost always had an interest in getting their own candidates appointed, and their interests rarely coincided completely with the president's.

To further enhance the president's leadership role in the appointment process, the Kennedy personnel staff was enlarged to a size double that of any previous administration.[6] In the past, the selection of noncareer executives had been intermingled with the less important task (from a management perspective) of filling minor patronage positions. The Kennedy personnel staff separated these, thus permitting the bulk of its attention to focus on those few hundred appointments of most consequence to an administration's success.

What Fenn established was not a perfect solution to the president's personnel selection problems. Kennedy himself circumvented Fenn's operation completely on a number of occasions, and political forces in the appointment process often overcame the personnel staff's effort to harness them. But in the larger perspective of presidential personnel management, what occurred in the Kennedy administration was of no small significance. The executive recruitment operation in the White House was substantially institutionalized. The freeing of the president from a long tradition of deference to others in the selection of "his" executives was greatly advanced. And some initial, but important, steps were taken toward a reversal of prevailing expectations about the president's responsibilities in the executive selection process. The president's role had begun the change from one of stewardship to one of leadership.

The White House personnel staff continued in operation and came to new prominence during the Johnson administration—largely because Lyndon Johnson wanted it to. Although the president did not always heed the advice of his personnel staff, he found it useful to create the illusion that he was deeply wedded to it. Lyndon Johnson was personally responsible for most of the important personnel choices made during his presidency, but his repeated statements of dependence on his personnel staff allowed him to evade the full thrust of most external efforts to influence those decisions. John Macy, his chief personnel aide, explained how he did this: "A number of times it was reported back to me that somebody would come in and complain about a particular appointment that the President had made and he was quoted as having said, 'Well, don't blame me. It's that God damn Macy. He insists on having merit.' And that tended to terminate the conversation as far as the complainant was concerned."[7]

In an indirect way, this abetted the institutionalization of the personnel selection support system in the White House. Those political actors who typically seek to influence appointment decisions—party leaders, members of Congress, interest groups, and the like—began to see the personnel staff as their logical contact point with the White House on personnel matters. This development of habits of interaction with the personnel staff increased its utility to Johnson and subsequent presidents as a prime conduit for negotiations over personnel selection decisions. Ultimately, this helped to solidify the place of the president's personnel staff in the appointment process.

The components and character of the personnel support system developed under Dan Fenn and John Macy appear now to have become a permanent feature of the contemporary presidency. Presidents Ford and Carter adopted selection procedures and staff structures very similar to those in use during the Kennedy and Johnson years. The Nixon administration, in pursuing its "administrative management strategy" after 1970, committed more resources to the selection and management of political executives than its predecessors or immediate successors. But, although its aggressiveness in pursuit of its operational objectives was extraordinary, these objectives remained remarkably similar to those that guided every White House political personnel staff in the two decades after 1960. Stated simply those objectives were to establish:

- An effective outreach capacity allowing an administration to identify potential executive candidates beyond the circle of friends and acquaintances of the president and his staff and beyond the names that are thrust upon the White House by those primarily concerned with serving their own interests.
- Systematic procedures for carrying out the background investigations and political clearances that are necessary to avoid embarrassing or impolitic nominations.
- A planning capability permitting an administration to anticipate its personnel needs in advance and to begin a search for replacements soon enough to avoid long-term position vacancies.
- Active coordination of departmental and presidential concerns in the selection process.
- Staff resources of sufficient size and professional quality to manage adeptly each of these functional responsibilities.

Not all of the problems of noncareer executive selection have been solved by these developments, and the management challenge in this area is a constant one. Turnover in executive positions remains alarmingly high, and the time never comes when an administration can stop looking for talented and responsive executives. Indeed, in many ways the difficulty of executive recruitment has been exacerbated in recent years by the tougher scrutiny of Senate confirmation procedures, by the rising cost of living in Washington, and by the progressive tightening of conflict-of-interest requirements.

But the structures and procedures of noncareer executive selection that have accumulated gradually over the past three decades represent a serious and significant effort to improve the president's management capabilities. Personnel selection remains a process over which presidents must struggle for control. They do not always win. But the changes of the recent past have created better *opportunities* for the White House to manage the executive selection process—better opportunities, that is, to pinpoint the president's needs and to protect his options.

Career Executives

At the end of 1979, there were approximately 11,000 men and women working in civil service grades GS 16 through 18 or their equivalent. These are the cream of the federal career service—its technical specialists, its most experienced administrators, the repository of much of its institutional memory.

These career executives, the so-called supergrades, are immensely important to a president. Their substantive expertise, their managerial skills, their hands-on understanding of the internal operations of the executive branch, and their enduring relationships with the Congress can make or break a president's efforts to successfully direct the actions of the federal government. If those resources are used to support the president, they greatly enhance his leadership possibilities. If they are used to impede the accomplishment of his objectives, the success of his administration will inevitably be diminished. The president wants their allegiance and their help.

But wanting their allegiance and actually winning it, as recent presidents have quickly discovered, are two quite different things. Although he is the elected leader of the executive branch and they are its employees, the ties that bind them do not adhere to conventional lines of authority and hierarchy. The president does not hire the career executives, he has little power to fire them, his control over their assignments and compensation is peripheral, and—in many ways, most disabling of all—he is a transient interloper in their world of long-standing traditions and relationships. These are the compelling and often severely complicating realities he must confront in trying to put the talents of the career executives at the service of his policy objectives.

In attempting to do this, the president has two overarching management problems. The first is to get the right people with the right skills in the right places. The second is to ensure their responsiveness to his administration's goals once they are there. To solve these problems, a president needs a corps of career administrators properly trained and prepared for the jobs he wishes to assign them. And he needs sufficient authority to move career executives around, to create incentives to inspire their efforts and their loyalty, and to remove those whose incompetence or whose personal views improperly interfere with the administration of public policy. Presidential personnel advisers have argued for this, indeed have fought for it, for more than forty-five years. But their successes have been small and infrequent. In recounting that struggle, we encounter many of the practical difficulties that have long frustrated American presidents in their efforts to create a flexible and responsive personnel management system.

Management Ideas and Initiatives, 1935 to 1976

The issue of specialized management procedures for those in the senior civil service grades was first brought to public notice by the report of the Commission of Inquiry on Public Service Personnel in 1935. Employing as its models the American Foreign Service and the British higher civil service, that commission recommended the creation of an administrative service of the United States. The administrative service would be composed of high-ranking civil servants who would be available for assignment to nonpolitical executive and administrative positions requiring "correlation, planning, and the central direction, arrangement, and delegation of work."[8]

The principal objective of this proposal was improved administrative flexibility and executive control. The assignment of senior career administrators would be centralized in the Civil Service Commission or in a special office in the White House. Members of the administrative service could be transferred from one bureau to another within a department or even across departmental lines. This would give political executives the ability to remove and reassign reluctant or incompatible career administrators, and it would give the White House greater latitude to put talented career administrators where they could be of most service to the administration.

This particular proposal lacked influential proponents in Congress and in the White House, but its echoes sounded through all of the major personnel studies of the following four and a half decades. They quickly reemerged, for instance, in 1937 in the *Report on Personnel Administration* that Floyd W. Reeves and Paul T. David wrote for the President's Committee on Administrative Management (the Brownlow Committee).

Although they did not call for a separation of the higher and lower civil service grades quite as distinct as that preferred by the Commission of Inquiry on Public Service Personnel, Reeves and David heavily emphasized "the advantages that would accrue to the Chief Executive and to the Cabinet officers from the existence of a highly trained corps of mature career administrators." They noted that in fact such a corps of administrators already existed, and they lamented the failure of government policy to provide them with "the recognition in dignity of office, emoluments, or security of tenure to which their actual contribution to the business of government entitles them." Their positions, Reeves and David argued, "do not hold out the incentives and opportunities . . . that are so necessary to attract new talent to the service and to improve the morale and performance of that already present."[9]

Despite the Reeves and David recommendations, the Brownlow Committee chose to say very little about specialized treatment for senior civil servants in its final report. And, except for normal increases in pay, little was done over the ensuing decade and a half to improve the status of the government's senior career administrators or to strengthen their managerial relationship with the president.

A new and significant response to this problem emerged from the work of the second Hoover Commission in 1955. The first Hoover Commission had been silent on this issue, but the second one addressed it directly and developed an elaborate proposal for the creation and nourishing of a distinctive corps of senior civil servants. These were its main elements:

- A senior civil service (SCS) would be established, composed initially of about 1,500 career administrators selected from throughout the federal service. (The commission thought that the service might ultimately grow to 3,000 people, a large enough group to fill almost all of the top nonpolitical management positions in the federal government.)

- Members of the senior civil service could move from one job to another or from one department to another without a sacrifice of pay or status.
- As in the armed forces and the Foreign Service, senior civil servants would have personal rank status, independent of the jobs they held.
- Individuals would be nominated for the SCS by their employing agencies and appointed by a bipartisan senior civil service board with the consent of the president. The board would be composed of the chairman of the Civil Service Commission, a member of the president's Executive Office staff, and three private citizens appointed by the president and confirmed by the Senate. The board would conduct periodic appraisals of the work of the senior civil servants and would have power to authorize pay raises for those who performed effectively and to drop from the SCS those who did not.
- Members of the SCS would be expected to serve responsibly in any administration, regardless of party, and to refrain from political activities that would adversely affect their ability to perform fairly and responsively.

Unlike the earlier proposals for specialized treatment of senior career administrators, this one attracted considerable attention and support. It also generated no small amount of controversy and debate. The plan caught the interest of President Eisenhower's Presidential Advisory Committee on Government Organization (PACGO) and of other key members of his administration, and the Civil Service Commission staff soon went to work to develop a presidential proposal modeled on the Hoover Commission plan.

At the same time, the personnel and public administration journals began to be filled with penetrating and often heated debates over the probable impact of the Hoover Commission proposal for a senior civil service.[10] All of these arguments were speculative, of course, as there was no comparable experience or analogy upon which judgments could be founded, but they were full of skeptical questions. Would those eligible to serve in the SCS find that prospect very appealing if, in fact, it minimized the value of their substantive knowledge or jeopardized the security of the positions they had established through a career of service in a single agency or department? Would genuine managerial benefits result from this proposed substitution of administrative generalists for career executives highly familiar with and deeply committed to agency programs? Would the benefits the president would gain in managerial flexibility sufficiently offset the decline in overall government performance likely to result from reductions in the commitment and efficiency of career administrators? And, finally, there wove through these debates the specter of a new political force, an inward-looking senior civil service possessed of its own corporate identity, with a potential for thwarting those presidential initiatives that challenged its management orthodoxy or the career interests of its members.

Important as these intellectual arguments were in shaping the environment in which the Hoover proposals were received, the greater threat to their success came from two groups of political actors who felt, on balance, that the proposals promised more harm than good. One of these was the senior civil servants themselves. Few of them had any difficulty in keeping their enthusiasm for this plan under control. Their fears of disruption of career progression, of the diminished value of their substantive expertise, and of loss of tenure generally outweighed the new challenges and increased compensation promised by these proposals.

The plan for a senior civil service generated even less enthusiasm in the Congress. Both Clarence J. Brown and Chet Holifield, members of the House of Representatives serving on the Hoover Committee, appended dissents to the commission's report, *Personnel and Civil Service*, in which they took issue with the concept of a separate corps of senior civil servants. Holifield called the idea "fanciful" and argued that there was "no compelling reason for establishing a special category of top Government executives with privileges and obligations which set them apart from other career employees."[11] Brown wrote that "the creation of a select group of relatively nonexpendable executives to be endowed with great administrative power within our Government tends to destroy government by representation. It is a risk that I do not wish to take."[12]

But congressional opposition had other roots as well. Most notable was the fear that rotation of career administrators would break up long-standing and mutually profitable relationships between congressional subcommittees and career officials in the line agencies and bureaus of the executive branch. Because of the short tenure of most political appointees, the Congress had traditionally relied heavily on the expertise and experience of senior career administrators, the most knowledgeable people in the government about the programs they supervised. But many in Congress believed that the SCS proposal, with its emphasis on career executive mobility, would undermine that important source of congressional information. Support for the Hoover plan was weakened further by the absence of any requirement that the appointments of members of the SCS be subject to Senate confirmation, as was the case for other career executive services like the armed forces and the Foreign Service. The rotation of experienced hands, the destruction of traditional working relationships, and the lack of direct influence on the assignments of members of the SCS left little in this proposal for the Congress to like.

Although reluctant to push too hard into the teeth of this political opposition, the Eisenhower administration went ahead nevertheless with its plans for implementing a scaled-down variant of the SCS. In August of 1957, President Eisenhower issued Executive Order 10724 creating the Career Executives Committee within the Civil Service Commission, appointing its five members, and providing its charge: "After taking into consideration the views of the departments and agencies and making such inquiries as it deems appropriate, the Committee shall develop specific recommendations with respect to the establishment of a Career Executive Program within the civil service system." In January of 1958, the committee reported a set of proposals very similar to the recommendations of the Hoover Commission. In March of 1958, President Eisenhower put as much of the program into effect as he could through the issuance of Executive Order 10758.

This brought an immediate reaction from some members of Congress. They had not much liked the idea of a distinctive corps of senior career officials, but they were especially angry at Eisenhower for bypassing legislation and establishing much of the career executive program through executive order. The Subcommittee on Manpower Utilization of the House Post Office and Civil Service Committee passed a resolution calling on the president to withdraw Executive Order 10758 and to suspend the career executive program until it had been enacted through legislation.[13] Eisenhower refused. Early in 1959, members of the House Appropriations Committee, at the request of their colleagues on the Post Office and Civil Service Committee, struck out the president's request for funds to operate the Career Executive Program and attached an amendment to the fiscal 1960 appropriations bill for the Civil Service Commission prohibiting the use of any of its funds for that program. The Congress had made its point.

But the idea of a career executive program did not die easily. The interest of contemporary presidents and the arguments of personnel management specialists kept it on the reform agenda in spite of the practical opposition of senior executives and certain members of Congress. Other plans of varying scope were introduced in the 1960s and early 1970s: the Civil Service Commission's proposal for an executive assignment system (1966), President Nixon's effort to establish a federal executive service (1972), and the federal executive development program (1973). Like their predecessors, each of these initiatives provoked academic debate, political suspicions, and congressional skepticism. None improved in any substantial way the limited ability of a presidential administration to utilize and develop the talents of career officials in the supergrades. By the mid-1970s, most of the goals of the Second Hoover Commission remained unfulfilled.

The Civil Service Reform Act of 1978

The fallen standard was picked up again by the Carter administration in 1977. Included in its sweeping proposals for reform of the civil service system was a program for the establishment of the Senior Executive Service (SES). Agencies would designate positions to be filled by members of the SES. Senior executives would be drawn primarily from those serving in the supergrades; a maximum of 10 percent could be selected from outside the career service. Incentives for entry into the SES and for performance within it were primarily financial. Merit pay increases and lucrative performance bonuses would be available as rewards for good work. Senior executives would carry rank-in-person and could be assigned to positions throughout the government. Those who failed to satisfy appropriate performance standards could be removed from the SES without long delays or massive entanglement in complicated removal procedures.

Its main elements bore striking similarities to the earlier plans reviewed here, but the Carter proposal was different in one important way.[14] It won congressional approval and was enacted into law. After four decades of unsuccessful effort, the federal government finally had a comprehensive program for improved management of its top career executives.

The SES program, established with the passage of PL 95–454 in 1978, rests on many of the same intellectual underpinnings as its aborted ancestors. The first of those is *separatism*, the notion that senior career executives are a distinctive group of government employees with special problems and special needs. Recognition of that has been the steady driving force for four decades in the effort to build a senior executive service. Corporations have long paid special attention to the identification and nourishing of their most able managers. The armed forces have done so since the development of the general staff system. So too has the Foreign Service. It is less remarkable that the federal executive branch has also come around to this view than that it took so long for that idea to be formalized.

Executive *mobility* is a second principle that weaves through the history of this development. Practitioners and students of public administration have long bemoaned the tradition of American public service in which career employees spend all or most of their work lives in the confines of one agency. Neither scope of ability nor breadth of perspective is well served by that habit, and every effort to create a senior career service has sought to break it. In its place they have proposed a system that encouraged the movement of executives across agency lines. The aim in this was to hone the talents of executives by broadening their experiences and to improve the performance of agencies by providing them with periodic infusions of new people whose views and skills were not constrained by socialization solely within a single organization.

A third principle is the concept of a separate and effective executive *incentive system*. Good performance ought to be encouraged and rewarded; poor performance ought to be discouraged and punished. That notion has been at the core of every serious proposal for a senior executive service. There are many incentives in the life of a senior bureaucrat: to stick with the familiar, to attend primarily to the whims of congressional committees and clientele groups, to avoid actions that might jeopardize job security. A major part of the task of good management is to create other, more attractive incentives that will tie executive performance to the objectives of an agency's appointed leaders and of the president himself. The urge to create just that kind of appealing incentive system has been a constant in the tortuous history that led finally to the establishment of the Senior Executive Service.

A final principle—and perhaps the most important, given the political history of this effort—is *collective responsiveness* to political leadership. It is hardly a coincidence that efforts to distinguish a top managerial corps within the career service have always stemmed either from the initiative of American presidents or from study groups organized to improve the quality of presidential management. One of the architects of President Carter's proposal, Wayne Granquist of OMB, has said, "The underlying theory of the SES is that the top layer of bureaucracy will be more responsive to the President."[15] That is precisely why presidents have expended so much political capital on these proposals over the years. The responsiveness of career executives to presidents and their appointees is fundamental to the success of an administration. But without an appropriate administrative structure and the necessary management tools, that kind of responsiveness is hard to secure and maintain. It is so important, however, that many recent presidents have been willing to fight difficult and usually unsuccessful political battles to establish that structure and create those tools.

The story of the struggle to create a senior executive service reveals two persistent dilemmas that confront American presidents when they try to improve their own ability to manage the personnel resources of the federal government. One of those is the tension—inherent and pervasive in our system of government—between devotion to principles of merit and political neutrality in the career service, on the one hand, and the desperate need of any administration to be able to put the knowledge of its most experienced employees at the service of its own policy objectives, on the other. The former is rooted in notions of nonpartisanship; the latter is inherently partisan. It has been extraordinarily difficult to find and occupy a satisfactory middle ground.

A second persistent difficulty that presidents have encountered has been with the Congress. In principle, many members of Congress have sympathized with the objectives of recent presidents who sought to improve their abilities to direct the executive branch. But, at the same time, the Congress has been jealous of its relationships with senior career executives and hesitant to support new programs, whatever their administrative desirability, that might jeopardize those relationships. Opposition to these proposals has most often taken the shape, not of one branch against the other, but of a "permanent government," composed of congressmen, their staffs, and senior career officials, posed against a "transient government" of presidents and their noncareer appointees. When the sides are thus drawn, the former have most of the advantages. And this accounts for much of the presidential frustration that this effort has produced.

The SES provisions of the Civil Service Reform Act of 1978 embodied ideas that had been on the reform agenda for four decades. Their enactment might well become a significant landmark in the evolving relationship between American presidents and the corps of senior career officials that their administrations inherit. That, of course, will depend on the support the Senior Executive Service receives from the agencies, from the Congress, and from the senior executives. If that support is forthcoming and if the SES is sensitively administered, the personnel management capabilities of the modern presidency will be substantially enhanced.

Personnel Organization in the Executive Branch

The president is not, nor can he be, a personnel manager. The demands on his time and the limits of his resources simply do not permit him to participate with any regularity in day-to-day personnel management decisions throughout the executive branch. But the manner in which those decisions are made and their collective outcomes are important to him and to the aims of his administration. His success as a political leader with a short lease on the White House can only be hindered by a federal personnel system that is unresponsive, inefficient, or unduly expensive.

It is not surprising, therefore, that all of our recent presidents have taken a more than passing interest in the federal personnel system and have sought to develop central management institutions to improve their ability to guide its operations. For the most part their concerns have been broadly focused, on general policies rather than specific operations. Their most common substantive concerns have been with the quality of personnel, the fairness of procedures, responsiveness, cost, and the relationship of the parts to the whole. The principal objectives of this presidential involvement have been to ensure the establishment and maintenance of federal personnel systems that would enhance centralized policy management and satisfy fundamental democratic values.

The Civil Service Commission Under Challenge

Tinkering with the central personnel machinery began in the 1930s, and it continued through the 1970s. Through statute, through executive order, through reorganization plans, by hook or by crook, each president in the modern period has sought to shape central personnel institutions to fit his own political needs and administrative orientations. This has rarely been easy. Every effort to alter those institutions has encountered the massed opposition of all of those—members of Congress, federal employees and their unions, good government organizations, public administration scholars—who had grown comfortable with or who benefited from the status quo.

The Civil Service Commission was established by the Pendleton Act of 1883 as the government's central personnel agency. Designed primarily to be nonpartisan and largely independent of the president, it was composed of three members, no more than two of whom could be of the same party, and who served terms that were fixed in length and staggered in duration. Its format was a perfectly understandable response to the excesses of the partisan spoils system that originally inspired the creation of the civil service system.

But its structure and collegial mode of operation were not very compatible with a significant presidential role in government personnel management. And as the dual thrusts of administrative theory and practical administrative necessity began to demand more active presidential direction in the early decades of the twentieth century, the structure and operations of the Civil Service Commission became an increasingly frequent target of scrutiny and criticism.

The report of the Brownlow Committee in 1937 marked the real beginning of a long and exasperating effort to improve presidential capabilities for central management of the federal personnel system. That report singled out the Civil Service Commission as a major impediment to a well-managed federal personnel system:

> This form of organization . . . has everywhere been found slow, cumbersome, wasteful, and ineffective in the conduct of administrative duties. Board members are customarily laymen not professionally trained or experienced in the activities for which they are responsible. They remain in office for relatively short periods and rarely acquire the degree of expertness necessary to executive

direction. . . . Board administration tends to diffuse responsibility, to produce delays, and to make effective cooperation or vigorous leadership impossible.[16]

To correct these problems, the Brownlow Committee recommended that the Civil Service Commission be replaced by a civil service administration, headed by a single administrator serving at the pleasure of the president. This single administrator would have responsibility for the duties and functions then vested in the Civil Service Commission. A separate civil service board composed of seven distinguished private citizens would meet from time to time to conduct investigations, act as a watchdog on the operations of the merit system, and advise the president on personnel policies.

The key to this proposal was the relationship it established between the president and the federal personnel system. The civil service administrator would "act as a direct adviser to the President upon all personnel matters and would be responsible to the President for the development of improved personnel policies and practices."[17] It was clearly intended that he would be the president's agent, and through his actions, presidential direction of the federal personnel system would take shape.

President Roosevelt endorsed the Brownlow Committee's recommendations on personnel and submitted a recommendation for their enactment to the Congress. But the proposal attracted little congressional support, and it never became law. Its principal opposition came from obvious sources. Federal employee organizations and the patrons of the nonpartisan reform movement saw the Brownlow recommendations as a significant potential threat to the merit system, as a dressed-up reversion to the unhappy period when presidents dominated the processes of hiring, retaining, and promoting federal employees. A good many members of Congress opposed the Brownlow plan out of fear that it would lead to an undesirable enlargement of presidential authority.

None of this dimmed Roosevelt's enthusiasm for the committee's conclusions and, where his authority permitted, he began to carry them out through executive order. In 1938, he required each executive agency to set up its own personnel office headed by a single director, the double aim being to improve the quality of personnel management in the agencies and to lay the groundwork for an administration-wide personnel network. In 1939 the Council of Personnel Administration was established by executive order, and in 1940 it became a unit within the Civil Service Commission. The council (later renamed the Federal Personnel Council) was headed by Frederick M. Davenport, and each of the agency personnel directors were ex officio members. Its job was to undertake studies of the federal personnel system and to provide ideas and advice on new personnel policies to the president. Because of the high caliber of its membership and the presidential directive that established its mission, it was able to retain a substantial degree of operating independence even after it was transferred to the Civil Service Commission. The Bureau of the Budget in this period also maintained a small but active staff that concentrated on personnel issues of concern to the president. To coordinate the activities of the council, the Budget Bureau, and the Civil Service Commission, Roosevelt in 1939 created the Liaison Office for Personnel Management within the White House.

Taken collectively, these actions were about as close as the president could come to centralizing authority for management of the federal personnel system in the absence of legislative support from the Congress. But this was hardly perfection; indeed, it was barely satisfactory. There was still no single line of personnel authority from the agencies to the White House. And responsibility for the management of federal personnel activities was still diffused throughout a number of organizations, all with different mandates, often acting at cross-purposes.

The first Hoover Commission looked closely at this arrangement a decade later and found little in it to admire. The theories underlying the Hoover Commission proposals were not unlike those that had inspired the Brownlow Committee. Both aimed at improving the efficiency and at emphasizing the policymaking role of the government's central personnel agency. Both also sought to clarify and tighten the relationship between the president and the federal civil service. But the Hoover Commission recommendations were perceived at the time of their publication as a somewhat milder concoction than the medicine earlier prescribed by the Brownlow Committee. Most significant perhaps was the decision of the Hoover Commission not to recommend the eradication of the Civil Service Commission. For all its inadequacies, the Civil Service Commission still had a good many friends in Congress and still retained the respect of the "good government" types who wanted to hold the line against any threats to the merit system.

This was a matter of some importance when President Truman sent to Congress a reorganization plan to implement many of the Hoover Commission's personnel proposals.[18] The Congress did not veto the reorganization plan, and in August 1949, the head of the Civil Service Commission was assigned sole responsibility for the administrative direction of the commission's work. Truman, however, refrained from establishing an office of personnel in the EOP as the Hoover Commission had proposed and was satisfied instead merely to work directly but informally with the chairman of the Civil Service Commission.

The formalization of this relationship was one of the first actions undertaken by the Eisenhower administration. An executive order in 1953 created the position of presidential adviser on personnel management and specified that the duties of that office would be performed by the chairman of the Civil Service Commission.[19] To wear these "two hats," Eisenhower appointed Philip Young, the former dean of the Graduate School of Business at Columbia University. Young played an active and visible role during Eisenhower's first term. He had a close working relationship with the president, he was invited to participate in Cabinet meetings, and because of his dual responsibilities, he was widely regarded as the principal contact point with the administration for those who had an interest in shaping federal personnel policies.

But if the two-hat arrangement produced some benefits for the president, it also created some natural tensions for the wearer. The 1950s would have been a trying time for any chairman of the Civil Service Commission. Profound concern with the loyalty of public employees made the civil service a constant target of congressional investigations and media attacks. Its chairman had to convince congressional committees of his dedication in pursuit of subversives in government at the same time that he had to serve as the leading defender of the reputation and loyalty of public employees. Beyond that, he was part of a new Republican administration trying to assert its authority over a federal bureaucracy much of which the Democrats had created and all of which they had dominated for the previous twenty years.

It became increasingly difficult for the chairman of the Civil Service Commission to simultaneously act as protector of the partisan neutrality of the federal civil service and as principal spokesman for the personnel policies of a Republican administration anxious to remove federal employees devoted, in the president's words, "to the socialistic doctrine and bureaucratic controls practiced over the past two decades."[20] As time passed, it became more and more apparent that the two-hat arrangement was untenable.

In response to a growing consensus among his own advisers and to the recommendations emanating from the Second Hoover Commission's Task Force on Personnel and Civil Service, Eisenhower in 1957 decided to terminate the two-hat arrangement. He issued an executive order eliminating the position of presidential adviser on personnel management and replacing it with a new office, that of special assistant to the president for personnel management.[21] The clear intention was that this new post would *not* be filled by the chairman of the Civil Service Commission. Rocco C. Siciliano was appointed as its first incumbent.

The position of special assistant for personnel management remained on the books through the early 1960s, but neither the Kennedy nor the Johnson administration chose to fill it. Both presidents decided instead to rely upon the chairman of the Civil Service Commission as their principal adviser on personnel policy issues. John Macy, who chaired the commission through both administrations, did not have the public visibility that Philip

Young had enjoyed during the early Eisenhower years. He did not regularly attend cabinet meetings and he was never invested with a formal White House title, as Young had been. During the Kennedy years, he spent nearly all of his time at the commission and devoted the bulk of his attention to problems affecting the career service.

That began to change after the Kennedy assassination. Macy and Lyndon Johnson had become well acquainted while working together on some committees the latter chaired as vice-president. Johnson emphasized his intention to rely on Macy early in his administration by abolishing the position of special assistant for personnel management and writing to Macy asking him to provide "advice and assistance to me in all areas of the President's responsibility for civilian personnel at home and abroad."[22]

The Macy-Johnson relationship marked a new chapter in the search for a presidential role in federal personnel management. Macy's responsibilities soon became the broadest of any person ever to serve as a personnel adviser to the president, broader even than Philip Young's. In addition to his chairmanship of the Civil Service Commission and his role as adviser to the President on government personnel policies, Macy also took charge of administration efforts to recruit political executives. It was a three-hat, not merely a two-hat, arrangement. Johnson liked it because he had great faith in Macy and because they were in close agreement on most personnel issues. Macy liked it because it allowed him to see the picture whole, to deal with personnel policy in an integrated rather than a disintegrated way.

But a good many other people did not like this centralization of personnel responsibilities in a single presidential adviser. Members of Congress are naturally wary of any relationship in which a single person fills a dual role as an agency head and a presidential counselor.[23] It becomes too easy for that person to avoid testifying on agency-related issues by hiding behind the shield of executive privilege that traditionally protects conversations between the president and his aides. Leading students of public personnel administration worried that the Macy-Johnson arrangement would foreshorten the necessary distance between the political and the career personnel systems. Even those who admired Johnson and Macy were skeptical that this arrangement could work without their unique personal relationship. They worried deeply over the havoc that such a setup could wreak in the hands of an administration bent on dominating the federal career service. The idea of combining direction of political and nonpolitical personnel processes in the job of a single presidential adviser flew in the face of the recommendations of every commission that had studied presidential personnel management since the mid-1930s. No subsequent administration chose (or was permitted) to replicate it.

Neither Richard Nixon nor Gerald Ford chose to designate a member of his staff as chief presidential personnel adviser. In both administrations an office was set up in the White House to supervise the selection of presidential appointees, but no centralized White House structure was established to facilitate the president's role in government-wide personnel management.

In part, this reflects the initial reliance that Presidents Nixon and Ford sought to place on the Civil Service Commission for policy guidance. But it is also an indication of the enlarged role the Office of Management and Budget—and particularly its Division of Executive Development and Labor Relations—came to play in personnel policymaking. While publicly declaring that the chairman of the Civil Service Commission would be their principal adviser on matters pertaining to career government employees, both Nixon and Ford lent an increasingly sympathetic ear to personnel proposals emanating from OMB. Like their predecessors, they continued to search for an administrative structure *under their control* to which they could turn for assistance in personnel policy leadership.

The Reform Act Again

The absence of such a structure became an issue of immediate concern to the Carter administration and to Alan K. Campbell, the newly designated chairman of the Civil Service Commission. Working with ideas developed by the commission's Federal Personnel Management Project, the administration developed a proposal for a major reorganization of the federal career personnel system. It was submitted to Congress in March 1978.

The main provision of Carter's proposal (in addition to the SES plan discussed earlier) was to replace the Civil Service Commission with three separate agencies:

- Office of Personnel Management. OPM would take on most of the personnel management and policy development responsibilities of the Commission. It would be headed by a single director, appointed by the president with the advice and consent of the Senate, and serving at the president's pleasure.
- Merit Systems Protection Board. MSPB would have primary responsibility for protecting the integrity of the merit system. It would review OPM rules and other personnel practices, and it would hear appeals on employee grievances. MSPB would be a three-member, bipartisan body. Board members would be appointed by the president with the advice and consent of the Senate to seven-year, nonrenewable terms.
- Federal Labor Relations Authority. The FLRA would hear complaints about unfair labor practices in federal employment and, in general, supervise the relationship between federal employers and

organized federal workers. It would be a bipartisan, three-member board, with members appointed by the president with the advice and consent of the Senate and serving five-year terms.

The Carter proposal included a number of other provisions of importance to the operation of the federal personnel system. The impact of veterans' preference would be reduced. A genuine merit pay system would be established for managers and supervisors in grades GS 13 through GS 15. The rights of federal employees to join labor unions and engage in collective bargaining would be guaranteed by law. And civil service procedures for removal of incompetent employees would be simplified.

Like similar proposals by his predecessors, Carter's civil service reform bill encountered no small amount of opposition.[24] Veterans' groups took a strong stand against the bill's proposed weakening of veterans' preference. Some Republicans in Congress saw the creation of OPM and the SES and the introduction of a real merit pay system for the middle management grades as fraught with opportunities for a president who wished to politicize the civil service. Many federal employees, though sympathetic to some of the provisions of this bill, felt that its overall effect would be a diminution of the rights and familiar protections of those in the merit system.

The tone of this opposition was less bitter, however, and less unyielding than it might have been at other times. The effective legislative leadership provided by the Carter administration had something to do with this; so, too, did the peculiar political mood of the late 1970s. On this bill, and in spite of the administration's reputation to the contrary, the president's legislative efforts were intelligently conceived and well organized. The president himself made a strong and visible commitment to civil service reform. He appeared in public on several occasions, sometimes by himself, sometimes with Civil Service Commission Chairman Alan K. Campbell, to promote the bill. He and Campbell secured the strong support of a bipartisan group of former cabinet members. The administration's lobbying effort was intensive and featured the active solicitation of individual congressmen by every member of the President's Cabinet.

Facilitating the administration's efforts was the perceived mood of the electorate in that congressional election year. At every opportunity, Carter tried to paint this bill as a significant step toward making the federal bureaucracy more efficient and more responsive, an echo of themes he had emphasized in his election campaign in 1976. He apparently struck a sympathetic chord in the electorate and ultimately made this a difficult bill for congressmen to oppose. It was, perhaps at last, an idea whose time had come. By votes of 87 to 1 in the Senate and 385 to 10 in the House, the Congress in 1978 provided

President Carter with many of the personnel management tools that his predecessors had unsuccessfully pursued over the previous forty years.

The provisions of PL 95–454 departed from the past personnel proposals and practice in one important way. OPM is an independent agency and, although its director is assigned important advisory responsibilities, he has no special designation on the White House staff or within the Executive Office of the President. Not only does this distinguish the present arrangement of personnel management authority from most of the nonstatutory practices that preceded it, but it also sets the design and organizational location of the president's central personnel agency apart from those of his central budgeting agency and his principal support staffs in substantive policy areas like economics and defense. This is not accidental. The unique alignment of the career personnel management structure was necessary to strike a balance between the two competing objectives that have dominated the long, tortuous history of personnel reform proposals: the desire, on the one hand, for an effective central personnel management agency directly responsible to the president and the widely-held desire, on the other, to protect the merit system from partisan political intervention. The passage of the Civil Service Reform Act of 1978 rested in no small part on its apparent success in striking this difficult balance.

In nearly every other way, however, the creation of OPM represented a culmination of, not a departure from, the persistent efforts of the previous decades to find a suitable means of improving the president's ability to manage the personnel resources of the executive branch. It formalized and institutionalized the central personnel management functions that have been performed in the Executive Office, with few interruptions, since 1939.

Conclusion: The Search for a Presidential Role

The personnel dilemmas described in this chapter are recurring ones. Like his predecessors, Ronald Reagan came to office in 1980 with some firm ideas about personnel management, but quickly came to realize how difficult these ideas could be to implement.

President Reagan's determination to "hit the ground running" was thwarted by the difficulty he encountered in filling hundreds of important jobs in the few weeks between the election and inauguration. His desire to recruit talented individuals from the private sector was complicated by stringent confict-of-interest requirements, just as the effort to retain experienced career executives was confounded by the compression of salaries at the top of the civil service. And in a pattern repeated quadrennially, attempts to construct the new administration were buffeted by winds of self-interest emanating from every point on the political compass. None of this is unique or surprising, for these are some of the most persistent paradoxes of presidential personnel management.

The federal personnel system is differentiated both vertically and horizontally. In reality it is not one system, but almost a dozen separate systems. The armed forces, the Postal Service, the Public Health Service, the Tennessee Valley Authority (TVA), the Federal Bureau of Investigation (FBI), and the State Department—employing more than half of all federal workers—have distinctive personnel processes that set them apart from the rest of the federal civil service. The president's lines of authority to these discrete personnel systems tangle through a confusing web of decentralized personnel structures. But even that is not the extent of a president's personnel duties for, as we have noted, the rank-and-file employees in the federal career systems compose only one aspect of the president's personnel management task. He must be concerned as well with the experienced experts and executives at the top of the career structure and with the noncareer executives whom he has the power to appoint. There are fracture lines all through the federal personnel structure, and the task of coordinating and integrating its parts is no small enterprise. Up close, the federal personnel system looks little like a system.

But that is only one of the complications with which a president bent on effective personnel management must cope. Another is that this personnel system was not designed with responsiveness to executive leadership as a chief objective. Indeed, in important ways, precisely the opposite is true. The federal personnel structure was built on the bedrock of independence from changes in White House occupancy. Presidents have been accorded formal and theoretical responsibility for the direction of federal personnel operations, but rarely have they been provided with the authority necessary to fulfill that responsibility. The principal tools of personnel management are the power to hire, fire, and reassign employees; the ability to create an effective system of incentives through the rational allocation of money; and the power to create structures and procedures that facilitate optimum utilization of personnel resources.

An American president has complete access to none of these management tools. His real authority over personnel is constrained by a century of operational procedures and traditions that he inherits, by the many-handed interventions of a Congress jealous of its own personnel controls, by the political influence of a surprisingly large number of special interest groups, and by the entrenched power of federal employees and their unions.

When one adds to this catalog of difficulty the shortness of a president's term and the regrettable lack of personnel management experience that he and his aides generally bring with them to office, it is not surprising that frustration with the inaction and unresponsiveness of federal employees is so common a presidential affliction. Presidents themselves, and many others sympathetic to the need for a more effective presidential role in federal personnel management, have spent the past four decades trying to find a cure for these chronic maladies.

Their problem has not been a lack of ideas. Indeed, the effort to strengthen the president's role in central personnel management has been blessed with a profusion of ideas. The recommendations of the Brownlow Committee, the Hoover Commissions, the Committee for Economic Development, members of Congress, and presidents themselves have provided a constant transfusion of new intellectual blood into this debate over the appropriate presidential role in federal personnel management. The principal reason why this effort has been so long and exasperating has been the reluctance of the Congress to concede the personnel authority sought by recent presidents and to provide the managerial instruments necessary to exercise it. That reluctance we can attribute to three characteristics of the debate over central personnel leadership.

It is clear, first of all, that some of the congressional opposition to an enlargement of presidential personnel management capabilities resulted from a straightforward concern over institutional power. Personnel controls have traditionally been one of the Congress's most reliable "handles" on executive authority. Whether by reviewing presidential appointments, establishing job qualifications and benefit levels, or setting personnel ceilings in agency budgets, the Congress has often used its ultimate authority over personnel matters to constrain executive discretion and to help influence the shape and direction of public policy. Among the proposals generated in the past four decades to enhance the president's role in federal personnel management, there were few that did not threaten to diminish the utility and effectiveness of the Congress's traditional controls over executive branch personnel. In view of this, congressional foot-dragging should have come as no surprise.

But there is a good deal more to this history than a simple institutional power struggle. For what is interesting—and ironic—is that over this entire period of four decades, one finds little significant opposition in Congress to the fundamental objective of this reform movement, that is to the notion that federal personnel management should be centrally directed by the president of the United States. That *principle* has never lacked for supporters in Congress. Most disagreement has come over the more mundane problem of putting it into practice. Once you believe that the president should play a leadership role in managing the federal personnel system, how then do you shape that role and institutionalize it? It is on this issue that most of the haggling has occurred.

The difficulty in developing a legislative consensus has stemmed from the second and third characteristics of this debate. The second is that arguments over the proper shape of the president's personnel management role have taken place in a haze of theoretical conflict and ambiguity. So many issues were involved here, and so many conflicting values, that it would have been difficult even for a compelling consensual theory of public administration to have provided a road map out of the confusion. But in fact no such theory has existed to provide a homing beacon for this debate.

Public administration theory has itself been going through a period of extensive reexamination and innovation over the past four decades,[25] generating provocative questions, but providing few sturdy theoretical pegs to aid the efforts of the practitioners to sort out a host of competing interests. It is telling that almost every proposal to strengthen the president's role in personnel management has been debated as vigorously in the professional journals of public administration as in the halls of Congress. These are not isolated occurrences. They suggest – correctly, I think – that the principal difficulty in deciding on the presidential role in personnel management is rooted in the larger question of an appropriate presidential role, both theoretical and practical, in the management of the executive branch in general. Without consensus on the broader question, it has been extraordinarily difficult to come to consensus on the narrower one.

The debate in Congress over personnel management reform proposals reflected a serious effort to strike a satisfactory balance among a complex set of conflicting values and goals: merit versus representativeness, procedural efficiency versus procedural justice, political neutrality versus political responsiveness, and presidential direction versus democratic accountability. In its efforts to untangle and negotiate these traditional conflicts, the Congress moved with a painstaking deliberateness that often exasperated American presidents and the proponents of personnel management reform. But the resolution of fundamental conflicts of this sort is the reason we have a Congress, and we should have been surprised and saddened had it done any less.

This debate might have been brought to quicker resolution, even in the absence of some guiding theoretical imperative, had the weight of public opinion provided it with a political direction and momentum. But it did not, and that is the third reason for the slow germination of the personnel management ideas that loitered on the reform agenda for nearly four decades. Until the 1970s this was almost entirely a debate among elites. There was little public interest in the issues and almost no public comprehension of their implications. The circle of concern was tightly drawn around a few committees of the Congress, the policy levels of the Civil Service Commission, presidents and a handful of their aides, and the small group of practitioners and academics who composed the interested segment of the professional public administration community. But their interactions, occurring in a kind of political vacuum, failed to produce any significant alterations in the organizational and statutory foundations of the federal personnel system, many of which were created in the nineteenth century and were broadly perceived to have outlived their utility.

The legislative logjam finally broke in the late 1970s, but only after some significant changes in the scope of the conflict and the political appeal of the issues over which it was waged. The Congress that approved the Civil Service Reform Act of 1978 was different from the Congresses that rejected earlier personnel reform proposals. A majority of the members of both houses had served for six years or less, hardly time enough to build up the sinewy relationships with agencies and interest groups that had been such a barrier to civil service reform in earlier decades. A good many of those younger members, in fact, had won and held their seats by feeding on the antigovernment spirit so prevalent among their constituents. They had been sent to Washington—or so many of them felt—to shake things up, to redirect government operations away from business as usual.

The combination of their increased numbers, of changes in the internal power structure of the Congress that permitted their influence to equal their numbers, and of a public mood anxious to support any idea that promised to improve the efficiency and reduce the cost of government created a more favorable environment for civil service reform in 1978 than at any time in the previous generation. This did not guarantee that Carter's reform proposals would succeed—there were several occasions when that was in doubt—but these changes in the legislative environment did grease the skids for the committed and skillful effort generated by the Carter administration.

The Civil Service Reform Act of 1978 marks the end of an era in the history of presidential personnel management. With its passage, most of the important organizational and procedural goals of the personnel reform movement have been accomplished. The Civil Service Commission is gone, replaced by a different kind of central personnel agency, one that has a single head, is more responsive to the president, and is concerned principally with broad policy issues. The best of the supergrades have been organized into a mobile corps of career government managers, operating under a system of genuine incentives and affording much more staffing flexibility to political executives. The structure of performance criteria and merit pay in the middle management levels (GS 13–15) has been renovated. With these changes and with the significant improvements that have been made in the selection and recruitment of political appointees, the reformers have succeeded in building the structural supports for the presidential role in federal personnel management that they have so long thought necessary.

But completion of these efforts marks only a turning point, not a solution. If the past holds any lesson at all, it is that executive management in the federal government is an extraordinarily difficult enterprise. There are no quick fixes, not even slow fixes. Good organization and intelligent procedures only improve a president's management opportunities. They do not guarantee good management. A good management system can make a president's management task easier, but it cannot perform that task for him.

Even if the reformers were correct, even if the tools they have created are in fact the right ones, the quality of central personnel management will still be heavily dependent on the way those tools are utilized. There will always be people of different persuasions and different perspectives with whom the president will have to compete for the loyalty and commitment of those who work in the executive branch. Ultimately his success in that struggle—and *struggle* is the right word—will depend on the skills, the sensitivity, the experience, and the vision that he brings with him and retains in office. If we have created the right framework, then the important remaining ingredient in the recipe for effective central management of the government's personnel resources is the election of presidents who are up to the task.

Notes

1. Herbert Kaufman, "The Growth of the Federal Personnel System," in Wallace S. Sayre, ed., *The Federal Government Service* (Englewood Cliffs, N.J.: Prentice-Hall, 1965), pp. 23–24.

2. John W. Gardner, *No Easy Victories* (New York: Harper & Row, 1968), p. 6.

3. Oral history of Martin L. Friedman, undated, Harry S. Truman Library, Independence, Missouri, p. 44.

4. Memorandum for the Record from Martin L. Friedman, July 14, 1950, Friedman Papers, Box 11, Harry S. Truman Library.

5. There were in practice a general contact list and a number of specialized contact lists. The makeup of these changed constantly as the personnel staff had opportunities to evaluate the quality of the advice it was receiving.

6. According to Fenn, the normal staff complement was three professionals and three clerical staff working on presidential appointments. Patronage and "honoraries" were handled by a separate staff supervised by Dorothy Davies. (Interview with Dan H. Fenn, Jr., Waltham, Massachusetts, March 26, 1976.)

7. Quoted in Richard L. Schott and Dagmar Hamilton, "The Politics of Presidential Appointments in the Johnson Administration," paper delivered at the annual meeting of the Southern Political Science Association, November 4, 1977, p. 6.

8. Commission of Inquiry on Public Service Personnel, *Better Government Personnel* (New York: McGraw-Hill, 1935), p. 36.

9. Floyd W. Reeves and Paul T. David, *Report on Personnel Administration* (Washington, D.C.: Government Printing Office, 1937), pp. 63–64.

10. For examples of this debate, see Paul T. David and Ross Pollock, *Executives for Government* (Washington, D.C.: Brookings Institution, 1958); Leonard D. White,

"The Case for the Senior Civil Service," and Herman M. Somers, "Some Reservations about the Senior Civil Service," in *Personnel Administration* (January-February 1956); Paul P. Van Riper, "The Senior Civil Service and the Career System," *Public Administration Review* 18 (Summer 1958); and William Pincus, "The Opposition to the Senior Civil Service," *Public Administration Review* 18 (Autumn 1958).

11. Commission on Organization of the Executive Branch of the Government, *Personnel and Civil Service* (Washington, D.C.: Government Printing Office, 1955), pp. 93-94.

12. Ibid., p. 90.

13. For the discussion that preceded this, see U.S., Congress, House, Committee on Post Office and Civil Service, Subcommittee on Manpower Utilization, *Hearings on Manpower Utilization in the Federal Government (Career Executive Program)*, 85th Congress, 2d Session, 1958.

14. Despite its legislative success, the Carter SES proposal, like its predecessors, stimulated no small amount of intellectual debate. For a taste of that, see Bernard Rosen, "Merit and the President's Plan for Changing the Civil Service System," *Public Administration Review* 38 (July–August 1978), pp. 301–304; Frederick C. Thayer, "The President's Management 'Reform': Theory X Triumphant," *Public Administration Review* 38 (July-August 1978), pp. 309–314; and Alan K. Campbell, "Civil Service Reform: A New Commitment," *Public Administration Review* 38 (March-April 1978), pp. 99–104.

15. Quoted in "Every Good Bureaucrat Deserves Favor," *Forbes* (September 3, 1979), p. 33.

16. President's Committee on Administrative Management, *Administrative Management in the Government of the United States* (Washington, D.C.: Government Printing Office, 1937), p. 9.

17. Ibid., p. 10.

18. Reorganization Plan Number 5 of 1949.

19. Executive Order 10452 (May 1, 1953).

20. Memorandum to Cabinet Members from Dwight D. Eisenhower, March 13, 1953, Ann Whitman File, Cabinet Series, Box 1, Dwight D. Eisenhower Library, Abilene, Kansas.

21. Executive Order 10729 (May 8, 1958).

22. The letter is reproduced in full in Donald R. Harvey, *The Civil Service Commission* (New York: Praeger Publishers, 1970), p. 29.

23. See, for instance, the colloquy between Macy and several members of the House in U.S., Congress, House, Committee on Post Office and Civil Service, Subcommittees on Manpower and Civil Service, *Hearings on Supergrade Requirements*, 90th Congress, 1st Session, 1967, pp. 14–15.

24. This discussion of the effort to enact the Civil Service Reform Act of 1978 is based on the following sources: Harlan Lebo, "The Administration's All-Out Effort on Civil Service Reform," *National Journal* 10 (May 27, 1978), pp. 837–839; Joel Havemann, "The Catch to Civil Service Reform," *National Journal* 10 (February 25, 1978), p. 317; "Congress Approves Civil Service Reforms," *Congressional Quarterly Almanac, 1978*; contemporary accounts in the *New York Times* and the *Washington Post*; and interviews with participants in the effort to enact this legislation. For his

perceptive analysis, I am most especially indebted to Ronald P. McCluskey, staff director and counsel, Subcommittee on Compensation and Employee Benefits, House Committee on Post Office and Civil Service.

25. For perspectives on this debate, see Alan K. Campbell, "Old and New Public Administration in the 1970s," *Public Administration Review* 32 (July-August 1972), p. 343; Dwight A. Ink, "The President as Manager," *Public Administration Review* 36 (September-October 1976), pp. 508–515; Donald C. Stone, "Achieving a Capable and Manageable Federal System," *Public Administration Review* 35 (December 1975), pp. 728–736; Marver H. Bernstein, "The Presidency and Management Improvement," *Law and Contemporary Problems* 35 (Summer 1970), pp. 505–518; Herman M. Somers, "The President, the Congress, and the Federal Government Service," in Wallace S. Sayre, ed., *The Federal Government Service* (Englewood Cliffs, N.J.: Prentice-Hall, 1965); Frederick C. Mosher, *Democracy and the Public Service* (New York: Oxford University Press, 1968), especially Chapters 1 and 3.

5

Federal Regulation: A New Arena for Presidential Power?

Lester M. Salamon

SENATOR EAGLETON: The dilemma I face on this Presidential intervention business is that if the President is one whom I politically favor and if he intervenes in issues that pander to my voice . . . then I am going to give him all kinds of rights of authority to intervene to bring about the desired result.

Conversely, if it is a President of an opposite political persuasion and of an opposite philosophy, then I don't want him intervening. . . .

It is difficult to draft a statute that panders to one's likes and dislikes, isn't it.

MR. CUTLER: I can only answer that, Senator, by saying that most of us, I think, are looking for the elected officials to form a government and to be accountable for what that government in its totality does. . . .

Congress is not going to be accountable for what the President does. But for the President to be able to say, "I am not accountable for what the agencies within the executive branch do" it seems to me is absolutely intolerable. We should hold him accountable and we should give him the tools he needs to discharge that duty. Otherwise we are not forming a government.[1]

Few recent developments have as much potential significance for the evolution of the modern presidency as the intense interest that has surfaced during the past decade in federal regulatory activities. Yet in few areas are the dilemmas created by Vietnam- and Watergate-induced inhibitions about

This chapter was originally prepared for presentation to the Panel on Presidential Management of the National Academy of Public Administration in July 1980. I am grateful to Alan Abramson for assistance in its preparation.

presidential power more clearly and more painfully apparent.

On the one hand, it is now widely acknowledged that the world of govern-ment regulation has grown far beyond the "haphazard deposit of irresponsi-ble agencies and uncoordinated powers" that the Brownlow Committee be-wailed in 1937 and colorfully characterized as "a headless 'fourth branch' of the government."[2] By Brownlow standards, the federal regulatory apparatus today has mushroomed into a sprawling empire, an immense shadow government with wide-ranging powers and with what one official recently termed "a virtual blank check on the national income accounts."[3] Although the current situation is still far removed from the picture Senator Martin Madden (R–Ill.) painted of federal budget making in 1919 when he conclud-ed that "the Government has been running wild. the ship has been rudder-less, the captain has been off watch, and there has been no head who might be held responsible,"[4] the parallels are striking. Most importantly, almost sixty years after the creation of the modern system of federal budgeting, there is no widely accepted, organized system for making coherent decisions on the sizable resources allocated by the federal government through regulations.[5]

On the other hand, however, although current federal regulatory decision making bears striking similarities to federal budget making prior to the Budget and Accounting Act of 1921, the dispute over how to cope with the situation is more problematic today than it was then. Many of the agencies now involved in the regulatory field were explicitly designed to be indepen-dent of the chief executive. Also, recent abuses have left serious doubts about whether the solution embodied in the Budget and Accounting Act of 1921 – i.e., empowering the chief executive to coordinate agency ac-tivities – should still be trusted. Not until well into the Ford administration, therefore, were the first halting steps taken toward establishment of a presidential role in the regulatory process. The Carter administration went beyond these first steps, establishing formal procedures and improved in-stitutional machinery for presidential oversight of regulatory decision mak-ing, but in a cautious, sometimes halting fashion. The Reagan administra-tion, during its first weeks in office, threw caution to the winds in a way that raises immediately the questions of how extensive presidential involvement in regulatory decision making should be and what form it should take.

The purpose of this chapter is to shed some light on these questions by ex-amining the basic issues involved in the current debate over the manage-ment of federal regulatory policy and particularly the implications this debate holds for the presidency. No attempt is made here to assess the merits or drawbacks of particular regulatory provisions, let alone of regulation in general. Nor does this account purport to review the full range of problems attributed to federal regulation or all the solutions that are under discussion. Rather, the focus here is on those problems that have particular relevance for the role of the president and the operation of the presidency. In particular, this chapter explores three key questions: (1) What are the problems in the regulatory arena that most clearly raise questions about the role of the presidency? (2) What approaches are available to deal with these problems? and (3) What criteria are most appropriate for assessing these approaches, and which approach seems best in terms of these criteria?

Background: The Presidential Stake in Regulatory Reform

Despite the urgings of a succession of study commissions, presidents have generally adopted a hands-off attitude toward regulatory agencies and regulation in general. Indeed, the traditional pattern of presidential involvement in regulatory matters provides an interesting insight into how the limited presidency now being advocated by many students of presidential power might work. As William Cary, chairman of the Securities and Exchange Commission under Presidents Kennedy and Johnson, observed, "The President had no time for, and indeed in normal course should devote no time to, our problems unless there was 'trouble.' . . . the White House is interested and involved in a regulatory agency only if there has been a scandal or wide newspaper publicity about the industry it regulates."[6] As Cary saw it, the independent regulatory commissions were "stepchildren whose custody is contested by both Congress and the Executive, but without very much affection from either side."[7] And moreover, the same was true of regulatory bodies inside the executive branch. Preoccupied as they have tended to be with the high drama of policy formulation, presidents and their advisors have had little time or inclination to concern themselves with the mundane business by which legislation is translated into action.

To the dismay of both those who champion a limited presidency and those who have fought so hard for environmental, health, and safety protection, this pattern is now beginning to change. Indeed, a veritable stampede is on to reform federal regulation, creating immense pressures for changes in the role of the president and in the functions of Executive Office institutions and processes.[8] This stampede has its origins in three factors that have fundamentally altered the incentives for presidential involvement in regulatory affairs:

- A growing awareness of the costs of regulation and their potential implications for efforts to restrain inflation and carry out traditional presidential economic management responsibilities.
- Concern about conflicts both among various regulatory activities and among these activities and other national policies resulting from the recent major expansion in the scope of federal regulation.

- The evident willingness of Congress and the judiciary to move into whatever vacuum presidential inaction leaves in the management of federal regulatory affairs through such devices as the legislative veto and judicial review.

Let us look briefly at each of these factors.

The Costs of Regulation

The recent impetus for regulatory reform and for changes in the management of the regulatory process comes not from traditional public administration preoccupation with the organizational tidiness of the executive establishment, but from newfound concerns about the costs of regulation. To understand these concerns, however, it is necessary to distinguish between two major types of regulation: economic regulation and social regulation. *Economic regulation* involves controls over the terms of entry and the conditions of operation in particular industries. Much of the early regulation of industry in the United States took this form, as efforts were made to avoid excessive prices in such naturally monopolistic industries as utilities or to prevent destructive competition and ensure market stability. *Social regulation,* by contrast, involves the establishment of standards for certain types of activities or the imposition of controls to limit the effects of these activities. Much of the recent growth in federal regulation has taken this latter form, as efforts have been made to prohibit or discourage actions that endanger workers or consumers, pollute the environment, or violate important social goals, such as equal employment. In both cases, federal regulation imposes costs that are not reflected in the federal budget or in any other explicit statement of governmental accounts. And these costs have not only grown substantially over the years, but in many cases have come to be seen as unjustified and counterproductive, in whole or in part.

As the earliest form of federal regulation, economic regulation was the first to attract significant criticism. Economists studying its effects in the 1950s and 1960s generally concluded that its results were mostly perverse, creating government-supported cartels that limited competition, raised prices unjustifiably, and inhibited technological change.[9] Created to cope with the economic circumstances of the early twentieth century, or to shield an industry from competition, most of these forms of protection had lost their economic rationale by mid-century, yet they lingered on at the insistence of the protected industries.

This evidence of the costs of economic regulation became a matter of presidential attention and concern because of the serious inflation that gripped the American economy in the late 1960s and early 1970s. Suddenly turgid economic treatises on the "opportunity costs" of back-haul trucking regulation became urgent White House reading material, as political leaders came to see in the dismantling of economic regulation a way to show their anti-inflationary resolve. At an "economic summit" in September 1974, President Ford added impetus to the movement by associating himself with a twenty-two-point hit list of inflationary regulations identified by a cross section of prominent economists, thus launching a major rethinking of governmental regulatory policy and processes.[10]

What really brought regulatory policy to center stage as a subject for presidential concern, however, was not the demonstrated costs of economic regulation, which Vice-President Nelson Rockefeller noted had "about as much political sex appeal as a sick alligator,"[11] but the purported costs of social regulation. This type of regulation grew massively in the late 1960s and early 1970s with the passage of a spate of new environmental, consumer protection, and workplace-safety laws. This is doubly ironic, however, because the costs of social regulation are not only associated with real public benefits that justify them at least in part (a claim that can no longer be made for most economic regulations), but also are far smaller than those attributable to economic regulation. Even if the total cost of social regulation were considered unnecessary and undesirable—which no one is seriously proposing—the cost of economic regulation would still overshadow it. For example, the most widely cited estimate of the costs of regulation, coauthored by Reagan's Council of Economic Advisors Chairman Murray Weidenbaum, attributes 60–70 percent of the estimated regulatory costs to economic regulation.[12]

Unlike economic regulation, however, the costs of social regulation are visible and concrete. They take the form of seat belts and scrubbers and water treatment plants. In addition, these costs seem more dramatic and disruptive because, unlike the costs of economic regulation, which accumulated over many decades, they have been added in rapid succession over a period of little more than a decade. What is more, there is growing concern that at least some of the costs of social regulation may be as unwarranted as the costs of economic regulation because of the tendency of statute-writers and regulators to rely on unduly burdensome forms of intervention—e.g., the use of detailed "design standards" instead of more flexible "performance standards," or the use of "command-and-control" techniques instead of economic incentives.[13]

Finally, and perhaps most importantly, the distribution of the costs and benefits of social regulation differs markedly from that of economic regulation. With economic regulation, the benefits typically accrue to the regulated industry, but the costs are borne by consumers, who tend to be less well organized and have little individual incentive to protest.[14] With social regulation, however, it is the benefits that are diffused while the costs fall squarely on producers and businessmen, who tend to be far better equipped to object. Furthermore, businesses and other nonfederal organizations sometimes find themselves bearing the costs of several different types of regulation, each of which is imposed by a different regulatory agency without much knowledge of the costs being imposed by others. The result can be a sizable cumulative impact with important implications for the viability of particular firms or industries, creating a strong incentive for political activism. As a result, the expansion of social regulation, even more than the demonstrated irrationality of economic regulation, has fundamentally altered the politics of regulatory affairs, adding a potent political force for regulatory reform and creating new pressures for presidential involvement and concern.

Coordination and Priority-Setting

In addition to adding new and more visible costs to the national regulatory bill, moreover, the rapid expansion of social regulation in the 1960s and 1970s generated serious problems of coordination and priority-setting by enlarging the range of goals government sought to promote through regulation and thereby increasing the prospects for conflict.

The origins of this problem are partly legislative, partly organizational, and partly political. In the first place, regulatory statutes tend to specify rather narrowly the goals to be achieved and the considerations that can be taken into account in pursuing them. The resulting narrow authorities are then parceled out to a host of separate agencies, each of which acquires jurisdiction over a limited range of issues and finds itself constrained by political pressures to respond to a relatively few substantive concerns to sustain support from the congressional committees and interest groups ultimately responsible for its fate. The result, as the Council of Economic Advisors pointed out in its 1978 report, is that:

> Regulatory requirements from different agencies have sometimes conflicted with each other, and particular industries, firms, or communities are confronted with a series of regulatory requirements imposed by different Federal agencies. No one of these may pose serious problems, but taken together they may have serious economic consequences: increasing costs or requiring large capital oulays in a short time. There is now no mechanism to assess these combined effects and take them into account in regulatory decisions.[15]

In its recent study of federal regulation, the American Bar Association came to much the same conclusion, identifying the absence of "effective mechanisms . . . for coordinating the decisions of one agency with those of other agencies, or conforming them to the balancing judgments of elected generalists, such as the President and Congress" as the "basic defect of the American regulatory system."[16]

Congressional Assertiveness

The third key factor impelling a reconsideration of the presidential role in the regulatory sphere has been the evident determination of the Congress to take matters into its own hands in response to the twin problems of regulatory costs and priority-setting discussed above. The vehicle for this has been the legislative veto, through which individual committees, or one of the two houses, gains the power to veto the regulations proposed by executive branch agencies to carry out particular congressional enactments. More than 200 separate legislative veto provisions are now on the books, more than half of them added during the past decade.[17] During 1979 alone, 8 bills with legislative veto provisions were signed into law, and an additional 100 were introduced or reported during the first eighteen months of the 96th Congress.[18] Beyond this, Congress has recently had under serious consideration bills that would apply the legislative veto in blanket fashion to all regulations.

The significance of the legislative veto is that it affords Congress a far more direct and more detailed form of control over the operations of executive branch agencies than has traditionally been available on a broad scale. As a result, it challenges long-standing doctrines about the relative roles of the executive and legislative branches. Whatever the virtues or drawbacks of the legislative veto as a response to the regulatory problems mentioned above (a subject that will be treated below) the widespread adoption of the device has inevitably forced some rethinking about the traditional presidential approach to regulatory affairs. Indeed, it seems clear that much of the presidential attention to regulatory management over the past several years has been substantially motivated by a desire to avoid congressional preemption.

Four Routes To Reform

Contrary to widespread belief, neither the president nor Congress is powerless to deal with these problems under existing circumstances. To the contrary, some rather significant controls have long been in place, even over the "independent" agencies. These include:

- Judicial review of agency decisions
- The procedural requirements of the Administrative Procedures Act
- OMB budget control
- OMB forms clearance (except for the independent agencies, forms

clearance responsibilities for which were transferred to GAO in 1973)
- OMB legislative clearance
- Presidential power to appoint commissioners and, in the case of executive branch agencies, to remove them
- Presidential selection and removal of commission chairmen
- Federal personnel laws and regulations for permanent employees
- Dependence on the Justice Department to bring lawsuits and to decide on appeals to the Supreme Court
- Congressional control of appropriations

In response to the problems identified earlier, however, pressures have arisen for additional means of control or for better ways to orchestrate the existing ones. Two critical issues are at stake: first, whether to shift a larger share of the responsibility for regulatory decision making from the individual regulatory agencies to higher-level overseers and policymakers; and second, which of a number of potential overseers should receive what authority. These issues hinge in turn, however, on the importance that is attached to the need to balance regulatory goals against other national goals and on judgments about how this can best be done.

Against this backdrop, it is possible to discern four basic approaches to regulatory reform. The first involves changes in the basic statutes governing regulatory programs. The second involves the establishment of procedures to encourage greater coordination among the regulatory agencies themselves. The third involves mechanisms to review individual regulations centrally. And the fourth involves changes in the regulatory process intended to inject particular types of considerations into regulatory decision making on a systematic basis. Let us look at each of these in turn.

Deregulation and Legislative Revision

The first approach to regulatory reform is to alter the basic statutory framework of particular regulatory programs. Broadly speaking, this can take two different forms: deregulation, the partial or complete elimination of regulatory controls; and clearer goal-setting, the clarification of regulatory objectives to constrain the exercise of administrative discretion.

Deregulation. Deregulation is clearly the most fundamental form of regulatory reform, but also the most difficult. It has value chiefly where the original rationale for regulation has been overtaken by events (e.g., railroad and truck regulation) or where regulation produces perverse consequences that outweigh its benefits (e.g., price regulations on natural gas). Generally speaking, therefore, deregulation is most applicable to economic regulation, for it is here that the economic justification for regulation has worn thinnest. Hence, the Ford and Carter administrations invested substantial political capital in major battles to deregulate the airline, trucking, banking, railroad, petroleum, and communications industries and thereby substitute market forces for regulatory controls. Although much of this work is now well under way, it seems likely that the dismantling of outdated economic regulations will require continued presidential attention and support for the foreseeable future.

Goal Clarification. Deregulation holds far less promise in the field of social regulation. However, other types of legislative changes have been proposed here, most notably the clarification of regulatory goals. Proponents of goal clarification argue that much of the excessive cost of federal regulation results from the overly broad discretion given to regulatory officials by Congress when it writes the statutes. Thus, they favor more precise statements of congressional purposes and the narrowing of administrative discretion.[19]

Although this approach has much to recommend it, its drawbacks are substantial. Most important, it overlooks the inevitably political character of regulatory decision making; regulatory decisions almost invariably require some balancing of competing interests, if for no other reason, because they involve substantial uncertainties. What is more, policies and priorities change too rapidly to vest much confidence in a system that too narrowly constrains the exercise of discretion. The resulting rigidity can easily become counterproductive. In fact, many of the existing regulatory statutes are already so specific and narrow that they make it impossible for regulators to take account of costs and other important factors in setting regulatory standards. As a result, selection of the least costly way to achieve regulatory goals may sometimes be of questionable legality.[20]

Far from easing the problems identified earlier, therefore, this approach may exacerbate them. In fact, a better approach might be to move in the opposite direction, broadening the range of considerations that can be weighed in designing regulations and thereby permitting the kind of balancing of competing concerns that sensible decision making in areas of great complexity frequently requires.

Interagency Coordination

Deregulation or the broadening of legislative authorities may reduce the costs of regulation, but it does not address the problem of regulatory coordination. One way to deal with this latter problem is through the time-honored device of interagency coordination.

Not surprisingly, this approach is overwhelmingly favored by the regulators and their allies, as it involves the least infringement on their autonomy, institutional integrity, and existing authority. Indeed, when proposals for bolder regulatory reform began circulating within the Carter administration in 1978, the chiefs of the major regulatory agencies, under the leadership of Environmental Protection Agency Administrator Douglas Costle, countered with a proposal to create a Regulatory Council composed of the regulators instead. Trumpeted as a major regulatory reform step, creation of this council was conceived by the regulators as a way to take the sting out of the attack on social regulation and to forestall efforts to subject the agencies to outside control by providing evidence that the regulators themselves were hard at work on the problems. Accordingly, the council was empowered to publish a regular calendar of forthcoming regulations, to encourage coordinated approaches to complex regulatory problems for which responsibility is scattered among several different agencies (e.g., toxic substances control), to examine the cumulative impact of the regulations of different agencies on particular industries, and to explore innovative approaches to regulation.

The great advantage of interagency coordination devices like the Regulatory Council is that they leave basic decision-making responsibility where Congress formally vests it: in the heads of the regulatory agencies. They also avoid the build-up of large Executive Office bureaucracies operating in the president's name but often without effective presidential supervision. To the extent that such devices can instill greater sensitivity to the crosscutting impacts of multiple regulations in the minds of the regulators, they can be a powerful vehicle for improved regulatory decision making and one that is far less threatening to the goals of regulation.

The problem, however, is that such devices lack any power other than moral suasion and have no reliable mechanism for resolving conflicts or enforcing decisions. As a result, they frequently find it difficult to bring a government-wide perspective to bear and to make it stick. A proposal originally advanced by Senator John Culver (D–Iowa) would attempt to deal with this shortcoming by creating a regulatory policy board with statutory authority and including on it Executive Office personnel as well as representative regulators. But there is reason to doubt whether even this modification would yield a regulatory coordination apparatus that could work effectively.

Regulatory Clearance and Review

As an alternative to the essentially voluntary approach embodied in the first two routes to regulatory reform, considerable interest has arisen in more direct mechanisms of control to make regulatory decision making more accountable to elected officials who, in our constitutional system, are the ones to whom the public formally entrusts the responsibility for resolving difficult conflicts of values and interest.

How to provide for that accountability systematically and reliably, however, has become a matter of hot dispute. One approach, endorsed by presidential study commissions from the Brownlow Committee to the Ash Council, is to end the special status of the independent regulatory commissions and make these agencies part of the executive branch. However necessary this might be—and there are real doubts on the issue[21]—the record of the numerous regulatory agencies already part of the executive branch makes it clear that it is hardly sufficient, for these latter agencies have not been notably more responsive than the independent agencies.

Accordingly, attention has come to focus on the more direct approach of regulatory clearance and review. The distinguishing feature of this approach is the establishment of some mechanism for direct review and clearance of individual regulations before or soon after their promulgation. Where the several different variants of this approach differ is in how they would structure such a review mechanism and where they would vest control. In particular, three major variants of this approach are available, depending on whether clearance authority is vested in the courts, the Congress, or the president.

1. Judicial Review. One variant of the regulatory clearance approach would substantially broaden existing grounds for challenging regulations in court. Proposed by Senator Dale Bumpers (D–Ark.) and incorporated in a Senate Judiciary Committee regulatory reform bill in May of 1980, this approach would remove the presumption that regulatory agency rules are valid and require agencies to show, if they are challenged, that they have clear legislative authority for any rule in question. By contrast, under current circumstances judges generally attribute presumptive validity to an agency's interpretation of its statute unless it is clearly unreasonable.

This judicial approach has the advantage of building on existing review mechanisms with established procedures. It would do so, moreover, without adding greatly to the burdens or powers of the presidency and thus without upsetting the delicate balance between Congress and the presidency that has evolved in the regulatory field over the years.

However, this approach has at least three problems. First, it could strain an already overburdened judicial system and introduce additional delays in cumbersome and delay-ridden regulatory processes. Second, the proposal favors interests that can afford to bring cases to court.[22] Third, and most important, the proposal assumes that regulatory statutes can and should be written narrowly and specifically. Otherwise, judicial review would shift to the courts the power to resolve difficult conflicts of values and interests that our constitutional system has preferred to vest in elected officials. If, as suggested earlier, the degree of latitude in regulatory statutes is increased to avoid handcuffing regulators and to permit the balancing of a variety of considerations, this expanded judicial review approach is likely to produce more problems than it solves, creating an "imperial judiciary" every bit as pernicious as the "imperial bureaucracy" said to exist now.

2. *Legislative Veto.* A more appropriate place to vest regulatory clearance and review responsibilities would be in the Congress. It is Congress, after all, that ultimately authorizes federal regulation. It is reasonable, therefore, for Congress to take an interest in how the authority it grants is actually carried out.

As I have noted, Congress has already traveled a substantial distance down the road toward establishing procedures for such review and clearance of individual regulations, most strikingly in the form of the "legislative veto."[23] More than 200 such veto provisions, each one applying to a particular program or authority, are already on the books. These provisions vary widely in form, but the two most common are the one-house veto, which provides for disapproval of proposed agency rules and regulations by a simple resolution passed by *either* the House or the Senate within a fixed period of time (usually thirty or sixty days), and the committee veto, under which the appropriate committees in both houses must approve executive proposals before they can go into effect.[24] The House, moreover, seems inclined to travel even farther down this road by endorsing a blanket one-house veto provision applying to all regulations or a modified blanket one-house veto under which a veto passed by one house of Congress could be revoked by the other.

Despite its political popularity, however, the legislative veto has serious drawbacks. For one thing, because it short-circuits the constitutional procedure for enacting legislation—which requires approval by both houses of Congress and by the president—it involves significant constitutional problems that have yet to be resolved. Certainly, to the extent that such provisions permit a single committee, a pair of committees, or a single chamber to subvert the will of the entire Congress, they are of dubious wisdom.

Beyond this, if applied in wholesale fashion to all regulations, or even all "major" regulations, the legislative veto would involve the Congress in a level of detail that could easily overwhelm it and that could tie the regulatory process in knots. Even with sizable expansions in staffs, it is doubtful if Congress could do an adequate job of analyzing the thousands of regulations issued each year and second-guessing agency decision makers. One probable result might therefore be to open the way for extensive reliance on outside interests to spot "objectionable" rules, an arrangement that, in former President Carter's words, could "turn regulatory enforcement into an endless process of capricious negotiation with special interests."[25]

Finally, given the fragmented structure of congressional decision making, there is reason to doubt whether the legislative veto can contribute to the kind of coordination and priority-setting needed in the regulatory arena. In fact, the opposite result is more likely. Proposed regulations will be reviewed by separate committees—usually the same committees that established the original authority—with little opportunity for effective scrutiny by the Congress as a whole. It is useful to recall that the total output of Congress in a typical session is usually no more than 400 pieces of legislation. By contrast, the total number of regulations issued each year is now in the neighborhood of 7,000. How Congress could apply its collective wisdom to even a fraction of these rules without immense, and inevitably distorting, internal delegation is hard to imagine.

Despite these problems, however, the widespread congressional support for the legislative veto evident in the rapid expansion of this device during recent years makes it clear that some more direct means of congressional review of agency rule making than has traditionally been available is probably needed. Under the circumstances, it is probably more prudent to devise an approach that responds to these pressures in a way that avoids the most objectionable features of the legislative veto than to persist in a course that is likely to add further to the unmanageable, crazy-quilt pattern of interventions that is already developing.

One such approach is embodied in a proposal advanced in 1980 by a House Rules Subcommittee chaired by Congressman Joe Moakley (D–Mass.) under which a new House Select Committee on Regulatory Affairs would be created with the authority to report resolutions of disapproval of any proposed regulation to the House. Such a resolution would require the approval of both houses of Congress and the signature of the president before it would become effective. A similar proposal has been advanced by Senators Carl Levin (D–Mich.) and David Boren (D–Okla.), without the select committee concept, but with a provision permitting Congress to override a presidential veto by two-thirds votes in both chambers. Both of these approaches would provide an orderly "safety valve" for congressional hostility to particular rules and regulations, but without opening the floodgates for a torrent of detailed regulatory reviews, violating constitutional safeguards, or further extending the chaotic, ad hoc pattern of veto authorities that has already taken shape.

3. *Presidential Review.* Even if some kind of blanket legislative veto were enacted, the third variant of the regulatory clearance approach, which would establish a presidential process for regulatory clearance, might still make sense as a way to complement congressional action.

This third variant certainly finds ample support in the work of the major commissions on executive reorganization that have recently looked at the problem. Almost all of them have stressed the need for clear lines of administrative authority stretching from the president to agency officials in order to ensure accountability and promote coordination.[26] This view has been endorsed as well by the American Bar Association, which concluded in its recent report on regulatory reform that "the President is the elected official most capable of making the needed balancing decisions as critical issues arise."[27] A strong case can be made, not only that the president has the authority to perform this role, at least with respect to executive branch agencies, but that he also has a responsibility to do so because of the charge in Article II of the Constitution to "take care that the laws be faithfully executed."[28] Finally, the Executive Office of the President already has substantial experience in managing a process that could serve as a model for regulatory clearance—the legislative clearance process. More than that, this model was actually put to the test in the regulatory sphere between 1971 and 1976 through what was known as the "Quality of Life Review."

Launched by OMB Director George Schultz, the Quality of Life Review required major executive branch regulatory agencies involved in the health and safety fields, especially the Environmental Protection Agency (EPA), to submit their proposed rules and regulations to review by other affected agencies and by OMB prior to publication for comment. As the process ultimately took shape, EPA regularly circulated its proposed rules to the other agencies, collected the comments, and reported to OMB on which it had accepted, which it rejected, and why. OMB then determined whether any of the rejected comments were sufficiently important to reopen discussion between EPA and the objecting agency, and, if necessary, to send to the director or the president for final resolution.[29] Before it was abruptly terminated in the final week of the Ford administration by Acting EPA Administrator John Quarles, the Quality of Life Review had won grudging respect even in some quarters of EPA on the grounds that, despite some delays, it generally improved the quality of EPA decisions and laid a firmer political and analytical foundation for the agency's proposals.[30] But because the process applied to EPA, it came to be viewed as discriminatory and biased against environmental protection.

This concern that presidential intervention will be biased against needed health, safety, and environmental regulations has, in fact, turned much of the consumer-environmental-liberal-labor community against the idea of systematic presidential regulatory review.[31] Indeed, a series of legal challenges has now been raised to presidential intervention in regulatory decision making on the grounds that under the Administrative Procedures Act, the president should be treated like any other ex parte petitioner, with all his communications with the regulators on the record and confined to the public comment period.[32] Because of this concern, the American Bar Association, in proposing an expanded system of presidential regulatory clearance in 1979, felt obliged to propose an elaborate set of procedural checks on this system as well. Drawing on a concept first advanced by lawyers Lloyd Cutler and David Johnson, the ABA proposal would give the president statutory authority to modify or reverse the decision of any regulatory agency (independent or not) on critical regulations, but subject this authority to the following substantive and procedural conditions:[33]

- The president could not require the agency to take any action or consider any factor not authorized in the agency's governing statute.
- The president could take such action only by executive order published in the *Federal Register*.
- A finding would be necessary that the regulation was "critical."
- The president would have to state the reasons for his action, and where agency actions are required to be based on the record, these reasons would have to be reflected in the record.
- The president would have to signal his intention to issue such an order thirty days in advance and invite comments.
- The president's action would be subject to judicial review.

Whatever the virtues of a presidentially operated regulatory clearance system, it seems clear that this particular version would be an excessively cumbersome and ill-advised way to achieve it. Rather than enhancing the president's ability to balance competing national goals, establish priorities, and guide the exercise of administrative discretion, this proposal would be very likely to work in the opposite direction, transforming the president into a kind of trial judge issuing formal opinions to his own appointees and destroying the critical informal processes by which policy formulation and direction take place. What is more, these procedures have a "massive retaliation" quality to them that seems more likely to keep presidents from ever using them than to deter headstrong regulators from risking their use. What president would incur the wrath of environmentalists, after all, by attracting this much public attention to himself in order to ease the standard on emissions of some particulate by two parts per million, even if he could claim a saving to some industry of $500 million per year without appreciably increasing the risk to the public?

Even beyond this particular proposal, however, there are important questions about the adequacy and wisdom of the whole regulatory clearance and review approach, even if managed by the president. These questions take three different forms. First, there is the issue of scale. As noted in the discussion of the legislative veto above, the sheer volume of regulations each year makes the thought of subjecting even a fraction—say 500—to detailed substantive review at the center somewhat mind-boggling, unless great care is taken to focus only on the most significant regulations and to rely on agency expertise. This is especially so in view of a second issue—the lack of a shorthand "bottom line," such as that afforded by the budget in the case of regular legislation, for assessing proposed rules and regulations. In the absence of such a litmus test, each regulation has to be separately assessed on its merits. What is more, the review has to be done centrally since there is no simple "decision rule" that can be communicated easily to others and applied in a decentralized fashion. Third, this approach is inevitably ad hoc and reactive. It considers proposed regulations individually as they are submitted, with little opportunity to scrutinize the existing base or analyze cumulative effects.

The thrust of these comments is not to suggest that there is no place for a systematic process of regulatory review in the Executive Office of the President. To the contrary, such a process, properly focused and organized, has much to recommend it, particularly if it (1) relies chiefly on the analytical resources and perspectives of the various departments and agencies, as the Quality of Life Review did, (2) restricts itself to major regulations, (3) avoids any involvement in adjudication or licensing, (4) can count on presidential intervention when necessary, and (5) is accompanied by formal congressional review procedures of the sort suggested in the preceding section. What these comments do suggest, however, is that this approach, although useful, is not sufficient and should not be overtaxed. "Effective management of the regulatory process," as the Council of Economic Advisors pointed out in its 1979 report, "must go beyond measures dealing with individual regulations."[34] It must, in short, involve a fourth approach as well.

Regulatory Management

The fourth approach to regulatory reform involves the use of essentially procedural means to achieve substantive regulatory change. Rather than focus on individual regulatory statutes, or particular regulations issued under these statutes, this approach emphasizes the management of the regulatory process and seeks to improve the content of regulations by influencing the method by which they are formulated. The advantage of this approach is its greater efficiency, its use of a relatively narrow set of management tools to influence a broad range of regulatory decisions. By the same token, this approach permits a greater decentralization of responsibility, as it involves the establishment of criteria that can be applied by the agencies themselves and reviewed on an "exceptions only" basis at the center.

Two variants of this approach to regulatory reform are available, one involving procedures for improving internal agency regulatory decision making, including the use of regulatory analyses, and the other involving the more rigorous discipline of a regulatory budget.

Regulatory Analysis and Internal Agency Regulatory Management. The first of these two variants has its origins in Executive Order 11821 issued by President Gerald Ford in November 1974. This order was the first effort to induce regulatory agencies to give explicit attention to cost considerations in designing their regulations. Under it, agencies were required to submit to OMB and the Council on Wage and Price Stability an analysis of the full range of costs and benefits associated with any proposed new regulation or legislation. Although agencies were not required to adopt the most cost-effective approach, the foundation was laid for a broader consideration of the factors to be taken into account in regulatory decisions and a beginning made in establishing an analytical capacity both in the agencies and in the Executive Office to assess the consequences of regulatory action.

Building on the lessons learned in this Inflation Impact Statement program,[35] the Carter administration took a second major step toward establishing a systematic regulatory management process by issuing Executive Order (E.O.) 12044 in March of 1978. This new executive order elaborated on and refined the earlier process in a number of critical ways.

1. It established procedures for internal agency policy oversight. Prior to the issuance of E.O. 12044, most large departments left decisions on regulations almost exclusively to the subunits with direct program responsibilities, with no review by department or agency-level policy officials. This procedure contrasted sharply with that in place for both operating budgets and legislative proposals. As a consequence, agency heads not only lost an opportunity to coordinate regulatory activities within their spheres and help balance the regulatory goals of the separate bureaus with broader administration policy objectives, but also found themselves unaware of what regulations their own departments were issuing.

In what would later be described as "the key to the success of the President's regulatory reform program,"[36] E.O. 12044 required that agencies establish internal regulatory clearance processes that involve agency heads and other policy-level officials in the initial decision to develop a regulation and in the sign-off of the final version.

2. It provided for the publication of semiannual agendas of regulations. To alert the public and other affected agencies of forthcoming regulations far enough in advance, E.O. 12044 required each agency to publish a semiannual list of significant regulations under development or review, complete with a schedule for action and a point of contact. These agendas, pulled together in periodic "regulatory calendars" by the newly formed Regulatory Council, were to provide opportunities to improve coordination of regulatory policymaking and ease some of the obstacles to effective public participation in agency rule making.

3. It established a broader "regulatory analysis" requirement that im-

proved on the original inflation impact analysis requirement in the following ways:

- Beginning the analysis earlier in the process of developing a regulation and requiring completion of a preliminary analysis at the time the regulation is published for comment.
- Requiring explicit analysis of various alternatives for achieving the regulatory objective.
- Expanding the focus beyond inflationary effects to include a broader range of economic effects.
- Dropping the rigid benefit-cost analysis requirement and permitting qualitative assessments where needed.
- Providing for a Regulatory Analysis Review Group (RARG) cochaired by the Council of Economic Advisors and OMB to review a small number of "regulatory analyses" each year and therefore provide a mechanism for quality control.
- Making the analyses available to the public at the time the rules are issued.

4. It required agencies to establish schedules for systematically reviewing existing regulations.

From all indications, the procedures put in place by E.O. 12044 have had a generally positive effect, sensitizing regulators to a broader set of approaches, exposing the process to a wider set of inputs, and generally improving the internal procedures by which regulatory policy decisions are made. At the same time, however, progress has been uneven, and not only because the process is still so new. The approach also suffered from some more fundamental problems. Most important, perhaps, is the fact that it lacked teeth. Agencies were required to analyze the costs of various alternative approaches but not to select the least costly route. In addition, despite the potential peer pressure involved in RARG review, there were few incentives for agencies to do careful analyses. The more thorough the analytical job, the more ammunition the agency gives to its potential critics, who would be able to cite the agency's own regulatory analysis to demonstrate that better alternative approaches were available. In fact, there were strong incentives for agencies to duck the regulatory analysis requirement altogether by taking a very narrow definition of what constitutes a "major" regulation.[37]

What this meant in practice is that the success of the process came to depend critically on the rather weak reed of administrative jawboning. And that jawboning was generally limited. Enforcement responsibility was vested in a special OMB unit, but that unit lacked clout either within the agency or in the departments. Budget examiners, busy with other responsibilities, gave it scant attention. The upshot was that the analysis, on the whole, was disappointing, and numerous important regulations evaded the new procedures.[38]

To remedy these deficiencies, several modifications were proposed in the latter part of the Carter administration. Most important, legislation was introduced, both by Senators Ribicoff and Percy and by the administration, to give these new procedures the force of law. The theory was that this would strengthen OMB's hand in securing compliance with the new procedures and relieve whatever doubts might exist about the willingness of Congress to have regulators consider costs and other effects in making their regulatory decisions. The administration bill stipulated, in fact, that regulators must choose the least costly regulatory alternative or explicitly explain why they did not. In addition, the Ribicoff-Percy bill authorized the Congressional Budget Office to review regulatory analyses in an effort to increase the pressure for competent and thorough analytical work. Finally, several groups urged that provision be made in this legislation for judicial review of the regulatory analyses to give outside parties grounds for insisting on agency compliance.

Some of these modifications have great merit; others are more dubious. The judicial review proposal, for example, would be likely to do as much harm as good by forcing courts to judge the quality and adequacy of complex economic analyses about which experts will doubtless disagree. Beyond this, however, there remains the more basic problem that procedures such as those embodied in E.O. 12044, although promising some improvement in the quality of individual regulations, still do not provide a mechanism for setting overall priorities in the use of the national resources allocated through the regulatory process, for assessing the aggregate and sectoral consequences of regulation, or for making explicit policy trade-offs. For this, something more is needed.

Regulatory Budget. To cope with this problem, attention has recently come to focus on the concept of a regulatory budget. The basic notion here is that the total cost of federal regulatory activities to the economy would be calculated and a limit set on additional costs to be permitted each year, either in an aggregate sense or by sectors, industries, or regions. These allowable costs would then be apportioned among agencies and programs much as the current budget allocates spending authority. Indeed, the regulatory budget could adopt a process very much akin to the one used in the expenditure budget—involving agency submissions, OMB review, presidential approval, and submission to Congress—although this is not essential.

In its present state of development, the regulatory budget has formidable analytical problems, a problem it shares with regulatory analysis generally.[39]

Most serious, perhaps, are the technical difficulties of computing cost estimates. Moreover, because agencies may have incentives to exaggerate the
costs of their programs initially in order to build up a "reserve" for future activities, it would also be necessary to establish procedures for after-the-fact
assessments of actual costs, something that is not needed on the expenditure
side.

Despite these obstacles, the regulatory budget may be far more practical
than is frequently assumed. In the first place, substantial work is already
under way to assess the costs of regulation, and the results, although incomplete, are encouraging.[40]

In the second place, some of the purported problems with the approach,
such as the difficulty or impossibility of computing the value of the benefits
generated by regulation, betray a misunderstanding of the concept. A
regulatory budget need no more include benefit estimates than the existing
expenditure budget does. Whether the costs shown in the budget are
justified by the social benefits generated is an important question, but one
that has to be resolved in the political process generally, not in the budget.
A budget, in short, is not the same as a cost-benefit analysis, as critics of
waste in the expenditure budget will readily attest.

Finally and perhaps most important, much of the discussion of the regulatory budget, by analogy with the expenditure budget, has tended to emphasize the budget's function as a resource allocation mechanism to the
neglect of what might really be its more important function as a management tool. What a regulatory budget would achieve is to supply the enforcement mechanism needed to make the regulatory analysis and
regulatory management processes of E.O. 12044 work. And it would do so
by creating incentives for voluntary agency compliance instead of having to
rely on constant administrative jawboning. This is so because, by setting the
maximum allowable cost a particular agency could impose on the economy
through its regulations, the regulatory budget would create a powerful in-
ducement for agency heads to find the least costly way to carry out each
regulatory mission, so that more such missions could be accommodated. In
this way the energies and inventiveness of the agencies could be harnessed
to the goals of regulatory reform without the need for detailed, regulation-
by-regulation review. The regulatory budget thus promises a way to manage
the complex regulatory processes of the government in an efficient, decentralized way while still providing a measure of central control for priority-
setting and coordinating purposes. For these management purposes,
moreover, the cost estimates for a regulatory budget may not need to be
anywhere near as precise as those in the expenditure budget, making the
whole undertaking far more feasible than is sometimes thought.

Interestingly, important steps that could eventually lead to a regulatory budget are already being taken. In January 1980, OMB circulated a proposed regulatory cost accounting act to the agencies for review. This act would establish overall procedures and methodology for calculating regulatory costs and would require agencies to compute the costs of their existing regulatory activities. In addition, on November 30, 1979, President Carter issued an executive order calling for the establishment of a "paperwork budget." As reflected in the implementing OMB Bulletin, issued in June 1980, the resulting Information Collection Budget (ICB) offers a prototype of the procedures that could be used in a regulatory budget. In both cases, a budget approach is being used to deal with nonbudget costs or burdens imposed on nonfederal actors as a consequence of federal action.[41]

Not surprisingly, both the Regulatory Cost Accounting Act and the Information Collection Budget encountered vigorous resistance, particularly from the social regulatory agencies and their supporters, who rightly observed that both devices, as well as the regulatory budget per se, are systematically biased against social regulation because they expose costs without showing benefits. This suggests that the establishment of a presidential role in the regulatory arena must proceed with great care and with due regard for the substantive stakes and legal traditions involved. At a minimum, efforts to limit the costs of regulation must take account of the real benefits. Beyond this, it would probably be prudent to link an effort to establish a regulatory budget to efforts to extend the budget discipline to other currently nonbudget federal activities as well, including loan guarantees, tax subsidies, insurance, and others.[42]

Conclusions and Future Directions

Several conclusions about the role of the president flow from this discussion of the problems of regulatory management in the federal government. Taken together, they suggest a possible strategy for dealing with what has become a central issue of national life. In particular, these conclusions include the following:

1. The traditional pattern of presidential inattention to regulatory matters is no longer tenable. The regulatory activities of the federal government have grown too large, too complicated, too controversial, and too much in need of government-wide management for a responsible president to ignore.

2. Because of the scope and scale of the regulatory arena, presidents cannot afford to get involved in a way that requires centralized substantive review of all, or even a fraction, of the regulations issued. At the same time, presidents must retain the ability to intervene in regulatory decision making when they deem it appropriate for valid public policy reasons.

3. The appropriate presidential role in the regulatory arena is to focus on

a limited range of priority concerns like overall resource allocation and regulatory coordination and to do so through essentially procedural means, leaving as much of regulatory decision making as possible to the agencies.

4. Presidential involvement in the regulatory process must make provision for extensive and meaningful cooperation with the Congress.

To what extent has the Reagan administration, as of late March 1981, heeded these conclusions? The record to date is revealing.

In the first place, the Reagan administration has moved actively to assert a strong presidential role in regulatory decision making. Within two days of taking office, and before the heads of most regulatory agencies had been chosen, the president announced the creation of a Task Force on Regulatory Relief chaired by the vice-president to "review major regulatory proposals by executive branch agencies" and help formulate regulatory policy. A week later, the president announced a sixty-day freeze on all pending or recently issued regulations, and within several weeks, many of these were revoked. Then, in mid-February, a revision of Executive Order 12044 was promulgated, imposing a stricter cost-benefit test on all proposed regulations, tightening the regulatory analysis requirements, and strengthening OMB's role in determining which proposed regulations should be subjected to regulatory analysis, reviewing the resulting regulations, and establishing procedures for estimating regulatory benefits and costs. To police this executive order, moreover, a more coherent institutional mechanism was put in place, centered in OMB and explicitly tied to the paperwork control apparatus established during the Carter administration. Because most new regulations require some new information-gathering form, this setup provides OMB and the new presidential task force considerable leverage in securing agency compliance with Executive Office views on the proper content of agency regulations.[43]

By moving so quickly, the Reagan administration caught the opponents of expanded presidential involvement in regulatory decision making off guard. Whether this strategy will pay off over the long run, however, is more problematic. The "regulatory relief" promised by these actions is immensely popular, but the procedural safeguards built into the regulatory process are deeply rooted, as are the commitments to the substantive goals of many of the regulatory programs. How these concerns will be reconciled with the substantial concentration of regulatory power that the Reagan proposals vest in the presidency, however, is not yet clear. The new Task Force on Regulatory Relief, for example, is dominated by Executive Office officials and excludes most of the key regulatory agencies. The new executive order on regulations was promulgated with no opportunity for comment and review by either the agencies or the public, violating long-standing procedures in the regulatory field. By stipulating OMB review of minor, as well as major, regulations prior to promulgation, the new provisions have increased the regulatory work load of the Executive Office immensely. By specifying that agencies shall not take regulatory action "unless the potential benefits to society from the regulation outweigh the potential costs to society," the new executive order ventures into territory hotly disputed by Congress, even though it makes the concession of noting that this new requirement applies only "to the extent permitted by law" (Sec. 2).

In short, Reagan has boldly asserted presidential power, building on a foundation carefully and slowly constructed during the Carter administration, but going beyond it in ways that could, unless handled well, bring the whole structure crashing down. This would be an unfortunate outcome indeed in view of the growing importance of regulation and the widespread popular distress about the lack of control over regulatory decision making on the part of elected officials. As the Council of Economic Advisors (CEA) noted in its 1980 report: "Regulation has joined taxation and the provision of defense and social services as one of the principal activities of government; it has just as much need for effective management."[44] For better or worse, in our system of government that means increased responsibility for the presidency. But like other presidential responsibilities, this one too must be designed and operated with due regard for the limitations of the office and with due respect for the legitimate roles of other key actors and institutions.

Notes

1. U.S., Congress, Senate, Committee on Government Affairs, *Regulatory Reform Legislation: Hearings*, 96th Congress, 1st Session (1979), Part 2, pp. 132–133 (hereafter *Regulatory Reform Legislation: Hearings*).

2. U.S., President's Committee on Administrative Management, *Report of the Committee*, Submitted to the President and the Congress in Accordance with Public Law No. 739, 74th Congress, 2nd Session (Washington, D.C.: U.S. Government Printing Office, 1937), p. 40 (hereafter *Brownlow Committee Report*).

3. James Tozzi, assistant director for regulatory and information policy, Office of Management and Budget, personal interview, July 18, 1980.

Counting federal regulatory agencies is not a simple matter. Nearly all government agencies have some regulatory functions. President Ford's Domestic Council Review Group on Regulatory Reform tried to cut through the confusion with the following definition of regulation: *"Federal laws or rules which impose government established standards and significant economic responsibilities on individuals or organizations outside the federal establishment"* (U.S., Domestic Council Review Group on Regulatory Reform, *The Challenge of Regulatory Reform* [January 1977], p. 47). The review group's report (pp. 50–57) lists 64 federal regulatory agencies. Congressional Quarterly's *Federal Regulatory Directory, 1980–81*, describes 102 agencies (Robert E. Healy, ed., *Federal Regulatory Directory, 1980–81* [Washington, D.C.: Congressional Quarterly, 1980]).

Figuring out whether regulatory agencies are independent or nonindependent is another difficult job. The labels have no universally agreed upon meanings. Statutes creating an agency do not necessarily assign it unambiguously to one category or the other. Only three agencies, all created since 1973, are designated "independent regulatory commissions" in their enabling acts, but one of these—the Federal Energy Regulatory Commission—is located completely within an executive department. The Environmental Protection Agency was created by a 1970 reorganization plan that called the agency "independent," but it is within the executive branch and is not commonly considered independent (U.S., Congress, Senate, Committee on Governmental Affairs, *Study on Federal Regulations*, 96th Congress, 1st Session [1977], Vol. 5, pp. 34–35 (hereafter *Ribicoff Committee Study*).

The *Ribicoff Committee Study* (Vol. 5, pp. 38–39) considers an agency independent if it satisfies three conditions.

1. Multiple membership, appointed for set terms that expire at staggered intervals;
2. Restrictions against removal by the president except for cause; and
3. The exercise of quasi-judicial powers concerning economic regulation of business activities, which almost without exception is not subject to review by any executive official.

The Governmental Affairs Committee study does not, however, contain a complete list of independent or executive branch regulatory agencies according to this definition. Ford's Review Group report (pp. 50–57) names eighteen regulatory agencies headed by collegial bodies, twenty-nine agencies in executive departments and agencies, and seventeen other federal agencies that have some regulatory impact on specified geographical regions or parts of the economy. Congressional Quarterly's *Federal Regulatory Directory, 1980–81* identifies twenty-eight independent and seventy-four executive branch agencies.

4. *Congressional Record*, October 17, 1919, p. 7093, quoted in James L. Sundquist, *The Decline and Resurgence of Congress*, Draft manuscript, Brookings Institution, 1980, p. III-7.

5. Domestic Council Review on Regulatory Reform, *Challenge of Regulatory Reform*, p. 4.

6. William L. Cary, *Politics and the Regulatory Agencies* (New York: McGraw-Hill, 1967), p. 7.

7. Ibid., p. 4.

8. As of March 1979, 128 bills had been introduced in the House, and 29 in the Senate, to restructure the regulatory process (*Congressional Quarterly Weekly Report*, March 31, 1979, p. 560).

9. For a summary of this research, see Roger Noll, *Reforming Regulation* (Washington, D.C.: Brookings Institution, 1971); and *Ribicoff Committee Study*, Vol. 6, pp. 9–75.

10. Domestic Council Review Group on Regulatory Reform, *Challenge of Regulatory Reform*, pp. 19–27; personal interview, Stan Morris, July 15, 1980.

11. Interview with Nelson Rockefeller by A. James Reichley, March 24, 1978,

quoted in A. James Reichley, *Conservatives in an Age of Change*. Draft manuscript, Brookings Institution, 1980, pp. 17–26.

12. Of the $66 billion in costs that Weidenbaum and DeFina attributed to regulation in 1976, $22 billion resulted from industry regulations and $25 billion from paperwork, including income tax forms. Murray Weidenbaum and Robert DeFina, *The Cost of Federal Regulation of Economic Activity*, Reprint No. 88 (Washington, D.C.: American Enterprise Institute, 1978), p. 2.

13. "Design standards" specify particular procedures or equipment that must be used to achieve a particular regulatory goal (e.g., installation of fire hydrants *x* feet from the ground to avoid fire hazards in the workplace). "Performance standards" specify only the goal to be achieved (e.g., reduction in the incidence of fire by a specified rate) and leave it to the discretion of the regulatee to determine how to achieve the goal. For a succinct analysis of this distinction and of the virtues of incentive approaches generally, see Charles L. Schultze, *The Public Use of Private Interest* (Washington, D.C.: Brookings Institution, 1977).

14. Economists refer to this as the "free rider" problem. For a fascinating analysis, see Mancur Olson, *The Logic of Collective Action* (Cambridge, Mass.: Harvard University Press, 1965).

15. U.S., Council of Economic Advisers, *Annual Report, 1978* (Washington, D.C.: Government Printing Office, 1978), p. 215.

16. American Bar Association, Commission on Law and the Economy, *Federal Regulation: Roads to Reform, Final Report 1979 with Recommendations* (Washington, D.C.: American Bar Association, 1979), p. 68. See also James M. Landis, "Report on Regulatory Agencies to the President-Elect" (unpublished manuscript, December 1960), p. 85 (cited hereafter as "Landis Report"); and *Ribicoff Committee Study*, Vol. 5, p. 21.

17. Clark Norton, *Congressional Veto Provisions and Amendments: 96th Congress*, Issue Brief Number IB 790944, Congressional Research Service (June 1980), p. 1.

18. *Congressional Quarterly*, March 8, 1980, p. 661.

19. This view finds expression in Emmett S. Redford, "The President and the Regulatory Commissions," unpublished manuscript prepared for the President's Advisory Committee on Government Organization, pp. 9–12; Henry J. Friendly, *The Federal Administrative Agencies: The Need for Better Definition of Standards* (Cambridge, Mass.: Harvard University Press, 1962); Theodore J. Lowi, *The End of Liberalism* (New York: Norton, 1969); and *Ribicoff Committee Study*, Vol. 5, p. 13. For a summary of this position, see American Bar Association, Commission on Law and the Economy, *Federal Regulation*, p. 16.

20. U.S., Council of Economic Advisers, *Annual Report, 1979* (Washington, D.C.: Government Printing Office, 1979), pp. 125–127; Elmer Staats, testimony before the Senate Governmental Affairs Committee, *Regulatory Reform Legislation: Hearings*, Part 2, p. 63.

21. Congress has clearly been moving over the past few years to strengthen, not weaken, regulatory agency independence, creating four new independent commissions, exempting these commissions from executive branch reorganization authority and OMB forms clearance powers, and extending their powers in litigation and budget making. See *Ribicoff Committee Study*, Vol. 5, 1977, pp. 25–26. In its report

on federal regulation, the Senate Governmental Affairs Committee endorsed an approach that would preserve and increase the independence of the regulatory commissions, but would also increase their accountability to the president and Congress. See *Ribicoff Committee Study*, Vol. 5, p. xiii.

22. Senator Robert Dole has warned, for example, that this proposal "will become merely another device in the hands of large corporations to block or slow the promulgation of regulations which affect their interests." *Congressional Record*, September 7, 1979, p. S 12152.

23. Other devices for detailed congressional review of particular regulations include a variety of notification requirements, project review procedures, and waiting period provisions. See Clark F. Norton, *Congressional Review, Deferral and Disapproval of Executive Actions: A Summary and an Inventory of Statutory Authority*, Congressional Research Service, Report No. 76-88G (April 30, 1976), pp. 2–10.

24. Norton, *Congressional Veto Provisions*, p. 1.

25. President Jimmy Carter, speech to the Consumer Federation of America, quoted in *Congressional Quarterly*, March 8, 1980, p. 663.

26. See, for example, *Brownlow Committee Report*, pp. 40–41; U.S., President's Advisory Council on Executive Organization, *A New Regulatory Framework* (Washington, D.C.: Government Printing Office, 1971), p. 16 (cited hereafter as the *Ash Council Report*); "Landis Report," pp. 81–87.

27. American Bar Association, Commission on Law and the Economy, *Federal Regulation*, p. 73; See also Lloyd N. Cutler and David R. Johnson, "Regulation and the Political Process," *Yale Law Journal*, Vol. 84, No. 7 (June 1975):1410–1411.

28. The following exchange during Senate hearings on proposed regulatory reform legislation in 1979 is instructive on this point:

> SENATOR EAGLETON: I think it is very conceivable that this Congress will give to the President of the United States the authority to overrule Mr. Costle or overrule Dr. Bingham or overrule any other regulatory agency.
>
> MR. SCHULTZE: With all due respect to Mr. Costle, my strong belief, in fact, conviction, is that the President already has that authority.

29. Based on conversations with James Tozzi, the OMB official in charge of the process, July 17, 1980. See also "Office of Management and Budget Plays Critical Part in Environmental Policymaking," *Environment Reporter*, Vol. 7, No. 18 (September 3, 1976), pp. 693–697. Interestingly, the quality-of-life process was managed by the relevant OMB budget staff, not the legislative clearance shop.

30. See *Environment Reporter*, Vol. 7, No. 18 (September 3, 1976), pp. 693–694.

31. See the testimony on behalf of Congress Watch, the Environmental Defense Fund, and the Public Citizen Litigation Group in *Regulatory Reform Legislation: Hearings*, Part 1, p. 1083; Part 2, pp. 113–115.

32. Endorsing this position, U.S. Circuit Court Judge David Bazelon told the Senate Governmental Affairs Committee that "this is an area where courtesy doesn't extend to risking the integrity of the administrative process." Ibid., Part 2, p. 8.

33. Cutler and Johnson, "Regulation and the Political Process," pp. 1414–1416; American Bar Association, Commission on Law and the Economy, *Federal Regulation*, pp. 79–84.

34. U.S., Council of Economic Advisors, *Annual Report, 1979*, p. 88.

35. For an evaluation of the inflation impact process, see U.S., Council on Wage and Price Stability and Office of Management and Budget, "An Evaluation of the Inflation Impact Statement Program," (principal author, Thomas D. Hopkins), December 7, 1976, mimeographed.

36. U.S., Office of Management and Budget, *Improving Government Regulations: A Progress Report* (Washington, D.C.: Office of Management and Budget, September 1979), p. 9 (hereafter OMB *Regulatory Progress Report*).

37. OMB has acknowledged this point in its own evaluation of experience under the executive order, noting, "we must come to grips with this paradox and avoid creating disincentives for agencies to do careful regulatory analyses." Ibid., p. 21.

38. OMB *Regulatory Progress Report*, 1979, pp. 19–21 and passim. For an outside analysis of the lack of compliance with the executive order in one agency, see the statement of the American Hospital Association, in Senate Governmental Affairs Committee, *Regulatory Reform Legislation: Hearings*, Part 2, 1979, pp. 154–175.

39. For a good analysis of the strengths and weaknesses of the regulatory budget concept, see Christopher DeMuth, "The Regulatory Budget," *Regulation*, Vol. 4, No. 2 (March-April 1980), pp. 29–44.

40. See, for example, U.S., Environmental Protection Agency, "Comparisons of Estimated and Actual Pollution Control Cost for Selected Industries" (prepared by Putnam, Hayes, and Bartlett, Inc.), February 1980, mimeographed.

41. U.S., Office of Management and Budget, Bulletin No. 80-11 (June 19, 1980).

42. On this point, see Lester M. Salamon, "The Budget—A Weak Reed," *Wall Street Journal*, December 8, 1980.

43. Executive Order on Federal Regulation (E.O. 12291), February 17, 1981; White House Press Office, Fact Sheet, "President Reagan's Initiatives to Reduce Regulatory Burdens," February 18, 1981; personal interview, James Tozzi, Assistant Director of OMB, March 9, 1981.

44. U.S. Council of Economic Advisers, *Annual Report, 1980*, p. 127.

PART THREE
Policy Management

We are accustomed to thinking of the presidency in terms of momentous decisions made by individuals—Truman and the steel seizure, Kennedy and the missile crisis, Carter and the Iranian hostages. The reality of policy development in the executive branch is far different, however. Against the handful of momentous decisions made by solitary presidents stand thousands of decisions made each year without any direct presidential involvement at all and hundreds of others in which the president is directly involved only at the end of an elaborate process that has substantially narrowed his range of choice.

Under these circumstances, understanding the substance of presidential decisions is just the beginning of a true understanding of presidential participation in policymaking. Of equal or greater importance is a comprehension of the procedures and circumstances that determine which issues come to the president's attention, in what form, at what stage in the decision process, at whose initiative, and in what context.

As the range and complexity of policy issues facing the nation has increased over the past half century, specialized, institutionalized processes have evolved to handle these matters, often with unexpected results. The four chapters in Part 3 examine these processes as they have taken shape in the three major spheres of national policy: domestic, economic, and international. In Chapter 6, Lester Salamon traces the evolution of the specialized, institutionalized domestic policy capability in the presidency and then identifies the major issues and options that surround the design of this presidential role. Roger Porter then undertakes in Chapter 7 a similar task with regard to the economic policy machinery of the presidency. This machinery was given shape by the Employment Act of 1946, but it has grown far more elaborate, if not yet far more effective, in response to the multiple challenges that have emerged since then. Finally, in Chapters 8 and 9, Anna Kasten Nelson and I. M. Destler analyze, respectively, the early history and subsequent evolution of the machinery for presidential involvement in foreign and defense policy, particularly the National Security Council apparatus, and, especially in Chapter 9, the rise of the national security assistant. Here, again, the picture is one of groping improvisation leading ultimately to a set of processes and patterns of behavior that few intended and many now regret.

In the establishment of formal mechanisms for presidential participation in policymaking, we see the ultimate extension of the concept of presidential government. And in the difficulties these mechanisms have encountered, we see clearly the dilemma this concept entails and the illusion to which it gives rise.

6

The Presidency and Domestic Policy Formulation

Lester M. Salamon

Less and less can it be presumed that the negative process of piecemeal review, rejection, and modification of individual proposals flowing up from administrative units to the Office of the Chief Executive will eventuate in the sort of integrated program of objectives that evolving conditions seem certain to require. . . . Thus it may be expected that the need for positive origination at the center of broad but intelligible objectives will become more pressing.

—V. O. Key, 1942[1]

Introduction

The presidential role in the formulation of national policy has its legal roots in the constitutional invitation to the president to "give to the Congress Information on the State of the Union, and recommend to their consideration such measures as he shall judge necessary and expedient" (Art. III, Sec. 3). Not until the early twentieth century, however, did this role take institutional form, and even then only in a negative sense—to tame free-wheeling agency spending and policy activism by subjecting agency proposals to central executive review. It is therefore ironic that the central question surrounding this presidential policy role today appears to be how to tame *presidential* policy activism, how to avoid excessive centralization of the

This chapter is a scaled-down version of a paper prepared for the Panel on Presidential Management of the National Academy of Public Administration in May of 1980. I am grateful to Alan Abramson for research assistance in its preparation. Unless otherwise noted, unreferenced quotations are drawn from interviews I conducted in late 1979 and early 1980.

policymaking function in the Executive Office of the President, and how to restore a meaningful policy role to the departments and agencies where most of the government's expertise and experience ultimately reside.

The heart of the issue is that modern problems are so complex that most public issues cross departmental lines and therefore call for some integrating influence. Yet by law the department and agency heads, not the president, are formally responsible for the operation of public programs and regularly answerable to Congress and the courts. How, then, can the need for coherence—which the president, both politically and practically, is best equipped to provide—be reconciled with the need for accountability and expertise—which the department and agency heads can more easily supply?

During the past sixty years, a variety of models have evolved to cope with this dilemma. The purpose of this chapter is to examine these models and to assess the lessons that they hold for the design of the domestic policy role of the presidency in the future. The discussion is divided into four parts. The first part briefly outlines the major models that have emerged for handling the policy formulation responsibilities of the presidency over the past several decades. Behind this evolution is the fact that the character of presidential involvement in policy development is at base a political, not simply an administrative, issue: It affects which interests have effective access to the policy process, at what stage, and in what form. As a result, it involves important substantive and political stakes and not infrequently intense political debate.

Against this backdrop, the second part identifies a number of key issues that underlie the design of the policymaking role of the presidency and suggests a number of criteria for sorting out these issues. The third part then extracts from this discussion of issues and criteria four alternative designs for presidential domestic policymaking machinery and subjects each to a critical appraisal. The fourth part, finally, steps back from the details of particular Executive Office machinery to draw some general conclusions, emphasizing the importance of reliable institutional processes to give structure to executive branch policy development activities.

Although the discussion here focuses primarily on the formulation of domestic rather than national security or macroeconomic policy, separate treatment of domestic policy in the apparatus of the presidency is not in any sense inevitable or desirable. To the contrary, a strong case can be made that such differentiation no longer makes sense in view of the growing interdependence of domestic and international affairs and in view of the shift in economic policy toward greater concern with microeconomic, sector-specific concerns.

By the same token, the focus on the machinery and processes of presidential decision making does not imply institutional determinism. Quite obviously, numerous other factors influence the shape of presidential decisions—for example, the president's philosophy, outside political pressures, the nature of the problems that the president faces, and just simple chance. Moreover, presidents have ways to escape the tyranny of executive branch decision processes—they can reach outside for advice and counsel, they can reject what comes up from below, or they can mold given structures to their own personalities and needs. Beyond this, the decision-making structure of American government stretches well beyond the presidency, embracing Congress, the courts, other levels of government, interest groups, and numerous other players as well.

The argument, therefore, is not that the processes and structures of the presidency determine policy, only that they can influence it in important ways—by affecting which issues reach the president for decision, how much time he has to decide them, what options are developed, what perspectives are represented, and what constraints make themselves felt. Despite the image of an individual president, in a government as complex as ours these matters must usually be handled through regularized—often institutionalized—processes if they are to be handled at all. Making sure these processes are sensibly designed and effectively operating is therefore a worthwhile and necessary concern.

Evolution of the Presidential Domestic Policy Apparatus

Although presidential involvement in the formulation of domestic policy began early in the nineteenth century, this involvement remained ad hoc, sporadic, and largely unorganized until early in the present century, when a regularized system of presidential review of agency legislative proposals was appended—almost as an afterthought—to the newly created presidential budgeting mechanisms mandated by the Budget and Accounting Act of 1921. Subsequently, the capabilities of the presidency, as distinct from the departments, in the field of domestic policy became steadily more institutionalized and ultimately more differentiated and specialized. This evolution took place, moreover, in four more or less distinct phases stretching over some fifty years.

Central Legislative Clearance: The Classical Model[2]

The first phase of this evolution began, innocently enough, as a response to House Appropriations Committee concern about agency end-running of the executive budget procedures established by the Budget and Accounting

Act. To prevent this, the Bureau of the Budget in late 1921 issued a circular requiring all agencies to submit to the bureau, prior to sending to Congress, all agency proposals for legislation or comments on legislation that might involve an expenditure of federal government funds or a commitment to expend funds in the future. Agency proposals judged not in accord with the president's financial program were not to be transmitted to Congress, and agency comments on pending legislation, if not in accord, were to note this fact. Thus was forged a regular mechanism for direct presidential involvement in a process formerly handled almost exclusively by agency heads and their counterparts in the Congress.

Under Presidents Roosevelt and Truman, this process underwent further evolution. First, its reach was extended to the substantive content, rather than just the fiscal impacts, of proposals. Second, beginning in 1946, it was used to pull together an annual presidential legislative program for inclusion in the regular State of the Union message.

By the time the Democrats surrendered the presidency to General Eisenhower in 1953, therefore, a regularized system for presidential participation in national policymaking and, even more, for the formulation of a comprehensive, "presidential legislative program" was largely in place. During the next eight years it became entrenched. The product of a curious admixture of conscious design and accidental accretion, the legislative clearance function during the Eisenhower years completed its journey from an instrument of presidents to an institution of the presidency. In broad outline, the process that resulted, and that still exists, has the following basic characteristics:

- Agency submission of proposals for legislation along with budget submissions each fall.
- Review of these proposals by a specialized Legislative Reference staff in the Bureau of the Budget and circulation for comment to budget examiners, other potentially interested agencies, and other relevant Executive Office of the President staffs.
- Collection of comments by the Legislative Reference staff; resolution of outstanding issues, drawing on White House staff where appropriate; and issuance of "advice" to the sponsoring agency indicating that the proposal is sufficiently important and sufficiently supportive of presidential goals to warrant making it a presidential priority ("in accord with the program of the president"); not in violation of administration policy but not of highest priority ("consistent with the program of the president"); merely not objectionable ("no objection"); or in violation of administration policy ("not in accord" or "not consistent with" the president's program). Proposals in the latter category are not to be transmitted to Congress.

- Assembly of proposals judged "in accord with the president's program" into the State of the Union message, the budget message, or other presidential messages by budget and White House staff. Review of these messages in draft.
- Review through similar channels of all agency comments on legislation requested by congressional committees and of all testimony by agency officials before Congress.
- Distribution for comment and review by agencies, budget staff, and other relevant EOP officials of all bills passed by Congress and awaiting presidential action, and preparation of "enrolled bill memorandums" recommending approval or disapproval by the president.

The Task Force Approach:
Differentiation Without Institutionalization

Despite its strengths as a systematic process for giving presidents regular access to policy decisionmaking throughout the executive branch, the classical legislative clearance process was quickly judged inadequate by the legislative activists who took over the reins of government in 1961. In the first place, because of its fundamental reliance on agency initiative, the process was vulnerable to the parochialism and loss of creativity that afflicted even the most vibrant New Deal agencies as they made peace, through the 1940s and 1950s, with their congressional overseers and interest group allies.[3] In the second place, the process lacked a countervailing source of positive invigoration from the center, as the Bureau of Budget, which managed the process for the president, was still primarily a budget agency committed to keeping a lid on agency funding requests, not promoting new initiatives.[4] The presidency, as a consequence, was exceptionally well equipped to reject or modify departmental initiatives, but not to seize the policy initiative on its own where agency timidity or the need for a multidepartmental approach made this necessary.

Lacking in-house domestic policy staff, President Kennedy, and President Johnson even more elaborately, therefore turned outside the government for help and established an alternative policy development apparatus constructed around a network of expert "task forces." As it took shape under President Johnson during the period 1964–1967, this task force approach involved a massive mobilization of the nation's intellectual talent in the service of presidential initiatives in domestic policy. In a sense, the task forces constituted a "second track" for executive branch policy formulation outside the established, agency- and BOB-dominated clearance channels.[5] "My Brain Trust, operating almost as a separate arm of the government," is how Lyndon Johnson later described the operation.[6] The result was a massive surge of new legislative proposals bearing the L.B.J. imprint in virtually every sphere of domestic affairs, a remarkable burst of creativity and presidential policy activism.

The Domestic Council:
Institutionalization Without Professionalization

If the task force approach made up for the lack of creativity of the traditional clearance approach, it had the drawback of surrendering one of the greatest strengths of this traditional model: the capacity to design new proposals that fit into the ongoing operations of government without overwhelming existing systems. "The task force routine," as long-time Budget Bureau official William Carey later recalled, "was regarded and treated principally as a kind of instant policy blender to whip up tasty concoctions to meet the message schedule in January."[7] In the process, little attention was paid to problems of implementation, to overlap with other programs, to legitimate technical problems, or to the capacity of the operating agencies to understand what was intended and to carry it out. With the task force approach, in short, the policy development capability of the presidency was further differentiated from other ongoing processes, but also became far less institutionalized.

After several frantic years of "task-forcing," therefore, a vigorous search began for yet another approach, one that could combine the virtues of the task force and legislative clearance models without succumbing to the serious defects of either. This search took place in three different arenas: a Bureau of the Budget self-study launched in late 1966, the blue-ribbon Task Force on Government Organization appointed by Lyndon Johnson in late 1966 under the chairmanship of Chicago industrialist Ben Heineman (the Heineman Commission), and the Advisory Council on Executive Organization appointed by Richard Nixon in April 1970 under the chairmanship of Litton Industries executive Roy Ash (the Ash Council).

Significantly, all three of these study groups concluded that an institutionalized presidential capability for domestic policy formulation, differentiated from the budget and legislative clearance operations, was critically needed.[8] Although the bureau self-study and the Heineman Commission recommended that such a capability should be added to the Budget Bureau in order to develop the needed expertise and professionalism, the Ash Council favored a White House–based operation modeled on the National Security Council, with a cabinet-level domestic council and a separate domestic council staff reporting to a special presidential assistant for domestic policy. This approach was preferred on two major grounds: first, that it would permit greater involvement on the part of department and agency heads by giving them a statutory position on a special cabinet-level council; and second, that it would avoid the submersion of the policy development function under the single-minded budget preoccupation of the Budget Bureau.[9]

As Lyndon Johnson never acted on the recommendations of the Budget Bureau self-study or the Heineman Commission, it was the Ash Council view that ultimately was translated into reality through a reorganization plan introduced by Richard Nixon in the spring of 1970. As it evolved under Nixon and domestic adviser John Ehrlichman, the resulting domestic council model involved increased presidential control over the substance of policy; heavy use of interagency task forces, frequently involving agency staff in direct contact with White House staff without the intervening participation of department heads; extensive reliance on the council staff and its director as a buffer between the president and the domestic departments; and over time, the isolation of cabinet officers and other Executive Office of the President units, including the new Office of Management and Budget.[10]

In terms of the evolution of Executive Office machinery for the formulation of domestic policy, the domestic council model thus represented the continuation of a trend toward greater differentiation and institutionalization of the presidential policy development role. It did not, however, complete that trend as the Ash Council hoped. For the Ash Council had specified that the council be staffed by a combination of career and non-career personnel,[11] whereas in practice the professional career staff never materialized. What is more, the Ash Council anticipated a much more active role for the Domestic Council qua council, a collective decision-making body involving cabinet members directly, whereas in practice the council staff and its director took the reins instead. Finally, as it turned out, the Domestic Council was but one of a number of separate Executive Office units that Nixon established to increase his control over domestic policy. Not only did the new Office of Management and Budget equip itself with a politically attuned layer of policy officials in an effort to retain a meaningful policy role for itself, but also mini-bureaucracies formed around each of a host of other key advisers—Colson, Klein, Ziegler, Finch, Rumsfeld, Moynihan, and Harlow. In addition, special offices were created for drug abuse prevention, consumer affairs, the aged, volunteerism, energy, and inflation.

In a sense, the two precepts on which the domestic council model, as interpreted by Nixon, was based—first, the president should exercise policy control with the aid of the White House staff over all matters of importance throughout the executive branch; and second, that all such matters should be channeled to the maximum extent possible through one or two major decision processes—came into conflict. Given the scope and complexity of government activity and the proportion of the decisions that the Nixon team wanted to control from the center, there was no way that even a powerful domestic council staff of thirty professionals could handle all the business. The result was a proliferation of separate staffs and offices to the point that, according to Richard Nathan, "it was often impossible to find out who was handling a particular matter, much less to decide which one of several crosscutting decision systems in the White House should be assigned any given issue."[12]

The White House–Monitored Interagency
Task Force Model: Deinstitutionalization?

In the wake of Watergate, the whole concept on which the domestic council model was based came in for serious questioning. The basic notion that the presidency should be better equipped institutionally to give policy direction to the executive branch, a notion that went back at least as far as the New Deal and that found forceful intellectual expression in the Brownlow Committee report of 1937, turned out, it now appeared, to have within it the seeds of its own destruction: Presidential influence could be too great, not just too weak. Accordingly, a search began for yet another model of presidential participation in the formulation of executive branch domestic policy proposals, one that would equip the president to promote a needed degree of coherence in policy decision making without unleashing an institutional dynamic that would end up usurping the legitimate roles of other key actors, including those in the agencies and the Congress.

What took place, first under President Gerald Ford and then under President Jimmy Carter, was a significant de-institutionalization of the White House domestic policy role. Without disbanding the separate White House domestic policy staffs, Ford and Carter significantly loosened their grip on executive branch policy development, establishing instead a series of interagency policy task forces chaired by department or agency heads and monitored by the White House policy staff. Generally speaking, these task forces were more highly structured under Ford than under Carter, with several—especially the Economic Policy Board—acquiring a degree of permanence and institutional structure.[13] Under Carter, by contrast, each issue produced a different constellation of players and frequently a different decision process.

As a way to combine active White House and agency involvement in the formulation of policy, the White House–monitored interagency task force approach worked well. Departmental participation in the formulation of administration policy was extensive, indeed often endless. But at least as it operated during the Carter years, this approach had its own rather serious defects. These defects were the mirror image of those that afflicted the domestic council approach, but they produced a negative political reaction nonetheless. They included a high degree of relatively unrestrained inter-agency rivalry and dissension, a resulting lack of timeliness and coherence in policy decisions, insufficient attention to orderly process, and a tendency to bypass the career personnel of the Executive Office as deals were made directly between agency advocates and White House staff, frequently without analysis of historical patterns or long-run implications.

Redesigning the Presidential Policy Machinery: Underlying Issues and Criteria

The preceding discussion makes clear that the structuring of a presidential role in the formulation of national policy involves a number of important trade-offs. In order to determine how the performance of this role can be improved, it is necessary to look more closely and more systematically at what these trade-offs entail.

The Major Design Issues

Three major issues lie at the heart of the design of the presidential role in policy decision making. Although hardly exhaustive, these three issues define the core of the problem of designing presidential policy machinery.

1. Agency Versus Presidential Responsibilities. The first of these issues involves the allocation of policymaking responsibilities between the departments and the Executive Office of the President. Historically, as we have seen, agencies exercised substantial autonomy in the formulation of policy and the submission of legislative proposals to Congress. Only in the third decade of the twentieth century were regularized procedures for presidential review of departmental proposals developed, and only in the past twenty years have presidents developed the capability to perform a more active, initiating role.

Based on this pattern of evolution, four major options for the presidential role in policymaking vis-à-vis the departments seem available: a largely reactive role, a largely facilitative role, a largely stimulative role, or a controlling role.

2. Institutional Versus Personal Staff. Historically, a sharp distinction prevailed between the institutional and personal staffs of the president, with the personal staff kept small and the major ongoing burdens of the presidency (e.g., preparation of the budget, legislative review) entrusted to a permanent institutional staff, largely in the Bureau of the Budget. In more recent years, two things have changed: First, the personal staff has grown and absorbed functions formerly left to the professional staff; and second, a more substantial personal staff layer has been added to the institutional staff agencies. Although sole reliance on one or the other of these types of staffs to assist the president in policy formulation seems highly unlikely, several alternative configurations are possible: personal staff dominance, institutional staff dominance, or a mixed approach involving both types of staff at each stage of the policy development process.

3. *Consolidated Versus Compartmentalized Staffs at the Center.* The White House and Executive Office have recently grown not only in terms of numbers of persons but, even more important, in terms of numbers of separate units or staffs. The White House has become a complicated organization in its own right. In 1980, for example, the White House–Executive Office complex consisted of thirty-five different units or staffs reporting directly to the president. Whatever the division of responsibilities between the president and the departments, or between the institutional and personal staffs, therefore, how these various presidential responsibilities and staffs are themselves organized and grouped constitutes a separate issue. The choice here is essentially between numerous small units and staffs and fewer larger ones.

Design Criteria

Given these basic design issues, on what grounds should choices be made among them? What are the criteria by which the machinery for presidential involvement in policy formulation should be judged? What are the components of a "good" design? Quite clearly, no single answer can be given to these questions. Ultimately, how one prefers to design this machinery depends on the relative emphasis one gives to a number of different, and partially competing, criteria. It is therefore important to know what these major criteria are and what the trade-offs are among them. Although the list is hardly exhaustive, nine such criteria seem especially important.

1. *Substantive Soundness.* Ultimately, the basic test of any decision-making system is its ability to tap the best knowledge in existence in the time available and bring it to bear at the point of decision. Substantive soundness is not simply a product of factual information, however. It also involves the application of a suitable analytical framework so that the full dimensions of a problem can be perceived and the appropriate aspects emphasized. Other factors ultimately enter into any final decision, but the availability of the pertinent factual information and the use of an appropriate analytical framework seem basic, and a process that systematically—even if inadvertently—excludes such information or applies the wrong framework must be judged faulty.

2. *Responsiveness to National Needs.* The policymaking apparatus of the executive branch must be capable of identifying major national problems,

formulating effective options to deal with them, and bringing them to the attention of top decision makers in time to allow corrective action. This complex process of problem definition, option development, and decision making requires a combination of analytical insight, openness to new ideas, and effective procedures.

3. *Responsiveness to Presidential Priorities.* As there are always more problems in need of solution than political or economic resources to solve them, priorities must be set. In the American political system, the president holds a unique position in this priority-setting process by virtue of his status as the only nationally elected political leader. Because of this, the presidential perspective deserves special attention, especially in the formulation of executive branch policy positions. Although the presidency represents only one of many authoritative expressions of public preferences, it is certainly one of the most important and therefore one that the decision-making machinery should be designed to help clarify and respond to.

4. *Coherence.* Powerful centrifugal forces are at work in the American polity. Yet national problems are more complex and interdependent than ever. What is urgently needed, therefore, is a policymaking apparatus that can overcome some of the prevailing institutional and political fragmentation and encourage increased coherence and consistency in national efforts, including close integration of policymaking and resource allocation.

5. *Accountability and Political Sensitivity.* A policymaking system that generates policies that are coherent, responsive to national needs, and substantively sound can nevertheless fail if it is insufficiently sensitive and responsive to the other sources of political power in the American political system. At a minimum, the executive branch must be attentive in its policy prescriptions to the preferences of the Congress, as well as to those of outside interest groups, state and local governments, and others. Policymaking is only partly an analytical process. Important political dimensions must also be considered. In addition, in the wake of Watergate, special precautions are needed to make sure that the formal channels of accountability, under which the Congress holds agency heads legally responsible for the operations of the executive departments, are not subverted.

6. *Representativeness and Orderliness.* For a government as complex as ours to work with even a modicum of efficiency, those involved must have some assurance that orderly procedures will be followed in the handling of important matters. Everyone with a stake in a decision must have confidence that he or she will have his or her "day in court," that an opportunity will be provided for serious input at a meaningful point in the process, unless extraordinary circumstances clearly make this impossible. The more uncertain or chaotic the process, the more anxiety is created, the more time is wasted, and the more likely the chance of slipups.

7. *Timeliness.* At some point, further deliberation and soundings of opinion must stop, and decision processes must yield decisions. The more elaborate and cumbersome the process, however, the more difficult this becomes. There is thus a potential trade-off between representativeness and timeliness in the design of the decision process.

8. *Manageability and Selectivity.* A decision-making system can easily channel so many issues to a single point in the process that bottlenecks develop and overloads, sloppiness, and other malfuntions result. Clearly, only a tiny fraction of the total decisions made in the name of the federal government can be made at the center. What is needed, therefore, is a process that can screen out the less important issues while still reserving for top-level attention those matters that cannot, or should not, be handled anywhere else.

9. *Institutional and Organizational Sensitivity.* Ultimately, policy decisions must be implemented to be felt. What is more, policies must be constantly readjusted, reshaped, monitored, and reformed. For either of these to occur, however, ongoing institutions and processes and "institutional memories" are needed. A policymaking process that is insensitive to the way implementing institutions operate or that fails to draw on or contribute to the available institutional memory can therefore be self-defeating over the long run even if it is highly responsive and adaptable in the short run. As one long-time budget professional noted: "The whole process of government breaks down if top career officials like me don't get the up-to-date information; we can't do our job to make the wheels of government turn."

The Trade-Offs: Applying
the Criteria to the Design Issues

Given these criteria, how should the design issues identified above be resolved? How well do the various options spelled out under each design issue fare in terms of these criteria? To answer these questions, it is necessary to look back at each of the major design issues in light of the criteria just discussed.

1. *Presidential Versus Departmental Responsibilities.* As reflected in Table 6.1, departmental approaches to policy formulation, like that embodied in the central clearance process, have an edge over president-centered approaches in terms of substantive soundness, accountability, representativeness and orderliness, manageability, and institutional sensitivity. Where such approaches fall short is in terms of their responsiveness to national needs, their responsiveness to presidential priorities, their coherence, and their timeliness.

This is so for a variety of reasons. In the first place, the whole structure of American politics creates dual loyalties for agency officials. Despite its ap-

TABLE 6.1. An Evaluation of Alternative Presidential (versus Departmental) Roles in the Formulation of Policy

	Criteria	Alternative Presidential Roles			
		Reactive	Facilitative	Stimulative	Controlling
1.	Substantive soundness	Moderate-High	Moderate-High	Moderate	Moderate-Low
2.	Responsiveness to national needs	Moderate-Low	Moderate-Low	High	High
3.	Responsiveness to presidential priorities	Low	Low	High	High
4.	Coherence	Low	Moderate	Moderate-High	High
5.	Accountability	High	High	Moderate-High	Low
6.	Representativeness, orderliness	High	High	Moderate	Low
7.	Timeliness	Low	Moderate-Low	Moderate-High	High
8.	Manageability, selectivity	High	High	Moderate	Low
9.	Institutional sensitivity	High	High	Moderate	Low

parent hierarchical structure, the executive branch is in practice a loose confederation of semiautonomous baronies. As Norton Long wrote thirty years ago, power in the American bureaucracy does not flow down from the top along the chain of command. Rather, it flows "in from the sides" and "up from the bottom."[14] Bureau and agency chiefs occasionally receive support and encouragement from the president. But over the long run, their success or failure is in the hands of the interest groups with a direct stake in their operations and the Congressional subcommittees that authorize their activities and appropriate their funds. Defiance of presidents can mean temporary inconvenience. Defiance of clients and Congressional overseers can mean termination. Left to their own devices, therefore, agencies on the whole will generate proposals more responsive to the narrow constituencies with which they regularly interact than to broader national needs or presidential priorities.

In the second place, because of the absence of a fully developed civil service concept and the limited movement of personnel among agencies, agency cadres tend to develop a parochial perspective that defines personal success in terms of agency durability. The result is a turf-consciousness that makes it difficult to achieve coordinated action among agencies or to develop coherent policies across bureau and agency lines. In the process, moreover, these characteristics can reduce the basic substantive soundness of decisions by narrowing and skewing the analytical framework within which problems are perceived and addressed.

In the third place, the organizational structure of the federal establishment accentuates some of these trends by placing at the cabinet table officials with rather narrowly defined portfolios and limited maneuvering room vis-à-vis dominant client interests. Although this hardly prevents statesmanship, neither does it encourage it. Indeed, the incentives, traditions, and expectations all encourage advocacy of agency perspectives.

In practice, all of this means that presidents incur great costs when they rely totally on the agencies and departments to formulate policies. As Theodore Sorensen noted in 1963, "Each department has its own clientele and point of view, its own experts and bureaucratic interests, its own relations with the Congress and certain subcommittees, its own statutory authority, objectives, and standards of success. No Cabinet member is free to ignore all this without impairing the morale and efficiency of his department, his standing therein, and his relations with the powerful interest groups and congressmen who consider it partly their own."[15] Because of this, Sorenson noted, Kennedy "could not afford to accept without seeking an independent judgment, the products and proposals of departmental advisers whose responsibilities did not require them to look, as he and his staff looked, at the government and its programs as a whole."[16] If anything, this situation has grown even more acute since Kennedy's tenure, as problems have grown more complex and the need for interdepartmental approaches more pressing.

To say that a departmentally dominated policymaking process has serious flaws, however, is not to say that the opposite extreme—a presidentially controlled process—is best. To the contrary, as Table 6.1 indicates, such an approach has serious drawbacks in the areas of accountability, representativeness, manageability, and institutional sensitivity, and potential drawbacks with respect to substantive soundness.

The real choice, therefore, may come down to whether the president should play merely a facilitative role or whether he should be equipped to stimulate and initiate policies as well, at least in priority areas. The choice here hinges on the relative weight that is assigned to the greater responsiveness to national needs and presidential priorities and the greater policy coherence that is possible from a stimulative role, as opposed to the greater risk of attracting too many issues to the center, limiting accountability, and reducing the substantive soundness and institutional sensitivity of decisions that such a role can also entail. Some of these problems can be mitigated, however, by the staffing pattern that is chosen. The alternative staffing possibilities must therefore be assessed next.

2. *Personal Versus Institutional Staff.* If a strong argument can be made for a substantial—though not controlling—presidential role in the formulation of national policy, the question still remains whether this role is best performed primarily by personal staff, primarily by institutional staff, or by some better combination of the two than now exists.

Using the Carter Domestic Policy Staff (DPS) and OMB as the frame of reference for the "primarily personal" and "primarily institutional" staff categories, respectively, Table 6.2 shows that the choice of staffing pattern, like the division of responsibilities between the Executive Office and the

TABLE 6.2. An Evaluation of Alternative Staffing Patterns for the Presidential Role in Policy Formulation

	Staffing Pattern		
Criteria	Primarily Personal[a]	Primarily Institutional[b]	Mixture[c]
1. Substantive soundness	Moderate-Low	Moderate	Moderate-High
2. Responsiveness to national needs	High	Moderate-Low	Moderate-High
3. Responsiveness to presidential priorities	High	Moderate-Low	Moderate-High
4. Coherence	Moderate	Moderate	High
5. Accountability, political sensitivity	High	Moderate	Moderate-High
6. Representativeness, orderliness	Low	High	Moderate-High
7. Timeliness	High	Moderate	Moderate-High
8. Manageability, selectivity	Low	Moderate	Moderate-High
9. Institutional sensitivity	Low	High	Moderate-High

[a]Assumes primary reliance on Domestic Policy Staff (DPS) as it existed in the Carter administration.

[b]Assumes primary reliance on current or slightly modified OMB, with scaled-down DPS.

[c]Assumes new institutional capability (e.g., original Ash Council conception) or the build-up of a politically sensitive policy capability in OMB.

departments, can have important ramifications in terms of the evaluative criteria I have suggested. In particular, the choice here comes down to one between the greater responsiveness to national needs and presidential priorities, the greater political sensitivity, and the superior timeliness of the personal staff option compared to the enhanced substantive soundness, orderliness, manageability, and institutional sensitivity available through the institutional staff route.

This configuration of advantages and disadvantages reflects, of course, the particular characteristics of the existing institutional and personal staff resources. As such, it reflects one of the striking realities of the institutionalized presidency: Presidential institutions, like all other organizations, develop their own distinctive personalities and outlooks. Whether by choice or happenstance, for example, the Office of Management and Budget, the oldest of presidential institutions, had its destiny stamped when it emerged as a budget agency instead of the more general "agency of the President" that the Brownlow Committee anticipated. Though it performs a variety of functions for the presidency, budget making dominates not only the agency's attentions but also its personality and its soul. Despite its claims of neutral competency, the agency has historically had a mission and a point of view. The mission has been to limit expenditures, and the point of view has been critical of new initiatives.

The problem is that although these are important parts of the presidential perspective, they are not the only parts, or always the most important ones. Relying chiefly on the institutional staff represented by OMB to carry out the president's policy responsibilities is thus to stack the cards against activism, innovation, and responsiveness and in favor of a more restrictive and conservative approach. As one Carter administration official explained, "OMB is a tremendous force for the status quo. It's off in a world of its own, not wired into Presidential decision-making. They don't seem to realize that the President has domestic priorities he's trying to push. They think OMB is supposed to speak for the President's conservative side and the Domestic Policy Staff for his liberal side. The agencies, of course, are caught in the middle."

By the same token, however, the personal presidential staff involved in policy development has its own biases and characteristics. Most serious, perhaps, are the tendencies to stimulate program initiatives with little regard for their fiscal consequences, to disregard orderly processes in order to force decisions through the system, and to attract far too many issues to the center for resolution, putting the president on the line in too many places and usurping departmental responsibilities. As one Carter budget official recently put it, "The staff in the DPS have a real incentive to surface issues, get Stu [Eizenstat] to sign off on them, and get them to the President. Their jobs depend on their ability to keep the President focused on their area." "They float freely with too little grasp of what has gone on before," is how another prominent budget official described the problem.

This discussion suggests the need for a better amalgam of institutional and personal staff resources to support the presidential role in policy formulation. The creation of the Program Associate Director (PAD) level in the Office of Management and Budget was one step in this direction. From this perspective, the PAD level can be viewed not as a "politicization" of OMB,[17] but as an effort to counteract the existing bias of the agency and provide a politically reliable transmission belt for conveying professional advice into presidential decision making. As one presidential adviser in the Carter administration explained, "If you didn't have those PAD's there, OMB's credibility with the President would be minimal or worse. He'd see OMB as largely outside his close circle."

Alternatively, greater professionalization of the White House policy staff, as the Ash Council recommended, could accomplish a similar end. This would require the establishment of a stronger tradition of reliance on policy professionals instead of campaign aides in these critical positions and possibly the establishment of a core secretariat of careerists who would staff at least the procedural aspects of the policy development function.

3. *Consolidated Versus Compartmentalized Executive Office Organizational Structure.* Which of these alternative courses to follow finally depends on how the third key design issue identified above—whether to consolidate the Executive Office policy functions into a few large units or leave them fragmented in numerous smaller units—is resolved. As Table 6.3 indicates, much more than the aesthetic appearance of the resulting organizational chart is involved in this decision. Important substantive consequences can also be at stake.

In particular, a consolidated structure is likely to contribute to greater coherence, timeliness, and orderliness. For example, an arrangement that merges the national security, domestic policy, and economic management staffs of the president would facilitate the integration of policy among these spheres below the presidential level and thus contribute to policy coherence. By reducing the number of separate checkpoints that decisions would have to clear, moreover, such an arrangement would also improve the orderliness of the decision process and reduce the chances of holdups and delays. Finally, to the extent that current problems require an integrated analytical approach that embraces both the foreign and domestic aspects of issues, such an arrangement could also contribute to the substantive soundness of decisions.

But this kind of arrangement also has drawbacks. For one thing, it is likely to impede responsiveness to national needs, because large organizations

TABLE 6.3. An Evaluation of Alternative Executive Office Organizational Structures for Presidential Involvement in Policy Formulation

	Alternative Organizational Structures	
Criteria	Consolidated	Compartmentalized
1. Substantive soundness	--	--
2. Responsiveness to national needs	Moderate	High
3. Responsiveness to presidential priorities	Moderate	High
4. Coherence	High	Low
5. Accountability, political sensitivity	Low	Moderate-Low
6. Representativeness, orderliness	High	Low
7. Timeliness	High	Low
8. Manageability, selectivity	Moderate	Low
9. Institutional sensitivity	--	--

tend to get bogged down in current responsibilities and to lose sight of emerging issues. By the same token, such an arrangement could limit responsiveness to presidential priorities by making it harder for presidents to highlight critical issues for special attention and to attract visible, high-powered talent to work on these issues, as high-powered talent tends to demand a direct reporting relationship to the president. Finally, a highly consolidated structure raises important issues of accountability. For one thing, congressmen have a well-known aversion to unelected Executive Office "czars" for this and that. How much greater would be their concern about a comprehensive czar. More important, presidents themselves might find such consolidated centers of power unattractive, for they could create in-house competitors to the president's own authority.

Here as well, therefore, the realistic question is whether some mixed approach is possible that would retain the basic pluralistic structure of the Executive Office but promote greater coherence and order in the flow of decisions.

From Issues to Options: Possible Avenues for Change

Three basic conclusions flow from the analysis of the evolution of presidential involvement in the formulation of policy and from the more detailed analysis presented here of trade-offs and underlying design issues. To be sure, these are "conclusions" in a special sense, for they are based on a particular weighting of the design criteria spelled out earlier, a weighting that puts its emphasis on the need for an executive policymaking mechanism that is responsive to national needs and capable of promoting coherence yet still accountable and substantively sound. Such a weighting reflects personal values and preferences as well as a reading of current political and institutional realities. Beyond this, however, it is consistent with the "consensus" view of the role of the presidency reflected in the report of the Brownlow Committee, the *Federalist Papers*, and elsewhere.

The first of these conclusions is that reliance on the departments and agencies is an inadequate way of organizing policymaking responsibilities of the executive branch in the current situation. Some better way to assert the presidential perspective is needed. A purely reactive presidential role thus seems inappropriate, but a controlling role seems even more undesirable. What is needed, therefore, is an arrangement to equip the president to take the initiative in key areas without inducing him to try to control everything from the center. The second key conclusion is that this presidential role cannot be adequately performed by sole reliance either on institutional staff or on personal staff. Some better combination of the two than now exists seems called for. Finally, it seems clear that the current trend toward fragmentation and compartmentalization of the Executive Office of the President must be halted and reversed. At the same time, however, drastic consolidation of responsibilities within the president's office seems likely to carry with it drawbacks every bit as serious.

Given these conclusions, what changes should be made to improve the operation of the presidency in the formulation of domestic policy? Is there a way to combine the alternatives specified under each of the major design issues discussed above in a way that promises to improve the performance of the presidential policy role?

The Options

Broadly speaking, four such sets of changes can be identified. Although some of the detail for each of these options is spelled out here, it should be emphasized that what is more important is not the detail but the direction of change each represents.

Option 1: Maximum Reliance on Departments and Agencies. This option would involve a sharp reduction of the specialized policy staff—both personal and institutional—available to the president—and an increased reliance instead on the departments and agencies. The presidential role in this model would clearly be "facilitative" and "reactive" rather than "stimulative," as suggested in Table 6.1. Under it, cabinet members would identify major problems in need of administration attention, secure presidential approval to convene interagency groups as needed to work on these problems, resolve disagreements within the interagency groupings, and present the president with major options for action. Presidential decisions would then be transmitted back to the relevant departments and agencies for translation into legislative or administrative form, with the departments and agencies primarily responsible for securing passage and monitoring implementation. The presidency, in this model, would serve a central clearance and attention-focusing function, but would leave to the departments and agencies most of the detailed development of proposals.

Option 2: A "Heinemanized" OMB. This option would involve a sharp reduction of the specialized White House Domestic Policy Staff and the creation of an upgraded policy development capability in the Office of Management and Budget along the lines suggested by the Heineman task force in 1967. The policy development staff in this option would be professionalized, though with some flexibility to accommodate skilled in-and-outers. The policy development staff would conduct some in-house analysis, would staff interagency task forces, and would work with departments and agencies in preparing major policy options for presidential attention. To function effectively, the policy development staff would have to enjoy a certain autonomy within OMB and be in a position to work directly with a scaled-down presidential policy staff of four to six people. In all likelihood, a new high-level office of program development would be needed in OMB, though an alternative configuration would be to use the existing Special Studies Divisions within each of the four major OMB program areas to perform the policy development role, as has been done in the energy field in the Carter administration. Under any circumstances, the top OMB leaders involved in the policy development work would have to be presidential appointees.

Option 3: A National Policies Staff. This option would leave OMB largely unchanged but would consolidate the major presidential policy staffs outside OMB into a single unit. In particular, the national security, domestic policy, and economic policy staffs (the NSC, the DPS, the CEA, and COWPS) would be merged into a single, integrated National Policies Staff (NPS) composed of sixty to a hundred professionals operating as a separate Executive Office unit outside the Office of Management and Budget. The function of the NPS would be to bring potentially important national problems to the president's attention, to review departmental policy proposals for their consistency with presidential priorities, to work with departments and agencies in the formulation of major administration policy initiatives, to help organize and staff interdepartmental task forces, and to monitor important economic, national security, and domestic issues on behalf of the president.

The NPS would be staffed by a combination of career professionals, skilled in-and-outers, and top presidential appointees. It would include a career executive secretariat whose function it would be to establish and maintain orderly processes for the development of major presidential policy initiatives. The remainder of the staff would be grouped and regrouped along project lines in accord with presidential priorities and national needs. Fundamental to the NPS concept, however, is an integrated, institutionalized, and professional staff to serve the president's facilitative and stimulative role in the policy process.

Option 4: A Modified Status Quo. This option would leave largely intact the basic institutional structure that has evolved to serve the president's policy role, but would alter certain internal characteristics of some of the key units and generally improve the prevailing decision processes. Among the changes that might be encompassed in this option are the greater professionalization of the Domestic Policy Staff (DPS); a reduction in the size of the Domestic Policy Staff and increased emphasis on the policy development functions of OMB; the creation of a secretariat in the White House or in the DPS to establish and maintain a less chaotic and more structured decision process for the development of major policy initiatives; and the development of a regularized mechanism for linking domestic, economic, and national security policymaking. The last change might involve a daily or weekly "national policies briefing" for the president prepared jointly by the staffs of the four major presidential policy units (DPS, OMB, NSC, and CEA) with cooperation from the affected departments; designation of regular liaison officials and mechanisms among these staffs; or regular meetings among the principals. Such process changes might be accompanied, moreover, by certain structural changes—e.g., placing responsibility for microeconomic policy and foreign economic policy matters in the Domestic Policy Staff, thereby broadening its scope and bringing some of the most important crosscutting issues under unified direction while preserving a certain pluralism in the president's policy advisory system.

Analysis of the Options

None of the options portrayed here, nor any others that can be imagined, is free of drawbacks. Yet some seem better than others, at least in terms of the evaluative criteria set forth earlier. In particular, the record of the White House–monitored interagency task force approach suggests quite strongly that Option 1, despite its advantages in terms of accountability and institutional sensitivity, carries with it unacceptable costs in terms of lack of timeliness, lack of coherence, susceptibility to agency instead of presidential perspectives, and difficulty in bringing information to bear on complex problems in an integrated fashion.

Option 2 has equally serious difficulties because of the major transformation it would require in the operation of OMB and because of the amount of influence it would concentrate in one presidential adviser. Despite the advantages it would have as a broader, professional staff agency, OMB has a special role to play that presidents, probably wisely, have been reluctant to subvert by altering the basic mission of the agency from budgeting to policy development. OMB should never be shut out of the positive policy development process (which could happen in the absence of something like the PAD level to keep it wired into presidential decision making and to insulate the professional staff from increasingly active outside political pressures); neither can it afford to be the principal actor in that process. As one high-ranking OMB official in the Carter Administration put it, "OMB is the only place with a detailed program review function and the only place that says 'no'. It should not give that up." Transforming the agency into something fundamentally different might do exactly that.

If this is so, then the real choice comes down to Options 3 and 4. As a full integration of the various policy staffs in the Executive Office seems unlikely, moreover, these two may in practice merge into a single option. The core of this option would be some meaningful–though not total–consolidation of the existing policy staffs (e.g., the creation of a partial national policies staff composed of the existing DPS with the addition of microeconomic and foreign economic policy responsibilities); greater professionalization of the resulting policy staff; and greater attention to systematic processes for policy decisions, including the processes for involving the agencies and the OMB. This might be accomplished by attaching a permanent secretariat to the broadened policy staff. Such an option lacks drama, but it provides a reasonable response to current ills, seems least likely to create new problems, and not insignificantly, is most likely to be generally embraced.

Interestingly, as of March of 1981, it appears that this is precisely the course that the Reagan administration is adopting in its first months in office. So far, this course has three elements: first, a mechanism for synchronizing the flow of policy advice to the president by having the domestic policy advisor, the national security policy advisor, and the economic policy advisor all report to the president through a single senior counselor, Edwin Meese, and by having more frequent cabinet sessions; second, a greater focus on the orderliness of decision processes through the establishment of a chief of staff to oversee the flow of paper; and third, an expansion of the policy role of OMB and hence of the professional staff input into policy decision making. It will be interesting to see whether this pattern proves durable, and whether it develops its own peculiar debilities.

Conclusions: Toward a New Presidential Policy Management Doctrine

One of the great ironies of recent American political development has been that the growth of the "institutionalized presidency," about which so much has been written, has resulted less from presidents' pursuit of their constitutional duty to see that the laws are faithfully executed than from the pursuit of their perceived political obligation to see that laws are energetically proposed. It is as a formulator of programs and policies, not as a manager of them, that the presidency has gained power, visibility, and bulk.

This chapter has examined the historical evolution of the specialized staff capability that presidents have developed to assist them in performing this policy role and has analyzed the drawbacks of current arrangements and the dilemmas involved in changing these arrangements. Opinions may differ on many of the crucial issues examined here, but at least one conclusion seems undeniable. Specialized presidential staff resources in the area of domestic policy formulation have now survived four changes in administration, two of them involving changes in party control as well. Presidents of quite different temperaments, operating styles, political philosophies, and political parties have thus apparently found such resources necessary and useful in the performance of their functions. Under the circumstances, it seems reasonable to assume that these resources are here to stay.

What this means in practice is that the standard, ritualistic presidential pledge to "return policy direction to the cabinet members," a pledge reiterated at the start of each new administration and then quietly, or noisily, disregarded, is as dated as the national nominating conventions. Repetition of this pledge is not only unconvincing; it has also been counterproductive, for it has inhibited the search for a new doctrine that better suits the prevailing realities of national policymaking.

In an era of complex national problems and interdependent policies, in which the need for coherence is great and the president is the political leader in the best position to provide it, what is the appropriate doctrine to guide president-cabinet relations in the formulation of policy? The answer suggested here is that neither "all power to the departments" nor "all power to the president" can suffice. What is needed instead is a new emphasis on process, a commitment to orderly procedures for collaborative decision making. "The process is the policy" is how Marshall McLuhan might put the new doctrine being proposed here. Instead of promising maximum discretion to the departments, this suggests that presidents should promise maximum reliance on agreed-upon processes for raising and resolving policy issues. Such a promise would make it clearer to cabinet officials that they are part of a larger enterprise and to presidents that they have a stake in an orderly system of collaboration with understandable and reliable operating rules. At a minimum, such a promise is more likely to be kept.

Notes

1. V. O. Key, "Politics and Administration," in Leonard D. White, ed.,

The Future of Government in the United States (Chicago: University of Chicago Press, 1942), pp. 155–156.

2. The account here draws heavily on Richard Neustadt, "Presidency and Legislation: The Growth of Central Clearance," *American Political Science Review* 48, No. 3 (September 1954), pp. 641–671; Richard Neustadt, "Presidency and Legislation: Planning the President's Program," *American Political Science Review* 49, No. 4 (December 1955), pp. 980–1021.

3. See Lyndon Johnson's critique in Lyndon B. Johnson, *The Vantage Point: Perspectives of the Presidency, 1963–1969* (New York: Holt, Rinehart & Winston, 1971), p. 326.

4. Arthur Maass, "In Accord with the Program of the President? An Essay on Staffing the Presidency," *Public Policy* 9 (1953), p. 82. For an internal bureau critique that makes a similar point, see memorandum, Phillip Hughes to William Carey, August 5, 1960, quoted in Larry Berman, *The Office of Management and Budget and the Presidency, 1921–1979* (Princeton, N.J.: Princeton University Press, 1979). See also "Roles and Missions of the Bureau of the Budget," in U.S., Bureau of the Budget, "Evaluation of the Organization and Management of the Bureau of the Budget," 3 vols. (unpublished manuscript, 1967; Office of Management and Budget Library), Vol. 1, p. 11 (hereafter "1967 BOB Self-Study").

5. See Norman C. Thomas and Harold L. Wolman, "Policy Formulation in the Institutionalized Presidency: The Johnson Task Forces," in Thomas Cronin and Sandford Greenberg, eds., *The Presidential Advisory System* (New York: Harper & Row, 1969), pp. 128–132.

6. Johnson, *Vantage Point*, p. 328. Emphasis added.

7. William D. Carey, "Presidential Staffing in the Sixties and Seventies," *Public Administration Review*, Vol. 29, No. 5 (September-October 1969), p. 450.

8. The discussion of the "1967 BOB Self-Study" here draws on interviews with Jack Young (the staff director), Sam Hughes (then deputy director), William Capron, and Dwight Ink, as well as a review of the self-study documents, including a final staff summary and the supporting working papers and meeting notes. On the Heineman Commission, see U.S., President's Task Force on Government Organization, "The Organization and Management of Great Society Programs, a Final Report," Working Paper No. 1, June 15, 1967. I am grateful to Peter Szanton for making this unpublished paper available to me. This discussion also draws on interviews with task force members William Capron and Herbert Kaufman, staff director Frederick Bohen, and staff members I. M. Destler, Peter Szanton, and Alan Schick.

For a description of the Ash Council proposal, see U.S., Congress, House, Committee on Government Affairs, *Hearings on Reorganization Plan No. 2 of 1970*, 91st Congress, 2d Session, 1 (April-May 1970), p. 11; and Memorandum to the President of the United States from the Advisory Council on Executive Organization, October 17, 1969.

9. Larry Berman suggested that a third reason was involved: John Ehrlichman's determination to use the Ash Council to consolidate his power in the Nixon White House. According to Berman, Ash originally preferred a Budget Bureau location for the policy development function but changed course to suit Ehrlichman and ultimately brought the council around. Murray Comarow, staff director of the Ash Council, categorically rejected this thesis, noting that the "National Security Council

model" was embraced by the staff as the best option prior to council deliberations and that the council was composed of strong, independent men like Walter Thayer and Frederick Kappel (chairman of A.T.&T.) who were not about to take orders from Ehrlichman and who made a special point of emphasizing the independence of their deliberations. See Larry Berman, "The Office of Management and Budget That Almost Wasn't," *Political Science Quarterly* 95, No. 2 (Summer 1977), p. 298; Murray Comarow, personal interview, May 28, 1980.

10. Richard P. Nathan, *The Plot that Failed: Nixon and the Administrative Presidency* (New York: John Wiley & Sons, 1975), pp. 45–53; Ronald C. Moe, "The Domestic Council in Perspective," *Bureaucrat* 5, No. 3 (October 1976), pp. 258–259, 269; John Ehrlichman, "How it All Began," *National Journal* (December 31, 1975), pp. 1690–1691; John Kessel, *The Domestic Presidency: Decision-Making in the White House* (North Scituate, Mass.: Duxbury Press, 1975), especially pp. 101–112; and Raymond Waldmann, "The Domestic Council: Innovation in Presidential Government," *Public Administration Review*, Vol. 36, No. 3 (May-June, 1976), p. 266.

11. Testimony of Roy Ash, U.S., Congress, House, Committee on Government Affairs, *Hearings on Reorganization Plan No. 2 of 1970*, p. 11.

12. Nathan, *Plot That Failed*, p. 53. See also Stephen Hess, *Organizing the Presidency* (Washington, D.C.: Brookings Institution, 1976), p. 133; Kessel, *Domestic Presidency*, pp. 101–102; Moe, "Domestic Council in Perspective," p. 260.

13. Daniel Balz, "Juice and Coffee and the GNP—The Men who Meet in the Morning," *National Journal*, April 3, 1976, pp. 429–431; and Dom Bonafede, "The Fall Out from Camp David," *National Journal*, November 10, 1979, p. 1894.

14. Norton Long, "Power and Administration," in Norton Long, *The Polity* (Chicago: Rand-McNally, 1962), pp. 50–63. (Originally published in *Public Administration Review* 9, No. 4 [1949].)

15. Theodore C. Sorensen, *Decision-Making in the White House* (New York: Columbia University Press, 1969), p. 69.

16. Theodore C. Sorensen, *Kennedy* (New York: Bantam Books, 1965).

17. For the alternative perspective, see Hugh Heclo, "OMB and the Presidency: The Problem of Neutral Competence," *Public Interest*, No. 38 (Winter 1975), pp. 80–96.

7

The President and Economic Policy: Problems, Patterns, and Alternatives

Roger B. Porter

The economy has been a major concern for the president at least since the administration of Herbert Hoover and the onset of the Great Depression half a century ago. In 1956 Clinton Rossiter in his book *The American Presidency* wrote that the president had a new function, "still taking shape, that of Manager of Prosperity" (one of ten major areas of responsibility).[1] The 1953 *Economic Report of the President* outlined a role for government in the economy that could easily be repeated today with only minor modification:

> The demands of modern life and the unsettled status of the world requires a more important role for government than it played in earlier and quieter times. . . .
>
> Government must use its vast power to help maintain employment and purchasing power as well as to maintain reasonably stable prices.
>
> Government must be alert and sensitive to economic developments, including its own myriad activities. It must be prepared to take preventive as well as remedial action; and it must be ready to cope with new situations that may arise. This is not a start-and-stop responsibility but a continuous one.
>
> The arsenal of weapons at the disposal of the Government for maintaining economic stability is formidable. It includes credit controls administered by the Federal Reserve System; debt-management policies of the Treasury; authority of the President to vary the terms of mortgages carrying Federal insurance; flexibility in administration of the budget; agricultural supports; modification of

the tax structure; and public works. We shall not hesitate to use any or all of these weapons as the situation may require.[2]

Old Problems

Inflation, unemployment, and sustained growth—the principal concerns of macroeconomic policy—are old problems for the president. The major tools for dealing with the economy at his and the government's disposal are essentially unchanged: government spending, taxes, and the money supply. And the principal institutional arrangements for exercising the president's role in these areas are similar to those that existed three decades ago. The Council of Economic Advisers (CEA), established by the Congress in the Employment Act of 1946 to advise the president on economic policy issues, remains a central element in the Executive Office of the President. The Troika (an informal group composed of the secretary of the treasury, the chairman of the CEA, and the director of OMB) has existed in one form or another since 1961 and advises the president on most macroeconomic policy questions. In terms of the tools of macroeconomic policy, the federal budget as a portion of the gross national product has risen but slightly from around 18 percent to roughly 22 percent over the last quarter century. Government spending as a whole has experienced a greater increase, but most of the growth has occurred at the state and local levels. Similarly, monetary policy has largely remained the preserve of the Federal Reserve System. Despite much discussion about limiting the traditional independence of the Federal Reserve Board of Governors, its autonomy and effective control over the major instruments of monetary policy remain intact.

Yet, despite these elements of constancy, dealing with macroeconomic policy issues is more complicated for the president in 1980 than it was thirty years ago, largely because of increasing fragmentation within both the executive branch and the Congress. A 1978 study of 132 economic policymaking units at the bureau level in the executive branch found that authority for many actions was widely distributed. Likewise, the growth of "off-budget" items—loan guarantees, interest-rate subsidies and so on—has added a large and important element to macroeconomic policy that is largely outside the president's effective control. The Congress has assumed a somewhat more prominent role in the budgetary process since the reforms of the mid-1970s that created the Senate and House Budget Committees and the Congressional Budget Office.

For the most part, then, the president's general responsibilities and the institutional framework through which he must operate are similar today to what they were at mid-century. But although the problem of macroeconomic policy also has altered little, five new challenges for the presidency have arisen.

New Challenges

First, the 1970s ended with economic difficulties very different from those of either the 1950s or 1960s. High inflation (the consumer price index [CPI] increased 13.3 percent in 1979—the highest annual increase in the last quarter century), relatively high unemployment (5.9 percent at the end of 1979), low rates of real growth, and low productivity growth (virtually no increases in productivity for the past two years) now characterize the economy's performance. This is coupled with a growing dependence on foreign sources of oil. No longer does the president preside over a buoyant, expanding economy. The realistic policy alternatives available to him today involve distributing pain rather than dividing greater wealth. The tools remain the same, but the environment is less favorable. This presents a new challenge. To the extent that those who look to the president for leadership in addressing the economy's ills refuse to accept these changed circumstances, their expectations often exceed what the president can deliver.

A second new challenge is the greater complexity of policymaking. The federal government's aggregate dollar share of the GNP has not altered markedly, but the number and scope of its programs have. One driving force behind the growing complexity is the expansion of government activity. Charles L. Schultze, CEA chairman under Carter, has aptly described the changing environment of government:

> Until perhaps fifteen or twenty years ago, most federal activities in the domestic sphere were confined to a few broad areas: providing cash income under social security programs for which eligibility was fairly easily determined; investing in the infrastructure in a few sectors of the economy, principally highways, water resources, and high-rise public housing; regulating selected industries allegedly to control monopoly or prevent certain abuses; and operating various housekeeping activities such as the Post Office, the national parks, the merchant seamen's hospitals, and the air navigation system. But in the short space of twenty years the very nature of federal activity has changed radically. Addressed to much more intricate and difficult objectives, the new programs are different; and the older ones have taken on more ambitious goals.[3]

The expansion of federal concerns and the enlarged scope of federal programs have increased the demands on the president. He is not merely responsible for administering these arithmetically expanding programs; he is also responsible for resolving the geometrically expanding conflicts among their objectives and priorities.

The growing number of factors that must be taken into account also contributes to the complexity of policymaking. Environmental considerations acquired a new prominence in the 1970s. The end of the cheap energy era has added another dimension. Consumer interests are more visible than a decade ago. Moreover, these interests are now much better organized to press their claims. The growth of highly organized private-sector groups is mirrored by an increasing fragmentation of power within the Congress. Congressional leaders have less influence over committee or party members, making the task of negotiations between executive and legislative branches more difficult.

Third, microeconomic problems and sectoral issues assumed a new prominence in the 1970s. An explosion of federal regulatory activity has fueled this development. During the two decades following 1955 the number of pages published annually in the *Federal Register* increased from slightly more than 10,000 to more than 60,000. This growth has accelerated in recent years and is concentrated in the period since 1970. Between 1970 and 1975, the average annual rate of growth was nearly 25 percent—up from just under 5 percent between 1955 and 1970.[4] Another measure of the growing importance of microeconomic and sectoral issues is the division of labor among staff members of the Council of Economic Advisers. Whereas microeconomic issues occupied a modest fraction of the staff resources and time of the council two decades ago, today microeconomic problems consume at least as much of the council's resources as do macroeconomic policy issues.

A fourth change is the blurring of the traditional distinction between domestic and foreign economic policy during the past quarter century. A significant reduction in the natural, artificial, and psychological barriers to foreign trade and international capital movements has occurred. National economies have become more open and more sensitive to developments in the economies of their trading partners. A variety of developments demonstrate the increased openness of the U.S. economy. One key measure of increasing international economic interdependence is the marked increase in trade-to-GNP ratios.[5] The export share of the U.S. gross national product has doubled in the past fifteen years, and the import share has doubled in just seven years.[6] The United States exports approximately 20 percent of its industrial production and more than one-third of its farm output. About one-third of U.S. corporate profits come from overseas activities, primarily direct foreign investment. And the United States presently imports more than 50 percent of its needs for nine of the thirteen key industrial raw materials.[7] The American economy, in short, is becoming increasingly dependent on foreign markets and foreign products. This blurring of the distinction between foreign and domestic policy is also revealed by the interest of members of the national security community in using economic means to advance foreign policy objectives.

A fifth challenge for the president in dealing with economic policy issues is the U.S. position in the world economy. Not only are the domestic and international economies increasingly interrelated, but the relative economic power of the United States is less than it once was. The preeminence of the dollar in international markets is now challenged, and its strength relative to other currencies has eroded substantially over the last decade. Dependence on foreign sources of oil and slow U.S. productivity growth have damaged U.S. trade competitiveness. Moreover, U.S. firms increasingly must compete with state-controlled or -supported enterprises. Foreign governments typically have more concentrated mechanisms for dealing with economic policy issues.

Implications for the President's Role

As a result of these changes in the last twenty-five years, economic policy issues are likely to consume more of the president's time without the promise of major achievements. The fundamental characteristics of our economy are not encouraging. Most macroeconomic and microeconomic problems that the president faces have no easy solutions, but public hopes and expectations for presidential performance will probably remain high. Moreover, the fragmentation of congressional power and the strengthening of organized interests make the president's task of building consensus and developing support for his policies more difficult.

Barring fundamental constitutional revision, the fragmented structure of Congress and the power of organized interests are unlikely to change significantly. Similarly, the intrusion of the government into the economy is unlikely to recede. The increasing international interdependence and the pressures for social-value regulation (safety, health, and environmental standards) are likely to persist.

In such a complex and fragmented environment the president has several crucial needs. First, he needs help in sifting and sorting, in selecting what issues he should personally get involved in and how. A president who consents to become involved in a host of issues may soon find that others hold him accountable for successfully resolving them. Yet, the president has limited time and resources. He cannot respond to every need and cure every ill. He must focus his energies on major, not minor, issues.

Second, the president needs help in integrating policy. He wants the parts to bear some relationship to the whole, as he is uniquely accountable for the comprehensiveness and coherence of his administration's policies. Indeed, the integration of policy "is the overriding problem of policy making under conditions of diffused power."[8]

Third, the president needs help in structuring his decisions. He has an interest in balancing the competing forces and interests in major areas of public policy. His decisions will be best informed if the objectives and considerations presented to him reasonably correspond to their real importance. Thus, he needs organizational arrangements that provide representation for all important interests without significantly favoring one perspective over another.[9]

Finally, the president's success in dealing with economic policy issues is tied to the cohesion of his administration. Not only must he present coherent policies, but he needs a united administration — key officials who see their responsibilities in a broad setting and who understand and support his policies. The fragmented structure of the executive branch and the Congress often frustrates overall direction of policy. The president needs institutional arrangements and incentives to bring and keep together his administration team.

Economic Advice to the President: Institutional Arrangements

Economic advice to the president since the end of the Second World War has varied widely, reflecting the decision-making styles of the presidents and their leading administration officials. Three entities or types of institutional arrangements have characterized economic policy advice to the president: the Council of Economic Advisers, interdepartmental committees, and a White House assistant for economic policy.

The Council of Economic Advisers

The Employment Act of 1946 created the Council of Economic Advisers to advise the president and the newly created Joint Economic Committee of the Congress on economic policy matters. President Truman did not request creation of the council, and it rated only passing mention in his memoirs. Composed of three members, equal in authority over the council's staff and operations, it was assisted by a small professional staff.

Reorganization Plan No. 9 of 1953 reconstituted the council, establishing the chairman as preeminent.[10] Responsibility for employing staff, specialists, and consultants was transferred from the council to the chairman, as was the formal function of reporting to the president on the council's views and activities.[11] There was a modest increase in the size of the council staff under Walter Heller at the onset of the Kennedy administration, but the characteristics and functions of the CEA have remained remarkably constant.

The three council members and the staff of twelve to twenty professionals are drawn disproportionately from academia. There is high turnover among staff members. Most remain with the council no more than two years. This high turnover rate limits the institutional memory of the staff. However, many of the council members and senior staff previously served as junior staff members. Arthur Okun was successively a senior staff member, a council member, and finally chairman of the council. Of the eleven CEA chairmen, seven previously served with the council in some capacity before their appointment as chairman. Party affiliation has had little influence on the selection of the professional staff. The council has been extremely successful in attracting well-trained and highly motivated professional staff.

The CEA has avoided assuming operational responsibilities and instead has served exclusively as a staff arm of the presidency. Although its members regularly testify before the Joint Economic Committee and other congressional committees, it is clearly the servant of the chief executive and not of the Congress. Its principal functions have been: (1) forecasting trends and the future pattern of overall economic activity; (2) general analysis of economic issues for the president (in the past two decades microeconomic issues have consumed more and more of the CEA staff time, and the staff has become somewhat more specialized); and (3) preparing an annual economic report for the Congress.

Presidents have sought the advice of the CEA with varying frequency over the post–World War II period. The principal function of the CEA has been expert analysis, but it has, from time to time, served as a coordinator of views for the president. In almost every administration the CEA has participated in many interagency committees, some of which it chaired. But the CEA was not originally designed to serve as a coordinator or broker. Executive departments and agencies view it not as a broker but as an advocate—not for a constituency, such as farmers or labor unions, but for the views of professional economists, usually favoring markets and opposing subsidies. It has no "constituency"; rather, it has a *client*, the president. This is true for both Democratic and Republican administrations. In interagency discussions, CEA members take positions and press for particular policies as avidly as do other department or agency representatives.

There is general agreement among former CEA chairmen that the council should stay small and avoid administrative responsibilities. There is little support for a more active CEA role in coordinating or brokering. A highly qualified expert staff has served the council well in the past and presumably will continue to do so in the future.

Interdepartmental Committees

Almost every president, usually early in his administration, talks of reviving the cabinet as an institution and indicates that he intends to hold regular and frequent cabinet meetings. Yet most presidents come to regard the full cabinet as an unsatisfactory forum for considering major policy issues. Few problems engage either the interest or the expertise of all members of the cabinet. The sheer volume of work and demands on their time suggest the wisdom of focusing their expertise rather than using the entire cabinet to seriously deliberate policy issues.

Regular participants in cabinet meetings held by the last five presidents uniformly describe them as mainly exercises in exchanging information and getting direction from the president. Reports on how the administration's program is faring in the Congress, an account of the latest foreign mission of the secretary of state or the prospects for successfully concluding current negotiations with foreign countries, a description of the current state of the economy and the principles underlying the administration's economic program—these are representative of the standard agenda items at cabinet meetings.

The most systematic use of the cabinet as a body occurred during the Eisenhower administration, when the cabinet met 230 times during Eisenhower's eight years as president, an average of 28.75 meetings each year. (This compares with 366 National Security Council meetings during those same years.) Both Gerald Ford and Jimmy Carter indicated that they planned on weekly cabinet meetings. This fairly soon shifted to every other week and then to once every four to six weeks.

During the Eisenhower years a small cabinet secretariat was established with responsibility for the cabinet meeting agendas, papers, and minutes, and for overseeing the implementation of any decisions made. Although the Eisenhower administration probably generated more documents relative to cabinet meetings than most administrations, the papers and minutes do not suggest that full cabinet meetings were where the action was. Options were not seriously discussed. The papers prepared were more for informational purposes than to help structure a debate. These were occasions for setting a general tone—conveying what was going on, what the general philosophy on budget matters was, and so on.

The cabinet itself has generally not had committees under the direction of a cabinet secretariat or cabinet office. Rather, all presidents have established various independently operating cabinet-level committees and councils.

Some councils have been created by statute (the National Security Council, the Energy Resources Council); others by executive order (the Advisory Board on Economic Growth and Stability, the Economic Policy Board); others by presidential memorandum (the Council on Economic Policy, the Agricultural Policy Committee); others by letter (the Council on Foreign Economic Policy); and some merely by mention in a presidential speech (the Cabinet Committee on Export Expansion).

The evolution of councils and committees dealing with economic policy issues reveals some interesting patterns. Dwight D. Eisenhower early in his administration created, at the urging of Arthur Burns, the Advisory Board on Economic Growth and Stability (ABEGS) as essentially a committee advisory to the CEA. It was designed as a forum at which the thinking on economic policy of the various departments and agencies could be compared and coordinated. It originally consisted of eight cabinet-level departments and agencies and was subsequently expanded to ten.

A year and a half later ABEGS was joined by another high-level interagency body, the Council on Foreign Economic Policy, which also met regularly to discuss and coordinate foreign economic policy issues. These two bodies remained active for the remainder of the Eisenhower years. They were joined by other committees—the Cabinet Committee on Small Business, the Trade Policy Committee, the Committee for the Rural Development Program, the Committee on Government Activities Affecting Prices and Costs, the Cabinet Committee on Price Stability for Economic Growth (chaired by the vice-president), the President's Special Committee on Financial Policies for Postattack Operations, the Interdepartmental Committee to Coordinate Federal Urban Area Assistance Programs, to name just a few.

John F. Kennedy, who considered the Eisenhower decision-making process too highly structured, not only quickly dismantled the National Security Council apparatus, but also abolished ABEGS and the Council on Foreign Economic Policy. He encouraged less formal arrangements instead, and several new committees were created in 1961 to deal with specific economic problems. These ranged from an ad hoc committee on housing credit to a White House committee on small business; from an advisory committee on labor-management policy to "new machinery for interagency cooperation in formulating fiscal estimates and policies"—later referred to as the "Troika," consisting of the chairman of the CEA, the secretary of the treasury, and the director of the Budget Bureau. An Interdepartmental Committee of Under Secretaries on Foreign Economic Policy and informal arrangements under the direction of Carl Kaysen, deputy special assistant to the president for national security affairs, handled most foreign economic policy issues other than monetary affairs. On the domestic side, the Troika was joined by the broader Cabinet Committee on Economic Growth, which was established in August 1962 and included the secretaries of treasury, commerce, and labor, the Budget Bureau director, and the chairman of the CEA.

Under Lyndon Johnson, the Troika and the Quadriad (the Troika plus the chairman of the Federal Reserve Board) continued to meet regularly and to formally undertake every three months a forecast of the economy that was sent to the president and personally reviewed with him if the Troika members felt some action was needed. Interestingly, these were consensus memorandums hammered out so that all three members could feel comfortable signing them.

Richard Nixon took office in 1969 determined to establish a more formal and more systematic approach to policy development. The National Security Council staff was enlarged, and the committee structure that supported it was expanded. Moreover, Nixon created an Urban Affairs Council, a Rural Affairs Council, and a Cabinet Committee on Economic Policy (established by executive order on January 24, 1969) chaired by himself and including the vice-president; the secretaries of the treasury, agriculture, commerce, labor, housing and urban development; the counselors to the president (Burns and Moynihan); the director of the Budget Bureau; the deputy under secretary of state for economic affairs; and the chairman of the CEA. These committees were to be the principal mechanisms for shaping administration policies. In January 1971 they were joined by another cabinet-level body, the Council on International Economic Policy (CIEP).

But Nixon was never very happy with this phalanx of committees and, over time, met with them less and less frequently. His appointment of John Connally in December 1970 as secretary of the treasury marked the second phase in Nixon economic policymaking. Nixon selected Connally in part because he wanted an economic czar to whom he could comfortably delegate most economic policy decisions. In Connally he found the czar he wanted. Formerly the meetings of the Troika, held roughly every other week, rotated among the offices of the three leading officials. Connally announced shortly after his arrival that henceforth they would be held at the Treasury Department. He subsequently was publicly designated by the president as the administration's chief spokesman on economic policy matters.

Connally was succeeded in the spring of 1972 by George Shultz, formerly secretary of labor and director of the Office of Management and Budget. Shultz held the same title as Connally, but by temperament was more collegial in his approach. In January 1973, he was appointed assistant to the president for economic affairs (in addition to his treasury portfolio) and made chairman of a cabinet-level Council on Economic Policy designed to coordinate all economic policy decision making. The council formally met infrequently, but Shultz personally succeeded in presiding over a process that involved most senior administration officials in issues that affected their interests.

As Shultz prepared to leave government in the spring of 1974 Nixon faced the choice of his successor. William Simon, Shultz's deputy at the treasury and the energy czar, and Roy Ash, director of the Office of Management and Budget, were both anxious to succeed Shultz as the administration's leading economic figure. Rather than choose between them, Nixon selected Kenneth Rush, deputy secretary of state, as his counselor for economic affairs, making him chairman of most of the interagency economic committees.

Within weeks, Nixon had resigned and Gerald Ford had replaced the Nixon machinery with a new Economic Policy Board, chaired by the secretary of the treasury, but managed by an assistant to the president for economic affairs, designed to coordinate both foreign and domestic economic policy.

Two and a half years later, Jimmy Carter abolished the Economic Policy Board and created an Economic Policy Group (EPG), initially cochaired by the secretary of the treasury and the chairman of the CEA. Although the EPG existed throughout the Carter administration, its influence at the White House and with the president waxed and waned. Frequently, it struggled unsuccessfully with the Domestic Policy Staff for control of issues having a major impact on the economy. The EPG, with no firm White House base, was seldom a match for the relatively large Domestic Policy Staff—approximately seventy staff members, including twenty-five to thirty professionals—and the president's domestic policy assistant, Stuart Eizenstat. A regular channel and predictable pattern for handling major economic issues never emerged.

This thumbnail sketch of economic policymaking arrangements in the last six administrations sheds some light on the role of interdepartmental committees. There has been no real counterpart in economic policy to the National Security Council staff in foreign policy. The CEA, which was established at approximately the same time, is not an interdepartmental council, nor does its charter include coordinating advice to the president on economic policy issues. Some broad-based committees, dealing with all issues in a general policy area, have been created in every administration—some formally, others informally. They have generally been created by executive order or presidential memorandum, rarely by statute.

Most administrations have had separate cabinet-level committees or councils to deal with foreign and domestic economic policy issues. Most councils or committees have not survived from administration to administration. The narrowly focused National Advisory Council on International Financial and Monetary Problems (NAC) and the informal Troika and Quadriad arrangements are exceptions. Moreover, virtually every administration has created a number of cabinet committees to deal with specific issues. They have tended to proliferate over time for several reasons: (1) Creation of a new council or cabinet-level committee reporting directly to the president demonstrates presidential concern and action both to the participants and to the public; (2) it may help soothe the bruised feelings of a specific constituency (the March 1976 creation of the Agricultural Policy Committee, chaired by the secretary of agriculture, was a symbolic action calculated to improve the president's sagging popularity in the farm community); (3) most presidents view such groups as inexpensive ways of building political support and demonstrating some movement in addressing a problem; and (4) often these groups are the work of a skillful entrepreneur within an administration.

These committees have operated with little overall direction. When Gerald Ford succeeded Richard Nixon as president he instructed William Seidman, his assistant for administration, to attend any cabinet-level meetings relating to economic policy. Seidman set about trying to find out what committees existed and where they were meeting. After asking OMB and the Treasury Department independently to prepare lists of cabinet-level committees dealing with economic policy issues, he discovered that there were a score of such committees.

Most of these committees have been chaired by the department or agency that is seen as having lead responsibility for the problem. The U.S. trade representative chairs the Trade Policy Committee; the Treasury Department chairs the NAC; OMB chairs the interagency committee on PL-480 allocations.

Few of these committees have had direct access to the president. Most have quickly become in effect subcabinet-level committees; cabinet officers do not attend the meetings. The Economic Policy Board, which met 520 times at the cabinet level in two and a quarter years, averaging almost 5 meetings each week, and which President Ford used to make virtually all his economic policy decisions, was an exception to this pattern.

In the place of genuinely effective formal structures, most administrations have evolved a set of informal relationships among the leading officials. A version of the Troika has existed in every administration over the past quarter century. A rough division of labor between the three principal agencies has generally held. Treasury has provided revenue estimates, the Office of Management and Budget federal spending estimates, and the CEA forecasts of the future pattern of economic activity. For the most part, other agencies within the federal government have been, or were for many years, effectively excluded from Troika deliberations and from macroeconomic policy issues. Labor, commerce, and other departments viewed as "constituency-oriented" by Troika members did not play a major role. But in the 1970s this pattern began to shift as departments and agencies throughout the executive branch developed new internal capacities. The number of professional economists increased in virtually all departments. One recent senior administration official, who returned to government after more than a decade, described the change that had occurred:

> In the 1960's there were a lot of people who would have liked to get into the game but just did not have the staff. They were unsupported and when you weren't supported, you couldn't carry the issue. Nobody had a group of economists to evaluate all these issues for them. CEA had a monopoly on it along with a few people at the Treasury. What has changed today is that every agency has an economic policy and planning group and it is not easy to tear their arguments apart. CEA cannot blow people out of the water with the depth of its analysis like it could in the 1960's. Few people understood what the term "multiplier" meant in the 1960's much less were able to argue with CEA's arguments about a tax policy to stimulate the economy. When CEA said the effect of a specific tax action on investment was such-and-such there wasn't any other agency doing its own empirical work to argue with it. But now, Treasury may say, "No, it's Y." and Labor, "It's Z." The Labor Department has turned their economic policy planning group into a mini-CEA. There is no issue that they don't regard as absolutely vital.

In surveying economic policymaking patterns over the past thirty years, one finds that interagency committees and groups have played a major role in organizing advice to the president on specific issues, but that presidents have generally not relied principally on general-purpose, formal entities. More frequently, they have relied on a trusted adviser or group of advisers, settling many issues bilaterally with the interested parties. The increasing complexity of the economic policy arena and the growing interest and capability of departments and agencies to influence a wide range of economic policy issues, foreign and domestic, represents a challenge to this traditional pattern. This is particularly true for those concerned with developing a coherent and integrated administration program.

A White House Assistant for Economic Policy

Reliance on senior White House aides with responsibility for economic policy has varied greatly from administration to administration. The Eisenhower White House had, first, Arthur Burns (before the Council of Economic Advisers was reconstituted and Burns was named as its chairman), then Gabriel Hague and Don Paarlberg. The Kennedy administration had no senior official whose principal duties were economic policy matters, although Theordore Sorensen, White House counsel, coordinated some economic policy issues and attended the sessions of the Troika with the president. On the foreign economic policy side, Carl Kaysen coordinated several issues as McGeorge Bundy's deputy at the NSC. In the Johnson administration Joseph Califano played a similar role to that of Sorenson in the Kennedy years, and Francis Bator a similar role to that played by Kaysen.

Richard Nixon did not initially appoint a senior White House official to deal with economic policy issues, although Arthur Burns as counselor to the president with cabinet rank actively participated in White House economic policy discussions. In 1970 Burns was appointed chairman of the Board of Governors of the Federal Reserve System. It was not until January 1973 that a small White House economic policy office was established and Treasury Secretary George Shultz was given a second hat and a small West Wing outpost as assistant to the president for economic affairs. Following Shultz's departure in the spring of 1974, Kenneth Rush was appointed counselor to the president for economic affairs and chairman of most of the major economic policy committees, including the Council on International Economic Policy and the Council on Economic Policy.

When Gerald Ford became president, he appointed L. William Seidman as assistant to the president for economic affairs and as executive director of the Economic Policy Board. Apart from Rush's brief tenure, this was the first time that a White House economic assistant had been given responsibility for managing the process of policy development on economic issues. Hague and Paarlberg during the Eisenhower administration were responsible for handling many day-to-day issues for the president, but they did not principally coordinate interagency processes.

Jimmy Carter made the explicit decision at the outset of his administration not to appoint a White House assistant for economic policy (a precondition for Charles Shultze's accepting the CEA chairmanship). The Economic Policy Group replaced the Economic Policy Board; the secretary of the Treasury and the chairman of the CEA were named cochairmen; and the executive director who was ultimately appointed had neither a White House office nor a White House title. Subsequently, Carter named first Robert Strauss and later Alfred Kahn as his inflation adviser and as chairman of the Council on Wage and Price Stability, but they were not given responsibility for managing an interagency process, although they sat on the Economic Policy Group Steering Committee and did have reasonable access to the president.

A somewhat different pattern has existed for dealing with foreign economic policy issues, which have frequently been treated apart from domestic economic policy problems. Joseph Dodge and Clarence Randall served as chairmen of the Council on Foreign Economic Policy during the Eisenhower administration and simultaneously held the title of special assistant to the president. Likewise, Carl Kaysen and Francis Bator held the title of deputy special assistant to the president for national security affairs while serving on the Bundy and Rostow National Security Council staffs. Unlike Randall, who had little personal contact with the president, Kaysen and Bator had a good deal of access to Kennedy and Johnson. Peter Peterson and Peter Flanigan also held White House staff titles while serving as executive directors of the Council on International Economic Policy. During the Carter administration, Ambassador Henry Owen managed preparations for the annual international economic summit conferences and coordinated some other foreign economic policy issues. He and his small staff were technically part of the larger National Security Council staff.

In summary, presidents have generally not relied heavily on White House economic policy assistants to organize the pattern of economic advice and decision making to the same degree that they have for national security affairs (Cutler, Bundy, Rostow, Kissinger, Scowcroft, and Brzezinski) or domestic affairs (Sorensen, Califano, Ehrlichman, Cole, Cannon, and Eizenstat). Most have handled day-to-day concerns rather than overseeing a policy development process.

Issues and Alternatives

The Council of Economic Advisers has performed a valuable function for the president: introducing the viewpoints of professional economists, detached from departmental perspectives or operational responsibilities, into his deliberations concerning economic issues. There is a general consensus that the CEA should remain relatively modest in size (three members and fifteen to eighteen professionals staff), that it should avoid administrative responsibilities, and that it should not have the principal responsibility for policy coordination. Three issues concerning the president and economic policy decision making, however, merit consideration.

Issue 1: Developing Coherent Economic Policies

The first issue concerns the means for coordinating policy advice and achieving policy coherence. The president must seek to integrate policy. The aggregate of microeconomic and sectoral decisions can have a tremendous impact on the president's ability to influence the pattern of overall economic activity. Some machinery is needed to mesh macro and micro concerns. There are at least four broad alternative ways of achieving such coordination and integration.

Option One: Creating a Super Department. Many countries have a department of economic affairs or a finance ministry that combines in one what is normally performed by the U.S. Treasury Department, the Office of

Management and Budget, and the Council of Economic Advisers. One of the central criticisms made by students of federal organization is that departments are too closely tied to particular constituencies and special interests. The recommended solution is creating super departments with comprehensive interests that therefore will be able to resist the pleas of special interests. In 1964 the President's Task Force on Government Organization recommended creating a department of labor and commerce. In 1967 the Heineman Task Force report made a similar proposal. In 1970, the President's Advisory Council on Executive Organization (the Ash Council) recommended that "four major executive departments which handle highly interdependent economic matters: Commerce, Labor, Agriculture, and Transportation" be combined into a department of economic affairs. Richard Nixon, in his State of the Union address on January 22, 1971, proposed a sweeping reorganization of the executive branch, calling for four new super departments to join the four "inner cabinet" departments — state, defense, treasury, and justice.[12]

Proponents of the large-department concept point to several potential advantages. First, to the extent that those at the top of such departments exercise effective control of the department's activities, such a department would aid in the integration of policy. Those "who deal with common or closely related problems would work together in the same organizational framework." The department "would be given a mission broad enough so that it could set comprehensive policy directions and resolve internally the policy conflicts which are most likely to arise."[13] As the Ash Council pointed out in its report: "The present organizational structure encourages fragmentation when comprehensive responses to social and economic problems are needed. Problems are defined to fit within the limits of organizational authority, resulting in piecemeal approaches to their solutions by separate departments and agencies."

Second, it would help the president provide overall direction to economic policy development. In Nixon's view: "As this single new Department joined the Treasury Department, the Council of Economic Advisers and the Federal Reserve Board in shaping economic policy, it would speak with a stronger voice and would offer a more effective, more highly integrated viewpoint than four different departments can possibly do at present."[14] Moreover, when the responsibility for realizing basic objectives is clearly focused in a specific governmental unit, that department can be held accountable for achieving them.

Finally, a large, comprehensive department could also ease the president's decision-making burden. "Decisionmaking responsibility is often shifted to the Executive Office of the President because no official at the departmental level has the authority to decide the issues."[15] Thus, it may help in pushing some problems away from the president. As one seasoned Executive Office veteran remarked: "Our difficulty is that we clutch tightly to us every problem that appears on the horizon."

There are several potential advantages — greater concentration of authority to resolve problems before they reach the president, focused responsibility and thereby enhanced accountability, a greater likelihood of comprehensive rather than piecemeal approaches to policy problems, and an easing of the decision-making burden on the president, consistent with the concept of an "economizing presidency" — but the concept of a super economic department has several limitations.

Many who press for the larger and more comprehensive executive departments do so in the belief that consolidation will undermine narrow departmental perspectives. Yet there is reason to question whether aggregating responsibilities within larger entities will produce the desired effect. Few would argue that the size and scope of the Department of Defense or the Department of Health, Education, and Welfare eliminated, or even significantly reduced, the power of special interests and specific constituencies. Aggregating functions into larger departments may transfer the resolution of certain disputes and the weighing of certain trade-offs from the White House to the office of the departmental secretary, but competing narrow interests remain. Consolidation may result in fewer major decisions naturally flowing to the White House, with no guarantee that the president's interests will prevail in those decisions made at the departmental level. From the president's vantage point, even large consolidated departments will have a different outlook, perspective, and constituency from his. Moreover, as problems become more complex, it is increasingly difficult to concentrate authority in one place without the entity soon looking like the entire executive branch.

Option Two: Designating a Super Secretary or Czar. As an alternative to the creation of a comprehensive department of economic affairs, the president might either designate one cabinet official as a super secretary for economic affairs or effectively delegate responsibility for economic policy decisions to a czar.

John Connally, as treasury secretary, had a public and private mandate from the president that extended well beyond his treasury portfolio. Connally used this grant to dominate economic policy decision making. As he explained his relationship to the president:

> Most of the meetings that I had with the President were one-on-one. In the economic field, he made it clear that I was his chief economic adviser. Throughout my entire time there, it was a situation in which he clearly delegated the authority to me. I kept in constant contact with George Shultz, with

Paul McCracken, with Arthur [Burns]. When we had all these meetings in Rome and London and Washington on the international monetary currency exchange rates, we were the only people who had any authority to do anything. There wasn't a finance minister in the room in any of those meetings, in my judgment, that could commit to anything. But the President had clearly said to me, "Just go ahead and do what you think you have to do." He just gave me almost unlimited authority and delegation of authority. Of course, I kept him fully informed all the way along.[16]

Later, unable to obtain favorable congressional action on his departmental reorganization proposals, President Nixon briefly instituted a system of super secretaries. Four cabinet secretaries were designated as super secretaries, with offices in the Old Executive Office Building, to coordinate the activities within their jurisdictions, which were similar to the four major departments proposed earlier. The experiment was short-lived. One of the super secretaries related that within three months after his designation, following a cabinet meeting the day after the resignations of H. R. Haldeman and John D. Ehrlichman, he was told that the concept had been scrapped.

The czar approach has many of the same potential advantages as the super department approach—resolving disputes before they reach the president, concentrating responsibility and hence accountability, and clarifying the public perception of who speaks for the administration (shortly after taking office, Connally was officially designated as the chief administration spokesman on economic policy matters). Moreover, it may be congenial to a president who has limited interest in economic policy questions and is anxious to delegate to one individual.

But there are also problems. It is perhaps even more difficult to concentrate power in a czar than to effectively consolidate power under a super department. Bits and pieces of economic policy responsibility are scattered throughout the federal government because they are linked to other important governmental responsibilities. Decentralization of operating responsibilities will remain a central fact of life; this presents a formidable challenge to concentrating authority in any one set of hands. Moreover, the czar approach depends heavily on the person selected. If he is to have any opportunity for success he must not only enjoy the confidence of the president, but he must be perceived by other department and agency heads, external groups, the press, and the Congress as having the clout and the powers of persuasion to be truly first among equals.

Thus far we have identified several difficulties with the super department and super secretary approaches. But a capacity for central oversight is badly needed. There is a need to raise issues to the presidential level when his personal decision is desirable and to ensure that he receives the views of his senior advisers whose responsibilities are most relevant to the issue.

Option Three: Creating a National Economic Council Staff. One response to the parochialism with which executive branch departments are frequently charged would be to create a centralized White House staff similar to the Nixon-Kissinger NSC or the Nixon-Ehrlichman Domestic Council staffs. Such a staff would be large enough—perhaps forty or fifty professionals—that it could not only manage the flow of day-to-day communications between economic departments and the president, but could also pull the strands of a policy problem together and provide an assessment of the relevant information and alternatives.

As Alexander George has pointed out, a centralized management approach sees the president as a "unitary rational decision maker, shielded from raw disagreements over policy."[17] This approach gives primary responsibility to the president's Executive Office and immediate staff. It emphasizes careful, systematic examination of policy questions, with control vested in individuals familiar with the president and his views. Executive branch departments and agencies might have substantial input on particular issues but would generally play a distinctly secondary role, as centralized management is designed to overcome what is viewed as departmental parochialism and inertia.

Such a staff could increase the president's control over the policymaking process, raise issues for his attention that might not otherwise reach the White House, and increase his likelihood of controlling the timing and announcement of a new policy or initiative, but a large centralized management staff would also involve substantial costs and risks for the president. Heavy reliance on his immediate staff would inevitably undermine morale and initiative in departments and agencies. Moreover, the objectivity of a presidentially oriented staff may be an illusion if the staff ends up mirroring and reinforcing perceived presidential inclinations. It cannot mobilize the same resources nor reflect the range of concerns that exist in departments and agencies. Implementing a large number of issues requires the cooperation of departments and agencies who will withhold it if they feel alienated. Thus, centralized management widens the gulf between policy formulation and implementation and the gulf between the president and his executive branch.

Option Four: Establishing a Cabinet-Level Multiple Advocacy Council. A fourth alternative would be to establish a cabinet-level body designed to bring together regularly the administration's leading economic policy officials to advise the president on a broad range of economic policy issues. The core of such a collegial enterprise would be the three elements of the Troika (treasury, OMB, and the CEA), but its mandate would extend well beyond the issues traditionally considered by the Troika. It could include, as part of the core group, other leading administration officials – the secretaries of state, commerce, and labor, for example. Whatever the size of the core group, its deliberations would include representatives from all departments and agencies that had a legitimate interest in an issue under discussion. This group of officials would have collective responsibility for advising the president on all major economic policy issues. Its thrust would be to bring departments to see their responsibilities in a broader setting. Its purpose would be to mobilize rather than to transcend the resources of departments and agencies. Such an approach would involve combining the principles of multiple advocacy (that the president should be exposed to competing arguments and viewpoints made by the advocates themselves rather than having viewpoints filtered through a staff) and collegiality (a continuity among advisers who share responsibility with the president for policy development over a broad area).

There are many limitations of such a system in practice. Disparities in resources, talent, and abilities among the advocates can distort the process. As Theodore Sorensen has observed: "The most formidable debater is not necessarily the most informed, and the most reticent may sometimes be the wisest."[18] A genuine competition of ideas may be undermined if one or more advocates consistently dominate the process because of superior skills and resources. Moreover, there is no guarantee that the advocates will represent all viable policy alternatives and not merely lowest-common-denominator recommendations. Group norms that stifle creativity and reflect a single ideology may emerge. Such a system can consume enormous amounts of time, it runs the risk of leaks on sensitive issues, it can force a large number of decisions to the top, and it can weaken the ability of senior executives responsible for particular policy areas to "deliver" on commitments to their constituencies and to the Congress.

No structure can consistently transcend the abilities and limitations of individual actors. But many of the collegial experiments in providing policy advice to the president have been undermined by structural deficiencies. Several organizational guidelines can help minimize the potential limitations of such a system in practice.

Unquestionably, the council or committee's effectiveness depends on its having the president's imprimatur. Departments and agencies must perceive it as the president's vehicle. If he permits individual officials to consistently circumvent the collegial process, departments will cease to take it seriously. Thus, such a system depends heavily on the president's commitment to it.

Equally important, an "honest broker" or process manager should control the council's operations. He must be perceived as dispensing due process. He should not have other, competing responsibilities. He must be intelligent enough to be considered a peer by his colleagues, and he must enjoy the president's confidence. He should find his satisfaction in pulling the strands of a problem together rather than in driving the process toward a particular outcome. In seeking a balanced presentation to the president he must be willing and able to reach for advocacy as an instrument of brokerage rather than undertaking brokerage because he is told to do so. He should have what the Brownlow Committee called "a passion for anonymity."

The staff for such a council should be small and should consist of generalists. A large staff can exercise greater quality control, but invariably such staffs have become specialized, have tended to ignore departments and agencies (and are viewed as competitors by departmental staffs), and are tempted to circumvent the council's decision-making process themselves.

Such a council should meet regularly and operate at the cabinet level. Its clout will depend on the capacity of its members to speak authoritatively for their department or agency. If given responsibility for advising the president over a broad policy area, the council could help ensure that a comprehensive approach is taken to a wide range of policy problems, that the president is not left to integrate interrelated issues on his own, and that senior departmental officials are likely to view problems in a framework that transcends their departmental responsibilities.

Multiple advocacy is a difficult system to operate. Its success is contingent on consistent presidential support. Powerful officials with access to the president may attempt to circumvent the collegial process to advance a particular interest. Multiple advocacy depends on having the "right" people to manage it. The other participants must view them as fair and evenhanded in their coordination of policy development. The necessary combination of skills that an honest broker needs are frequently not found in those people most closely associated with presidential candidates. And there are often powerful personal factors and political forces that guide a president-elect in the selection of his immediate staff. These people will have the most decisive influence on organizing the pattern of advice he receives. In short, such a system depends on the president's recognizing its value, appointing individuals with the requisite abilities (and temperament) as the managers of his policy development process, and then demonstrating his commitment to such a system by not allowing individual officials to circumvent it.

Issue Two: The Relationship of Foreign and
Domestic Economic Policy Formulation

For most of the past thirty years, different processes have existed for considering foreign and domestic economic policy issues. Parallel cabinet-level committees have often existed—the Council on Foreign Economic Policy and ABEGS, the Council on International Economic Policy, and the

Cabinet Committee on Economic Policy—and the most continuous informal arrangements, the Troika and the Quadriad, have concentrated almost
exclusively on domestic economic policy questions. Not until the Nixon
Council on Economic Policy under George Shultz and the Ford Economic
Policy Board have foreign and domestic economic policy questions been
considered regularly by a single entity.

The creation of such bodies as the Council on Foreign Economic Policy
and the Council on International Economic Policy has sprung from the conviction that international economic policy questions are important, merit
high-level attention, and are being insufficiently addressed under the existing machinery. While Carl Kaysen and Francis Bator were with the National Security Council during the 1960s they effectively coordinated a host
of foreign economic policy questions. But they were trained economists who
were given the mandate to do so by their superiors, Bundy and Rostow and
Presidents Kennedy and Johnson. Under the Kissinger and Scowcroft National Security Councils there was less interest in economic policy questions
and, on Kissinger's part, a reluctance to delegate. Moreover, CIEP never acquired the clout to fill the gap adequately. With the abolition of CIEP, international economic policy coordination was once again partially returned to
the NSC in the person of Henry Owen, who played a role similar to that of
Kaysen and Bator.

Yet the attraction of reestablishing a formal entity to advise the president
on foreign economic policy questions remains strong. There are two principal arguments against it. First, it is increasingly difficult to distinguish
issues as either foreign policy, domestic economic, or foreign economic problems. As argued earlier, the distinctions have blurred with the growing complexity of considerations and interests that presidents must weigh. Second,
the experiments with entities established to address foreign economic policy
issues suggest that they have not succeeded in consistently engaging the
president's interest and attention, largely because they have not been tied to
a regular work flow with which he must deal.

However, deciding against creating a separate channel to advise the president on foreign economic policy issues still leaves open the question of
whether foreign economic policy issues, to the extent that they can be identified, should be tied to the national security or the economic policy
machinery. There are good arguments in support of both positions, and an
excellent discussion of them can be found in I. M. Destler's *Making Foreign
Economic Policy*.[19] Destler argues, and I concur, that the substance and
politics of current foreign economic issues "encourage the conclusion that it
is more realistic to build their coordination around economic policy officials
and institutions." The substance of most foreign economic policy issues re-
lates more closely to domestic economic policy concerns than to foreign policy
ones. Moreover, senior foreign policy officials have generally been

able to effectively influence economic policymaking processes more easily than economic officials have been able to penetrate foreign policymaking processes.

Issue Three: A White House Economic Policy Assistant?

A third issue meriting consideration is whether the president should appoint an assistant for economic affairs. The positions of assistant to the president for national security affairs and assistant to the president for domestic policy now have a tradition extending back through at least four administrations, but the position of White House assistant for economic affairs is less solidly entrenched. The pattern over the past thirty years has been for Republican presidents to generally favor the idea and for Democratic presidents to consider the position unnecessary, although there is nothing partisan in the concept.

There is no compelling need for such an assistant to handle the day-to-day concerns of the president that are related to economic policy issues. Several administrations have demonstrated that a national security assistant and a domestic policy assistant, aided by adequate staffs, can handle most of the day-to-day responsibilities of keeping the president apprised of current developments.

The issue of a White House economic assistant hinges in large part on the type of integrating machinery, if any, that the president should establish. Creating a super department or delegating most economic policy decision-making authority to a czar reduces the need for a White House economic assistant. Establishing a national economic council staff or a cabinet-level economic policy entity would create a need for such a White House assistant: A relatively large centralized staff to shape alternatives for the president on economic policy issues would obviously need a senior official to oversee it. Experience with cabinet-level coordinating mechanisms suggests the usefulness of a White House–based assistant to manage the process unencumbered by departmental or agency responsibilities.

The potential for tension between a White House economic assistant and the chairman of the Council of Economic Advisers exists, but conceptually there is no necessary conflict. To the extent that the economic management process works well, it provides the CEA chairman and council members with the opportunity to become involved in presidential deliberations across a broad range of issues that transcend macroeconomic policy. A White House economic assistant can also share the work load and help reduce CEA involvement in many activities that are not central to its mission, such as personnel appointments, dealings with special-interest groups, and handling numerous small but nondeferrable items that the Office of the President cannot ignore.

The role of the CEA is to provide substantive economic advice and analysis. A White House assistant, responsible for managing the process of providing advice to the President, would have a coordinating, facilitating role. He need not become a major adviser with regard to substantive questions, and indeed doing so may well reduce his effectiveness as a coordinator. There is the risk that a White House economic assistant may acquire a taste for shaping policy outcomes to the extent that he becomes a regular competitor for the president's ear with the CEA chairman and other administration economic officials. But a White House assistant who tends to managing the policy development process could prove a great asset to his colleagues.

Presidents are inclined to devote their time and energies to those areas in which they have the greatest interest and in which they feel they have the greatest opportunity to influence events. Most presidents have spent disproportionate time on foreign policy matters, in part because of fewer domestic and congressional constraints, but also because their national security policymaking machinery has been relatively well developed. The National Security Council apparatus, for all its limitations, has generally produced high-quality products—issue papers and options memorandums—for presidential consumption.

Consistently engaging the interest of the president in shaping the major economic policies that his administration will pursue requires machinery that can effectively identify alternatives and generate quality analysis across a wide range of issues. The challenge of an unfavorable economic environment and the intertwining of foreign and domestic economic policy interests make it more crucial than ever that the president have the benefit of a structure that will enhance the prospects for developing coherent policies to address the economic problems facing the nation.

Notes

1. Clinton Rossiter, *The American Presidency* (New York: Harcourt Brace, 1956), p. 21.

2. *The Economic Report of the President* (Washington, D.C.: Government Printing Office, 1953).

3. Charles L. Schultze, *The Public Use of Private Interest* (Washington, D.C.: Brookings Institution, 1977), p. 9.

4. Testimony of William Lilley III and James C. Miller III before the Subcommittee on Economic Stabilization, Committee on Banking, Currency and Housing, U.S. House of Representatives, December 17, 1976. See also William Lilley III and James C. Miller III, "The New 'Social Regulation,'" *Public Interest* 47 (Spring 1977), p. 50.

5. See Peter J. Katzenstein, "International Interdependence: Some Long-Term Trends and Recent Changes," *International Organization* 29 (Autumn 1975), pp. 1021–1034.

6. These ratios are rapidly approaching those in Japan and the European Common Market as a group. C. Fred Bergsten and William R. Cline, "Increasing International Economic Interdependence: The Implications for Research," *American Economic Review* 66 (May 1976), p. 155.

7. Ibid.

8. Graham Allison and Peter Szanton, "Organizing for the Decade Ahead," in Henry Owen and Charles L. Schultze, eds., *Setting National Priorities: The Next Ten Years* (Washington, D.C.: Brookings Institution, 1976), p. 253.

9. As George Schultz and Kenneth Dam put it, the president "must have some way of balancing competing interest groups against one another while at the same time building a policy structure that can take account of broader considerations." *Economic Policy Beyond the Headlines* (Stanford, Calif.: Stanford Alumni Association, 1977), p. 5.

10. The chairman is an EL-II; the other two members are EL-IV's (EL is Executive Level in the federal job structure).

11. The position of vice-chairman of the council was abolished.

12. See *Papers Relating to the President's Departmental Reorganization Program* (Washington, D.C.: Government Printing Office, March 1971).

13. President's message, March 25, 1971, in ibid., p. 11.

14. Ibid, p. 18.

15. Ibid., p. 235.

16. Interview by the author, Cambridge, Mass., Fall 1979.

17. Alexander L. George, "The Case for Multiple Advocacy in Foreign Policy Making," *American Political Science Review* 66 (September 1972), p. 752.

18. Theodore Sorensen, *Decision Making in the White House*, (New York: Columbia University Press, 1963), p. 62.

19. I. M. Destler, *Making Foreign Economic Policy* (Washington, D.C.: Brookings Institution, 1980).

8

National Security I: Inventing a Process (1945–1960)

Anna Kasten Nelson

The Constitution, with characteristic brevity, mentions the president's diplomatic powers and role as commander in chief but gives no hint of how these functions are to be organized. For this nation's first hundred and fifty years, presidents, relying on their secretaries of state and war, improvised in various ways to meet the foreign threats that occurred periodically. To manage the international affairs of the United States seemed to require no enduring staff, organization, or procedures in the presidency.

This situation changed dramatically after 1940. The Second World War and the growing U.S. assumption of world responsibilities in the postwar period led a relatively small number of top policymakers to rethink the traditional ad hoc arrangements. Clearly it was necessary to invent some new method of bringing central coordination to bear on the continuing problem of "national security." The result of these efforts was the National Security Act of 1947. Like most legislation, this act was a compromise. It did not represent the views of its sponsors in all respects. And in subsequent years, changing circumstances and personalities altered national security management in unforeseen ways.

During the years 1945 to 1960, when the modern presidency as a relatively large bureaucratic institution was haltingly emerging, policymakers were struggling to define America's new role in the world. The two developments were in fact inextricably linked. Thus the 1947 National Security Act took the unprecedented step of establishing a council the sole function of which was (and is) to advise the president. Although participation in the National Security Council (NSC) and the council's operations have varied, the intended function of the NSC, as described by the 1947 act, has remained the same. It is "to advise the President with respect to the integration of domestic, foreign, and military policies relating to the national security" so that the military services and other agencies can "cooperate more effectively in matters involving national security."[1] One interpretation counted this new council arrangement a restriction on the presidency, a vote of no confidence in the results to be achieved by continuing to allow presidents to organize and manage national security problems in whatever way they might personally chose. By another interpretation, the new arrangement entrusted the president as no legislation had done before with an explicit and immense responsibility to coordinate all domestic, foreign, and military policies affecting the nation's security. By either reading, the National Security Council was a landmark in the development of the modern presidency.

However, the creation of the NSC was not only a manifestation of a changing presidency. It was also an organizational reflection of the cold war. The assumption underlying the concept of "national security policy" (a term coined in the 1940s) was that the United States was engaged in a long-term battle with the Soviet Union and the forces of world communism. Traditional foreign policy was no longer adequate in the postwar world; U.S. security now required a military and intelligence component. Determining national security policy included decisions on psychological strategy, intelligence and covert operations, the building of sophisticated weapons, such as hydrogen bombs or missiles, and the crucial budget decisions that pitted domestic against international demands.

Viewed from our own troubled era, the policies and presidencies of 1945–1960 have a reassuringly clear thrust. A closer examination of developments inside and atop the executive branch shows abundant confusion, miscalculation, and uncertainty about how to manage such a vital policy area; and yet there were certain constants during these years, too. Despite partisan differences, both Presidents Truman and Eisenhower resisted developments that would have created a staffing system in the White House much like the one that actually developed after 1960. And in both administrations, certain problems of coordinating national security policy seemed to be inherent, yielding to neither study nor reorganization. Between 1947 and 1960, these two presidents and their top aides, experimenting with an untried process, gradually developed a nebulous presidential advisory unit into the core of a White House–centered national security process.

An Uncertain Beginning

Ideas for the coordination of national security were stimulated by the "administrative chaos" of the Roosevelt administration.[2] Impressed by experience during World War II with the Combined Chiefs of Staff and the British Committee of Imperial Defense, General George C. Marshall and Secretary of the Navy James Forrestal advocated similar structures in the United States. Their efforts resulted in little more than the de facto creation of the Joint Chiefs of Staff and finally, late in 1944, a State-War-Navy Coordinating Committee (SWNCC) to improve communication between the United States military and the State Department.

The impetus for a formal and more permanent coordinating council gained much greater strength when President Truman turned to the postwar task of unifying the armed services. As former chairman of a Senate committee investigating operations of the national defense program during the war, the new president who succeeded F.D.R. in April 1945 had become a firm believer in the necessity of a unified department of national defense. Since the earliest days of the republic, the War and Navy Departments had been separate. The critical role of air power during the Second World War brought even greater fragmentation, as the army, navy, and the marines each created separate air forces. As early as 1943 General of the Army George Marshall began proposing a single department for war. Navy Secretary Forrestal also began working behind the scenes to create some "machinery" similar to the British system. As Forrestal put it, without such machinery for "coordinated and focused government action," the United States would not be able to deal with the "problems and relationships arising during the postwar period."[3] To Forrestal, the new president's desire to unify the military establishment provided an opportunity to create this new machinery.

The Unification Issue and the NSC

President Truman proposed the unification of the armed services in a special message to Congress on December 19, 1945. A storm of controversy raged for the next year and a half until the final passage of the National Security Act in July 1947. As Robert Donovan has written, the unification issue "aroused passion in Washington because it affected careers, pride, tradition, the roles of air, sea, and land power, political influence and allocation of funds among the military services."[4] The National Security Council was a product of this controversy. Rather than the carefully conceived body its later prominence would indicate, the NSC was a creature of compromise. Its inclusion in the National Security Act of 1947 was part of the price Truman had to pay to gain support within his own administration for his unification proposal.

The first mention of a council originated in a study prepared for Secretary Forrestal in the summer of 1945. The navy, although acknowledging the need for coordination, objected to the ramifications of a single defense department. Aside from the desire to keep its air force intact, it objected to any system that would deprive the navy secretary of his seat in the cabinet and of direct access to the president.

Seeking an alternative to the army plan for unification, Forrestal asked a friend and former business associate, Ferdinand Eberstadt, to study the effect of unification on national security and recommend the form of government organization that would be most effective in protecting the country. In the report he submitted to Forrestal in September 1945, Eberstadt proposed several mechanisms for policy coordination: a cabinet secretariat; a national security council composed of representatives from state, war, and navy and chaired by the president; a national security resources board to coordinate information necessary for industrial mobilization; and a central intelligence agency. Although the proposal for a national security council was a clear reflection of Forrestal's earlier support for such a coordinating council, under the Eberstadt plan it was also a necessary component of a decentralized military establishment that would rely upon interdepartmental committees rather than on departmental unification. The national security council would be the most important committee of all, coordinating policy while still assuring access to the president by independent secretaries of the military services.

There was no necessity for a national security council in the proposal sent to Congress by President Truman, which suggested the unification of the armed services into a single department with a single chief of staff. But largely because of the personal influence of Secretary Forrestal, the Senate subcommittee that fashioned the president's message into a bill—and every other serious proposal for unification placed before the Congress until the final act was signed—included the idea of a coordinating council composed of the secretaries of state, army, navy, and air force.

Finally, Truman accepted the idea of a council as part of the compromise necessary to gain Navy Department support for unification. The council would allow the service secretaries to present personally their points of view to the president without their inclusion in the cabinet. The council was a small price to pay for Forrestal's support of a single civilian head for the armed services.

Acceptance of the concept of a council did not, however, mean agreement among members of Congress, the military establishment, and the presidential staff on the nature of the council. Various aspects of the projected council as it emerged from legislative proposals particularly worried analysts in the Bureau of the Budget. A council with statutory power threatened to undermine the president's unique position in the decision-making process. Under the direction of Harold Smith, the Bureau of the Budget (BOB) had become the institutional heart of the Executive Office of the President.

Smith's successor, James Webb, made the bureau doubly valuable to President Truman by expanding its role in the development of the president's legislative program and by providing the small White House staff with experts and analysts from the bureau's staff. Under Webb's direction, Truman grew to trust advice given by the bureau above that of agencies seeking support for their more parochial interests. As Webb has noted, "he thought we really were there to serve him as the President" and the institution of the Presidency.[5] Therefore Truman's White House aides worked carefully with staff from the bureau to redraft the proposals, rewriting a phrase here, eliminating another there. The result was to transform the Forrestal and Eberstadt proposals for a rather precisely defined council with statutory duties and an executive director confirmed by the Senate into the present National Security Council—a purely advisory group with no authoritative functions in statute and a staff appointed at the sole discretion of the president.[6]

Aside from the rather special concerns of the White House staff, the creation of the NSC was of minimal interest to those caught up in the long battle over unification. That part of the testimony before the Senate Armed Services Committee that did not emphasize the effect of the legislation on the military establishment concerned itself with the impact of an intelligence agency on the intelligence-gathering function of the government. There was very little mention of the NSC and, with one exception, nothing to indicate that within two decades the NSC would become one of the principal instruments of U.S. foreign policy.

Only Secretary George C. Marshall seemed to understand the possible implications of the council for future foreign policy. Although the State Department was obviously not involved in a bill to reorganize the military establishment, Marshall expressed his concerns to the president in early 1947 when the legislative drafts still described a council with statutory powers and responsibilities. Such a council, Marshall wrote, would introduce "fundamental changes in the entire question of foreign relations." Even though the final act described a weaker, purely advisory council, Marshall's analysis was essentially correct.[7]

The Struggle for Control

The ambiguous language of the act in describing the NSC ensured a first step toward unification of the military services, but provided little guidance on the establishment of such a council. Except for the list of statutory members, the White House staff had succeeded in eliminating specifics. Thus, to implement the function of advising the president, the council was to "assess and appraise the objectives, commitments, and risks of the United States in relation to our actual and potential military power" and to consider policies "of common interest to the departments and agencies" concerned with national security. This language masked two completely different views of the council held by the defense establishment, on the one hand, and the Budget Bureau, on the other. Within ten days after the passage of the act, both Forrestal and Webb had developed quite different plans for the new NSC.

Forrestal's plan emerged from a meeting held in his conference room on August 4, 1947. Ferdinand Eberstadt was among the participants, and Forrestal, it was noted, "participated in the meeting from time to time."[8] The defense group envisioned an NSC over which the president would rarely preside, as the major function of the council was to reduce the president's work load. For example, matters within the scope of policies already approved by the president would not need to be referred to him again. Therefore, one question to be decided was when the council "would recommend action to the individual departments and agencies, without first referring the matter to the President." Participants agreed that "it would seem to be appropriate for Mr. Forrestal's office to draft a suggested directive" for the president on the operation of the council.

The original view of Forrestal and Eberstadt that the council was a part of the defense establishment reappeared at this meeting in recommendations that the council and its staff be "housed as close as possible to the Secretary of Defense" and that the president clearly indicate at the first formal meeting of the NSC that the secretary of defense would preside over the meetings in his absence. It was, no doubt, the importance of the latter point that stimulated a memorandum from one of Forrestal's principal assistants, Marx Leva. The act, he wrote, provided that the "Secretary of Defense shall be the principal assistant to the President in all matters relating to the national security"; the comparable provision in the British organization for defense definitely named the minister of defense as deputy chairman of the committee; and the legislative history of the act indicated that the secretary of defense would "perform many functions—including that of presiding over the National Security Council—as the agent or alter ego of the President."[9]

Quite a different picture of the NSC emerged in a Budget Bureau memorandum that Webb sent to the president just one day later. Emphasizing the advisory roles of both the NSC and the National Security Resources Board (NSRB), the bureau's memo noted that the full-time staff of those two bodies constituted a "further enlargement of the Presidential staff." Webb advised the president to regard the executive secretary of the council as an administrative assistant. Presidential access to the executive secretary would not compromise his usefulness to the council "since the basic reason for the Council's existence is to advise and aid the President." The bureau therefore recommended that the secretariat of the council and the NSRB be housed in the Executive Office Building. The council and the board could become effective in assisting the president, it continued, "if organized and utilized in the proper manner," but the "proper manner" meant careful avoidance of circumscribing the ability of the president to make decisions freely. The president could take recommendations under advisement, but under no circumstances should he feel pressured to accept the advice of the council. In order to ensure the advisory nature of the council's actions, the memorandum urged the president to refrain "from attending the majority of Council meetings" and to designate the secretary of state as presiding officer in his place.[10] The bureau's plan, based perhaps upon conversations between Webb and the president, probably only reinforced Truman's own views by providing a workable alternative to the Forrestal plan. Truman's deep regard for Secretary of State Marshall would no doubt have precluded his acceptance of the defense secretary's predominance in any case.

Forrestal, however, continued to see the NSC as "an integral part of the national defense setup." Determined to ensure its success, he organized a practice session the day before the first meeting of the council. Nine members of the national military establishment and the new executive secretary of the NSC were called together to hear Under Secretary of State Robert Lovett discuss the situation in Italy "as something of a dry run for the following day's meeting."[11] As a measure of his continued commitment, Forrestal also played a very important role in initiating council projects until his resignation in 1949.

The appointment of Admiral Sidney Souers as the first executive secretary of the NSC was certainly a factor in Forrestal's active participation. Souers and Forrestal had met when both were bankers. When Souers was in Washington as an assistant director of naval intelligence plans in 1944, he was asked by Forrestal to serve on the Eberstadt Committee. Here, then, was a man Forrestal could trust even as Souers set about implementing a White House–oriented NSC. Souers was also extremely sensitive to the position of the State Department. For example, the first paper for the council was presented to the president by Acting Secretary of State Robert Lovett. The president informed Lovett of his approval, and Lovett in turn reported this to Souers. In a meeting between presidential adviser Clark Clifford and Admiral Souers, it was agreed that this was an "atrocious" procedure. The NSC required a more personal relationship between the president and the executive secretary, in spite of the State Department's predominance in foreign policy. Henceforth, all papers would be delivered to the president by Souers. Although a cautious Souers thought it might be proper for other members of the council to accompany him, Clifford convinced him that he should present the papers to the president alone. Thereafter, Souers would present two copies of council papers to the president, and Truman would indicate his approval or disapproval on one and keep the other. The executive secretary would then inform the members of the council of the president's decision.[12]

After this tentative beginning, Souers quickly established a role for himself and his staff within the Executive Office of the President. His perception of the NSC and of his role as executive secretary had a lasting effect upon national security policy in the White House.

The NSC in Action

The work process of the NSC began when a policy question was initiated by an NSC member. Souers would then check with the president to make sure that he wanted the NSC to consider the question. Souers shared Truman's view that, as the council's responsibility was to advise the president, at no time should the council force upon the president views or decisions that he had not requested. With the president's agreement, then, the working draft of a paper would be prepared. Normally this draft was prepared in the State Department by the Policy Planning Staff and then submitted to the NSC "staff." This staff was in fact a group of individuals from the lower echelons of each NSC member department. Coordination of this staff came from the State Department member.

After approval of the staff, the working paper was then returned for circulation to the offices concerned within each of the departments and agencies involved. Next the working draft would be considered by a staff of "consultants," individuals from senior levels representing each member of the NSC. If the consultants accepted the working draft, it would be circulated to council members and placed upon the council agenda. At this point, departments formed their positions on the matter, and the strategic military implications were referred to the Joint Chiefs of Staff (JCS). Finally, the council would consider the question, action would be taken, and the president, if he approved, would assign the responsibility for coordinating the implementation of the policy decision. Although Souers wrote that in at least one instance the NSC completed this process in one week, in fact the process generally took a matter of months.[13]

The substantive work of the NSC was done in the departments. Admiral Souers's staff performed the functions of a secretariat: circulating papers, preparing agendas, keeping the council advised of all items of business, reviewing the implementation of recommendations, and acting as the official channel between the council and other agencies.

Souers saw his role as that of "neutral coordinator," ensuring that the views of all the interested departments and agencies were reflected in the advice he gave the president. He had a keen understanding of the difficulties of simultaneously performing the tasks of national security adviser to the president and executive secretary of the NSC. The individual performing this role, he wrote, must be a "non-political confidant of the President." He should maintain continuous and intimate contact with the president, "be a trusted member of the President's immediate official family but should not be identified with his immediate staff of personal political advisers." Observing his own advice, Souers did not attend the nine o'clock staff meetings with the president, but instead saw Truman immediately after those meetings. Souers also put into practice his belief that the executive secretary was only a servant of the president and the members of the council. The executive secretary, he wrote, must be willing to be objective, to subordinate his personal views, and "forego publicity and personal aggrandizement" as he had neither the authority nor the responsibility of the president or council members.

It seems ironic that within months, the NSC, a creation of the defense establishment, came to be completely dominated by the State Department. Truman's sense of tradition as well as his deep respect for Secretary Marshall no doubt contributed, but there were also several institutional reasons for this dominance. An important factor was the dispersal of authority in the national military establishment, which resulted from the unification compromises. In fact, the secretary of defense had only general authority over the service departments. Each service secretary sat on the council, and together they could overrule the secretary of defense. Each member of the JCS answered to both the service secretary and the secretary of defense. There was, therefore, considerable confusion of authority within the defense establishment as opposed to the State Department. Even Secretary Forrestal could not overcome the institutional weakness inherent in the position of the secretary of defense.

A second reason was the result of the decision to keep the actual NSC staff as a small secretariat. Unwittingly, perhaps, this ensured the dominance of the State Department in the preparation of council papers. Several months before the passage of the National Security Act, Secretary of State Marshall had created within the State Department a staff to formulate and develop "long-term programs for the achievement of U.S. foreign policy objectives."[14] By September 1947, when the NSC was seeking departmental help in developing policy studies, this Policy Planning Staff (PPS) was in place. George Kennan, the director of the PPS, was the "consultant" from the State Department, and George Butler from the staff of the PPS was the "staff coordinator." Although the military establishment initiated as many studies as did the State Department, the latter—and specifically PPS—organized and wrote the papers and thus had a critical impact upon the council during the Truman administration.

In spite of repeated requests from the military establishment, the State

Department, under Kennan's influence, rejected the formulation of broad policy papers in favor of papers on very specific topics or specific countries. For example, at a meeting of the PPS on May 12, 1948, Kennan suggested the following subjects as "appropriate for decision by the National Security Council: Dhahran, Tsingtao, Austrian Treaty, Japan, Philippines, and Italian Colonies."[15] On the other hand, the reaction of the PPS to a National Security Council paper, "Position Of The United States With Respect To Soviet-Directed World Communism," was decidedly negative. This paper, dated May 19, 1947, began with broad analysis ("already Soviet-directed world communism has achieved alarming success in its drive toward conquest") and ended with sweeping conclusions (the United States should "encourage the formation of underground resistance movements in countries behind the iron curtain"). After six weeks of discussion and some rewriting, members of the State Department bureaus were still unimpressed with the paper, which was regarded as too general to be useful. Even though Kennan and his staff were aware that the "representatives of the military establishment felt strongly that some such paper as this should be adopted," they succeeded in temporarily removing the paper from the NSC agenda. Agendas and records of action of NSC meetings indicate that the State Department's approach dominated: Until 1949, most NSC papers were devoted to specific subjects.

From the very beginning, the process of preparing papers for policy decisions was very lengthy. Nothing more clearly illustrates this than the discussion of one of the original questions brought before the council, the possible consequences of removing American troops from Italy: If a communist republic were established in Northern Italy, should the United States encourage an invitation from the De Gasperi government to help the Italians reestablish their army so that they could resist communist domination? Lovett and Forrestal agreed that as neither the State Department nor the military services were equipped to evaluate the consequences of such a decision, it was a perfect example of the kind of problem to be brought before the NSC. Italy was the subject of the "dry run" of September 25 in Forrestal's office.

The PPS had already begun to prepare a paper on Italy, although the staff could not agree on certain important points, and the paper was unfinished when Lovett requested information from Kennan. Lovett nevertheless had material for his presentation to the first council meeting and noted that if alternatives were pondered in advance, then the quick decisions that might confront the United States in regard to Italy would not be made under the frenzy of last-minute crisis.

Fortunately, no quick decision was necessary. The PPS continued to discuss the paper on Italy at a meeting of September 30; the NSC began considering it in October; the State Department began clearing it in November;

and on December 15, the PPS was again considering revisions of the paper prior to a meeting of the working staff of the NSC. The forthcoming Italian election of April 18, 1948, prompted a revival of the Italian question in the PPS in March. Again a draft paper was prepared and sent to the NSC staff for discussion before being returned to the State Department. "The changed paper" was then considered by the "consultants" before going to the council—eight months after its initial consideration.

One cause for delay was the relationship between the PPS and the other bureaus in the State Department. Although papers would be written and approved by the planning staff before being sent to the NSC staff, they could not receive departmental approval until they had been cleared by the interested bureaus, which often disagreed with PPS positions. Finally, in March 1948, Souers's concern over the delays that plagued the process brought some changes. Geographical offices and bureaus were assured participation in the original preparation of papers by the PPS, but the preparation of NSC papers remained a lengthy process.

Continuing Uncertainty

The National Security Council had been in operation little more than a year when the Hoover Commission began its work on government reorganization. Two task forces, one on national security organization and another on foreign affairs, were created to study the NSC. The Foreign Affairs Task Force, reflecting the view of the State Department, saw the NSC as a well-run organization. Interviews with those staff members from the PPS who were most closely involved with the NSC produced few recommendations for change. There was not even much concern over the preponderance of the military, for at the staff level there did not seem to be a purely military or purely civilian view of the work of the council. The planning staff emphasized the view that the council should occupy itself with concrete problems and not abstract papers, but in general it was cautious and suggested to the members of the Hoover Commission that the council "meets a need in government planning" and that basic changes should await further experience.

On the other hand, the National Security Task Force, reflecting the views of the defense establishment, saw the NSC as the "keystone" of national security organization, but noted several deficiencies: It had not produced a comprehensive statement of long-range U.S. policies; it had not provided guidance on the 1950 budget; and it was not yet able to give the military the kind of guidance needed to judge the proper size of the armed forces for the needs of the nation. In addition, the desire to centralize the defense establishment led the task force to urge that only the secretary of defense (rather than the three service secretaries) sit with the council.[16]

In its final report, the Hoover Commission objected to the excessive number of military participants in the NSC and the designation of NSC members by statute. Both in its report on general management in the executive branch and in its report on foreign affairs, it emphasized the informal manner in which the president received staff assistance in the conduct of foreign affairs. The report on foreign affairs noted that the president needed machinery to bring him more competent, complete advice, as well as to handle the prompt resolution of interdepartmental disputes.

Amendments and Personalities. The 1949 amendments to the National Security Act that resulted from the Hoover Commission left the NSC largely untouched, apart from a slight revision in its membership. Significantly, the Congress refused to accept the Hoover Commission's conclusions that the council, as a purely advisory body to the president, should not have any statutory designation of members. Not only did Congress remove the service secretaries, it added the vice-president to the council and stipulated that others could be added only when appointed by the president with the advice and consent of the Senate. Having created the NSC, Congress seemed intent on keeping a hand in. Reorganization Plan number four, which further implemented the Hoover Commission report, made existing administrative practice official: The NSC and the NSRB were officially transferred to the Executive Office of the President.

These changes were largely cosmetic. Yet there was a decided change in the effectiveness of the NSC from January 1948 to the summer of 1949. As the Hoover Commission noted, the NSC was still little more than an interdepartmental committee with cabinet status. Its effectiveness was therefore highly dependent upon the structure of its member departments and the relationships between leading personalities in those departments.

Reorganization of the State Department, for example, shifted liaison work with the NSC from the PPS to the new deputy under secretary for substantive affairs. Members of the Policy Planning Staff still served on the NSC staff but no longer supplied the State Department's representative on the consultant level. This answered complaints within the department that the NSC received papers that had been completed without input from individual bureaus. It also shortened the time for State Department review and satisfied the desire of members of the PPS to return to "long-term" policy planning.

The 1949 amendments did change the character of the military establishment. The position of the civilian secretary of defense was strengthened, as he gained greater central authority over the three armed services within the new Department of Defense.

Organizationally, the NSC should have been strengthened by all these changes. Instead, it was weakened by the steadily deteriorating relationship throughout 1949 and early 1950 between Secretary of State Dean Acheson and Secretary of Defense Louis Johnson. Unfortunately, as the relationship between the two secretaries disintegrated, the council was further weakened by the departure of Admiral Souers in January 1950. Souers had played an important role in coordinating information, smoothing relationships, and serving the president as a staff assistant. James Lay, who replaced him as executive secretary, was competent as the director of the secretariat functions of the council, but regarded himself as a servant of the council rather than a staff assistant to the president. The situation was further complicated by the fact that Souers remained as a consultant to the president. His services in that role were intermittent, but his presence prevented anyone else from stepping into the vacuum.

The departure of George Kennan from the PPS was another important change. Aside from the changed relationship between the PPS and Acheson, who used it infrequently, Kennan and Acheson had basic policy differences. Kennan's departure and Acheson's belief in military preparedness cleared the way for the long-range appraisal studies that had long been desired by the military establishment. Secretary Johnson sought to formalize U.S. policy positions, and in May 1949, Souers was directing the NSC staff to prepare studies "assessing and appraising the implications for our security and the alternate courses of action open to us in those matters of major policy on which it is anticipated that the United States will be called upon to act." These studies, he added, should not recommend policy, but should furnish the comprehensive analysis as a basis for the preparation of policy statements.[17]

Although the 1949 amendments to the National Security Act had reduced the statutory membership of the council, the propensity of Secretary Johnson to bring numerous personnel from the Defense Department encouraged others to do the same. By early 1950 the meetings of the council had grown so large that more and more substantive work began to be done in ad hoc working groups outside the council framework. Ironically, by the time that President Truman was convinced that the NSC was an important mechanism, it had taken on the worst characteristics of government by committee.[18]

The Effects of War. The outbreak of war in Korea marked a turning point in the history of NSC, just as it signaled important changes in U.S. national security policy. This war represented precisely the set of circumstances foreseen by Forrestal and his supporters in the early days of the cold war. Here was a situation that required the most careful coordination of military and diplomatic affairs.

The Korean War and the reassessment of the military situation in Europe and elsewhere in the world required intimate cooperation between the

Defense Department, the State Department, and the Central Intelligence Agency (CIA), and Truman moved with alacrity to reorganize the NSC machinery for that purpose. On July 19, 1950, Truman wrote the members of the NSC that as a result of "the present international situation," he wished to discuss every policy matter concerning the national security within the NSC. Therefore, he directed the council to meet each week, with participation in the council meetings limited to fewer individuals to encourage free discussion. To lend his personal authority to the NSC process, Truman began to preside over the NSC meetings.[19]

Truman also asked each member of the council and the Secretary of the Treasury, the Joint Chiefs of Staff, and the CIA to nominate an individual from his agency to be a member of an NSC Senior Staff. The Senior Staff was to provide participation by people close enough to the department or agency heads to ensure proper staff work and implementation of NSC decisions. The consultants of the previous staff arrangement had devoted little time to NSC matters, largely approving or disapproving papers that had already been written. The Senior Staff (individuals at approximately the assistant secretary level) now began to meet at least twice a week and actively participate in NSC staff activities. In addition, whereas the previous NSC "staff" had been coordinated by the State Department member and the consultants had lacked any coordination, the new Senior Staff was directed by the executive secretary of the council. Like other changes to come, the net effect of this reorganization was to strengthen the hand of the White House at the expense of the departments.

NSC 68. Truman could move with such alacrity in July 1950 because the blueprint for change within the NSC had been in his hands since the previous April. In response to the critical events of late 1949, among them the evacuation of mainland China by the Nationalist government and the detonation of the atomic bomb by the USSR, an ad hoc committee from the State and Defense Departments had been directed by the president to reexamine the objectives and strategic plans of the United States. This group worked throughout February and March 1950 on a paper—NSC 68—that was presented to the NSC on April 7. The document, which painted a bleak picture of U.S. capabilities, was a call for rearmament. The thrust of NSC 68 was so far-reaching that the president immediately asked for more information on its budgetary implications as well as suggestions for coordinating the implementation of these new programs.

As the executive secretary delivered NSC 68 and the president's request for further information, he also distributed to council members a memo entitled "Proposed Procedure for Handling NSC 68." The subject of the memo was essentially the reconstitution and strengthening of the NSC staff. Lay's recommendations were those that the president placed in his directive of July

19, 1950, with an important exception—an exception that delayed council approval. Lay suggested that the Senior Staff include a "military advisory representative designated by the JCS." Secretary Johnson, who had been urged by each of his service secretaries and the chairman of the Joint Chiefs of Staffs to reject any suggestion that would compromise the full participation of the JCS, objected to the word "advisory." An "advisory representative" was considerably less than full representation. Johnson suggested and the council agreed to the establishment of a special committee to prepare recommendations for the strengthening of the NSC staff. This committee was still deliberating when the president issued his directive of July 19, which included the representative of the JCS as a full member of the Senior Staff.[20]

Meanwhile, at its April meeting, the council established a procedure to handle NSC 68. An ad hoc committee with several subcommittees was formed to prepare a complete response to the document. The subcommittee to recommend organizational changes was placed under the direction of the Bureau of Budget, and with its usual efficiency and thoroughness, the Administrative Management Division of the bureau immediately began its study with a series of interviews in the summer of 1950. This study and its recommendations later became Annex 9 (of ten annexes) to NSC 68/1.[21]

An Insider's Critique. President Truman made no further structural changes in the National Security Council after his July 1950 directive, and Annex 9 was largely forgotten in the future debates over the substance of NSC 68. Nevertheless, the bureau study remains valuable. After only three years of experience with an emerging national security process, the authors were able to pinpoint the very problems in that process that were—and still remain—the most intractable: the problem of a process that is only as strong as the internal organization of its major participants, the State and Defense Departments; the problem of implementing national security policy once it is determined; and the problem of creating a viable role for a staff assistant to the president for national security.

The study briefly considered new alternatives to coordination, such as a White House "czar" for policy coordination or a proposal for centering coordinating in the State Department, but quickly rejected these proposals. The Defense and State Departments were urged to strengthen the national security process through improving internal coordination of NSC matters. The Joint Chiefs of Staff, for example, often presented papers to the council after policy had been decided; staff members of bureaus in the State Department would often move forward on a policy quite opposite to that approved by the council.

Basically the document supported the newly appointed Senior Staff and turned its attention to the major problem of policy implementation. The authors, reflecting their interviews with council participants, pointed out that the difficulties of policy implementation frequently were caused by the lack of clarification of basic policies and programs approved by the NSC. Admiral Souers had pointed out to them that policy papers that still indicated disagreement among the authors, such as those on export controls, would often be presented to the council. Policy from such papers was poorly implemented, he noted, because of the lack of clarity, although he conceded that hammering out policy in committees could lead to generalities that were also difficult to implement.

The bureau did not take the logical step of suggesting that the council itself supervise implementation. Instead it suggested that the NSC should require periodic progress reports from the agencies to the president through the NSC.

The most innovative section of the study recommended the appointment of a special assistant to the president. On June 15, 1950, as the BOB was beginning its study, President Truman had, in fact, announced the appointment of Averell Harriman as a new special assistant to the president. Harriman assumed his duties shortly after the outbreak of the Korean War, and several NSC participants interviewed by bureau personnel were encouraged by the creation of this new position. Admiral Souers, for example, saw Harriman "as the President's man to follow up and assure implementation." Senior members from the Defense Department also welcomed Harriman as the "President's personal representative" who "would provide the driving force to make the machinery work." But Harriman's appointment proved misleading. It was assumed that the position of special assistant would be permanent, but in fact it was not so much that Harriman was chosen for the position as that the position was improvised to use his special talents. When Harriman moved on to direct the mutual security program, the position of special assistant was abolished.

The budget study saw the special assistant "as rounding out and balancing the Executive Office of the President." His functions would include keeping abreast of program and policy development and assisting in developing recommendations that involved both national security and domestic economic interests. He would intervene on behalf of the president when programs lagged or seemed out of balance and would serve to resolve program conflicts that could not be resolved by the agencies concerned. In addition, the assistant would follow up on instances where an agency may have been lagging in performing its national security responsibilities. Although President Truman ignored this recommendation, it provides an accurate description of the duties of the national security adviser in the years ahead.

In summary, the Truman administration bequeathed to its successor an imperfect instrument for policy coordination, but one that was a marked improvement over the chaotic conditions of World War II. Through the efforts of the president, his staff, and the Budget Bureau, the NSC was molded into a presidential instrument. The changes that had strengthened the coordination process since 1947 were those that strengthened the control of the president and his staff. The NSC was officially part of the Executive Office of the President, the executive secretary of the NSC was now in charge of the Senior Staff, and a member of his secretariat was in charge of the staff assistants.

President Truman had been suspicious of a legislatively mandated NSC, and after presiding over the first meeting, he did not attend a council meeting for another ten months. But he clearly supported Admiral Souers in his efforts to create a White House–centered national security process. His use of the NSC process was entirely consistent with his views on its purpose and value. Throughout his administration, the president and his secretary of state remained completely responsible for foreign policy. The NSC was there to advise the president on matters requiring specific diplomatic, military, and intelligence coordination once policy decisions had been made. Thus, in the summer of 1948, Truman made the decision to support West Berlin. He then attended NSC meetings from July to September 1948 to discuss the specifics of the Berlin airlift.[22] Similarly, the decision to defend South Korea was made by the president, who then met with the NSC for the coordination of military, diplomatic, and intelligence policy.

Throughout the second half of 1950 and 1951 the council and its staff were actively concerned with Korea and the tense international situation. A study prepared for the Brookings Institution in March 1951 concluded that, on the whole, the NSC was working as well as could be expected, but that the implementation of policy was still the weakest link in the national security process. General Eisenhower and his advisers disagreed completely with this rosy assessment.

The Eisenhower Consolidation

The famous World War II general in his campaign speeches criticized the Truman National Security Council as no more than a "shadow agency." He emphasized the importance of a revitalized NSC so that every significant act of government would be organized for the cold war battle over the minds of men and women throughout the world. Presidential candidate Eisenhower even suggested the appointment of nongovernment participants, elder statesmen, who could bring fresh viewpoints to the council's deliberations.[23] Temperament and training indicated that Eisenhower would attempt to reorganize, streamline, and restructure the entire executive branch of the government as well as the White House. Certainly his election promised a complete overhaul of the whole national security apparatus.

As a harbinger of the future, new studies devoted to the national security process emerged from the transition period and the early months of the new administration. Meanwhile, Robert Cutler (president of a Boston bank, friend of Henry Cabot Lodge, and active participant in Eisenhower's presidential campaign) had been asked by the president to join the administration in order to study the NSC, recommend changes, and move into the position of "executive" of the Council. Cutler received various transition reports, but enthusiastically went to work on his own study before the inauguration. Although he later wrote that the Eisenhower system was unlike that of President Truman, the outline for his study clearly shows that in 1952–1953 he was more interested in strengthening the council's mechanism than in overhauling it. He sought recommendations concerning membership in the NSC, changes in Senior Staff, procedures for follow-through on council policies, and the problem of cold war strategy—all of which had been topics of concern in all previous studies of the NSC.[24]

Cutler compiled his information from interviews with former participants of the NSC, including General George Marshall and Ferdinand Eberstadt. He discussed the council with the president and received a report from the President's Advisory Commission on Government Organization (PACGO) as well as from James Lay, the NSC executive secretary. Finally, in February, 1953, he called two conferences at which a half dozen participants examined every facet of the problem for seven hours at a time.

Although individuals differed on details, such as council membership or the title of the new NSC executive, from these discussions there emerged a distinct consensus: The council was too big; the president needed someone in charge of the council who could implement council action; and the Senior Staff needed to be upgraded and given a higher status in each department. Rejected by everyone but the president was the suggestion that elder statesmen should participate in the council. Also discarded was the suggestion that an NSC staff be created to implement the policy decisions of the council. As James Lay noted, such a staff would interpose the council between the president and his cabinet. It was much wiser, he wrote, to establish a new position of executive officer of the NSC whose function, in the words of the PACGO memorandum, would be "to prevent delays, follow-up decisions, and keep the Council ahead of crises."[25]

Cutler presented his report and recommendations to the president on March 7, 1953. The resulting changes were modest. A Policy Planning Board replaced the Senior Staff, and the council secretariat was augmented by a special staff in the EOP. The most important change was the designation of a special assistant to the president for national security affairs who would preside over the Planning Board and act as executive officer at council meetings. These changes bore a striking resemblence to the recommendations of Annex 9.[26]

A further change in the NSC structure came the following summer with the establishment of the Operations Coordinating Board. This part of the national security process, which will be discussed in the next section, has continued to be the least understood and most controversial aspect of the Eisenhower national security apparatus.

From "Psychological Strategy" to "Operations Coordination"

In the spring of 1951, President Truman had established the Psychological Strategy Board (PSB) in an effort to coordinate the psychological and foreign information activities of the government. Although the PSB was established outside the NSC structure, it reported to the council and its director was invited to attend council meetings. However, the PSB was not regarded as a successful answer to the problems presented by the psychological aspects of the cold war. Eisenhower and his advisers did not believe that psychological strategy could be separated from national security policy and sought a method of coordination that would encourage policymakers throughout the government to think in terms of the cold war relevance of each of their actions. It was logical, therefore, to place the coordination of the psychological aspects of the cold war in the hands of the organization that would implement national security policy, i.e., the National Security Council.

Immediately after his inauguration, Eisenhower established the President's Committee on International Information Activities to evaluate the activities in this field. The committee was chaired by William H. Jackson and included Robert Cutler, Gordon Gray (chairman of the PSB under Truman), and C. D. Jackson, who had been designated the president's special assistant for the cold war. In its report the following summer, the committee recommended the abolition of the PSB and the creation of a new Operations Coordinating Board (OCB). It conceived of the board as the executive arm of the NSC charged with a twofold duty: to carry out approved policy and to ensure that "each action is so executed as to make its full contribution to the particular climate of opinion which the United States is seeking to achieve in the world."[27]

Although the committee recommended that the board become part of the NSC, the Justice Department decided that the National Security Act was too narrow to allow the OCB to be financed from NSC appropriations. From 1953 until July 1, 1957, when that opinion was changed, the OCB was an interdepartmental committee financed by contributions from the member agencies. The board reported to the NSC, however, and functioned in much the same manner as it did after 1957.

The members of the OCB were the under secretary of state, who was the chairman; the deputy secretary of defense; the director of the Foreign

Operations Agency (which was later called the International Cooperation Administration); and the special assistant for the cold war. The president's special assistant for national security affairs also customarily sat with the board. Each Wednesday, just prior to their regular meeting, the board members would hold an informal lunch. This weekly luncheon, held without staff or other participants, was probably the most useful coordinating mechanism of the entire OCB system.

Each board member had an assistant whose entire assignment was OCB activities. These assistants met every Friday to prepare agendas and review papers going to the board. There was also an OCB staff divided into four groups; the area group, the special projects staff, the media programs staff, and the secretariat.

The main work of the OCB was done in OCB Working Groups, of which there were usually thirty-five or forty at any one time. The working groups, which had members drawn from each involved agency and were usually chaired by the representative from the State Department, had several tasks. They prepared an outline plan of operations to carry out the action listed in NSC policy, a progress report of a few pages every six months, and status reports of a sentence or two that were submitted weekly. The formal reports from the working groups went to the board assistants and then to the board itself. The board then sent progress reports to the NSC so that the full circle—NSC to OCB to NSC—was completed. Obviously this was a lengthy, complex, and time-consuming process. It often took six months for a working group to formulate an operational plan ready for the board's assistants!

The NSC in Action

The use of the NSC structure can best be understood within the context of the overall staff arrangements in the Eisenhower White House. The revitalization of the NSC in 1953 was consistent with the revival of the Council of Economic Advisers, the organization of a cabinet secretariat, and the addition of other formal advisory groups. The facilitating and coordinating role of the special assistant for national security affairs was consistent with a structure that had a special assistant for economic affairs, a cabinet secretary, a staff secretary, and an assistant to the president (Sherman Adams). Even the amount of paperwork in the NSC process was consistent with Eisenhower's emphasis on comprehensive staff work in the White House.

President Eisenhower placed great value on the planning procedure. The very process of planning kept staff and presidential advisers fully informed and involved. Eisenhower felt that through the planning process and meetings of the NSC, "the members of the NSC became familiar, not only with each other, but with the basic factors of problems that might on some future date, face the President." Thus, when the president was faced with a crisis, the planning process would be ready, and his advisers, accustomed to expressing their views to the president, would be prepared to offer critical judgment instead of simply becoming "yes-men."[28]

Eisenhower, like Truman, regarded the NSC process as only one of several components in the shaping of foreign policy. In general he used the council procedure for issues that profited from long-range planning and from coordination between departments of government. Some critical problems were fully debated in council meetings; others were never presented to the council.

Subjects for consideration at NSC meetings frequently involved military programs and intelligence. For example, the agenda for the meeting of November 22, 1957, included about an hour and a half on the U.S. military program for fiscal year 1959, a 25-minute briefing by the CIA director for Central America (especially Guatemala and Honduras), and a few minutes spent on the OCB progress report on Tunisia and Morocco just prior to a visit to the United States by the sultan of Morocco. Issues concerning the Military Assistance Program were also consistently on the agenda because they involved many departments.

Although there is only scattered information on the content of NSC papers and few summaries of NSC meetings are available, it would appear that there were candid discussions that were important to the president. For example, the discussion of NSC 5810 at the meeting of May 1, 1958, revolved around the fundamental question of U.S. response to aggression abroad. Would the United States fight limited wars? Did reliance on a nuclear deterrent prevent the United States from fighting limited wars? NSC 5810 involved the council members in a discussion of one of the most basic defense questions: the nuclear deterrent versus conventional forces. The participants in the discussion were primarily members of the JCS and the Defense Department, but the secretary of state entered the discussion to support the development of a supplementary strategy for "defensive wars which do not involve the total defeat of the enemy," although he recognized that budgetary problems would require further study. As the discussion progressed, the president remarked that "this one paper, NSC 5810 . . . was worth all the NSC policy papers which he had read in the last six months."[29]

The emphasis on structure, process, and formal meetings of council or cabinet did not mean that Eisenhower limited himself to formal advice at the expense of informal contact with members of his administration. The Eisenhower style of managing White House business was a continuing mix of the formal procedure and the informal conversation. Side by side with formal meetings was an informal network of consultation in the White

House that brought information to the president and to various members of his staff. The president, for example, would formally meet with the members of his commission on government reorganization (PACGO), but would precede such a meeting by an informal breakfast with members of the commission, such as his brother Milton or Nelson Rockefeller. Similarly, the president often held informal discussions or off-the-record meetings with participants in the NSC process while protecting the integrity of the NSC procedure. During the spring of 1954, for example, when the French asked for American aid at Dien Bien Phu, the president conferred constantly with individual advisers and relied heavily on the diplomacy of Secretary of State Dulles. The Planning Board, meanwhile, was assigned to investigate such topics as the necessity for a joint resolution from Congress authorizing armed action in Indochina and a contingency paper on economic measures to be taken against China in the event of U.S. intervention. The OCB quickly prepared papers on a plan for political warfare in Indochina as well as contingency papers on such topics as reducing the effectiveness of Chinese intervention should the United States act in Indochina.[30]

The President's Assistant and the Secretary of State

An understanding of President Eisenhower's style of mixing formal meetings with informal discussion partially serves to explain the apparent contradiction between the simultaneous existence of a strong secretary of state and a strong NSC apparatus in the White House. Immediately after his inauguration, Eisenhower indicated to John Foster Dulles that as senior representative on the NSC "he would have to dominate certain parts of it." Robert Cutler concurred in that opinion. In fact, the lack of conflict between Dulles and the special assistants in the White House was due both to Eisenhower's confidence in Dulles and to the perception of the role of special assistant developed by Cutler and continued by Dillon Anderson and Gordon Gray.[31]

Cutler firmly believed in his role as coordinator. Although he often gave the president his opinion (in spite of his view that "the desire for advancing a cause could be a very dangerous attribute") Cutler continued to regard himself as the president's assistant in charge of the NSC rather than of national security policy.[32] He was politically astute and preserved a good working relationship with Dulles. Gordon Gray shared Cutler's views. After the death of Secretary Dulles, the president rather than his national security adviser seemed to step into the vacuum of leadership on foreign policy.

Cutler also preserved the position of the State Department by firmly resisting all efforts to create for himself a permanent staff concerned with the substance of national security. Forwarding to the president yet another study on national security policy, this one by the Hoover Commission Task

Force on procurement, Cutler criticized at some length the recommendation by the task force of an NSC "national staff." Such a staff, Cutler wrote, would tend to become sterile because it would be divorced from operational responsibility. Because of the "direct access of the Special Assistant to the President, this kind of staff operation would tend to intervene between the President and his Cabinet ministers." In addition, he concluded, it would be unwise to increase the "functional prestige" of the special assistant.[33]

The personality of Dulles and his relationship with the president also had an important effect upon the work of the NSC. Although Dulles was often concerned about potential leaks from NSC meetings of twenty-five to thirty-five people, he was no less interested in protecting the prerogatives of the State Department and preserving his special relationship with the president.

Dulles firmly believed that matters of "day-to-day operations" should not be the subject of council discussion, and he never wavered from this position. In a conversation with the newly appointed special assistant, Gordon Gray, in 1958, Dulles emphasized that the council should continue its work in the preparation of long-range papers and their revision. For example, Dulles suggested that while the day-to-day decisions were being made concerning Taiwan or the Lebanon episode, the NSC could be discussing the lessons to be learned from the problems in those areas.[34]

An example of the secretary of state's constant vigilance in protecting his prerogatives can be found in a memorandum he wrote to the president concerning the chairmanship of the OCB. In considering the restructuring of the OCB in January 1957, it was suggested to the president that the vice-president should replace the under secretary of state as chairman. The president sent this proposal to Secretary Dulles, who strongly objected. Dulles pointed out to the president that replacing the under secretary of state with the vice-president would involve "a totally new concept for the OCB," as it would bring in a chairman and vice-chairman (who was a presidential assistant) who would speak for the president in directing the agencies. "I believe," he wrote, "that the relations of the Secretary and the Under Secretary of State to the President in regard to foreign affairs are and should be more intimate than those of the Vice President. If the time comes when the Vice President more authoritatively expresses the President's views on these matters than the Secretary of State, then a revolution will indeed have been effected in our form of government."[35]

Yet Dulles also knew that the NSC was an important mechanism for the president, and he performed his role there as well as in the Oval Office. In August 1956, Dulles argued that the issue of Egypt and Suez did not lend itself to council action, as it required day-to-day decisions. Although the president seemed to agree, a memorandum from the JCS concerning the military aspect of the crisis was placed on the council agenda for August 9th, and the president specifically asked Dulles to "introduce the subject" by advising the council on the status of the situation. Of course, throughout August, day-to-day decisions were made in the Oval Office since, as noted above, the discussion of critical problems simultaneously in small informal meetings as well as in larger structured ones fit very well into the Eisenhower pattern of management.[36]

New Doubts

Notwithstanding reminiscences and memoirs that sometimes describe a system of near perfection, the Eisenhower Administration entered its final phase amid growing discontent with the management of national security policy. Eisenhower spoke seriously of recommending the appointment of a first secretary of the cabinet to relieve the president of some of his managerial tasks.

The participants began to feel that the NSC was becoming mired in detail. In April 1958 Eisenhower urged Cutler to structure future council meetings so that they would focus less on the discussion of papers and more on issues. This would give the council a greater opportunity to guide the Planning Board in its work. The president also preferred to discuss "provocative issues which required high-level thought" instead of constantly reviewing all existing policy papers. He suggested that the NSC might follow the example of the cabinet, which from time to time would have a half-hour executive session devoted to oral discussion rather than to the formal papers prepared for the meetings. Cutler agreed to follow the president's guidelines, but he reiterated his commitment to carefully prepared papers. His insistence that such papers generated the most fruitful discussion and provided the most explicit guidelines must have contributed to the impatience of the president and other council members.

In 1958 Gordon Gray, who followed Cutler as a special assistant and who had participated in council meetings in varying capacities through two administrations, held a series of informal discussions with members of the administration in a continuing effort to improve the process. Those who talked with Gray (Secretary of the Treasury Anderson, the vice-president, the attorney general, the director of the BOB, and others) shared the view that there was much wasted time in the council meetings—that too much time and effort was spent on language changes in policy papers, that there was too much document reading, perhaps even too many meetings. Gray expressed his own concern over the increasing number of people coming to council meetings and the propensity to keep certain important issues outside the NSC process.

Finally, as the election of November 1960 drew near, the NSC staff formulated some suggestions for changes in the NSC for the edification of the next administration. At least one staff member suggested that the Planning Board should deal with fewer items, that the OCB mechanism "needs to be oiled," and that actual coordination could be substituted for the paperwork. The complexity of the NSC mechanism that had evolved since 1953 was illustrated by the attention given to the need for closer coordination between the several staffs in the NSC process. As often happens, the coordinators now needed coordinating.[37]

An Outsider's Critique. Members of the Eisenhower administration were satisfied with a structure they merely wished to improve. But to many outside observers, the highly structured NSC process, from Planning Board through council meetings to OCB, was time-consuming and laborious. It was also thought to destroy dissent and encourage consensus advice to the president rather than the diversity envisioned under the original National Security Act. As the Eisenhower administration came to an end, this view was widely publicized by the hearings and report of the Jackson Subcommittee.

In the summer of 1959, Senator Henry Jackson (D-Wash.) introduced a Senate resolution to provide funds for a study of the national security policy machinery by the Committee on Government Operations. The previous April, Jackson had delivered a speech at the National War College that had been very critical of the administration's national security policies. He expressed the belief that the United States was losing the cold war, that budgetary restraints were endangering national security, and that the NSC mechanism was unable to produce a coherent national program for U.S. survival. Members of the administration were therefore very concerned about the prospect of hearings conducted by Senator Jackson. Although the national security process had been the subject of many studies, these had been confidential analyses by the Budget Bureau or otherwise privileged studies for internal use. The hearings proposed by Senator Jackson would be the first public discussion of the NSC process.

An attempt to stop the hearings failed in spite of support for the president from the chairmen of the Senate Armed Services and Foreign Relations Committees. The administration finally reached an agreement with Senator Jackson on guidelines for the study so that it could offer cooperation, however limited. It was agreed that insofar as the NSC was concerned, the committee would undertake a study, not an investigation. It was further agreed that the study would be "directed to matters involving purposes, composition, organization and procedures" and would not require personnel of the executive branch to discuss substantive matters before the council. In addition, all testimony by present and former government officials who had been a part of the NSC apparatus would be taken first in executive session. As a result, to paraphrase an NSC official, the Jackson study thus witnessed *Hamlet* without the Prince of Denmark.[38]

The staff analysis and report of the Jackson Subcommittee launched a succession of criticisms at the Eisenhower NSC process. The council, in the opinion of the subcommittee, was originally conceived "as an intimate forum" in which the president and his chief advisers could engage in "searching discussion and debate" of both long-term and immediate problems. Instead the council had become the "apex of a comprehensive and highly institutionalized system" for generating proposals and carrying them out.[39] The council was only marginally involved in the resolution of the most important problems affecting the national security. The approval of policy papers was its major activity, but those papers did not necessarily affect the course of governmental action. They were often mere statements of aspiration produced by a process that weakened their content and seemed to reach for the lowest common denominator rather than innovation. The OCB, the study concluded, gave a false sense of security by inviting the conclusion that coordination was well in hand. In reality, it was a useless interagency committee that could only advise. Lacking command authority, it occupied itself with detailed paperwork and had little impact on real coordination of policy execution.

Implicit in the criticism of the Eisenhower system was the assumption that the president had relied far too much on his staff and had thus failed to exert his leadership in the decision-making process. Several times in the report, the subcommittee staff emphasized the importance of independent presidential decisions. The goal of completed staff work, it concluded, was not to spare the president the "necessity of choice," but to make his choices "more meaningful by defining the essential issues that he alone must decide."[40]

In effect, the subcommittee report suggested to the next president that he dismantle the Eisenhower NSC process. Council meetings limited to key advisers (excluding their staff members) could be held when he wanted advice on specific matters. Small working groups could replace the formal Planning Board, and the OCB could simply be abolished.

The criticism by former members of the Truman administration, the guarded testimony of Souers, Cutler, Anderson, and Gray, and the lengthy history of the NSC by Executive Secretary Lay and Robert Johnson, which painstakingly described the organizational layers of the national security apparatus, seemed to support the conclusion of the subcommittee that the NSC system had become bureaucratic, burdensome, inflexible, and inundated with unnecessary paperwork.

Understanding of the role of the council was further confused by the articles and speeches of Eisenhower's special assistants, whose loyalty to the NSC encouraged them to overemphasize its role. Dillon Anderson described the council as "the helm from which the President looks out toward the broad horizon ahead and charts the world course we are to follow"; Robert Cutler wrote in 1956:

> Assume that the National Security Council sits on the top of Policy Hill. On one side of this hill, policy recommendations travel upward through the Planning Board to the Council, where they are thrashed out and submitted to the President. When the President has approved a policy recommendation, it travels down the other side of Policy Hill to the departments and agencies responsible for its execution.[41]

The subcommittee's emphasis on structure, policy papers, and formal meetings, together with the emphasis on the importance of the NSC for policymaking that emerged from these published articles by Cutler, Anderson, Gray, and others, led many contemporary observers to misunderstand completely the use of the NSC during the Eisenhower years. The role of the council was so greatly overstated that its real usefulness as a policy mechanism was completely denigrated.

The hearings, studies, and conclusions of the Jackson Subcommittee were unusually influential. The subcommittee held extensive interviews with government officials and outside experts in preparation for the hearings. In conjunction with the annual meeting of the American Political Science Association, the subcommittee sponsored a seminar on its study that was attended by distinguished scholars. The Council on Foreign Relations made the subcommittee's study the subject of one of its study seminars. In addition to the publication of the hearings, the subcommittee issued a small volume of selected materials, and a commercial press published a compilation of selected testimony and documents. It is no exaggeration to say that virtually everything written on the NSC during the last twenty years has been based upon documentation gathered by the Jackson Subcommittee.[42]

Transition. There was little doubt in the minds of members of President Eisenhower's staff that Senator Jackson's investigation had been politically motivated and his report biased.[43] The election of John F. Kennedy, coupled with the publicity surrounding the subcommittee report, seemed destined to mark the end of the carefully constructed Eisenhower NSC process. Within a few months after his inauguration, President Kennedy had, in fact, completely dismantled the NSC machinery. Structured organization was, of course, alien to the Kennedy style, but the haste with which the dismantling took place clearly reflected the effect of the Jackson Subcommittee. Richard

E. Neustadt, a Columbia professor who had just written a book critical of
the Eisenhower approach to the presidency, served as a key adviser to both
the subcommittee and the young president-elect.

The transition from President Eisenhower to President Kennedy marked
the first time that a concerted effort was made by a departing administration
to educate the members of the new administration. The Eisenhower-
Kennedy effort was an example of "unparalleled bi-partisan cooperation and
planning."[44] President Eisenhower held two carefully planned meetings with
Kennedy and encouraged members of his staff to meet with their incoming
counterparts as often as necessary.

There were several opportunities, therefore, to discuss the NSC with Kennedy and his national security adviser, McGeorge Bundy. Careful notes
taken by President Eisenhower of his meeting with Kennedy and by Gray of
his meetings with Bundy indicate that both men went to some lengths in
their explanations of the NSC machinery. Of Kennedy's request for a discussion on the national security setup, Eisenhower wrote:

> I explained to him in detail the purpose and work habits of the Security Coun-
> cil, together with its two principal supporting agencies—the Planning Board
> and the Operations Coordinating Board. I said that the National Security
> Council had become the most important weekly meeting of the government;
> that we normally worked from an agenda, but that any member could present
> his frank opinion on any subject even on those that were not on the formal
> agenda.[45]

Gray also emphasized the structural arrangements of the NSC. He
described in considerable detail the conduct of meetings, types of papers going before the NSC, the Planning Board process, and the duties of the NSC
staff. At his meeting with Bundy on January 11, 1961, he spoke at length
about the importance of the OCB. He urged Bundy to avoid "hasty decisions to abolish any of the machinery that had been established and evolved
over the years." Gray pointed out that the functions of the OCB were vital
in government and that "it did not make sense to me to abolish the agency
and then find it necessary to recreate it." Although his conversations with
Bundy also ranged over the breadth of the duties of the special assistant,
there is little indication that Gray, any more than the president, placed the
NSC apparatus within the context of decision making in the White House.
In his notes, Gray describes several instances when he suggested possible improvements or sent up warning flags of trouble spots ahead, but none of
these involved the NSC process.[46]

Perhaps unwittingly, Eisenhower and Gray, through their emphasis on
structure and process, supported the conclusions of their critics. Unwilling

to share their own concerns over the unwieldy numbers at NSC meetings, the limitations of a paper-bound agenda, and the apparent need for a less bureaucratic process of implementation, they lost the opportunity to present a viable alternative to the Kennedy solution of starting over.

Conclusion

The creation of the National Security Council in 1947 filled a genuine need for coordination in the development of national security policy. Although initially suspicious of using a congressionally mandated advisory unit, by 1949 President Truman succeeded in turning the plan for a defense-dominated coordinating mechanism into the White House–dominated NSC. It is clear that the mechanism President Eisenhower inherited in 1953 was not the one James Forrestal envisioned in 1947. President Eisenhower's belief in the value of staff work and process led to a much greater emphasis on the council apparatus. It was the Eisenhower administration that institutionalized the NSC in the White House.

Unfortunately, this emphasis on process and structure misled President Kennedy and his advisers. The perception of a passive president surrounded by groups of people making policy decisions was no doubt a result of the partisan debate surrounding the Jackson Subcommittee, but it may have been unwittingly encouraged by the council staff and the president himself. This misunderstanding of the Eisenhower style led President Kennedy to dismantle the entire NSC structure rather than remolding it to fit his needs.

In spite of the partisanship of the Truman and Eisenhower eras, the perspective of time shows that there was considerable agreement between these two presidents on the management of national security affairs. Neither president used the NSC mechanism for making foreign policy decisions. Before 1961 (and after) these decisions were the result of private meetings in the Oval Office and of informal consultations. But from 1947 to 1960, the NSC process assured the president that these decisions would be informed by all relevant information and that implementation of these decisions would include those officials who had also participated in the advisory process.

Although the terms "foreign policy" and "national security" are now sometimes used interchangeably, they were kept separate in the minds of those conducting policy before 1961. Each described a separate organization. First, there was the State Department with its primary responsibility for foreign policy and diplomacy. Second, there was the coordinating machinery of the NSC, which placed foreign policy within the broader context of military and intelligence information. Thus the secretary of state remained the principal foreign policy adviser, and the assistant for national security largely coordinated the NSC process.

As noted above, the creation of a strong national security adviser with his own policy staff was not an idea original with the New Frontier. The proposal first surfaced in 1949 and was firmly resisted by both Presidents Truman and Eisenhower. Neither man confused the role of president with that of secretary of state. Truman and Eisenhower had neither the need nor the desire to preempt their secretaries of state, but deliberately chose men for that position who completely dominated the foreign policy mechanism. Therefore, the NSC process never led to a foreign policy staff in the White House during their tenures.

A study of the roots of national security management also indicates that certain problems of coordinating policy are inherent in the organization of the executive branch. In spite of a firm commitment to protect national security and the pervasive fear of world communism, neither president found the ideal way to achieve an integrated national security policy. Both President Truman and President Eisenhower were interested in good management. Both encouraged studies of government reorganization, and both made an effort to achieve good organization within the White House. Yet satisfactory management of national security eluded both, and both tinkered with the mechanism time and again in an effort to improve it. The problems enumerated in the first Hoover Commission studies, in Annex 9, in NSC 68/1, by PACGO, and by the Jackson Subcommittee were often the same problems described differently. Some problems of national security management have been and probably will continue to be subject to only partial solution.

The process developed by Presidents Truman and Eisenhower served these men well. Yet as a result of changes in presidential leadership, within only a few years, the National Security Council had effectively been replaced by the National Security Staff and the special assistant for national security affairs. Ironically, it was McGeorge Bundy, special assistant to President Kennedy for national security affairs who best expressed the value to the president of the council mechanism. In a memorandum dated January 24, 1961, he wrote,

> The Council can provide a regular and relatively formal place for free and frank discussion of whatever major issues of national security are ready for such treatment. I believe such discussion can do two things . . . it can (1) open a subject up so that you can see what its elements are and decide how you want it pursued; and (2) present the final arguments of those principally concerned when a policy proposal is ready for your decision. . . . The special service the Council can render to your associates is a little subtler: it can give them confi-

dence that they know what is cooking and what you want.[47]

That was the essence of the NSC process as it emerged from thirteen years of experimentation.

Notes

1. U.S., Congress, Senate, Subcommittee on National Policy Machinery of the Committee on Government Operations, *Organizational History of the National Security Council*, by James Lay and Robert Johnson (Washington, D.C.: Government Printing Office, 1960), p. 418. Statutory members of the NSC were originally the president; the secretaries of state, defense, army, navy, and air force; and the chairman of the National Security Resources Board. In 1949 amendments to the act eliminated the three armed service secretaries and added the vice-president.

2. Alfred D. Sander, "Truman and the National Security Council: 1945–1947," *Journal of American History* 59 (September 1972), p. 369.

3. James V. Forrestal, *The Forrestal Diaries* (New York: Viking Press, 1951), p. 19.

4. Robert J. Donovan, *Conflict and Crisis* (New York: Norton, 1977), p. 138.

5. Oral history interview by the author on the Truman White House, February 20, 1980, National Academy of Public Administration, p. 15.

6. This story is unfolded in the National Defense Unification Folders, George Elsey Papers, Harry S. Truman Library (hereafter HSTL), Independence, Missouri.

7. George C. Marshall to President Truman, February 7, 1947; Donald C. Stone, "Analysis of the Fourth Draft Army-Navy Unification Bill," February 3, 1947, Elsey Papers, Box 82, HSTL.

8. Minutes of meeting held on 8 August 1947 in Secretary Forrestal's conference room, declassified by the Department of Defense, January 1980.

9. Marx Leva, Memorandum for the file, August 12, 1947, declassified by the Department of Defense, January 1980.

10. Memorandum for the president, August 8, 1947, Clifford Papers, Box 11, HSTL. A copy of this memorandum was provided to the transition spokesmen for President Kennedy, 1960–1961.

11. Forrestal, *Diaries*, p. 316; Minutes of a meeting held in Secretary Forrestal's office, September 25, 1947, OSD, CD 9-1-10, RG 330, National Archives and Records Service (hereafter NARS), Washington, D.C.

12. Memorandum, Elsey to Clifford, November 5, 1947, Elsey Papers, Box 83, HSTL.

13. Information in this and the following paragraphs is taken from Sidney W. Souers, "Policy Formulation For National Security," *American Political Science Review* 43 (June 1949), p. 542; and John F. Meck, "The National Security Council," March 1951, Box 70, Series 39.32, RG 51, NARS.

14. George F. Kennan, *Memoirs, 1925–1950* (Boston: Little, Brown and Company, 1967), p. 327.

15. The following information on the Policy Planning Staff is from PPS, Boxes 32 and 33, RG 59, NARS.

16. Meck, "National Security Council," pp. 14–15; George Butler, Memorandum of conversation, July 12, 1948, and Memorandum for files, July 28, 1948, PPS, Box 33, RG 59, NARS.

17. Memorandum for the coordinator, NSC Staff, from Admiral Souers, May 26, 1949, declassified by NSC, December 7, 1979.

18. Minutes of NSC meeting, April 21, 1949, declassified by NSC, September 8, 1978. Truman noted that the NSC and CIA have "proved to be one of the best means available to the President for obtaining coordinated advice as a basis of reaching decisions."

19. Truman to Secretary of State Acheson, July 19, 1950, President's Secretary File, HSTL. Truman presided over twelve of the fifty-seven meetings held from September 26, 1947 to June 23, 1950, and over sixty-two of seventy-one meetings held from June 28, 1950 to January 9, 1953.

20. Miles to Stauffacher, May 22, 1950, Box 70, Series 39.32, RG 51, NARS. Lay, Memorandum for the National Security Council, Records of the U.S. Joint Chiefs of Staff, CCS 381 US(1-31-50) Sec 2, RG 218, NARS. For the comments received by Johnson see Records of OSD, CD 16-1-17, RG 330, NARS.

21. Annex 9 and the memorandums of interviews conducted during its preparation can be found in Box 70, Series 39.32, RG 51, NARS.

22. Agenda of meetings attended by President Truman, declassified by the NSC, 1980.

23. Robert Cutler to Dwight D. Eisenhower, December 27, 1952, Administration Series, Ann Whitman File, Dwight D. Eisenhower Library (hereafter DDEL), Abilene, Kansas.

24. The file on Cutler's activities is in NSC Organization, Project Clean-up, DDEL. Also see Cutler to Eisenhower, December 27, 1952, Administration Series, Ann Whitman File, DDEL.

25. PACGO, Memorandum to the president, February 11, 1953, p. 8, NSC Organization, Project Clean-up, DDEL.

26. Cutler, Memorandum to the president, March 7, 1953, NSC Organization, Project Clean-up, DDEL.

27. William H. Jackson to President Eisenhower, October 1, 1954, Administration Series, Ann Whitman File, DDEL. Information on the OCB from Roy M. Melbourne, "Coordination for Action," *Foreign Service Journal* 35 (March 1958), pp. 25–29; and Dale O. Smith, "What is O.C.B.?" *Foreign Service Journal* 32 (November 1955), pp. 26–27, 48–51, 56. The papers of C. D. Jackson at the Eisenhower Library are also rich in material on the OCB.

28. Robert Cutler, "Use of the NSC Mechanism," March 1968, Box 1, Gordon Gray Papers, DDEL. The quotation is from comments on the paper written by President Eisenhower.

29. Memorandum, discussion at the 364th meeting of the NSC, May 1, 1958, Ann Whitman File, DDEL.

30. Material on Indochina is scattered throughout the Eisenhower Library. See for

example, the Dwight D. Eisenhower Diary, Ann Whitman File, for the president's daily schedule. Also see the Hagerty Diary and the Shanley Diary during the spring of 1954 and recently declassified material concerning NSC 5421.

31. Conversation with the president, January 21, 1953, Telephone Series, Dulles Papers, DDEL.

32. Cutler is quoted to this effect by Bernard Shanley in his diary, p. 1151, Box 2, DDEL.

33. Cutler, Report to the president, April 1, 1955, Administration Series, Ann Whitman File, DDEL.

34. Memorandum of conversation, John Foster Dulles and Gordon Gray, October 10, 1958, NSC Organization, Project Clean-up, DDEL. In a conversation with Cutler, January 13, 1954, Dulles suggested that the problem of Iranian oil not be discussed in an NSC meeting because there might be a leak. Telephone Series, Dulles Papers, DDEL. Also, oral interview by author with Gordon Gray, Andrew Goodpaster, and others on the Eisenhower administration, June 11, 1980, National Academy of Public Administration.

35. The executive order that placed the OCB within the NSC in 1957 ultimately skirted the issue by allowing the president to designate the chairman from among its members. The president chose the under secretary of state. After the death of Dulles, Gray became chairman of the OCB in addition to his other duties. Dulles to Eisenhower, January 14, 1957, Administration Series, Ann Whitman File, DDEL.

36. Memorandum for the record, conversation between Eisenhower, Dulles and Dillon Anderson, August 6, 1956, DDE Diaries, Ann Whitman File, DDEL.

37. Guidance from the president on conduct of council meetings, April 2, 1958, Administration Series, Ann Whitman File; Cutler to President Eisenhower, April 7, 1958, Administration Series, Ann Whitman File. For opinions gleaned by Gray see memos dated from July 22, 1958 to October 1958, NSC General, Project Clean-up, DDEL. Also see memorandum from Philip J. Halla to Lay, November 16, 1960, Box 283, National Security File, John F. Kennedy Library (hereafter JFKL), Boston, Massachusetts.

38. Memorandum, Cutler to Persons, June 4, 1959, Box 17, Harlow Papers, DDEL; Memorandum for the record, June 29, 1959, and Eisenhower to Senator Lyndon B. Johnson, June 25, 1959, DDE Diary, Ann Whitman File, DDEL; Eisenhower to Jackson, July 10, 1959, NSC General, Project Clean-up, DDEL; Senator Richard Russell to Senator Johnson, June 11, 1959, Subseries E, Series I, Russell Papers (Athens, Georgia); S. Everett Gleason, "The National Security Council as an Instrument of National Policy," speech given at the National War College, January 14, 1957, Gleason Papers, HSTL.

39. Henry M. Jackson, ed., *The National Security Council* (New York: Praeger Publishers, 1965), p. 32.

40. Ibid., p. 38.

41. Dillon Anderson, "The President and National Security," *Atlantic Monthly* 197 (January 1956), p. 46; Robert Cutler, "The Development of the National Security Council," *Foreign Affairs* 34 (April 1956), p. 448.

42. See, for example, Keith C. Clark and Laurence J. Leger, eds., *The President and*

the Management of National Security (New York: Praeger Publishers, 1969). Recently revisionists have concluded that the NSC had virtually no impact upon decision making. See, for example, Douglas Kinnard, "President Eisenhower and the Defense Budget," *Journal of Politics* 39 (August 1977), pp. 599, 621.

43. Gordon Gray, oral interview on the Eisenhower Administration, June 11, 1980, National Academy of Public Administration.

44. Robert Donovan, *Herald Tribune* (New York), January 8, 1961.

45. "Account of My December 6th, 1960 Meeting with President-Elect Kennedy," Whitman Diary, Ann Whitman File, DDEL.

46. Gray, Memorandum for the record, January 17, 1961, Transition Series, Ann Whiteman File, DDEL.

47. Bundy, Memorandum to the president, January 24, 1961, Box 283, National Security File, JFKL.

9

National Security II: The Rise of the Assistant (1961–1981)

I. M. Destler

In the 1960s and 1970s, the major institutional development in the presidency with relation to foreign affairs was the increased influence—and prominence—of the assistant for national security affairs. The National Security Council became in practice not the powerful senior advisory forum envisioned at its creation, but the senior aide and staff instituted under the council's name. Presidents employed this aide and staff not just as a link to the permanent government but also as an alternative to it, at least for certain issues they deemed particularly important.

This development is particularly notable because, throughout this period, the foreign policy community was generally in favor of a very different sort of foreign policymaking system, one in which the secretary of state had clear primacy (short of the president) and the White House foreign policy aide stuck to a low-profile, coordinating role. By the 1980 presidential campaign, criticism of recent practice had become nearly universal. In a major television speech, candidate Ronald Reagan made "reorganizing the policymaking structure" the first of "nine specific steps that I will take to put America on a sound, secure footing in the international arena."

> The present Administration has been unable to speak with one voice in foreign policy. This must change. My administration will restore leadership to

This chapter draws substantially on "National Security Management, What Presidents Have Wrought," written as a background paper for the Panel on Presidential Management, National Academy of Public Administration, and published in the Winter 1980-1981 issue of *Political Science Quarterly*. The author wishes to thank Peter Szanton and Hugh Heclo for their helpful critical comments on earlier drafts.

U.S. foreign policy by organizing it in a more coherent way.

An early priority will be to make structural changes in the foreign policy-making machinery so that the Secretary of State will be the President's principal spokesman and adviser.

The National Security Council will once again be the coordinator of the policy process. Its mission will be to assure that the President receives an orderly, balanced flow of information and analysis. The National Security Adviser will work closely in teamwork with the Secretary of State and the other members of the Council.[1]

In the months following his resounding election victory, Reagan took a number of steps consistent with this pledge, including the choice of a strong, assertive man as secretary of state and the reduction of the national security assistant's visibility and power. Yet scarcely three months into his administration he was confronted with a major public quarrel between the secretary of state and senior White House aides. That dispute raised serious questions about whether the president and his chief advisers could resist the broader forces that had brought the White House staff to foreign policy prominence and sometimes dominance, notwithstanding the expressed intention of Reagan and most of his predecessors. Recent experience suggests that there is a serious tension, which has received insufficient notice, between the operational needs of presidents, as they perceive them, and the requirements of careful, constructive U.S. participation in world affairs. The assistant's role has grown because presidents came to see that position as responsive to them—even though over the long run, the assistant's role has tended to make their overall foreign policy less coherent and less effective.

The Consensus Prescription: Low-Profile Facilitator

For each of the five presidents of the past two decades, the primary manager of foreign policy issues was the assistant (special assistant until 1969) for national security affairs. Under the formal aegis of the National Security Council, this aide has headed a staff of foreign policy analysts and operators that has varied in size—no more than twelve under McGeorge Bundy (1961–1966), rising to eighteen under Walt Rostow (1966–1969) and to a peak of more than fifty under Henry Kissinger (1969–1975) before dropping to a number in the forties under Brent Scowcroft (1975–1977) and in the thirties under Zbigniew Brzezinski (1977–1981).[2] The staff has been a mix of "in-and-outers" and agency officials on temporary assignment, and its members have characteristically been foreign policy professionals rather than political appointees in the partisan sense. But they have been "political" in one crucial way—they have departed, to be succeeded by new staff, when the party affiliation of the president has changed.[3]

Over this twenty-year period, there developed a semiarticulated consensus among practitioners, scholars, and public observers as to what the national security adviser should—and should not—be doing.[4] This consensus, originating in the sixties, was further developed and reinforced by reaction to the first Kissinger regime (1969–1973) and Watergate. Its basic thrust was that the national security assistant and staff should play at least part of the linking and constraining role originally envisaged for the council. To this end, the assistant should concentrate on certain types of activities and avoid others (see Table 9.1). The basic argument for the job description in Table 9.1 was essentially twofold. First, the assistant's performance of "outside leadership" activities would preempt or undercut other senior presidential advisers and the formally responsible institutions, particularly the State Department and its secretary. Second, it would compromise the "honest broker" reputation for balance necessary to performance of the "inside management" functions, most of which (unlike the outside leadership functions in the right-hand column of Table 9.1) are best handled from within the White House. As Bromley Smith put it in 1969:

> The theory was that the special assistant's greatest usefulness to the President is to be absolutely neutral so that the principals have full confidence that their views will be presented to the President, and that the assistant is not taking ad-

TABLE 9.1. The National Security Assistant: The Professionals' Job Description

YES ("Inside Management")	OK IN MODERATION	NO ("Outside Leadership")
Briefing the president, handling his foreign policy in-box	Discreet advice and advocacy	Conducting particular diplomatic negotiations
Analyzing issues and choices: (a) Ordering information and intelligence (b) Managing interagency studies	Encouraging advocacy by NSC staff subordinates	Fixed operational assignments
	Information and "background" communicating with press, Congress, foreign officials	Public spokesman
Managing presidential decision processes		Strong, visible internal advocacy (except of already established presidential priorities)
Communicating presidential decisions and monitoring their implementation		
General interagency brokering, circuit-connecting, crisis management		Making policy decisions

vantage of his position by introducing his own views. Once uncertainty develops, then it's a very difficult situation.[5]

No one would expect that any real-life system would follow such guidelines completely, despite the tendency of presidents to stress the inside, low-profile role whenever an assistant is newly appointed. But even when allowances are made for personal idiosyncrasies, the divergence has been striking. National security assistants have frequently moved into the outside leadership tasks becoming (1) prominent public spokesmen; (2) diplomatic operators; and (3) advocates pushing their own policy lines. And the Bundy-Rostow-Kissinger-Brzezinski sequence has identified the assistant, in the mind of the press and the informed public, as the "president's intellectual" much more than a staff facilitator. In fact, one can infer from recent practice an alternative role conception, far less confining than that of facilitator—that of a most senior aide serving the president personally and flexibly as the institutionally encumbered secretary of state no longer can. One result has been congressional complaints of lack of access to the assistant and demands that he be subject to Senate confirmation and available for testimony to Congress. As Senator Edward Zorinsky puts it, "It's clear that we have two secretaries of state . . . and it's time we made the other one accountable, too."[6]

This divergence from the consensus prescription did not come about all at once. And it began with a president who wanted stronger State Department leadership and seems to have regarded his national security process reforms as means to this end. John F. Kennedy began by dismantling Eisenhower's network of formal interagency committees, with the avowed aim of giving greater initiative to senior departmental officials, above all the secretary of state. But Kennedy also, through the day-to-day handling of policy, redefined the role of the assistant. This provided the basis for the assistant's moving into more visible and operational activities if he were so inclined, and if his president allowed or encouraged it.

The Position in Practice: A Second Secretary of State

As Kennedy prepared to assume office, Senator Henry Jackson's Subcommittee on National Policy Machinery was beginning to issue reports highly critical of the Eisenhower NSC process: It was a cumbersome papermill; the new President should "deinstitutionalize" and "humanize" it.[7] The primary responsibility of Eisenhower's national security assistants had been to manage this process. Hence in his "Memorandum on Staffing the President Elect," written for the Eisenhower-Kennedy transition, Professor Richard Neustadt, a Jackson Subcommittee consultant, listed that job as one "on which to defer decision." He warned, "This post should be avoided by all means until you have sized up your needs *and* got a feel for your new secretaries of state and defense."[8]

Kennedy did not avoid the post, but he did transform it. He invited McGeorge Bundy, dean of the faculty at Harvard, to assume the position. Bundy's job description was initially rather unclear: in some fashion he was to be the president's personal aide on national security issues. But Bundy was admirably suited, by temperament and experience, to operating within the type of open, informal, freewheeling operation that Kennedy clearly preferred, developing staff and processes ad hoc to meet emerging needs. Numerous formal interagency committees were abolished. Formal NSC meetings were replaced, to a substantial degree, by issue-specific gatherings. Anticipating press questions about national security procedures, Bundy wrote Pierre Salinger on February 28, 1961:

> I think the best answer is the straight one: he [President Kennedy] is spending more time on national security affairs than on any other class of problems and he is meeting frequently with those most directly concerned with each specific question. He finds this method on the whole more effective than frequent scheduled meetings of the whole group, but he does expect to have formal NSC meetings from time to time when it seems appropriate.[9]

The dismantling of formal structures, combined with Bundy's role as personal aide to Kennedy, meant that Bundy was performing, in practice, the national security job handled under Eisenhower by staff secretary Andrew Goodpaster: staffing the president's day-to-day foreign and defense business. The system that emerged, in Bundy's words, "rubbed out the distinction between planning and operation."[10] With the position now tied to the day-to-day activities of an activist president, it had enormous potential for engagement and influence, as it combined the formerly separate responsibilities of providing staff assistance to the president and coordinating interagency decision making. Bundy remained basically a facilitator, oriented more toward making the system work than toward monopolizing the action himself and excluding others. But his personal strengths and broad competence attracted much business. So did his recruitment of a small number of particularly talented senior aides to carry the president's flag in interagency battles. In a 1964 interview, Robert Komer, one of the most aggressive of them, conveyed much of the flavor of the operation:

> [The NSC label was] merely a budgetary device. Since NSC already had its own budget, it was sacrosanct. So instead of adding people to the White House staff, Bundy carried them all over here. But, in fact, Kennedy made very clear

we were his men, we operated for him, we had direct contact with him. This
gave us the power to command the kind of results that he wanted—a
fascinating exercise in a presidential staff technique, which, insofar as I know,
has been unique in the history of the presidency.

The manner and style of the president's use of the Bundy operation, particularly of Mac and Walt and Carl Kaysen, but the rest of us, too, was never
to have more than five or six people in the thing. We had maybe twenty people
in all, but a lot of them were just normal liaison types of one kind or another,
or doing security jobs, or special details. The inner group was four, five, or six,
seldom more.

As Komer described it further, the staff acted as the "eyes and ears" of the
president, who wanted "a complete flow of raw information over here." It
was also a "shadow network which clued the president on what bidding was
before a formal, interdepartmentally cleared recommendation got to him."
Thus "the president had sources of independent judgment and recommendation on what each issue was all about, what ought to be done about it,
from a little group of people in whom he had confidence—in other words,
sort of a double check." Finally, it provided "follow-through," working "to
keep tabs on things and see that the cables went out and the responses were
satisfactory, and that when the policy wasn't being executed, the president
knew about it and he could give another prod."[11]

This type of staff could not help putting the slower-moving State Department (or *any* established organization) somewhat in the shade. And
although an internal memo stressed that the staff was "*not*—though this is a
hard rule—a place meant for men trying to peddle their own remedies
without presidential backing,"[12] particular members of the staff, like Komer
and Bundy's deputy Carl Kaysen, did become identified with strong policy
preferences that they worked to advance. But these were preferences generally encouraged by the president even when he felt unable fully to support
them.

Bundy channeled an enormous volume of information and advocacy to
the president, generally seeking to pinpoint and balance others' biases rather
than to press his own. In transmitting an early report by Dean Acheson on
strengthening West European defenses, he cautioned:

A quick look at the front page—a proposed statement of National Security
Policy—suggests to me that there may be more here than we should swallow
quickly. Acheson is so strong a partisan of NATO that at a number of points
he suggests a balance of policy that you may not wish to accept.

In spite of these reservations, I think the main body of the report is an extraordinarily useful document.[13]

He also played the role of presidential enforcer. When a September 1962 speech by Chester Bowles created something of a furor, Bundy reported to Kennedy: "Clearance of the Bowles Cuba speech turns out to be a semi-comedy of low-level errors." After describing pithily how various offices had failed to focus on the matter, he added:

> I have spread enough terror so that I doubt if this particular mistake will occur again, and I have sent a message to Bowles (who is still out of town) that he should not add a syllable to what he has said on the subject of Cuba. When he gets back, I am sure he will call me in an apologetic mood and explain that he was only trying to back up your press conference statement. I will then tell him again what I have told him by message: that in matters of this kind, when you have spoken clearly on a sensitive matter, it is generally best to leave things where you have left them.[14]

These activities were well within the consensus job description, as was most of what Bundy did for Kennedy. But the vigor and activism of Bundy and his staff nonetheless pulled power to them. As Bromley Smith put it:

> It is true that, although State officers had the authority, they did not exercise it. They did not exert leadership at the various levels. Therefore, when the President had to have something done, it was almost easier for McGeorge Bundy to call a meeting in the Situation Room, bang all the heads together and get things going. The tendency was to do it that way.[15]

Bundy stayed on as national security assistant under Lyndon B. Johnson. The basic job remained the same, and Johnson shared Kennedy's preference for informal procedures. But he was far less comfortable with foreign policy than his predecessor; thus he initiated fewer issues himself and spoke with fewer officials personally. Kennedy had dealt directly with Francis Bator (Kaysen's successor as Bundy's deputy) on international economic questions, for example, but it was many months before Johnson was ready to do likewise. For Bundy, this meant both greater visibility and pressure to assume new roles—Johnson felt that he needed him more than Kennedy had, yet simultaneously resented this need. Bundy went on a crucial "fact-finding" mission to South Vietnam in early 1965 and led a diplomatic mission to the Dominican Republic later that same year. As the Vietnam issue heated up domestically, Johnson pressed Bundy into service as "my debater," urging him to go on "Meet the Press" or to rebut critics like Hans Morgenthau face to face. Such activities foreshadowed greater involvement in negotiations and public advocacy by certain of Bundy's successors.

By the time Bundy was succeeded in early 1966 by Walt Whitman Rostow,

Vietnam had of course become the administration's overriding foreign preoccupation. Rostow had strong, quasi-ideological convictions about the war, which tended to disqualify him as an honest broker on this issue. He also lacked Bundy's strong orientation toward process, being more an "idea man" interested in personally generating new policies. Moreover, Rostow entered office under a handicap. Johnson, apparently determined to demonstrate he didn't need "another Bundy" to help him conduct foreign policy, denied him Bundy's full title. Rostow was designated simply "special assistant to the president," with "national security affairs" deleted. Nonetheless, there was basic continuity in the day-to-day functions performed, as Rostow acted as staff focal point for the president's personal foreign policy business and for interagency coordination.

In terms of institutional development, then, the Rostow incumbency was a holding action. It was left to Richard Nixon and Henry Kissinger to demonstrate the potential of the assistant position for foreign policy dominance, at least on the issues most important to the president himself.

Nixon clearly intended, from the start, to establish a highly centralized system of foreign policymaking, and his national security assistant, Henry Kissinger, was both his personal and institutional instrument to this end. Kissinger's appointment was announced a week before that of Secretary of State William P. Rogers, and Nixon declared also that his new aide was "setting up . . . a very exciting new procedure"[16] for presidential review of foreign policy issues. By December 27, 1968, Kissinger had ready for Nixon a comprehensive seventeen-page memorandum, "Proposal for a New National Security Council System," which suggested means "to combine the best features" of the formal Eisenhower and informal Johnson decision-making systems.[17] Nixon approved it in almost every detail. It created a new system of interagency policy studies and committees to coordinate them, with a key role to be played by a new NSC Review Group, which Kissinger himself would chair. This cast him as the initiator and screener of a large number of studies designed to generate options for presidential decision. The system was represented, not without sincerity, it appears, as an alternative to "catch-as-catch-can" Kennedy-Johnson policymaking. The agencies would be able, it was said, to weigh in when an issue was being considered and to know what the president decided. The Kissinger proposal was nonetheless resisted by Rogers, who argued unsuccessfully for continuation of a Johnson administration procedure giving the State Department the formal power to resolve interagency disputes (subject, of course, to others' right of appeal to the president).[18] But Nixon ordered that the Kissinger-designed system be put in place on inauguration day, and it was.

This formal system continued through the Nixon administration (and through the Ford administration). But before two years had passed, it had been clearly supplanted by the Nixon-Kissinger taste for secret management of public issues. Kissinger became the prime negotiator on Vietnam, China, and the strategic arms limitation talks (SALT). "Back channels" were employed to an unprecedented extent to exclude the normally responsible officials at the State Department from key communications with foreign powers. Gerard Smith, director of the Arms Control and Disarmament Agency (ACDA), who was formally in charge of the SALT I negotiations with the Soviet Union, learned from Kissinger at a May 1971 breakfast that the latter had just achieved a "breakthrough" SALT agreement after months of negotiating through a presidential channel of which Smith was unaware. Smith's only consolation was that Nixon "was just then advising the Secretary of State," and Secretary of Defense Melvin Laird would not learn anything until one in the afternoon![19] As Kissinger noted in his memoirs, such procedures also produced the opening to China, a Berlin agreement, and a Vietnam cease-fire; they also required progressively more egregious deception of the bureaucracy and corruption of the carefully designed policy studies system. In Kissinger's words:

> My staff was too small to backstop two complex simultaneous negotiations. The control of interdepartmental machinery served as a substitute. It enabled me to use the bureaucracy without revealing our purposes. I would introduce as planning topics issues that were actually being secretly negotiated. In this manner I could learn the views of the agencies (as well as the necessary background) without formally "clearing" my position with them. . . .
>
> These extraordinary procedures were essentially made necessary by a President who neither trusted his Cabinet nor was willing to give them direct orders. Nixon feared leaks and shrank from imposing discipline. But he was determined to achieve his purpose.[20]

In the process of developing and dominating these procedures, Kissinger made many specific policy decisions himself. He ended up chairing three major interdepartmental committees and three important specialized groups.[21] He became a strong advocate of particular policy courses inside the government. And last of all, mainly as a product of his obvious de facto role as Nixon's senior foreign policy subordinate, he became in 1972 the administration's prime public foreign policy spokesman. In short, Nixon-Kissinger practice obliterated all the old distinctions between what a White House assistant did and what a strong secretary of state would have done. The staff man became the key line operator in every important respect.

This use of the assistant gave Nixon considerable control and flexibility on those issues that he handled from the White House. On matters where the Departments of State and Defense or other established institutions inescapably had a major operating role, or on those to which the assistant could give only limited personal time, the outcome was less salutary. As Kissinger later described it, referring particularly to the India-Pakistan crisis of 1971, "the result was a bureaucratic stalemate in which White House and State Department representatives dealt with each other as competing sovereign entities, not members of the same team."[22]

This pattern changed, of course, with Kissinger's appointment as Secretary of State and Gerald Ford's ascension to the presidency a year later. Kissinger took his strong policy role with him and used the new public platform to cement his position. Brent Scowcroft, first as deputy assistant and then as assistant to the president for national security affairs, played the assistant's role as the consensus description says it should be played. One reason was that Scowcroft's professional convictions supported this conception of his role. A second was that Kissinger's predominance kept the role from growing. Scowcroft never appeared, for example, on "Meet the Press" or "Face the Nation." A third was that President Ford tended to accept the advisory arrangements he inherited or those that his aides developed for him, rather than to assert any strong preferences.[23]

Jimmy Carter came to power publicly committed to cabinet government, openness, and decentralization. He and those who influenced him were reacting, in the main, to Kissinger's one-man show, particularly the 1969–1973 White House years. Unlike Nixon, Carter appointed his secretary of state well before his national security assistant and his designee, Cyrus Vance, was an experienced foreign policy professional with overwhelming establishment support. Unlike Kennedy, Carter designated his secretary before making any subordinate State Department appointments, and he allowed Vance considerable leeway in filling these positions. Vance moved quickly to capitalize on this freedom. Carter seemed to be reinforcing him when he abolished the network of formal interagency committees that Kissinger had chaired from the White House.[24]

But Carter also saw himself as a policy initiator and manager who would make his own decisions from the range of views provided by his senior advisers. This "spokes of the wheel" operating style would make it difficult for Vance (or any other senior cabinet member) to establish and maintain a broad policy mandate, as there was no assurance that the president would support him on crucial decisions. And the man Carter designated for national security assistant, Zbigniew Brzezinski, was an ambitious, assertive intellectual who had been a valuable counselor from early in the presidential quest. At the Plains, Georgia, press conference at which Carter announced his appointment, Brzezinski deferred to the consensus prescription in describing the position: "I don't envisage my job as a policymaking job. I see my job essentially as heading the operational staff of the president, helping him integrate policy, but above all, helping him to facilitate the process of decision-making in which he will consult closely with his principal cabinet members."[25] But as *New York Times* correspondent Leslie Gelb noted, Brzezinski, unlike Vance at a similar press conference, did not hesitate to answer substantive questions. Perhaps most revealing, when Brzezinski was asked, "Is Secretary Kissinger going to be a tough act to follow?" he did not reject this standard as inappropriate. Instead he replied: "I will let you make that judgment a number of years from now."[26]

Brzezinski began by maintaining a relatively low profile and cutting the NSC staff (though the number of substantive professionals remained double that of the Bundy-Rostow period). But in staff recruitment he gave priority at the outset to "idea people" to support him in supplying the presidential market, at the cost of professional policy management competence and experience.[27] And though he spoke insistently of his collegiality with "Cy" (Vance) and "Harold" (Brown, secretary of defense), Brzezinski was active from the start in pressing his personal policy views, particularly on relations with the Soviet Union and the SALT II negotiations. By 1978, a serious Brzezinski-Vance split was publicly visible. A major Carter speech on dealing with the Soviet Union compounded the problem, as it was apparently a splicing together of Vance and Brzezinski passages, with no serious effort at reconciling the contradictions. At a peak of public confusion in June 1978, fourteen members of the House International Relations Committee sent the president a letter formally asking him to clarify just "what is U.S. policy on such issues as Soviet-American relations and Africa."[28]

Thus the Carter foreign policymaking system never developed a clear, coherent pattern. At times, especially early in the administration, Secretary Vance seemed to speak more reliably for the president; later Brzezinski seemed more often ascendant, although other White House aides also had foreign policy influence. But the pervasive impression was of incoherence in both process and content. Carter did not lack foreign policy accomplishments—the Panama Canal treaties, normalization of relations with China, and above all, the Camp David accords between Israel and Egypt. By Carter's fourth year, however, Soviet troops were in Afghanistan, fifty-three American diplomats were being held hostage in Iran, and Carter's laboriously negotiated SALT II treaty was stymied in the Senate. Yet visible administration divisions continued. March 1980 headlines underscored the malaise: The *New York Times* proclaimed "U.S. Foreign Policy in Deep Disarray"; the *Washington Post* reported "Errors and Crises: A Foreign Policy Against the Ropes" and "Europe: Allies View Carter White House as Unpredictable and Insensitive."[29]

In April, Carter sought to recoup his fortunes and those of his nation by ordering a secret raid to rescue the hostages held captive in Tehran. The mission failed. Secretary of State Vance—who had been out of Washington

when Carter decided to proceed and was unable to reverse the decision—resigned in protest. U.S. allies were further shaken: They had just
agreed to economic measures against Iran on the understanding that
military force would not be employed. At home, Carter got considerable initial credit for trying, and his choice of Senator Edmund Muskie as Vance's
replacement was widely applauded. But by summer Muskie was complaining
openly about his exclusion from deliberation on a major presidential directive on U.S. nuclear strategy. By early fall, he "let it be known that he wants
major changes in the way foreign policy is managed if he stays on in a second Carter Administration." Specifically, he said, "If I were President, I
would appoint somebody as Secretary of State and make sure that the
N.S.C. role is that of coordinating and not anything else."[30]

Muskie was not alone in zeroing in on Brzezinski; indeed, criticism of
Carter's national security assistant had become nearly universal. Some of it
addressed his policy positions, above all his "tough," combative line toward
Moscow. Some of it focused on his style, a certain impulsiveness, a tendency
to press for action without full thought as to consequences. But there was an
important critique of process as well. It focused on the badly needed
management job—which Brzezinski was neglecting—bringing order and
reliability to the policy process. (It was simply inexcusable, for example, for
the president to issue a new directive on the targeting of nuclear weapons
without the secretary of state even knowing about it.) And it focused on the
roles Brzezinski was playing that undercut the assistant's credibility and objectivity for the management task.

Unlike Kissinger, Brzezinski did not conduct most major negotiations
himself, although normalization of relations with China was an important
partial exception. But more than any of his predecessors he was identified as
an advocate of particular policy directions; his reported efforts to intervene
in Iran's revolution, in fact, seem to have reflected his own impulses rather
than any clear, presidentially determined policy.[31]

As Table 9.2 indicates, Brzezinski also became a highly visible policy
spokesman. Kissinger's visibility tended to follow his attainment of influence
and policy success; Brzezinski's, on the other hand, seemed more independently generated by his own flair for public expression, by Carter's
readiness to have him play this role,[32] and by the natural interest of the
press in a newsworthy incumbent once Bundy and Kissinger had
demonstrated the job's potential. In any case Brzezinski continued a trend
that had been interrupted by Scowcroft—the emergence of the assistant as a
major, visible foreign policy figure in his own right.

Interestingly, most of the assistants themselves have expressed strong
misgivings about the inflation of the assistant's role. Kissinger has "become
convinced that a president should make the secretary of state his principal

TABLE 9.2. Number of Entries for Assistants in *New York Times Index*

Bundy	Rostow	Kissinger	Scowcroft	Brzezinski
38 (1961)	31 (1966)	150 (1969)	16 (1976)	147 (1977)
15 (1962)	18 (1967)	145 (1970)		145 (1978)[a]
21 (1963)	56 (1968)	292 (1971)		112 (1979)
29 (1964)		592 (1972)		130 (1980)[b]
91 (1965)				

[a]The *New York Times* was on strike from August 10 through November 5, 1978, and published only an abbreviated, "for the record" edition during this period.

[b]Based on semimonthly indexes.

adviser and use the national security adviser primarily as a senior administrator and coordinator to make certain that each significant point of view is heard."[33] Rostow declared he was "inclined to deplore the radical expansion of the NSC staff that occurred in the Nixon Administration and the failure of the two subsequent administrations to perform an act of radical deflation."[34] Scowcroft has described the position as "very much a substantive job," but a "private" one that should give priority to coordination, adding that "by and large it is wrong for the national security adviser to be a negotiator."[35] Even Brzezinski, as earlier noted, declared on his appointment that he did not see the position "as a policymaking job," but rather as helping to facilitate the process of decision.

Some of this can be written off as ritual deference of White House aides to the norm of anonymity. Some can be seen as retrospective self-interest: As Henry Kissinger might paraphrase Sophie Tucker, "I been both national security assistant and secretary of state—secretary of state is better." But there is serious conviction here also. Bundy wrote in November 1980 that president-elect Reagan was "entitled to the comfort of knowing that there is one place where less would be more—in the job of Assistant for National Security Affairs."[36] And a number of years earlier he had expressed a broader concern:

One of the most astonishing phenomena of the years of our permanent engagement in world affairs has been the increasingly intermittent effectiveness of those members of the Cabinet—the Secretaries of State, Defense, and the Treasury at a minimum—who should be, individually and in concert, the President's most powerful and valuable associates in the conduct of foreign affairs. Ever since Franklin Roosevelt lost confidence in Cordell Hull, the occupants of the White House, more often than not, have contented themselves with ad hoc arrangements designed around major weaknesses in the Cabinet. The mutual confident relations of Kennedy with McNamara or Dillon, Johnson with Rusk, Truman with Marshall or Acheson, and Eisenhower with Humphrey have been the exception, not the rule. I do not know just why this should be so, but I do know it deserves correction. . . .

. . . [For] while [staff] can complement and reinforce a good relationship between the Presidency and a major executive agency, they can never create one by themselves. For that the Cabinet officer is the indispensable man. He works for the President, and the Department works for him. If these two propositions do not hold, because one relation or the other is inadequate, the President's need for action, combined with the natural tendency of any bureaucracy to bypass weakness, will tend to produce a distorted and eventually enfeebled process of executive action.[37]

Flexibility on a Pedestal:
The President as Enemy of Himself?

Why then do presidents accept such a "distorted and enfeebled process?" Why, indeed, do their own actions help to create it? Dean Rusk provided part of the answer when he observed, "The real organization of government at higher echelons is not what you find in textbooks or organization charts. It is how confidence flows down from the President."[38] For although presidents inherit certain structures and institutions, they also create their own through how they operate, whom they work with, and what they demand. Their day-to-day signals condition, over time, their senior officials' responses, the relative power of these officials and their agencies, how these senior officials deal with *their* subordinates, and so on. It is unlikely that presidents calculate many of these effects in advance, or even that they understand very much about them as they are occurring. Nonetheless, it is the president's operating style and personal relationships as they evolve that structure U.S. policymaking on the most important issues.

This is particularly true for national security policymaking. International issues (together with economic issues) are where presidents feel most accountable, more so than ever in the nuclear age, and where they may see the greatest opportunity for historic impact. Partly for these reasons, presidents are major foreign policy actors in an operational sense. They make foreign policy statements, epochal and trivial, in carefully prepared speeches and impromptu press conferences. They decide many issues personally. They consult and negotiate with foreign counterparts.

Such daily personal policy engagement has a decisive effect on presidentially generated foreign policymaking systems. In responding to the president's immediate needs, these systems tend to undercut the senior officials and the established institutions that the president also needs, over the longer run, to make his administration's foreign policy coherent and effective. In extreme form, this produces split-level government, as under Nixon and Kissinger from 1969 to 1973. Or it can produce chronic discontinuity in policy, as during the Carter administration. But these de facto foreign policymaking systems do tend to provide certain things that presidents value very highly, at least in the short-run, day-to-day world within which they must operate.

Such systems favor *innovation* (visible if sometimes transient) over continuity within an administration and *connection* between its efforts and those of its predecessors. Rather than serving as a bridge between administrations, presidential staffing widens the gulf. The personal tendency of Carter (and Defense Secretary Harold Brown) to go beyond Ford's Vladivostok formula on SALT II was reinforced by the simultaneous arrival of committed aides with strong SALT views—not just Brzezinski but also his deputy, David Aaron. The case for building on the past was heard but overridden, and Secretary of State Cyrus Vance was dispatched to Moscow with the egregiously unsuccessful "comprehensive proposal" of March 1977. This episode sowed the seeds of serious future SALT difficulty at home and abroad, with Carter one of the principal losers. But at the time, the system gave Carter what he wanted—*his* SALT proposal, not Gerald Ford's.[39]

Staff-dominated policymaking provides the president a *responsive personal environment* (*his* senior experts, just down the hall, a minute's walk away) while reducing the amount that he works personally with senior statutory aides who have competing institutional loyalties—the secretaries of state and defense, the Joint Chiefs of Staff—and thus shielding him somewhat from the political and institutional realities of the world outside 1600 Pennsylvania Avenue. The senior military early in the Carter administration were apparently unhappy, not just with the substance of some early Carter decisions, but with the way he made them. They felt excluded from serious advisory contact. Their frustration reinforced the argument of Carter critics that he was soft on national security, something that (again) cost him dearly. Yet in the short run, a president who has trouble developing new personal relationships will find it much easier to work with and through staff men both closer to him and more completely his subordinates.

While maximizing his capacity to pull specific decisions into his own hands, a staff-heavy system weakens a president's capacity to multiply his ultimate leverage through developing relationships of personal confidence with senior line subordinates. If issues are repeatedly appealed to him, and he supports one adviser sometimes, another at other times, the adviser charged with exercising day-to-day bureaucratic, congressional, and international leadership is undercut, because he is perceived as not speaking for the president in any consistent, continuing way. And effective policy execution may prove impossible. Contrast, for example, Carter's delegation of the multilateral trade negotiations to Robert Strauss and his continuous, detailed immersion in the SALT II treaty with which Vance and SALT negotiator Paul Warnke were struggling. Yet Carter almost certainly saw himself as increasing his control when he decided and redecided such questions as how to limit encryption of telemetric transmission of missile performance data.

Heavy reliance on the national security staff seems to serve the goal of policy integration—its purview is, after all, broader than that of any foreign policy agency, the State Department included. But in practice, integration is usually achieved only selectively and sporadically as aides give priority to serving the president's personal needs (and sometimes to seizing particular issues themselves). Thus, in 1963 Neustadt noted that "the 'personal side' [of Kennedy's foreign policy staffing] seems firm enough, but not the other side, the 'institutional side.'" And in September 1979 Philip Odeen's report for Carter sounded a similarly understated warning that "despite this stress on the personal advisory role, the [NSC] staff's institutional role must not be neglected."[40] In fact, not only is comprehensive integration seldom attained, but national security advisers and their staffs have tended above all to focus on State Department business and political and strategic relationships, paying considerably less attention to defense and foreign economic questions. This too may reflect presidential inclinations, but it also means that the staff coordinates less, and competes more with the State Department and its secretary.

In sum, the recent evolution of White House policy staffing responds to the president's immediate needs, and caters to his personal convenience, but does not serve his broader, long-term need to lead a strong, loyal, and responsive government. It serves the illusion of presidential power more than its reality. It reinforces an exaggerated sense of the importance of specific presidential decisions—even on third- and fourth-order issues—while neglecting the officials and institutions, empowered by statute and ongoing engagement, that must carry weight for policy on most issues most of the time. And it changes the role of staff from mediating between the president and senior officialdom to that of substituting for officialdom, reducing the president's perceived need to work with and through established institutions at all.

Conclusions

Consensus on the content of current American foreign policy eludes us, but several propositions may perhaps command broad agreement:

- Our relative power—military, economic, political—is less than it once was.
- The United States remains, for most world issues, the most important single nation; it is certainly the leading power in the West.
- The world is less orderly than it was from 1945 through the 1960s, with power diffused, international regimes under stress, dependence on unstable sources of oil, and so on.
- Effective coping within this world requires careful, continuous, consultative leadership by the United States in our dealings with allies and adversaries, linked to programs—defense, economic, energy—that support this leadership.

Filling this requirement for leadership is not solely, not even mainly a problem of process. No institutional arrangements could, by themselves, bring us agreement on the proper size and role of our military forces or on how best to reduce and manage our international economic vulnerability. But the nature of these problems suggests what sorts of institutions can best serve us, for the problems are both long-term and crosscutting. This suggests a need for foreign policy institutions that provide *continuity*—strong, permanent repositories of expertise, initiative, and operational competence within the executive branch—and structures and processes that promote *integration*—the linking of U.S. actions to one another and to broader purposes, and in Tom Hughes's phrase, the "management of contradictions" among them.[41]

In the best of institutional circumstances, there would be tension between these two goals. In practice neither seems well served, and one important reason is the way in which the president's foreign policy advisory and management systems have evolved over the past twenty years. Far from being consistent forces for policy integration, presidents themselves have too often become sources of uncertainty, discontinuity, and idiosyncrasy. Or so, at least, this chapter argues.

We would like a system that both reinforces the ongoing departments and agencies and broadens their outlook by linking them. The logical prescription for this is the traditional one: strong agency heads (above all the secretary of state) with close ties to the president; low-profile White House/EOP staffs that facilitate communication and questioning up, down, and across. This seems the best hope of promoting steady relations and personal alliance-building between executive and legislative leaders and between U.S. officials and their foreign counterparts.

There is only one problem. The president, whoever he is, has to agree. Not that he must endorse such a system formally; this would be useful but not necessary and certainly not sufficient. Rather, he has to behave in a way that reinforces rather than undercuts such a system. Organizational change will be durable only if linked to a viable pattern of presidential engagement in foreign policy, one that meets the president's needs as well as the broader needs of the nation.

Can presidents be brought to accept constraint on themselves, on their day-to-day flexibility? Can they, as a result, impose or accept constraints on their staff aides, to the end of reinforcing and regularizing the larger policymaking system? Can presidents be brought to make the real life policymaking "systems" that they generate conform more closely to what many looking at the broader system have prescribed? Our tradition is against such constraints. Institutionally, we are quite permissive with presidents. A British or Japanese prime minister is quickly supplied with "private secretaries" from the career service, people who are astute in serving politicians but who do so within established broader traditions of governing. By contrast, a U.S. president-elect is generally advised that there are few firm rules, that he should structure his policy staffs to meet his particular needs, that anything is legitimate if it serves him.

But once he is in office, Americans tend to expect far more from him than any human being could conceivably deliver. After the Iran rescue mission, for example, Hugh Sidey wrote in *Time*, "It is a season for new resolve, for a display of determination that this White House has never reached before. These days cry out for daring, defiance. . . . How [Carter] puts this all together will decide if he survives as President, if the U.S. marches ahead or cringes."[42] It was as if, through sheer personal will, Carter could somehow transcend the excruciating limits on U.S. options that the real world had imposed and that the mission had so starkly illuminated!

If we are to move toward greater continuity in executive policy institutions, we need a more realistic conception of presidential leadership that both presidents and president-watchers can find attractive: one that deemphasizes the president's role as a decider of specific issues and elevates his role as leader-executive in the broadest political sense; one of a president who works his will not just by great decisions but also by choosing, supporting, and influencing strong subordinates with broad policy mandates; one of a leader who uses his personal leverage to nourish policy conceptions and policy coalitions that will further his goals and who employs his staff to link him to these broader political-institutional realities rather than to shield him from them. In the end, his staff aides need to serve his subordinates' needs as well as his own.

Obviously, organizational changes will avail little unless they mesh with such broader presidential leadership patterns. The basic choice however, is relatively straightforward. A president can repeat the recent pattern, where idiosyncratic presidential engagement in day-to-day decision making drives the system. Or he can try to replace it with some pattern of stable delegation of authority to senior cabinet advisers, whose work is connected to his own by strong personal ties *and* first-rate, low-profile White House staff support.

How, as of March 1981, had the new Reagan administration addressed this choice? The major initial steps were in the second—and preferable—direction. Reagan followed up on his promise to make the secretary of state his "principal [foreign policy] spokesman and adviser" by choosing for the post an assertive veteran of previous policy wars, General Alexander Haig, who had sharpened his bureaucratic skills through service as Henry Kissinger's NSC deputy. As secretary of defense Reagan named Caspar Weinberger, a close associate who had been his California budget director before serving as OMB Director and Secretary of Health, Education, and Welfare under Nixon and Ford.

Haig moved quickly to exploit and expand his authority by speaking out publicly, by taking interagency leadership on a range of issues, and by moving quickly to place his own people in subordinate State Department positions. By contrast, Reagan's national security assistant, Richard Allen, was performing the "disappearing act" he promised when his appointment was announced in December. Like Brzezinski before him, he came to this post through advisory service in the presidential campaign, a role that had afforded him considerable public exposure. But he consistently endorsed the low-profile, facilitator conception of the job, telling the *New York Times* two weeks after the election that "the policy-formulation function of the national security adviser should be offloaded to the Secretary of State."[43] And unlike Brzezinski, his base was not academia but Washington, and his forte was not conceptualization but policy management and operations.

To underscore administration determination to cut the post down to size, White House organization charts placed Allen (and domestic policy assistant Martin Anderson) not directly under the president but under senior assistant Edwin Meese, a long-time Reagan associate. And it was Meese who moved into the symbolically important White House corner office that Brzezinski had occupied, with Allen located in the White House basement, where Bundy and Rostow had served. As of March, Allen was putting together a substantial staff—a mix of analysts and operators—though less rapidly than had Kissinger or Brzezinski. And he continued one of his predecessors' key roles—that of the president's daily national security briefer. But Reagan's apparent detachment from day-to-day decisions was likely to make Allen's job harder by reducing the flow of presidential policy business, the assistant's prime source of leverage in past years.

Where Haig ran quickly into difficulty, however, was in relations with the senior White House staff generally, as well as with his cabinet colleagues.

Not content with his de facto primacy, Haig sought to pin it down by seeking, on inauguration day, a formal grant of presidential authority much more sweeping than Nixon had given Kissinger twelve years before. The White House resisted, as did the secretary of defense, and Meese ended up brokering a February compromise in which the State Department, the Defense Department, and the CIA each chaired policy coordination committees for their respective spheres. Then, a month later, Haig objected to a pending proposal to establish an interagency crisis coordination committee chaired by Vice-President George Bush. When Haig went public with his reservations, Reagan quickly approved the proposal; the White House released a terse explanation that "management of crises had traditionally—and appropriately—been done within the White House."[44]

How Reagan foreign policymaking would work out in practice was anything but clear in late March 1981. It *was* clear that Haig had sustained a serious blow—at least partly self-inflicted—to his claim to foreign policy leadership. And this particular row seemed to reflect a deeper tension between Haig's individualistic, assertive approach and the collegial way in which Reagan and his long-time associates preferred to make policy.

The dispute therefore underscores the central dilemma that this chapter has identified. The president is both solution and problem. He is our only available source for central foreign policy leadership. Yet in practice, presidents often contribute idiosyncrasy and discontinuity. If our policymaking institutions cater above all to short-run presidential needs, to his day-to-day flexibility and even whim, they will compound the problem. But if they are designed to be connectors, bridges, responsive to others' needs also, giving some value to continuity, can the president live with them? Will he accept the constraints they impose on him? And will the American people allow him to accept them, by renouncing *their* illusions about the president and substituting a more realistic concept of what his leadership can and cannot accomplish?

Notes

1. Address of October 19, 1980, reprinted in *New York Times*, October 20, 1980.

2. The numbers refer to substantive professionals, mid-career level and above, not to support or communications personnel. Most have been in actual NSC slots, but a substantial minority have been "detailees" from the State Department and other national security agencies.

Kissinger held two positions—secretary of state and national security assistant—from September 1973 to November 1975. Scowcroft, as deputy assistant, generally managed the national security staff and process during this period, and his elevation to the assistant position in November essentially formalized an arrangement that already existed in practice.

3. Bromley Smith, a senior NSC staff member under Eisenhower, stayed on under Bundy and Rostow, becoming NSC executive secretary. Kissinger insisted on changing all the substantive aides except Harold Saunders (Middle East) and Roger Morris (Africa). William Hyland, deputy assistant to Scowcroft, stayed on the staff through most of 1977 to provide some continuity, and perhaps four other senior staff members under Ford stayed on for at least a year. These are, to the author's knowledge, the only significant exceptions to the rule of discontinuity in 1961, 1969, and 1977.

4. I have in mind former senior officials like McGeorge Bundy, Henry A. Kissinger, Brent Scowcroft, Andrew Goodpaster, Francis Bator, and Bromley Smith, and political scientists like Richard Neustadt, Graham Allison, Peter Szanton, Alexander George, David K. Hall, Robert H. Johnson (a former NSC aide), and myself. This view is also reflected in the Heineman Task Force Report to Lyndon Johnson in 1967, some of the analyses done for the Carter transition staff in 1976, the general philosophy of the EOP reorganization report presented to President Carter in June 1977, and most recently in the National Academy of Public Administration panel report, "A Presidency for the 1980s," which is reprinted as an appendix in this volume. Obviously there are variations in views among those named, and none bears any responsibility for the way this consensus is characterized here.

For recent statements of former senior officials, see U.S., Congress, Senate, Committee on Foreign Relations, *Hearing on the National Security Adviser: Role and Accountability*, 96th Congress, 2d session, April 17, 1980 (hereafter *National Security Adviser*), pp. 139–50.

5. Oral History Tape #1, July 29, 1969, p. 35, Lyndon B. Johnson Library, Austin, Texas.

6. *Washington Post*, May 11, 1979. See also *National Security Adviser*.

7. "The National Security Council," in U.S., Congress, Senate, Committee on Government Operations, Subcommittee on National Policy Machinery (Jackson Subcommittee), *Organizing for National Security*, 3 vols. (Washington, D.C.: Government Printing Office, 1961) 3:38.

8. Memorandum on Staffing the President-Elect, October 30, 1960, Transition Papers, John F. Kennedy Library, p. 20 (emphasis in original).

9. Memorandum from Bundy to Presidential Press Secretary Pierre Salinger, Presidential Office File No. 62, John F. Kennedy Library, Boston, Massachusetts.

10. Bundy letter of September 1961 to Senator Henry Jackson, reprinted in Jackson Subcommittee, *Organizing for National Security*, Vol 1, pp. 1337–1338.

11. Oral history interview with Robert W. Komer, Kennedy Library, Part 4, October 31, 1964, pp. 20–22. Quoted with permission.

12. Memorandum for the President: Current Organization of the White House and National Security Council for Dealing with International Matters, unsigned, June 22, 1961, National Security File, No. 283/15, Kennedy Library.

13. Memorandum from Bundy to the president, March 24, 1961, Presidential Office File No. 62, Kennedy Library.

14. Bundy to the president, September 17, 1962, Presidential Office File No. 62a, Kennedy Library.

15. Oral History Tape #1, Johnson Library, p. 18.

16. Henry A. Kissinger, *White House Years* (Boston: Little, Brown and Company, 1979), p. 38.

17. Memorandum for the president-elect, "Subject: Proposal for a New National Security Council System," p. 2. The author's copy, obtained from an unofficial source, is consistent with Kissinger's report of the document in *White House Years*.

18. Kissinger, *White House Years*, pp. 42–46. At the time of Rostow's appointment as national security assistant, President Johnson established a network of interagency committees, which gave the State Department coordinating responsibilities at the under secretary and assistant secretary levels. This proved to have limited impact in practice, but State Department officials—particularly senior career officer U. Alexis Johnson—saw it as an important precedent to maintain and build on.

19. Gerard Smith, *Doubletalk: The Story of SALT I* (New York: Doubleday, 1980), pp. 222–225; Kissinger, *White House Years*, p. 819.

20. Kissinger, *White House Years*, pp. 805–806.

21. See I. M. Destler, *Presidents, Bureaucrats, and Foreign Policy* (Princeton, N.J.: Princeton University Press, 1972), pp. 127–128.

22. Kissinger, *White House Years*, p. 887.

23. Ford's adaptability on this score is illustrated by his use of very different advisory systems for differing policy areas: On foreign policy he depended on one predominant aide; on economic policy he worked with and reinforced a formal, participatory policy review system based on a cabinet committee (the Economic Policy Board); and on domestic policy he worked with unstructured "ad hoc-racy."

24. Carter replaced them with two committees, both at cabinet level: the Policy Review Committee (PRC) and the Special Coordinating Committee (SCC). The distinction between the two was never entirely clear, at least to the outsider, but in general terms the former, chaired by the appropriate cabinet member, handled those issues in which one department had clear lead responsibility; the latter, chaired by the national security assistant, handled other issues, as well as crisis coordination. Interestingly, the SCC handled SALT from the outset, even though Vance and ACDA Director Paul Warnke had lead negotiating responsibility.

25. *New York Times*, December 17, 1976.

26. Ibid.

27. See Philip Odeen, "National Security Policy Integration," Report to the President under the auspices of the President's Reorganization Project, September 1979, reprinted in *National Security Adviser*, pp. 106–128.

28. Letter of June 7, 1978, released by the committee.

29. *New York Times*, March 21, 1980; *Washington Post*, March 16, 1980.

30. *New York Times*, October 6, 1980.

31. See William H. Sullivan, "Dateline Iran: The Road Not Taken," *Foreign Policy* 40 (Fall 1980), pp. 175–186; and Michael A. Ledeen and William H. Lewis, "Carter and the Fall of the Shah: The Inside Story," *Washington Quarterly*, Spring 1980, pp. 3–40.

32. By one account, "When President Carter took his new secretary of state . . . and his national security advisor . . . to Camp David to work out ground rules for the delicate relationship between the two, several key aides tried to persuade Carter to silence Brzezinski completely. They wanted Carter to make it clear that foreign policy speeches, television appearances and negotiations with foreign governments would be off-limits to all but the secretary of state. Carter flatly refused." See Alison Muscatine,

"Brzezinski is 'Closer' Among Policy Equals," *Washington Star*, June 18, 1980.

33. Kissinger, *White House Years*, p. 30.

34. Statement in *National Security Adviser*, p. 150.

35. Personal interview, February 5, 1980.

36. "Mr. Reagan's Security Aide," *New York Times* (op-ed page), November 16, 1980.

37. "Towards an Open Foreign Policy," December 1973, in Commission on the Organization of Government for the Conduct of Foreign Policy, Appendix A, June 1975, p. 37.

38. Quoted in *Life*, January 17, 1969, p. 62b.

39. See Strobe Talbott, *Endgame* (New York: Harper & Row, 1979), Chapter 3.

40. U.S., Congress, Senate, Committee on Government Operations, Subcommittee on National Security Staffing and Operations, *Administration of National Security* (Washington, D.C.: Government Printing Office, 1963), p. 81; and Odeen, "National Security Policy Integration," p. 109. Neustadt hoped that the secretary of state's office could play the primary institutional support role.

41. "Carter and the Management of Contradictions," *Foreign Policy* 31 (Summer 1978), pp. 34–35.

42. "Days That Call for Daring," *Time*, May 5, 1980, p. 25.

43. *New York Times*, November 19, 1980.

44. *New York Times*, March 25, 1981.

Conclusion:
Beyond the Presidential
Illusion—Toward a
Constitutional Presidency

Lester M. Salamon

The 1970s marked the end of the presidential era in American politics. For more than a half century before, the presidency gained steadily in power and prestige as a result of an unusual confluence of circumstances: a growing public faith in the ability of activist government to solve national problems; the fact that the opposition to activist government was centered in Congress and the courts; and the appearance of a new set of public administration theories exalting the chief executive as the natural leader of national affairs. In response to these circumstances, between the 1930s and 1950s the presidency emerged as the legitimating center of the national political order, the primary repository of national hopes and ambitions.

To be sure, as the Introduction to this book makes clear, the concept of presidential government that emerged during this era was always largely an illusion: Power was too dispersed, the presidency too ill equipped, and the range of federal involvement too limited to make the concept a reality. But this illusory quality of presidential government was generally regarded as a matter for concern, as a situation to be overcome in the interest of governmental responsiveness and effective administration. Indeed, a steady stream of official commissions, unofficial reports, scholarly treatises, and thoughtful editorials poured forth recommending ways to strengthen the office and to instruct its incumbent on how to use his political resources more skillfully in order to get his way.

But in the late 1960s and early 1970s the illusory quality of presidential government ceased being a cause for concern and became instead something to be applauded. The reason: for a brief period, the illusion of presidential government came close to being translated into reality, and the results turned out to be far different, and far more frightening, than its champions had expected. Both Lyndon Johnson and Richard Nixon made immense strides in extending the reach of the presidency, as the doctrine of presidential management recommended. Hence, presidential policy staffs were greatly expanded, new presidential management processes inaugurated, and the persuasive powers of the office mobilized with unusual energy and skill. Though neither president succeeded fully, here was presidential government at its fullest, with the perspective of the presidency brought to bear forcefully and effectively across the full range of national affairs.

Unfortunately, presidential government at its best turned out to be constitutional government at its worst. Abuses of power became widespread. Far more issues were dragged to the center for resolution than could reasonably be handled there without confusion. As a consequence, decisions were made on the basis of inadequate — or worse — information, and they were made not by the president but by anonymous assistants purporting to speak in the president's name even though they rarely encountered the president in person. "Too many people trying to bite you with the president's teeth," is how long-time budget official Roger Jones described what happened.[1] In the process, regular lines of authority and accountability were disrupted, and available expertise and experience ignored. Taken as a whole, the episode produced a serious deterioration of cherished democratic institutions and undermined existing mechanisms for popular control. Not surprisingly, it left the doctrine of presidential government in disgrace and reopened for debate the central question that the Founding Fathers confronted two hundred years before: how, as Hamilton put it in *The Federalist Papers* No. 70, to combine "an energetic executive" with "those other ingredients which constitute safety in the republican sense?"

It should be clear from the evidence in this volume and from the record of the past several years that this question has not yet been settled. Presidents Ford and Carter, for their part, reacted to the events of the previous decade by significantly disengaging and demystifying the presidency. But in backing away from the "imperial presidency," they created instead what was widely perceived as the "ineffectual presidency." Ronald Reagan, for his part, has moved in the opposite direction, refortifying the presidency, though only in part. Thus, while centralizing control of domestic policy in the White House and OMB, Reagan has significantly decentralized control of international policy, giving increased responsibility to the departments and agencies. Through it all, the question of what, if anything, will replace the concept of presidential government remains open.

The report reprinted in the Appendix to this volume suggests why this might be so. The problem of balancing the need for "an energetic executive" against the need for republican controls has, if anything, grown more difficult over the past two centuries. The dilemmas that must be resolved are both more numerous and more intractable, requiring more complicated and more delicate relationships and procedures. The task of redefining the role of the presidency in the latter third of the twentieth century must therefore be approached with even more creativity and care than it was in the latter third of the eighteenth century.

Fortunately, recent experiences suggest a number of insights that can help guide such a redefinition. Two of these insights deserve special attention lest they be overlooked in the work of reconstruction that is now going forward.

Rethinking the Presidential Illusion

Presidential Power and the Purpose of Policy

The first of these concerns the relationship between presidential power and the purpose of policy. In theory, of course, presidential power is substantively neutral. Its rationale derives not from its association with any particular set of policy views but from its relationship to basic democratic theory and administrative practice. Presidential government is desirable from this perspective because the presidency is the only nationally elected political office and is therefore the clearest expression of the public will, and because executive direction is the best guarantee of administrative efficiency and accountability.

In fact, however, the presidency is just one of several representative institutions in American government. If it can legitimately claim to be more broadly representative of the American people than any of the others, it cannot claim to be exclusively so. At the very least, the interests and perspectives represented in the presidency are significantly different from those represented elsewhere in the political system, if only because national elections aggregate interests differently than do state or local elections, so that groups that are weak locally can nevertheless be strong at the national level. Support or opposition to presidential power can therefore not easily be separated from support or opposition to the goals and interests of those who happen to be most effectively represented by the office.

What makes this observation especially important is that a significant transformation appears to be under way in the constellation of interests that the presidency represents. Generalizations are dangerous, but it seems fair to say that the presidency came to be identified during the early part of this century with a particular constituency that was deprived of effective access to the other centers of national power and that found in the presidency a vehicle for mobilizing governmental power to solve a number of pressing national problems—poverty, economic insecurity, unemployment, poor housing, and so on. The resulting "presidential coalition," solidified during the New Deal and made up of liberal, labor, ethnic, and farm elements, has constituted the axis around which American politics has turned ever since.

In recent years, however, this axis has begun to disintegrate, and not simply because popular faith in positive government has begun to decline. Of equal or greater importance has been a more complex political dynamic: Various segments of the liberal-labor-ethnic-farm coalition, having used the presidency to secure a niche for themselves in the structure of the executive branch, have moved to protect that niche through alliances with supportive bureaucrats and congressmen and then used the resulting power to fend off efforts on the part of subsequent presidents to impose limits on their behavior in the name of broader policy priorities and resource considerations.[2] Ironically, the vested interests struggling against presidential power today are therefore often the same ones that struggled to establish this power thirty years earlier.

Nowhere is this role reversal on the question of support for presidential intervention more striking than in the field of federal regulation. Up through the early 1960s, the New Deal coalition that had done so much to advance the concept of presidential government supported its extension into the regulatory realm, to seize control of what the Brownlow Committee had termed "the headless fourth branch of government." As "social regulation" replaced "economic regulation" in the 1960s and 1970s, however, this situation changed dramatically. Now that it was the Environmental Protection Agency and the Occupational Safety and Health Administration whose activities would be restrained, arguments for presidential intervention to improve policy coherence and serve broad national interests lost much of their appeal in liberal-labor circles. More generally, as "liberal" power has shifted from the presidency to Congress and the bureaucracy, presidential power has come to be the darling of conservative elements instead.

The Illusion Without the Reality

The fact that presidential power has been associated with concrete policy interests, and not simply with abstract political and administrative theories, helps to explain why the illusion of presidential government has been so vibrant a force in American politics. But it also brings us to a second and possibly more important—if paradoxical—point: The concept of presidential government survived and prospered precisely because it was an illusion, because the reality of presidential government seemed safely beyond reach. Only under these circumstances, after all, could presidential power be confidently endorsed without simultaneously endorsing presidential assumption of all decision-making authority. The most important illusion surrounding the concept of presidential government, therefore, may not be the illusion that it exists, but the assumption that it never could, at least not in the form in which it was frequently described.

This latter illusion rested comfortably on several seemingly reliable verities of American politics. It assumed, for example, that presidents would continue to be restrained by effective power wielders in the Congress, by locally based political parties, by broad-based interest group coalitions, and by active media. The presidency needed to be strengthened to deal effectively with these other natural centers of political power. But their presence meant that compromise would be needed and that excess could be checked.

While the presidency has been assiduously strengthened, both intentionally and unintentionally, however, these other potential centers of power have undergone changes in the opposite direction. Broadly based interest associations have been eclipsed by far more numerous single-interest splinter groups. Political party organizations have deteriorated, to be replaced by fleeting campaign organizations and media consultants. And congressional reform has undermined the role of congressional leaders and fragmented legislative power into hundreds of small pieces. The upshot has been to give presidents increased incentives to mobilize their own political coalitions while undermining the positions of those who can share with them the responsibility for governing. The result is a situation ripe either for stultifying paralysis or gross abuse of power.

Under these circumstances, what should become of the illusion of presidential government? Should it, as some have suggested, be abandoned altogether and the presidency returned to a more modest role? The discussion above suggests that this is an exceedingly unlikely eventuality. Whether we like it or not, the presidency has become too useful a political resource for anyone with any hope of capturing even a piece of it to consider impairing it permanently. The illusion of presidential government serves a critical role in our political system; personifying the national will, setting an agenda for national and congressional debate, and providing a focal point for political thinking.

But to say that the illusion of presidential government will survive is not to say that the reality must survive also. The real problem, therefore, may be not how to eliminate the illusion of presidential government, but how to sustain the illusion while avoiding the reality. How, then, can this trick of statecraft be brought off?

Toward a Constitutional Presidency

Fortunately, our political traditions suggest a way to deal with this dilemma. In particular, they suggest the need for what might be termed a modern "constitutional presidency," a presidency equipped to act effectively but also required to act cooperatively. In truth, this doctrine has been implicit in the concept of presidential government from the outset, but it lay dormant so long as that concept remained an illusion. Now that it is clear that presidential government could again become a reality, it is necessary to make the doctrine explicit and organize more consciously around it. At a minimum, this will require three sets of changes.

The President as Highlighter

The first such change is to acknowledge the real limits that time, available knowledge, and reasonable staffing place on the president in his role as policy decision maker. The doctrine of presidential government acknowledges no such limit and posits a presidential role as broad and as detailed as available staffing allows. It consequently leads to a presidency whose reach regularly exceeds its grasp, generating new pressures for more staff, which, in turn, produces further efforts to extend the presidency's reach.

If the chapters of this book suggest anything, it is that this dynamic is self-defeating. By inducing presidents to attempt to control all issues, it leaves them in effective control of none. By spreading the presidency too thin, it dissipates the comparative advantages of the office and exposes it to unnecessary strain.

Far more effective would be a more strategic approach to the office, one that conceives of the president not as the ultimate decision maker but as the preeminent "national highlighter," whose most important task is not to settle all issues, but to identify a handful of issues of truly national importance and focus on them the attention, visibility, and support that only a president can provide. Such a role is far more consistent with the unique advantages of the office of the presidency, and far more compatible with the capabilities of the institution and the demands of the job.

Attention to Process

A president functioning as a national highlighter cannot, however, afford to ignore the thousands of other issues that regularly end up in the executive office for resolution. The complexity of modern life guarantees that such issues will exist, and presidents may, in fact, have reason to stimulate them. If it is impossible for a president to resolve all these issues personally or to wish them away, something else must be done.

The answer, it seems, is that presidents must pay more attention to the establishment and maintenance of reliable processes through which these issues can be handled. Even when the president's direct stake in such decisions is limited, his stake in the process through which they are resolved is substantial. Such processes must be fair; they must be reliable; and they must yield decisions in a reasonable time. What is more, they must be broadly collaborative—within the executive branch, with Congress, and with other centers of national political power—to ensure outcomes that a critical mass of participants can tolerate without serious damage to the public weal.

As we have seen, many such processes exist at present, but they have developed in ad hoc fashion and are in a perpetual state of uncertainty and disrepair. In many cases, the roles of the respective participants—departmental officials, White House staff, the Congress, executive office career personnel, and agency professionals—are ill defined and subject to change in midstream.

Some degree of flexibility is doubtless needed, but the current situation seems unduly chaotic and counterproductive. If the presidency is to function effectively without continually entangling the incumbent in issues he would be better advised to avoid, greater attention will need to be devoted to perfecting processes of collaborative decision making that can shoulder some of the burden instead. Unless these processes are structured carefully and operate reliably, the pressures for direct presidential involvement will continue to be irresistible, and the resulting damage to other key actors—e.g., department heads—substantial.

External Institutions and Processes

Finally, and perhaps most important, the prospects for a constitutional presidency depend less on what happens inside the presidency than on what happens outside it, in the other political institutions and processes with which the presidency interacts. For, in the last analysis, it is not presidential self-restraint and forbearance, but the effective exercise of power elsewhere in the political system that is the ultimate safeguard of constitutional government. This is the central thesis on which our political system was created, and it retains its validity today.

Considerable progress has been made in this direction over the past decade, most notably in the Congress. In the wake of Watergate, a significant congressional resurgence occurred that led to the creation of the congressional budget process, the passage of the War Powers Act, the widespread adoption of legislative veto provisions, and an assault on the seniority system that has multiplied the independent centers of power in the Congress.

Although these changes may provide some assurance against the reemergence of an imperial presidency of the variety seen in the late 1960s and early 1970s, however, they do not yet supply, and may even subvert, the peculiar twist that the historic concept of balance of powers needs to make it applicable to the governance problem that is likely to confront the nation over the foreseeable future. For an eighteenth-century government, after all, it was reasonable to favor the widest possible dispersion of political power. Government's role was quite limited and the major problem was how to keep it that way. Today, however, government is a far more active partner in the affairs of the nation, and its incapacitation would be a serious cause for alarm. Yet, this is precisely what current political trends outside the presidency are doing—reducing the prospects for effective governance by establishing an immense number of veto points from which narrow constellations of interest can subvert the popular will.

These trends can be countered by strengthening the presidency, but recent history suggests that this is not enough. What is needed in addition is the strengthening of other institutions that can legitimately claim, along with the presidency, a share in the responsibility of governing in the national interest. These include national political parties, central congressional leadership, state and local officials, and broad-based interest group coalitions. If, as the conventional wisdom has it, all politics are local politics, under current circumstances all local politics have national implications. Unless other institutions capable of approaching national politics from a national perspective are strengthened along with the presidency, the prospect for constitutional government, as opposed to presidential government, will continue to be dim.

Conclusion

The American presidency stands today at a point in its evolution as pivotal as any in its history. Still the object of immense expectations, the office has become of late a source of considerable misgivings as well. Perhaps most important, the office's long-standing *raison d'être*, its basic doctrinal underpinning, has recently been seriously eroded and attacked, raising fundamental questions about how the office should be constituted and what role it should perform.

In the first instance, these questions will be answered by those who occupy the office and those who follow it professionally. Ultimately, however, they must be resolved by the American people, in the voting booths and in thousands of other subtle and indirect ways. Given the importance of these choices, it is imperative that they be based on a realistic understanding of the true nature of the office and on a clear appreciation of what it can accomplish and what it cannot. If this volume and the report appended to it have made a contribution toward that understanding and appreciation, they will have amply served their purpose. For the rest, it is up to the citizenry to decide.

Notes

1. Quoted in Joel Havemann, "OMB's Legislative Role," *National Journal* (October 27, 1973), p. 1592.

2. This point is explored more fully in Theodore Lowi, *The End of Liberalism* (New York: Norton, 1969).

APPENDIX

A Presidency for the 1980s: A Report by a Panel of the National Academy of Public Administration

A PRESIDENCY FOR THE 1980s

A Report on Presidential Management by a Panel
of the National Academy of Public Administration

Don K. Price and Rocco C. Siciliano, *Co-chairmen*

David E. Bell	Frank Pace, Jr.
Fletcher L. Byrom	James H. Rowe, Jr.
Lisle C. Carter	Abraham A. Ribicoff
William T. Coleman, Jr.	Donald Rumsfeld
Alan L. Dean	Irving S. Shapiro
Daniel J. Evans	Charles B. Stauffacher
Thomas R. Donahue	Sydney Stein, Jr.
Andrew J. Goodpaster	Donald C. Stone
James D. Hodgson	James L. Sundquist
Dwight A. Ink	Glenn E. Watts
Carol C. Laise	James E. Webb
Arjay Miller	Arnold Weber

Phillip S. Hughes, *Project Director*
John E. Harr, *Deputy Project Director*
Hugh Heclo, *Director of Research*

November 1980

CONTENTS

FOREWORD

"The President needs help." This concise assessment of the state of federal administration was made by the Committee on Administrative Management—chaired by Louis Brownlow and with Luther Gulick and Charles Merriam as members—created by Franklin D. Roosevelt in 1936. President Roosevelt concurred and in 1939 established by Executive Order the Executive Office of the President, with the Bureau of the Budget as the keystone agency. Thus was born the "institutional Presidency."

In the 40 years since the Executive Office was created, many have argued the need for further management reform of the presidential office. In 1976 a panel of this Academy prepared a special analysis of presidential management, one which was used extensively by the Carter transition team. A belief persisted, however, that more substantial steps were needed to enable the President to handle his increasingly complex responsibilities.

This belief led to a proposal to the Academy, in the summer of 1978, that an evaluation of the 40 years of experience with the institutional Presidency was essential to determine how it might be strengthened to enhance America's capacity to govern itself. The proposal, made by Donald C. Stone and Sydney Stein, Jr., questioned whether the principles that the Brownlow Committee set forth, and both Hoover Commissions and other special panels in the 1960s and 1970s reaffirmed, were equal to the challenges of governance in the 1980s.

The Academy responded enthusiastically to the proposal, and convened an ad hoc panel of 15 of its members. That panel concluded that the evaluation was important and, further, that a distinguished panel should be convened which, on the basis of that evaluation, would recommend

steps to strengthen presidential management in the 1980s. To implement the proposal, a steering committee composed of Alan L. Dean, Dwight A. Ink, James L. Sundquist, Elmer B. Staats, Sydney Stein, Jr., and James E. Webb was established. With a generous grant from Mr. Stein, the committee moved rapidly to initiate the project, which had the written endorsements of President Carter and former President Ford.

Hugh Heclo of the Department of Government at Harvard University agreed to become director of research. He began his efforts in early 1979 with the assistance of several distinguished scholars. Meanwhile, the steering committee proceeded to organize the Panel.

The steering committee, choosing the leadership of the Panel from the ranks of Academy members, asked Rocco C. Siciliano and Don K. Price to serve as co-chairmen. They agreed. The steering committee in collaboration with the co-chairmen then rounded out the Panel, reaching outside Academy membership when necessary to secure particular talents or expertise. The complete panel of 24 members emphasized diversity in experience and political affiliation, as well as a knowledge of government management and crucial national issues.

Phillip S. Hughes was chosen to serve as project director, and was charged with coordinating both the research staff and a panel support group which included John E. Harr, Frederick C. Mosher, Richard E. Neustadt, and Lester Salamon.

Between October 1979 and October 1980, the Panel held eight two-day meetings. On behalf of the Academy we wish to express our deep appreciation for the superior quality of participation from each Panel member. Special acknowledgment should be given to Rocco Siciliano, Don Price, and Sam Hughes. Working as a team, they kept the Panel focused on the primary issues, prodded the staff to meet always stringent deadlines, and brought the Panel to a consensus on schedule. As is Academy custom, the report is the product of and therefore the primary responsibility of the Panel.

We should also like to express our appreciation to the foundations, corporations, and individuals whose financial support made this project possible. The support was given without conditions as to the contents of this report, and helped ensure the objectivity of the Panel's work. We sought, and received, diversity in our support, just as we sought it in the Panel's membership. Likewise, we had the fullest cooperation from officials of the Carter administration as well as from individuals who held important posts in the prior administrations.

The Panel's report will not be the only product of this two-year effort. Several volumes of research and staff papers are planned for publication and should provide important resources for governmental officials, scholars, and students who, in the years to come, may seek a better understanding of the Presidency.

We are confident that the report will be useful to Presidents and their staffs in the decade to come. We hope, further, that it will be read and digested by members of Congress, officials in the executive branch, members of the media, and citizens concerned by the need for effective government. The ambiguities of our constitutional system are often frustrating; but its demands for a sharing of powers challenge each generation to find new ways to make our federal government responsive without sacrificing critical democratic values.

Alan L. Dean   George H. Esser
Chairman,   *President*
Board of Trustees

National Academy of Public Administration

Chapter I

THE PRESIDENCY AND THE CRISIS OF PUBLIC MANAGEMENT

Two centuries ago, Americans were struggling to invent a new form of government, aware that history would regard their work as a vital test of whether or not a free people could govern themselves.

Since then the nation has survived many crises. Yet today, under vastly changed conditions, the challenge facing us in the 1980s harks back to that of the 1780s. It is not primarily our wealth, nor our power, nor our technical inventiveness that is in question: *It is our capacity to govern ourselves.* If we cannot so manage our public affairs as to bring unity out of diversity, we will be able to meet no other challenge in the decades to come.

Effective self-government cannot be manufactured in Washington; much less is it a process that can be run from the Presidency. In our form of democracy, management of public affairs depends on all levels of government and all parts of society.

However, mismanagement in Washington can undermine all other efforts. This report focuses on the President's role in managing the federal government. To the framers of the Constitution, proper arrangement of the executive function was crucial to the success of their experiment in self-government. The Presidency remains no less crucial today. *A more effective Presidency can help strengthen the rest of our democracy.* That is the purpose and the message of this report.

THE CRISIS OF PUBLIC MANAGEMENT

The cumulative effect of many trends and events is threatening America's capacity for self-government. A clear danger is bearing down on us: At the same time that the problems we face are becoming more complex and interwoven, the power to deal with them is becoming increasingly diffused.

Interrelated Problems

In earlier times it seemed possible to treat the issues on our national agenda as reasonably self-contained problems, and to deal with them one at a time on their own terms. Today the challenges seem neither clear nor unifying. They are interlocked with one another in confusing and divisive ways.

On the international front, the United States, while seeking to sustain an overall nuclear balance, has become both more competitive with and dependent on the rest of the world. Foreign power centers increasingly affect our domestic agenda and at times take advantage of the openness and due process of our democratic institutions. Yet we are reliant on many of these same foreign sources for vital raw materials, with oil being only the most obvious of our dependencies. The share of our national product that we export has doubled in the past 15 years; the import share has doubled in half that time.

In domestic affairs, most major issues transcend the scope of any single government agency, cut across federal-state-local relationships, and often blur the boundary between the public and private sectors. Americans have asked and expected the federal government to assume a greater role in many areas of national life, from the economy to the environment, from health care to energy supplies. This expectation has led to a proliferation in the instruments of policy and administration—an enormous growth in regulatory activity, in federal assistance to states and cities, in loan and loan guarantee programs, in special tax provisions, and in the creation of quasi-govern-mental organizations.

These increased demands have produced a fundamental shift over the past several decades in the nature of government management—a shift from direct to indirect means. Rather than delivering services itself, Washington has sought to achieve its objectives by sponsoring activities and pumping resources through individuals, states and cities, non-profit organizations, the private sector, and foreign governments. During the last 25 years, activities performed directly by the federal government have declined as a share of the national budget. The number of full-time federal employees has remained stable at a little under 3 million persons, while the number indirectly employed through federally sponsored activities has grown to 8 million. The result has been a massive increase in the complexity and interdependence of the entire government system.

The Diffusion of Power

As problems have become more complex and interrelated, the power to deal with them has increasingly fragmented.

This dilemma is most obvious in world politics. Antagonism between the superpowers dominates the world scene at a time when social, economic, and political upheavals have led to a global fragmentation of power. Our resources for the continuing superpower confrontation are substantial. Yet our ability to influence events abroad has diminished as other centers of economic, political, and military power have grown. We must rely increasingly on our allies, yet all existing alliances —democratic and communist—have had to accommodate more independence from their members. The United Nations and other international agencies have made only limited headway. The posture of nonalignment has gained strength. Nuclear power has proliferated. Terrorism stalks all nations. Events abroad can and do have profound effects on our domestic life, yet our efforts to influence the course of those events can rarely be unilateral; almost always we must interact with other governments.

In recent years, Americans also have become more aware of the fragmentation of power on the domestic scene. There has been growing concern over such trends as:

- the progressive weakening of political parties;

- drawn-out nominating and campaign pro-

cedures that are often irrelevant to the realities of governing;

- the fragmentation of congressional leadership coupled with new aggressiveness and assertiveness by individual members of Congress;

- mounting costs and delays in the delivery of public services as the complexities of federalism increase;

- increased litigation on matters of public policy and detailed judicial involvement in program administration;

- a radical increase in the number, professionalism, and potency of special-interest groups;

- a declining faith of Americans in the fairness, integrity, and competence of their social institutions, particularly the institutions of government.

Several of these trends have been given impetus by worthwhile reforms, including the opening of the political process to more influences. Yet the undeniable cumulative effect of these trends has been a radical diffusion of power, a weakening of the forces for coherence and unity. Independence which is unrestrained by a sense of larger responsibility threatens our capacity for self-government. Without such responsibility there can be no real political accountability.

Just such a sense of responsibility and accountability has waned in recent years. Instead, confrontation has become more nearly the norm in our political life, accentuated by the attention of increasingly powerful news media. Rather than a tool of last resort, confrontation has become the point of departure on many issues of national importance. The result has been progressively lessened prospects for decisive action based on consensus or reconciliation of competing objectives.

The practical effect of these trends is an unprecedented need for coherence in responses at all levels of government and with the private sector, and with other countries.

Yet the diffusion of power militates against this very coherence. Our national government now has responsibilities that involve power centers over which it has little control. Our institutional tools and resources are ill-equipped to provide the needed unity. Traditional methods of organization, which separate international issues from domestic concerns, economic policy from national security policy, have hampered our ability to respond. We have yet to find a reliable means to bring a governmentwide perspective to interdepartmental and intergovernmental matters, within either the executive branch or the Congress—even though these are precisely the types of matters that dominate our national agenda and create the crisis in public management.

COPING WITH THE DILEMMA

In dividing powers among the branches and levels of government, our Constitution deliberately was designed to require cooperative unified action; in that was seen to lie safety from arbitrary power. By this criterion, the system has worked well in the past.

We now have to face the reality that political power has become fragmented beyond what the Founding Fathers could have imagined. The cooperation so essential for coping with our national problems is not merely difficult, it has become nearly impossible.

There are three possible courses of action in dealing with this dilemma. One is to await events in the hope that the system contains some self-correcting mechanism that will in time remedy the situation. Another is to alter the Constitution so as to encourage unified action. The third is to undertake timely reforms to make our constitutional system more governable.

Neither of the first two courses is attractive. To await events is to drift toward a dangerous future, the possibility of a manifest political breakdown and a decline into arbitrary power. Although changing the Constitution may be unattractive, it is surely preferable to the consequences of inaction.

Various ideas for amending the Constitution have been advanced in recent years. Motivated by concern over the way that effective action is blocked by the division of powers, particularly the stalemate that too often exists between the President and the Congress, some highly responsible public officials have called for constitutional change. Yet achieving agreement sufficient for action on any of these proposals would be extraordinarily difficult; we may well have to be on the brink of a breakdown in government for such change to be possible. At the least, it would entail years of debate which might only contribute to the divisiveness in our society. And basic reforms, however well intentioned, often have unintended adverse consequences, including in this case the danger of removing the safeguard against arbitrary power.

The preference of this Panel is for the third course: *To develop a strategy for change, within present constitutional boundaries, to improve the effectiveness of our national government in dealing with interrelated problems and diffused power.* To achieve this goal, change will be needed in many complex and difficult areas—in political parties, in our processes for nominating and electing officeholders, in the public's understanding of the need for change, in the attitudes and performance of the media, and in the Congress and the executive branch.

In the judgment of this Panel, the place to begin is at the institution of the Presidency. *We can begin to strengthen the forces of cohesion and integration in our political system by strengthening the capacity of the Presidency for leadership.* It is to this need that our report is addressed.

In strengthening the capacity of the Presidency, we do not propose to alter the balance of powers in the Constitution. Neither do we agree with those who have proclaimed that the President can become more effective only at the expense of Congress, or Congress more effective only at the expense of the Presidency. The current problem is much less a power contest between the legislative and executive branches than a struggle between the forces for coherence and continuity *within each branch* and the more narrow, specialized forces that lead to fragmentation and irresponsibility in the total system.

Both presidential and congressional power can be enhanced if each improves its capacity for coordinated action. Indeed, the Presidency would in all probability benefit if the Congress were more strongly united and disciplined, and thereby able to bargain as an entity with presidential officeholders and executive departments. In this report the focus is on the Presidency, not Congress. But we are mindful that a more effectively organized and managed Presidency would improve the capacity of Congress to fulfill its obligation of holding the executive accountable.

The world has become too complex, and power too widely shared, for anyone to believe that the nation and the government can be managed solely from the White House, that the President can solve every problem that arises. Yet the fact remains that the President and the Vice President are the only officeholders elected by the nation. The Presidency is thus vital to the reconciling of regional and factional interests, to the collaboration that is necessary to manage our pluralism in the interest of national goals.

Toward a More Effective Presidency

Our deliberations over the past two years have led us to support the following principles as a foundation for recommendations to strengthen the Presidency as an instrument of effective self-government:

1. *Presidential management is primarily a matter of working with others to achieve national purposes.* Presidents and the public should recognize that the President is politically accountable not for the day-to-day, detailed management of the executive branch, but rather for leading others to sensible, concerted action on the important matters facing the nation. Each President will adopt his own approach to this management task. Some will use a chief of staff; others will prefer a different arrangement. The exact structure is less important than the concept.

2. *The dominant approach by the President in dealing with others should be a collaborative one.* Both the Constitution and the nature of the current crisis in public management demonstrate that ours is a government of separated and shared powers. Presidents must normally strive to work in concert with others, especially the Congress.

3. *To exercise effective political management, Presidents need a reliable base of non-partisan, unbiased advice.* The institutional staffs reporting to the President should have a highly professional ability to supply objective and factual information. This need is particuarly stringent for those staffs responsible for policy development, administrative management and coordination, and budgeting.

4. *The number, uncertainty, and interdependence of issues necessitate a systematic means for sorting and organizing matters coming before the President and for rejecting those which should not.* Again, each President will have his own approach to this need, some preferring a regular flow of decision memoranda and others opting for a less formal arrangement of consultations. Whatever the method, a President should adopt and enforce an effective system to bring the necessary range of relevant information and conflicting opinion before him in a timely manner.

5. *Because Presidents manage primarily through other people, presidential appointments are of immense importance.* Presidential appointments, both to the Executive Office of the President and to departments and agencies, should be made with the utmost

care. A far higher level of managerial ability than has been customary will be required in the 1980s. Presidents are thus well advised to make effective use of career and non-career personnel in the new Senior Executive Service.

6. *The immediate staff of the President should be small.* A large staff of personal assistants will reduce the President's ability to control those persons who speak directly in his name.

7. *Except in extreme national emergency, broad operating responsibilities belong in the executive departments and agencies, not in the Executive Office of the President.* Generally, statutory authority rests with departmental and agency officials. It is there that detailed knowledge exists, and it is there that legal accountability resides.

8. *Limiting the operational responsibilities of the Presidency requires a corresponding increase in the ability of the Executive Office to intervene selectively on matters of substance and to promote a central perspective.* An effective Executive Office must be equipped to initiate, prod, convene, facilitate, educate, and follow-up on the processes of collaborative policy-making and administration—not as a blanket authority, but selectively and in a responsible and supportive manner.

9. *The Executive Office should not mirror special interests represented elsewhere.* There is often a short-term political advantage in adding units to the Executive Office which represent special interests. Unless this temptation is avoided, the Presidency will be hampered in bringing a governmentwide, national perspective to problems and will tend to second-guess or duplicate the work of departments and agencies that possess operating responsibilities.

10. *The Executive Office cannot promote steady courses of action on vital national issues unless it contains important elements of continuity and planning.* Without these elements of continuity and planning, personnel dealing with daily issues are unlikely to benefit from the perspectives and knowledge of those with longer term frames of reference.

Goals and Rationale of This Report

Accepting these principles, we have examined the organization, processes, and capacities of the Executive Office of the President and have found them wanting. Despite the efforts and good intentions of many people concerned, serious gaps and inadequacies have come to exist in the Executive Office. *The Presidency has acquired its own internal problems of governability.* The Office's internal structure and processes mirror, rather than help to resolve, the particularistic interests in our society. The Office's personnel reflect the larger discontinuities and fragmentation of our politics. Presidential decisions tend to become one more piece of adversarial politics, amplified by the media's interest in confrontation.

If the managerial capacity of the Presidency is to be significantly improved, support for this effort will be required not only from the President and his close advisers, but also from the larger political establishment and citizens in general. For such support to be forthcoming, a common understanding is needed of the powers and constraints of the Presidency and of the evolution and current state of the Executive Office. To pro-

vide this understanding is the first major goal of our report, and the burden of Chapter II.

On the basis of this analysis, we present our recommendations for improvement in Chapters III, IV, and V. In Chapter VI we consider some less tangible, but nevertheless important, aspects of the conduct of the Presidency. Chapter VII identifies government problems beyond the Presidency that require attention.

In preparing our recommendations we have recognized that no easy formula can remedy the problems we are addressing. Rather, we have proposed a range of practices and reforms designed to create a momentum in the right direction, arrangements that can work equally well under a variety of circumstances and in whatever legal manner a President may choose to perform the duties of his office. This is the second, also major, goal of our report.

Chapter II

THE PRESIDENCY TODAY

No other job is today subject to more intense public interest and scrutiny than that of President of the United States. This attention is the natural result of the power and importance of the office. As the elected leader of a large, wealthy, and strong nation, one that provides the core defense for an entire set of political and economic beliefs, the American President is widely regarded as the single most powerful person in the world.

At the same time, as former Presidents, their aides, and knowledgeable observers can attest, the President is severely constrained in his opportunities for individual action. Thus one can comprehend the Presidency only if one understands the office's limitations as well as its powers and responsibilities. One must understand the interactions between presidential authority and constraints, and the skill with which a given President manages these tensions.

POWERS AND RESPONSIBILITIES

Most Americans are familiar with the general powers and responsibilities of the President. Perhaps less well appreciated are the extent to which these have changed in scope and difficulty over time; how significant new roles have been added in relatively recent times; and how all interweave in complex ways to create perhaps the most demanding and exacting job in the world.

Some presidential roles are based on explicit provisions of the Constitution. Others that emerged later are strongly consensual in nature, in a manner analogous to what the British refer to as the "unwritten constitution." These are nevertheless as binding as if they had been specified in the written document.

In the following discussion, we have segregated the responsibilities of the Presidency into eleven broad roles: seven that have been traditionally associated with the office, and four that have been added in more recent times. Although such a dissection of functions can only hint at the full complexity of the office, it is helpful in delineating the boundaries of presidential authority and how these have shifted over time.

Traditional Presidential Functions

Presidential officeholders have customarily been expected to fill certain roles, varying from highly official responsibilities as chief executive to less formal duties as party leader. Although the roles themselves have remained unchanged, their content and practice have altered over the years. These roles are seven in number:

1. Chief of state: The United States requires that its elected national executive function as chief of state. The demands of the modern world, and the position of our nation within it, have intensified the duties of this role. Although the President is able to delegate some of these largely ceremonial and representational duties to others, much of the burden remains inescapable.

2. Chief executive: The Constitution assigns "the executive power" to the President and instructs him to "take care that the laws be faithfully executed." This mandate confers broad presidential authority to function as head of government, or more precisely as head of the executive branch. The all-embracing term of "chief executive" has become virtually synonymous in the public's mind with "President." However, the enormous growth of governmental activity over the past half century and the increasing fragmentation of our society have made this the most difficult and problematic of all presidential roles.

Controversy over the nature and extent of executive authority is frequent, and opinion differs widely regarding the degree to which the President should function as a "general manager" in directly supervising and being responsible for the government.

3. Commander-in-chief: The Constitution vests in the President the broad power of commander-in-chief of military forces. Except in time of war, this role was for past Presidents largely titular or ceremonial in nature, requiring little time or serious attention. Since World War II, however, the increasing attention demanded by national security considerations has made this role a continuing preoccupation of every President.

4. Diplomat: The President's role as chief of foreign policy has also changed from an intermittent one to one of unrelenting importance. Although few Presidents in our nation's past were considered world leaders, a President is today automatically placed in that position, with all the burdens and responsibilities it entails.

5. Legislator: Presidents have historically been associated with the legislative process because of two constitutional requirements: the President must approve or veto every bill passed by Congress, and he is instructed to recommend to Congress "such measures as he shall judge necessary and expedient." However, since the first administration of Franklin Roosevelt (with strong antecedents in several earlier administrations), presidential initiatives in the legislative area have radically increased. A 19th century legislator would be astonished at the involvement of modern Presidents in setting the congressional agenda, in budgeting and lobbying, and in using the veto power. This enlarged role as legislator is a function of the growth of government, of the need and demand for government activity and intervention.

6. Communicator: The genesis of the annual State of the Union message can be found in the constitutional injunction that the President "shall from time to time give to the Congress information of the State of the Union." From the framers' modest demand for information, one could little predict the extent to which presidential oratory and symbolic acts of leadership would become a feature of the Presidency, to the point that President Theodore Roosevelt referred to the White House as a "bully pulpit." Today a virtually constant stream of communications issues from presidential officeholders. This is attested to by the size of the Washington press corps and the presence in the White House of large staffs for public relations, communications, speechwriting, and interest-group relations.

7. Party leader: The role of party leader is a clear example of a presidential function that lacks a base in constitutional language. The framers hoped they had designed a system that could function without generating the "factions" they so disliked. Nevertheless, parties quickly became indispensable vehicles for nominating and electing candidates, for coalescing sentiments and needs into ideas and programs of action, and for providing representation and promoting compromise. Although of late the power of political parties has been weakening, it is not clear whether more or less of a burden is thus imposed on modern Presidents. Suffice it to say that a President must continue to devote time to party affairs, and must also now find ways to compensate for the reduced sphere of party influence.

Recent Presidential Roles

If the traditional roles of the Presidency have expanded over the years, the burdens on the President in recent years have increased enormously with the addition of four new roles. Although these four functions are not without historical antecedent, the changes leading to a formalization of these roles are so massive that they represent not a change in degree, but in kind.

1. Economic policy coordinator: Since the time of the Depression and the advent of Keynesian economic theory, government involvement in the economy has been a pervasive fact of political life. Although executive powers vis-a-vis the economy are fragmented and the President lacks the clear primacy in economic matters that he has in foreign affairs, he is nevertheless in a unique position to influence the nation's economic development. Indeed, he is expected to orchestrate a variety of economic instruments and to take whatever steps are necessary to make and keep the economy healthy. The worsening economic trends of very recent years have clearly intensified the complexity and difficulty of this task.

2. Social policy advocate: In a manner similar to his involvement with the economy, the President has assumed a major role in advocating policies and programs to enhance the quality of life. Beginning with the emergency measures of the New Deal, social programs and government assistance have come to be seen as the right of all citizens.

3. Pivot of the federal system: The Constitution reserved all unenumerated powers for the states and the people. However, the interstate commerce and general welfare clauses of the Constitution, as well as the addition of a national income tax, provided the means to increase federal influence. Since the 1930s, public demands have led to the emergence of an enormous and extremely complicated program of federal assistance to states and local governments. The results are a need for continuous interaction among the three levels of government and vastly increased presidential responsibilities and influence.

4. Crisis manager: Although one can of course find examples of Presidents taking action to resolve crises in the past, the difference today lies in the frequency and variety of foreign and domestic crises that the President is expected to resolve.

CONSTRAINTS AND THE ART OF POLITICS

Formal constraints on the President's power as "chief executive" are, of course, inherent in our Constitution, specifically in the sharing of powers among the three branches of government. The President derives broad authority from his constitutional mandate to ensure that the laws are faithfully executed. However, it is the Congress which makes and passes these laws. And it is the specific power of the judiciary to define these laws when the need for interpretation arises.

Thus the somewhat open-ended nature of the powers of the Presidency is counterbalanced by the formal powers of the other branches, and particularly of the Congress. The Congress creates and administratively shapes the executive departments and agencies, makes the laws, and holds the purse strings. Except for those enumerated in the Constitution, all formal powers of the President are, in effect, granted to him by Congress.

In attempting to exercise their open-ended powers, Presidents encounter other major constraints. One is the bureaucracy. Some Presidents have complained of their inability to obtain from the bureaucracy the responsiveness they would

like. At times Presidents and presidential candidates complain about and campaign against the very organizations and people who are essential to a President's success in carrying out government programs.

Rarely is the problem one of willful bureaucratic obstruction. Rather it is in major part a function of the sheer size and complexity of the government. A President can bring his governmentwide perspective to only a fraction of the government's business at any given time. Most of the work of government is handled by agency officials, who tend to see their own particular trees instead of the forest. This situation is heightened by the fact that most executive authorities are granted by the Congress not to the President, but to the heads of departments, agencies, bureaus, regulatory bodies, and, increasingly in recent years, to quasi-governmental organizations and corporations of every description.

The so-called subgovernments composed of agency program personnel, relevant congressional subcommittees, and the clientele or special-interest groups that have a stake in these programs can also constrain presidential initiatives. These subgovernments are responsible for the conduct of much government business, and are less influenced by presidential desires than by their own perceptions of their clientele and of the sources of their authority and money. In consequence, special interests, especially "single interest" groups, can be formidable barriers to presidential freedom of action. Like the bureaucracy, they are sometimes portrayed as an evil in the body politic, notwithstanding the fact that their legitimacy is firmly anchored in constitutional guarantees and the fact that they individually support important public objectives. Nevertheless, the cumulative effect of these special-interest groups has, in the judgment of this Panel, seriously handicapped presidential action in the national interest and have vastly complicated the President's role in managing the federal government.

Public opinion and the media have also historically acted as constraints on Presidents. Their effects have been intensified in recent times by the advent of polling techniques and the growth of the mass-communication media. Public protest of the Vietnam War, echoed by the mass media, influenced one recent President to retire from politics. And the combined influence of the press, the courts, the Congress, and public opinion caused another President to resign in the wake of Watergate.

All of the forces identified here as constraints

are at various times seen by the public as villains obstructing good government. It is therefore important to recognize two facts: that they are legitimate elements of the system and can be constrained only at the peril of irreparable damage to the system itself; and that they can serve as allies in, as well as obstructions to, the achievement of presidential goals.

This latter point brings us to the most important element in the American system, and also the most elusive and intangible—the art of politics, in the highest sense of that term. As we noted earlier, of equal importance to the structure of the Presidency are the skills which a given President brings to that office. These skills are inherently political ones, resting on such intangibles as "prestige," "leadership," and "influence" which can compensate for the weaknesses and accentuate the strengths of the President's statutory and constitutional powers. In short, the President is a political manager, as well as "chief executive" or "general manager." What counts in the long run is how well he manages the processes of politics.

There is no way to guarantee that a given President will have the political skills appropriate to the problems of the day, or that his political skills will be matched by his integrity, wisdom, fortitude, and managerial instinct. But, if we cannot guarantee the capabilities of an individual President, we *can* at least examine the tools and resources that should be available to every President to help him do his job—and to find ways to improve them.

THE EVOLUTION OF THE EXECUTIVE OFFICE

The Executive Office of the President came into existence as the result of a reorganization plan and an executive order promulgated in 1939 by Franklin D. Roosevelt. When it began, the Executive Office consisted of the White House staff, the Bureau of the Budget, and other units which have since disappeared. The basic origins of the Executive Office can be found in the recommendations of the President's Committee on Administrative Management, which Roosevelt established in 1936 with Louis Brownlow as Chairman.

The Brownlow Committee was formed because of the rapid growth of government activity occasioned by the Depression and New Deal programs. To help the President perform his expanding roles, the Committee developed the concept of the Executive Office of the President, envisioning it as a compact, well-organized entity relying heavily on career generalists experienced in staff and managerial functions. As this description suggests, these staffs were not seen as policy-makers who would take power away from executive agencies.

Quite the contrary, they were conceived of as information-gatherers and facilitators who would help the President to cope with major issues of policy and administration. In this manner, the Brownlow Committee intended both to increase the President's flexibility by relieving him of some of the minutiae of government, and to enhance his ability to oversee and coordinate those matters requiring his attention.

The approach of the Brownlow Committee was affirmed in 1949 by the Commission on the Organization of the Executive Branch of the Government—the first Hoover Commission. This Commission gave significant bipartisan support to the strengthening of presidential staff resources, indicating that the idea, far from being a New Deal chimera, was a response to a genuine need.

The Brownlow and Hoover commissions gave doctrinal expression to the concept of a strong and active Presidency, a reality that was emerging in any case as a result of a vastly changed and changing world. The doctrine was taken further by two subsequent groups, the President's Task Force on Government Reorganization (1966-67) and the President's Advisory Council on Executive Organization (1969-71), respectively known as the Heineman Task Force and the Ash Council. Their recommendations were aimed more at control than at coordination, calling for reorganization and for new and stronger staffs to make agencies more responsive and to aggressively translate the President's policies into action. To obtain these ends, it was recommended that staffs take a more direct hand in exercising presidential authority to settle interagency disputes.

In a sense, the quest for greater presidential control reached its logical culmination during the first Nixon administration with the Ash Council's proposal to create four "super departments" to administer domestic programs. These were to be organized around broad "major purposes" of government and were to replace seven executive departments and a number of independent agencies. However, Congress failed to act on these reorganization proposals. Following the 1972 election, Nixon attempted to achieve much the same effect by administrative measures and more aggressive staff action, but this experiment was cut short by the effects of Watergate. The principal recommendations put into effect were the creation of a Domestic Council and staff, and the conversion of the President's Bureau of the Budget into an Office of Management and Budget.

Despite the efforts of this succession of special study groups, the Executive Office of the President has not developed according to some master plan. Yet its growth has been substantial and varied. Scarcely a year has passed without an increase in its overall size or without the establishment of new staff units and the abolition or transfer of others.

Staff units have come into existence for a variety of reasons—because of congressional insistence, as a result of pressure by special-interest groups, to resolve a dispute among agencies, because a particular issue is suddenly prominent (e.g., drug abuse, cancer research, urban blight, civil defense, youth affairs, and numerous others no longer represented by special Executive Office staffs). The prestige of the Presidency is a powerful magnet, constantly attracting proposals and pressures for new staff units in the Executive Office.

Although the Executive Office has not developed as the Brownlow Report envisioned, two of the Brownlow recommendations have had enduring significance over the years. One was the proposal for six "administrative assistants," the genesis of the now numerous assistants to the President. The other was the transfer of the Bureau of the Budget from the Treasury Department to the Executive Office. In charge of the annual budget process, the coordination of the President's legislative program, and the improvement of administrative management throughout the government, the Bureau immediately became a powerful staff resource for the President. Renamed the Office of Management and Budget in 1970 as a result of an Ash Council recommendation, it presently accounts for approximately 40 per cent of total Executive Office personnel (see Figure 1).

The creation of other units in the Executive Office has reflected fundamental and enduring changes in the President's responsibilities. For example, the Employment Act of 1946, which created the Council of Economic Advisers, was a major step forward in governmental responsibility for overall guidance of the economy. Although its establishment was at first resisted by President Truman, the Council soon became a valuable resource to Presidents in rendering advice on macroeconomic issue.

Similarly, the creation of the National Security

Council in 1947 marked the emergence of the Cold War and full engagement by the United States in world affairs. The Domestic Council, created by President Nixon in 1970, was intended to be analogous to the National Security Council, assisting the President in coordinating policies and programs over a very broad sector of the government, and one that had undergone rapid growth. It was reconstituted as the Domestic Policy Staff by President Carter.

The White House Office has also mushroomed in recent years and now represents an array of special interests as well as such traditional personal and political functions as appointments, congressional relations, and so on (see Figure 2). The White House staff currently accounts for about 30 per cent of the Executive Office's total complement of more than 1,700.

The growth of the Executive Office has been so haphazard and varied that it is difficult at any given time to keep an exact record of its component elements. Moreover, key terms are used in different ways. Some consider the White House staff and the Executive Office of the President to be separate and distinct groups, the former consisting of personal assistants to the President and the latter referred to as the "institutional Presidency." In our usage, we include the White House staff within the Executive Office and within the concept of the institutional Presidency. Together, then, the White House staff and the Office of Management and Budget account for about 70 per cent of Executive Office personnel, with the remainder distributed among a host of smaller staffs.

It should be noted that according to the government's organization manual and budget categories, at least two important agencies responsible for governmentwide managerial functions are not part of Executive Office—the General Services Administration and the Office of Personnel Management (successor to the Civil Service Commission as a result of legislation passed in 1978). The Office of Personnel Management has approximately three times the personnel of the entire Executive Office, one reason for its remaining outside of the Executive Office of the President. In addition, many present functions performed by the Personnel Office are relatively routine and are not appropriate for the Executive Office. Moreover, the Personnel Office is limited by statute to the general civil service system; other aspects of personnel policy and administration are handled within the Executive Office.

Figure 1

SIZE OF UNITS IN THE
EXECUTIVE OFFICE OF THE PRESIDENT—1980
(Dates are for year established)

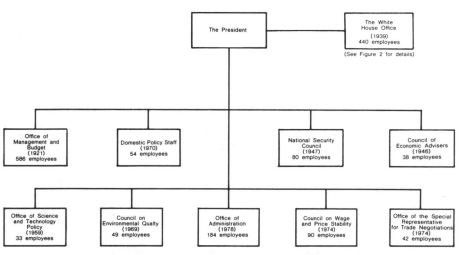

PROBLEMS, INADEQUACIES, AND UNMET NEEDS

Much of the more vocal criticism of the Executive Office of the President in recent years has been directed at its sheer size. There is no question that this is an area where smaller would be better, especially in regard to the size of the White House staff and the number of units in the rest of the Executive Office. It is only fair to note that some functions have been removed from the Executive Office over the years. An unrelenting effort should continue to transfer any functions that are not essential to fulfill presidential responsibilities on a governmentwide basis.

Our main consideration, however, is not directed to organizational symmetry, but to the "core" of staff processes vital in helping the President to: (1) deal with longer term, complex problems, (2) coordinate policies and programs across agency and functional lines, and (3) improve administrative capabilities throughout the government. Our study of these needs has revealed a number of shortcomings:

- The Executive Office is better attuned to the President's short-term political needs and to crisis management than it is to longer range policy and administrative considerations. Staffing arrangements cater to ad hoc presidential interventions and do not promote a review of those actions for their consistency and continuity with issues of enduring importance.

- There has been a pronounced shift away from the Brownlow Committee's recommendations that the Executive Office should be staffed heavily by career personnel. The Executive Office is thus deprived of people who are skilled in staff roles, experienced in government management, and suited to lend continuity and consistency.

- There has been a tendency toward control rather than toward coordination, with Executive Office staffs assuming powers and making decisions that should be the responsibility of executive departments and agencies or, in some cases, that should only be made by the President.

314

Figure 2

THE WHITE HOUSE OFFICE—1980

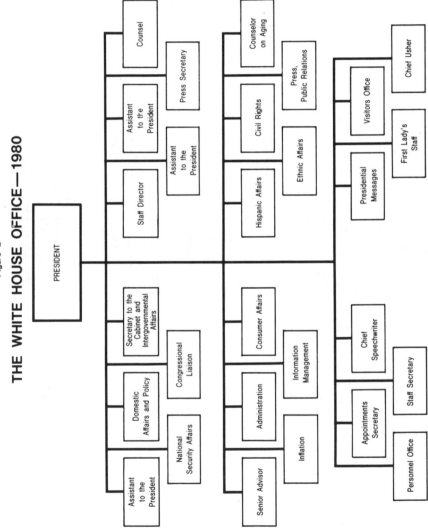

- In turn, this tendency has led to a lack of clarity in organizational roles and responsibilities, both within the Executive Office and between the Executive Office and the line agencies. It has also served to make these relationships more adversarial than is necessary or desirable.

- Although some division of labor is, of course, inevitable, given the large number of separate staffs in the Executive Office, there is too frequently no reliable means (short of direct presidential involvement) for integrating the specialized perspectives of these staffs, and those of the departments and agencies.

- In particular, the division of the key policy coordinating role into two compartments—the Domestic Policy Staff and National Security Council Staff—is ineffective. These two staffs are not comparable in important respects, and their work has been inadequately coordinated.

- Certain economic issues receive inadequate attention. Although Presidents receive an abundance of macroeconomic advice, information on the economic implications of policies and programs that cut across domestic and international lines is not well coordinated.

- In general, policy and program coordination lacks coherence and consistency; new policies are frequently developed without a sufficient analysis of the inadequacies of previous ones.

- The annual budget process has been weakened as the integrative discipline used in allocating resources in relation to policy objectives. The tendency to make many kinds of financial commitments independent of the budget process should be reversed.

- The Office of Management and Budget's administrative improvement capabilities have been impaired over the years by neglect, loss of experienced staff, and subordination of this role to the demands of the annual budget preparation cycle. The Office of Management and Budget's ability to serve the President in improving managerial performance throughout the government has in consequence been seriously weakened.

- There is no provision for a staff that, on a consistent and systematic basis, can look beyond short-term problems to study longer range trends and to anticipate problems.

In general, the many staffs and processes oriented toward the Oval Office present a vast flow of ideas, initiatives, and information to the President. *Unfortunately, these are not routinely and reliably integrated with one another or with the President's longer term governmental responsibilities.* Presidents thus too often base their actions on a sequence of partial views. They operate with little carryover of information, on either issues or procedures, from one administration to the next. They are likely to remain underexposed to longer term, institutional perspectives on their own work, as well as on the work of their personal aides and the government in general. The result of these tendencies is to impair the leadership potential of the Office of the President.

As an educational resource, the President too often renders messages that are unclear.

As a convenor of outside power centers, the President too often functions in a manner that is ad hoc and erratic, both at home and abroad.

As an initiator, the President too often operates without adequate knowledge of the longer term implications of policy choices and administrative realities.

Chapter III

DESIGN FOR THE EXECUTIVE OFFICE

Viewed against the crisis of public management, the Executive Office of the President exhibits weaknesses that demand correction. Inadequacies in that office reduce the ability of our national leadership to pursue coherent and well-considered courses of action. Remedying this situation will not solve all our problems of governing. It *will* represent a large step in the right direction.

This chapter offers six recommendations for restructuring the Executive Office of the President. The next chapter contains five recommendations for revitalizing the Office of Management and Budget—the single most important existing unit for implementing the President's management responsibilities. Our objective in making all these suggestions is to ensure that every President inherits an Executive Office equipped for the challenge of governing in the 1980s.

A STRATEGY FOR REFORM

Proposals for change in the Executive Office must recognize that the Presidency is occupied by an individual with personal preferences, needs, interests, and methods of operating. Formal designs for the Executive Office which go against the grain of this fundamental reality are useless.

However, this country can no longer afford the luxury of a de novo educational process every time a new President assumes office. Whatever a President's personality, the Executive Office must be adjusted to the needs of constitutional government in the modern era. The internal arrangement and staff resources of the Office must be able to serve a succession of Presidents and to cope with continuing national problems.

What is needed is a general framework, not a detailed blueprint for the Executive Office of the President. As Chapter II makes clear, the Executive Office as a whole has developed in the absence of any plan. It is time it was designed, and designed with national needs in mind.

Guidelines
Our recommendations are founded on the ten basic principles delineated in Chapter I. Taken together, they produce the conception of a Presidency that speaks for national interests but that does not ride roughshod over the divided and shared powers in our pluralistic society and world.

Any reforms must be sufficiently flexible to allow for an individual President's personality and interests, but not so flexible as to subordinate the central machinery of government to personal whim. The responsibility of a President for coping with immediate crises must not outweigh his responsibility for promoting orderly, ongoing processes of government management. Staff members are needed who will help to spark creative presidential policy initiatives as well as help to carry out the Constitution's injunction to "take care" that the laws passed by Congress are faithfully executed.

Guidelines for the appropriate reforms are implied by our diagnosis of the current situation. As policy and administrative problems have become more interconnected, Presidents need to be better equipped to perceive and act upon the interconnections. This need implies *the support of staff with broader competence than prevails today.*

If power has become greatly dispersed, the Presidency should have a heightened capacity to bring disparate and powerful interests together in a way that is orderly and sensitive to governmentwide and national needs. *Such a capacity implies an Executive Office that is organized to facilitate collaboration with others, not one that simply tries to impose the will of the President and his staff.*

If short-term political considerations inevitably (and legitimately) crowd into the Oval Office, Presidents must be assured access to individuals with continuing experience in the management of government affairs. *Such assurance implies the presence of people in the Executive Office who can help Presidents assess longer term policy and administrative problems and the larger implications of day-to-day presidential decisions.*

The Broad Proposal

Although it is necessary to present our proposals individually, the recommendations in this chapter and the next should be considered as an integrated unit. This set of proposals would reconstitute the core of the Executive Office of the President into a body of staff assistance for policy development, information coordination, and management improvement. More important than any one recommendation is the interrelationship among all.

In this chapter, we propose three staff units, each roughly comparable in function and status, to assist the President in the development of policies for international, domestic, and economic affairs. We also propose the creation of a small staff secretariat to help coordinate the information processes for presidential decision-making, and we suggest improving the capacity of the Executive Office to provide longer range policy studies. A small number of White House aides would serve the immediate personal needs of the President in his daily work. The following chapter sets forth our proposals to revitalize the Office of Management and Budget.

As the previous chapter showed, the Executive Office of the President and, within it, the White House Office have become a melange of units and staffs located there for all manner of reasons, but principally because of the higher status that comes from closer association with the Presidency. This desire for status should no longer be the guiding principle in the development of the Executive Office.

Instead, the Executive Office of the President should be reduced to encompass only those functions that are vital to the President in the performance of his governmentwide duties. To that end, we believe that if our recommendations for strengthening the core of the Presidency were implemented, it would become easier to analyze, one by one, other Executive Office units and to transfer many out of the Executive Office.

We are not proposing the creation of a closed bureaucratic elite in the Presidency. Each staff unit would be headed by a senior White House assistant appointed solely at the discretion of the current President. Below this top level should be a combination of non-career appointees and civil servants, including the federal government's new Senior Executive Service. It would be a mistake to equate political appointees with "policy" and career public servants with "administration." Career civil servants can and do function effectively in highly sensitive policy roles. Likewise, formal political appointees often have a technical competence that transcends their political-party credentials. Our proposals would integrate both types of personnel into the service of the Presidency.

The personnel performing in this Executive Office system, although they may have specialized backgrounds, must have advanced to the point that they have the governmentwide objectivity to comprehend, analyze, and coordinate information flowing to the White House. Like Presidents, they must be professional generalists.

We propose a new structure that would reverse the trend toward self-assertive, narrowly focused, haphazard assistance to Presidents. Staffs should play a facilitating role, helping the President to work out major policies and administrative problems with the leaders in Congress and in the executive departments and agencies.

This presidential staffwork cannot be a mechanical process. Those who do it must have a passion not simply for anonymity, but also for making the machinery of government work. Rather than handing down presidential decisions or fulfilling some personal policy agenda, their mission is to help the President frame and implement his national agenda in conjunction with the many other participants in our complex government system.

To play this facilitating (or "honest broker") role, staffs must be regarded both as loyal to the President and as fair and even-handed by the major parties involved. While remaining mindful of the President's interests, they must search for compromise wherever possible. Where issues must be brought to the President for resolution, the presidential staff must ensure that all positions are fairly presented, that the President is fully informed about all relevant facets of the problem, and that any staff recommendations have been subjected to vigorous scrutiny by the interested parties.

In other words, the system of presidential staffwork we propose would help to organize, scrutinize, and augment the information necessary for effective presidential leadership. Our design for the Executive Office would multiply the eyes, ears, and hands of the President as a constitutional chief executive.

SIZE AND FUNCTIONS OF WHITE HOUSE STAFF

Recommendation 1

The trend toward enlargement of the immediate White House staff should be reversed. Rigorous efforts should be made to keep this staff small. It should be structured to serve the immediate functional and personal needs of the President, not to reflect various special interests.

The optimum size of a staff cannot be determined by formulas and quotas. Therefore, the dictum that Executive Office staffs be kept as small as possible is one that should be applied on a case-by-case basis. The Office of Management and Budget, for example, presently has a complement of approximately 600 people for overseeing the budget and administrative work of the entire executive branch. As our recommendations in the next chapter imply, this is not sufficient to its responsibilities.

However, the pressure to keep Executive Office staffs small should be applied with special vigor to the White House. Major personnel increases in this staff can be forgone if the other, more institutional units of the Executive Office are adequately manned to do their jobs. The size of the White House staff should be limited for two reasons. First, it is here that the temptation to speak on behalf of the President and to "second guess" the line agencies is especially strong; the larger the staff, the wider the circle of persons who may yield to this temptation, and the greater the chances of building an image, if not the reality, of White House aggrandizement. Nothing more quickly destroys confidence in the "honest broker" function. Second, a vital function of elements of the White House staff is, under guidelines from the President, to filter information and preclude irrelevant material from reaching his desk. The larger the size of these staffs, the more likely they are to duplicate the expertise of executive agencies, to develop their own biases, intervene where they should not, and in short to create unnecessary work.

The desire for a trim White House staff is not intended to constrain, but rather to enhance, the

President's ability to function effectively. An examination of any typical day in the White House would reveal the importance to the President of those who serve him in such vital functions as appointments, media relations, congressional relations, speechwriting, executive recruitment, and others. These staff members should have a high order of political intelligence, functioning as presidential trouble-shooters and coordinators, not only in their own particular fields of interest but also to ensure that the other units of the Executive Office are working smoothly and well. It is to such vital presidential needs that the White House staff should be oriented, not to a proliferation of offices and assistants representing specialized interests in our society.

ECONOMIC AFFAIRS STAFF

Recommendation 2

An Economic Affairs Staff should be created within the Executive Office of the President, to be headed by a Director with the status of Senior Assistant to the President.

The complexity of economic issues and their significance in both the domestic and international spheres argue for the creation of a separate Economic Affairs Staff. The current division of the policy and program coordination function in the Executive Office between "domestic" and "national security" staffs has become increasingly unwieldy. Individuals with recent experience in these areas have told us that their most significant problems occurred in attempting to integrate the economic aspects of domestic and foreign affairs.

Virtually every domestic activity of the government has important effects on the economy, either directly or indirectly. And we have come into an age when problems, trends, and events abroad have profound effects on domestic programs and the economy. In turn, the state of the economy obviously has a vital effect on foreign as well as domestic affairs. The need to integrate these domestic/foreign/economic policy considerations might suggest the desirability of a single policy coordination staff encompassing all three, rather than the tripartite structure we propose. However, we think the latter is advisable to allow for a better division of labor and to preserve distinctions which, although broad and general, are nevertheless useful in a government as enormous and complex as ours. The domestic/ foreign/economic areas each comprehends a large community of executive agencies; each has a distinctive focus that should be maintained. Moreover, it would be more effective to allow the competing demands and tensions to surface among these three areas than to take the risk of submerging them.

Our recommendation for an Economic Affairs Staff is not intended to diminish the status of the Council of Economic Advisers or to duplicate the work of its staff. Rather, our recommendation preserves the status and role of the Council and prevents it from being drawn increasingly into additional considerations, including microeconomic and sectoral issues and the specific economic implications of agency policies and programs.

The Council of Economic Advisers' economic reports represent one of the four principal economic instruments of the government, the others being the role of the Treasury in tax policy, of the Federal Reserve Board in monetary policy, and of the Office of Management and Budget in fiscal policy. We are not satisfied that the ebb and flow of relationships among the economic policy streams is being monitored adequately by anyone at the present, not for purposes of control but for information, coordination, and clarity. This is a staff function, an important potential one for the Economic Affairs Staff.

DOMESTIC AFFAIRS STAFF

Recommendation 3
The Domestic Policy Staff should be reconstituted as the Domestic Affairs Staff, to be headed by a Director with the status of Senior Assistant to the President.

The Domestic Council was created during the Nixon administration in an effort to improve the ability of the Executive Office to coordinate the vastly burgeoning federal activities primarily concerned with domestic policy. It was reconstituted by the Carter Administration as the Domestic Policy Staff.

The creation of a White House unit concerned with domestic policy caused apprehension within the Office of Management and Budget because it impinged on some of the traditional responsibilities of that agency. Many line agencies also viewed the unit with misgiving, regarding it as another bureaucratic layer impeding access to presidential decision-making and at times functioning in a high-handed manner.

Although these problems appear to have eased over the years, the present situation remains less than satisfactory. One reason is the steady growth in the size of the staff, which now numbers approximately 60 persons. This creates a tendency for staff members to become specialized and for the "honest broker" function to break down.

We believe that the creation of an Economic Affairs Staff would ease the workload of the Domestic Affairs Staff and improve the division of labor, in addition to providing a valuable focus on the economic aspects of domestic and foreign concerns.

As emphasized earlier, the Domestic Affairs Staff, like the President's other policy coordinating groups, should be staffed to include professional generalists drawn from the Senior Executive Service and elsewhere. Among such persons one could expect to find greater resistance to pressures to specialize as well as temperaments better suited to the facilitative role. Moreover, such staff members would be more likely to survive changes in administration, and this likelihood would help to serve the goals of continuity and consistency.

INTERNATIONAL AFFAIRS STAFF

Recommendation 4
The staff of the National Security Council should be replaced by an International Affairs Staff, headed by a Director with the status of Senior Assistant to the President. The statutory National Security Council should remain as an interagency committee to be used as the President needs.

The National Security Council is an interagency committee consisting of the President, Vice President, Secretary of State, and Secretary of Defense, with the Director of Central Intelligence and the Chairman of the Joint Chiefs of Staff as statutory advisers. Since its inception, it has been a valuable presidential resource in the area of foreign affairs. However, the special status built up over the years by the National Security Council staff has not been conducive to the integration of domestic and foreign policies.

The Council's staff has tended to function recently as an agency unto itself, a power base for personal prominence, complete with public information officers. Yet at times in the past, the Council's staff has functioned as a model staff, operating circumspectly, anonymously, and with careful attention to the distinction between objective process and advocacy. This latter method of operating is obviously much to be preferred in the best interests of Presidents and of the society at large. One reason we now recommend the creation of an International Affairs Staff is to promote and reinforce this preferred style of operating in the international sphere.

Another reason for recommending the creation of the International Affairs Staff is that we believe the time has come to provide a mandate and perspective broader than the concept of "national security." The National Security Council's staff has traditionally focused on two areas of expertise—political and military affairs. These are clearly of primary importance and should remain paramount considerations of the International Affairs Staff. But we think it would be productive to place them within a larger frame of reference. Just as our society has become increasingly fragmented, so has the world. American influence has diminished, and we must now be partners as much as leaders and adversaries in world affairs. Economic, social, and cultural matters are assuming new importance on the international scene and must now be given attention equal to their importance.

POLICY RESEARCH AND ANALYSIS

Recommendation 5

The Executive Office of the President needs institutionalized arrangements for longer term policy research and analysis. One approach would be to establish a new office headed by a Director who reports to the President. Another would be to develop a more fluid system of long-term working assignments among the core staff of the Executive Office. In any case, this function should operate on a continuing basis within the Presidency.

Various recommendations have been made over the years for some type of planning agency within the Executive Office. Several attempts have been made to implement this idea, but none has survived. One reason, we believe, is that most of these proposals have been accompanied by grandiose expectations, which in turn have given rise to exaggerated fears and misunderstandings regarding what "government planning" is and can accomplish.

Partly for this reason, we eschew "planning" in favor of "policy research and analysis" in describing this function. Expectations should be kept within reasonable bounds, and it should be recognized that the products of future-oriented studies would not be "plans" in any rigid sense. They would instead be concerned with trends, developments, and alternatives that might have profound implications for U.S. policy.

We believe such an understanding of the role would dispel another major barrier to the establishment of this function—the fear of Presidents and their close advisers that a "planning agency" would embarrass the President by setting goals for him, controlling his agenda, and thus involving him in matters he would wish to avoid. We clearly intend this function to have no such effects. The products would constitute only one link in a chain of contributions to the process of policy formulation, coordination, and integration.

This link is missing at present, for all practical purposes. Given the complexities of the modern world that we have discussed thus far in this report, and the relative diminution of U.S. influence and margin for error, the time has come when a staff must be available to the President that can look beyond the short term in a systematic and ongoing way.

We see no inherent reason for future-oriented studies to be restricted to a single time horizon; in fact, we believe it would be advantageous if time frames were varied. However, as noted, one purpose of this staff would be to perform ongoing studies of longer range trends, 10 to 25 years out, in key areas.

In this regard, the recently concluded "Global 2000" study has some important lessons. This cooperative effort, involving some 15 executive agencies, was a herculean task because of the disparate nature of the forecasting, planning, and modeling capabilities of the agencies, disparities that made comparability and correlation extremely difficult. The study revealed a compelling need for a high-status function to give long-range studies a permanent mandate and framework, to set standards and requirements, and to coordinate results.

This implies what we in fact believe: that this function need not be performed by some massive agency that does all of the work itself. The participating agencies (and outside resources) should do most of the research and data processing. The role of Executive Office staff should be to stimulate, standardize, correlate, and coordinate.

The other major longer term work of the Executive Office staff would consist of special research assignments from the President or the three policy coordinating staffs, with time horizons of 2 to 10 years. In many cases, these studies would concern analyses of the possible consequences of alternative policies and courses of action.

We also believe that, whatever the structure of this policy research activity, its staff should have the discretion to select and undertake studies on its own initiative, within guidelines established by the President. Such discretion would stimulate intellectual ferment, as well as provide a measure of independence.

The staff must also have the authority to use grants and contracts to foster outside research. This ability would help to limit the number of staff members (it is important for this staff to be no larger than any of the three policy coordination staffs we have recommended). The staff should also have a particularly close working relationship with the President's Office of Science and Technology Policy. We believe that the existence of this function in the Executive Office would help to reduce the number of ad hoc presidential commissions required in the future. Many assignments could instead be done by temporary working groups. In those cases where special commissions were needed, Executive Office staff could help to systematize their work by providing a common administrative base and technical assistance.

WHITE HOUSE SECRETARIAT

Recommendation 6

A White House Secretariat, headed by a Senior Assistant to the President with a small staff of generalists, should be established to help ensure that materials come to the President's desk in an organized manner best-suited to his methods of operating and his needs for review and action. The Secretariat would not engage in substantive decision-making, but would be entirely process-oriented. It would develop procedures for summarizing and presenting materials and ensuring that relevant parties are consulted.

The volume and complexity of materials that now flow into the Oval Office argue persuasively for a more regularized system for organizing and presenting those materials. This statement is meant not to disparage those who in the past have performed ably in trying to organize the flow of initiatives and information to the President, but rather to indicate that this function must now be given a more formal and permanent structure.

The function of the Secretariat would be administrative in nature and neutral with regard to particular policies. The Secretariat should *not* be another layer in substantive decision-making. Instead, the Secretariat staff should be process-oriented.

We do not mean to suggest that the Secretariat would constitute a paper-processing mill that could be ignored with impunity by those intent on pressing their substantive view on the President. This is one reason we stress that the Secretariat should be headed by a Senior Assistant to the President. The overriding concern of the Secretariat should be to protect the integrity of central decision-making processes, making sure that incoming work consistently meets the President's standards of quality, that executive summaries are well and objectively done, that all relevant bases are touched. The Secretariat chief's abilities should be such that he or she could serve as a trusted adviser to the President on matters of process, evaluating the adequacy and reliability of existing sources of information and helping to find new sources. If the Secretariat's function, on both formal and informal dimensions, were performed with consummate professionalism, it would quickly come to be seen as a help by those wishing to reach the President on substantive issues.

By this we do not mean to suggest that the Secretariat would constitute the only channel to the President. On many occasions, time is vital and the head of an executive agency must contact the President immediately. This should not have to be done through formal Secretariat processes. Likewise, the annual budget process entails many months of work and countless transactions, and it would be pointless and duplicative to funnel this work through the Secretariat.

To a considerable extent, the Secretariat should concern itself with follow-through to ensure that a given matter is acted upon in an appropriate and timely fashion. This is the second reason for the head of the Secretariat to be a Senior Assistant to the President, able to keep track of materials after they have flowed through the Secretariat to the President, to be knowledgeable of needs for further consultations, to clarify assignments that are made, and to monitor some final disposition of the matter when necessary.

The head of the Secretariat should be helped in these tasks by a small staff—perhaps not more than 15. This number should be rigorously maintained, if for no other reason than that, at this staffing level, the workload itself should reduce the temptation of Secretariat staff to duplicate or second-guess the substantive work of others.

We stress that the Secretariat should follow a general "rule of reason" approach in its work. The essence of this work would be judgmental, not mechanical. Only a staff of the highest caliber could effectively judge whether a particular matter was exposed to the right people and to a broad range of views, and balance the need for consultation against the need for urgent action. Only a staff with the utmost discretion could be counted on to maintain the confidentiality of their information and the fairness of their actions. The Secretariat must not be a place for bureaucratic clerks, political opportunists, or policy advocates. Its staff members must be impartial, except in their commitment to an effective Presidency. It must be self-effacing, except in defending the integrity of its processes. It must be bureaucratically adept but politically sensitive, lest its process rigidify into a paper-shuffling operation that loses sight of its larger purpose in serving the President's needs.

In addition to the functions described above, the Secretariat could provide staff assistance to the Cabinet when it meets and, on a selective basis, to ad hoc groups. It could be especially useful in advising the President on when, and for what purposes, to rely on informal means of consultation across departmental boundaries and when to establish interagency task forces or committees of a temporary or continuing nature.

The existence of such a Secretariat would constitute a useful step forward in bringing consistency and continuity to the functioning of the Executive Office of the President. It would be an appropriate place to assign career personnel, thus helping to provide more of an institutional memory than the government now has. However, at a change of administration, the particular methods and procedures of the Secretariat should be adapted to the new President's personal needs and style of operating. For this reason the head of the Secretariat should be the President's choice, a person in whom he has confidence and who has the ability to adapt the Secretariat to the President's needs.

In the final analysis, the enforcement of proper discipline to protect the integrity of the Secretariat process would be the responsibility only of the President. Agency heads who abused the privilege of direct access and used it to short-circuit the Secretariat could be called to account by no one other than the President.

CONCLUSION

In our recommendations we have proposed four Senior Assistants to the President: three to head the policy coordinating staffs and one to head the Secretariat. We have also optionally proposed a director for long-range policy studies. These assistants, plus the Director of the Office of Management and Budget, would be responsible for what we have called the core processes of policy coordination, policy advice, information flow, and

management. These senior aides would constitute an informal "management committee" for the Executive Office as a whole, meeting as frequently as necessary to ensure that communications and the division of labor are working effectively on behalf of the President. A chief of staff, if one were chosen by the President, would be the natural chairman of this committee.

Our recommendations are based on a great deal more than specific institutional change. As important as these changes are is the way in which they are done. In particular, we draw attention to the comparability of our recommendations for the staffs represented on the management committee. Although the staffs concerned would be responsible for large sectors, overlaps could occur on many important issues. The stress on comparability is intended to encourage a close and fluid working relationship, with ad hoc project teams being drawn from different staffs when warranted.

Comparability in status among the heads of these staffs would encourage coordination, as would the function of the Secretariat. Another important factor is whether a chief of staff were appointed by the President and how the responsibilities of that role were defined. The appointment of a chief of staff is so clearly a matter of personal choice on the part of a President that, although our prevailing sentiment is in favor of such an appointment, we have not argued for it. If, however, a President were to appoint a chief of staff and wished him to be oriented primarily to process rather than substance, it would make sense for the chief of staff to also be head of the Secretariat. In addition, he could coordinate the remainder of the White House staff—the intimate associates of the President in his daily work, the political aides, congressional relations advisers, and others.

Crisis management is obviously an extremely important consideration that can occupy much of a President's time. Because crises are by definition unpredictable, we believe there is no certain way to organize and staff the Executive Office for specific crises. As we have previously pointed out, however, the Executive Office is already able to deal more effectively with short-term problems than with long-term ones. Our recommendations would help ensure that information and integrative mechanisms are at hand in advance and do not have to be created under the frenzy of last minute crises.

If the Executive Office staffs we have proposed were to fail in functioning as facilitators—if they were to act more as assistant Presidents than as assistants to the President—pressures by department heads for direct access to the President would mount, thereby increasing the burdens on the President and defeating the entire coordination process. Failure to perform the Executive Office staff role properly would inevitably intensify congressional demands to levy statutory requirements on the Executive Office and to bring unduly powerful presidential aides to account before the legislature. Our hope is that an implicit trade-off might be achieved in our unwritten constitution. In return for a more collaborative approach by the President, the Congress might be persuaded to refrain from encumbering the Executive Office with additional statutory requirements unless such were sought by the President, thus allowing him the maximum degree of freedom in organizing his staff and institutional resources.

Implemented in the ways suggested above, we believe our recommendations would resolve many of the problems we identified in the preceding chapter. They would improve the ability of the institutional Presidency to anticipate trends, to coordinate and integrate policies and programs, to give adequate attention to the economic aspects of domestic and foreign affairs, and to clarify relationships within the Executive Office and between the Executive Office and the line agencies.

Chapter IV

KEY MANAGEMENT PROCESSES: A STRENGTHENED OFFICE OF MANAGEMENT AND BUDGET

However high the quality of the new staff units proposed in the previous chapter, their work would be undercut if government were ineffective in carrying out approved programs and projected policies. Efforts at improved managerial performance clearly must extend to the large range of day-to-day and week-to-week government activities that rarely come to the personal attention of a President. Improvement of government administration is a responsibility shared by the Presidency and every department and agency of the executive branch. The next chapter offers recommendations for strengthening the performance of the departments and agencies. This chapter focuses on managerial resources in the Executive Office of the President.

A presidential agency for management improvement already exists: the Office of Management and Budget. What is needed is to strengthen this office to deal with the pressing problems of public management in the 1980s.

Once again, it is important to consider not only the separate recommendations but also their cumulative impact. Management may seem to be an abstract term, but it encompasses the everyday reality of the workings of government. The President's management agency—the Office of Management and Budget—should be the center for assessing and dealing with this reality. As a practical matter this means developing the plan for executive branch spending; assisting departments and agencies to operate as they should; helping different levels of government work together effectively; evaluating the policies and administration of government programs; developing a presidential perspective on legislation and government regulations; and facilitating the flow of information in all three areas.

The five recommendations in this chapter address ways to improve each of these functions in the Office of Management and Budget. Action on these recommendations would constitute a historic strengthening of the key agency for implementing the President's governmentwide management responsibilities.

THE DEVELOPMENT OF THE OFFICE OF MANAGEMENT AND BUDGET

Created in 1921, the Bureau of the Budget became a major resource to Presidents for central management capabilities, particularly after it was transferred to the Executive Office in 1939, at a time when the scale and complexity of government were rapidly accelerating. Although little known outside of Washington, the Bureau became of enormous importance as the agency responsible for preparing the President's annual budget, for clearing his legislative program, for acquiring administrative information, for proposing reorganizations, and for undertaking special managerial assignments.

As a result of these functions, staff members of the Bureau came into intimate contact with the administrative realities of every agency of government. The neutrality and competence that were hallmarks of the agency made it the trusted and reliable center of information networks that extended throughout the executive branch and into state and local governments. It became an invaluable source of intelligence, advice, and assistance for Presidents, White House assistants, legislative leaders, and state and international agencies. The Bureau not only compiled dependable information on people, programs, and problems, it also generated useful solutions.

The Bureau of the Budget thus came to have

a double value—for the specific functions it performed and for the informational and problem-solving capability it represented. In these ways, the agency for decades has been a reliable, professional resource for Presidents and their aides in maintaining a hold on the sprawling executive branch. A measure of its significance is that knowledgeable students of government would rank its Director among the half dozen most important presidential appointments.

In 1970, the Bureau was reorganized and renamed the Office of Management and Budget. The budget remains its most potent tool, one that has been the backbone of its effectiveness. The budget is by any definition a tool of *management*, as are the coordination of the President's legislative program and all other functions of the Office of Management and Budget. However, at almost the same time that the agency was reorganized, both its budget and management sides were being weakened.

After the reorganization, the administrative management functions were pared to a skeletal staff. Moreover, as pressures to cut the budget intensified, the agency's normal preoccupation with the budget became ever more dominating. A measure of political layering occurred and the agency became more political in its outlook, losing some of its anonymity and becoming more visible and subject to special-interest pressures. The Office of Management and Budget's congressional relations during this period became increasingly strained.

Serious efforts have been made in recent years to overcome some of these problems, but several key OMB functions remain weakened. Clearly, the Office of Management and Budget is not an end in itself. The end to be achieved is the need for improvement of the key managerial functions and processes that Presidents and their associates must rely on for information and for effective program implementation and coordination. The Office of Management and Budget has a history and tradition, however, which provide a foundation on which to build.

Several major functions must be addressed. All are represented within the OMB staff today, at one level or another. The problem is not that these functions are lacking within the agency, but rather that they have been weakened or have received insufficient leadership and resources.

There are obvious questions regarding the effect our recommendations would have on the organizational structure and leadership of the Office of Management and Budget, how various officials and staffs would relate to one another, and what the net effect might be in regard to revitalization of the agency. We present our comments on these questions in the conclusion of this chapter, after first presenting our individual recommendations.

STRENGTHENING THE BUDGET PROCESS

Recommendation 7

Strengthening the President's management capability requires an improved and expanded budget process. Steps should be taken to: (1) improve it as the vehicle for integrating presidential and congressional decisions about government income and the allocation of resources, (2) enhance its potential as an instrument for improving managerial discipline and the execution of federal programs, and (3) improve its accuracy as a measure of the effectiveness of governmentwide activity and expenditure.

As noted in Chapter I, the increasing size and complexity of government during the past several decades have contributed to a radical change in the character of most federal activity and expenditures, a fact still not fully realized by even the informed public. Although the effects of these trends in any given year may not be particularly noticeable or startling, their cumulative impact over a generation is definitely so. One of the most profound effects has been the progressive weakening of the annual budget process as a framework for decision-making, managerial discipline, and information.

Today, three-fourths of expenditures are "controllable" only over the long term and only by legislation. Most budget dollars are not expended in the purchase of goods or the delivery of services by the federal government itself. Rather, most of the federal budget comprises transfers to individuals (e.g., social security checks), payments to private contractors, grants to states and cities, and a host of other financial arrangements with the private sector and subnational governments.

At the same time, Washington has resorted extensively to federal commitments and actions not reflected in the budget, such as special tax provisions, loan guarantees, regulatory provisions, and various other techniques. Frequently, these are designed specifically to escape the discipline of the budget process or a budget ceiling imposed by the President or the Congress.

It would be a mistake to make the general judgment that all of these trends are inherently bad.

Considering all of the decisions made over many years that resulted in mandated expenditures or "off-budget" programs, it probably would be difficult to find many that did not seem reasonable and persuasive. They seemed so to their proponents who, at various times and in varying combinations, have included Presidents, executive agencies, congressional committees, and major interest groups. Many of those decisions represented ingenious solutions to problems which the normal budget process could not resolve. Nevertheless, the cumulative result of these decisions is undesirable, as are the degree to which these trends have come to dominate the process and the inability of the tools and resources of the Executive Office to cope with this changed situation. There has not been a sufficient countervailing force to protect the integrity of the budget process and to wage a consistent rear-guard action against the trends we have noted.

A major effort should now be made to resist these trends and to begin to reverse them. Not all mandated requirements are of equal value. Not all indirect expenditures are of equal value. We recognize that an extremely difficult, long and painstaking process would be required to incorporate the extra-budgetary expenditures into the budget process. It would require an unusual degree of mutual understanding and collaboration between the executive branch and the Congress, with leadership coming from key elements of both branches. Given such a concerted effort, the discipline of the budget process could be restored to a greater part of federal government activities.

The new congressional budget process is built around the two budget committees and the Congressional Budget Office. Far from being a threat to the Presidency, this process could be influential in bringing under control the specialized interests that now undermine the discipline of the budget system.

Simultaneously, a major effort should be made to simplify the actual work involved in compiling the budget in the Executive Office of the President. Over the years, the accretion of paperwork and the detailed requirements for data, many of them levied by Congress, have made budget preparation a nightmarish process. Budget examiners are rarely able to make field visits as they once did, and as a result know less about the grassroots operations of their assigned agencies. This lack of first-hand knowledge has introduced a certain air of unreality into the budget process and has contributed to the decrease in OMB's effectiveness. Many of the detailed requirements that have

helped produce these conditions are unnecessary and could be eliminated. A concerted effort to simplify the process, undertaken by the Office of Management and Budget and Congressional Budget Office with the support of the appropriate congressional committees, could yield very positive results.

In addition to a revival of the budget process as a tool for management and control, another goal should be an improvement in its informational value. In recent years, discussions have been held on a "tax expenditure budget" and a "regulatory budget" and other ideas, and some experimentation has taken place. Progress along these lines would make the annual budget a more accurate and understandable portrayal of federal activities and commitments. This would help clarify trade-offs, highlight responsibility, and inhibit those who attempt to short-circuit the budget process to attain their goals.

Although the budget process has been weakened, it remains the most effective single tool for management and the setting of presidential and congressional priorities. It is vitally important to prevent further erosion to the process and to build on this foundation in the ways that we have proposed. An essential first step here would be presidential and congressional recognition of the need and value in doing so.

STRENGTHENING ADMINISTRATIVE MANAGEMENT

Recommendation 8
Appropriate measures should be taken to strengthen the Office of Management and Budget's capabilities to improve administrative management on a governmentwide basis.

The crucial importance of effective administrative management is unfortunately not widely recognized. It is largely seen as routine in contrast to the high visibility and improtance of presidential decision-making. Yet the development and coordination of important government policies and programs will be undercut without consistently competent follow-through in the setting of standards, the provision of assistance, and the evaluation of results. Without such effective implementation, the creation of new government policies and programs may be futile exercises.

The mission of the Office of Management and Budget's administrative management staff should be to use its prestige and that of the President to improve organization and management throughout the federal government. Its functions should include the improvement of management and administration, information, personnel policy, productivity, program evaluation, and organization. The OMB is the only Executive Office agency in a position to perform these tasks. From its activities, OMB could derive a rich source of experience and information useful to other agencies, its own internal divisions, and to the President and his advisers. Properly conceived and given proper leadership, these functions would benefit and should be welcomed by the executive agencies.

Yet, as we have noted, the Office of Management and Budget is unable to meet the government's growing need for administrative management services. A virtual explosion of legislation now defines and regulates administrative authority, organization, processes, and procedures, as well as objectives and policies, often in inconsistent and contradictory ways. Programs have been launched without adequate planning as to how they would be administered, without using expert assistance in organizing them, and without prompt revisions based on experience. Policy developers frequently overlook the requisites of administration and often appear to assume that policies are self-implementing. Inadequate follow-through and implementation contribute to the stream of problems that eventually find their way to the President.

A major drive must in consequence be mounted to help improve management performance throughout the government, to protect the President from unnecessary problems, to help restore public and congressional confidence in government administration, and to make possible the proper devolution of decision-making and operational responsibilities to the line agencies. Such a revitalization of management capabilities would require a determined effort by OMB with the full support of the President, his close advisers, and the Congress. Administrative management functions should be given the proper organizational framework and status within OMB. An enlarged staff might be required; if so, emphasis should be given to recruiting the most seasoned and competent management experts that can be found.

STRENGTHENING PROGRAM EVALUATION

Recommendation 9
The Office of Management and Budget must be strength-

ened in its ability to improve program evaluation. A Program Evaluation Staff should therefore be created within the agency to set standards, provide assistance, monitor progress reporting and productivity improvement, and evaluate effectiveness in accomplishing objectives.

The previous recommendation included productivity improvement and program evaluation as two of the many functions that logically come under the general heading of administrative management within OMB. Regardless of the precise organizational arrangement, we believe these functions should be singled out for special attention and a new mandate.

In any rational management system, program evaluation is a vital function which provides essential "feedback" information for managerial, policy-making, legislative, and accountability purposes. Without reliable evaluation, it is impossible to know if a program is being administered effectively, if it is attaining its specified purposes, if its funds are being properly spent, and if its benefits are worth its costs.

We are well aware that program evaluation is a difficult task. It is more an art than a science, and no method or system is universally applicable. Yet advances are being made. The General Accounting Office has become competent in some aspects of evaluation, and most agencies have evaluation staffs and are making genuine efforts to advance their skill.

What is missing is a central focus for a sustained drive to improve executive branch program evaluation. This is a prime responsibility of every agency, but the agencies need help. Without objective standards, an agency's evaluation of its own programs is, fairly or unfairly, often regarded by congressional committees and others as self-serving.

In addition to assisting individual agencies, a central evaluation capability should monitor related interagency, intergovernmental, and intersectoral programs, and assess the effects of one agency's program on the program of another.

To fulfill these and other needs, a central program evaluation service of major dimensions would be needed. The Office of Management and Budget would be the obvious location of such a service. The Office of Management and Budget should establish a Program Evaluation Staff with a mandate to set standards, provide assistance, work for comparability in evaluation methods throughout the government, encourage productivity improvements, and monitor results. Properly supported and. led, this group should become a clearinghouse for the state of the art within the executive branch, working in cooperation not only with the agencies but also with the General Accounting Office, congressional groups, and private-sector resources.

ADMINISTERING INTERGOVERN-MENTAL ASSISTANCE

Recommendation 10
The federal government should make a firm commitment to a thorough and consistent effort to simplify, rationalize, and improve the many programs of federal assistance to states and local governments. The focal point of this effort should be a new Federal Assistance Administration Staff created within OMB.

One of the most difficult managerial problems confronting the federal government is the need to overhaul the system of federal assistance to states and local communities. This system has become overwhelmingly complicated.

Categorical grant programs to state and local governments now number over 500. More than 50 federal agencies are involved in administering assistance programs to states and local communities. There are now 59 "cross-cutting" requirements which apply national goals and values to the assistance programs of two or more agencies.

In addition to the problems generated by the sheer size of the system, a "crisis of confidence and competence" permeates federal assistance, according to a recent study by the Advisory Commission on Intergovernmental Relations. The study pointed to poor performance and inadequate results, excessive cost and waste, and lack of adequate control and responsiveness.

A determination to improve the system has often been voiced by political leaders, but to no avail. In truth, it is hard to imagine a more difficult task. The federal assistance structure has become the new form of political patronage, and as a result there can be no hope for significant improvement in the absence of a firm commitment from the President and the Congress.

The difficult and long-term nature of the task is apparent when one realizes that change in the most critical areas would require legislative action. A serious beginning would require a focus and pressure point—a dedicated staff with sufficient authority and resources, and with the requisite leadership and functional abilities.

The Office of Management and Budget has had an intergovernmental affairs staff for some time, but this staff is at a relatively low level in the organizational hierarchy and lacks the necessary mandate and resources. The Federal Assistance Administration Staff that we propose would represent a new beginning. It would elevate the status of the present unit and expand its staff. It would work cooperatively with federal agencies, recipients, and other involved parties in an ongoing program to simplify the assistance system. It should institute more structured management processes, help to resolve conflicts and problems, and propose needed legislative change.

IMPROVING REGULATORY DECISION-MAKING

Recommendation 11
Systematic procedures should be established in the Office of Management and Budget to enable the President and his advisers to review publicly major proposals for new regulatory rules so that they may (1) consider the proposed rule in relationship to other policy development activities, and (2) provide administration views to the rule-making agency.

A drastic increase in regulatory activity has occurred in recent years in such areas as health, safety, and the environment. Moreover, congressional enactments often leave substantial discretion to the implementing agency, to the extent that some crucial issues are resolved not in the development of the legislation, but instead in the preparation of the implementing regulations.

We are aware that substantial controversy exists over whether Presidents have the authority to overrule the decisions of regulatory bodies or to participate in regulatory decision-making outside of the public comment process. These are matters of deep constitutional concern that are now before the courts and about which it would be inappropriate for us to comment.

As a practical matter, a President is not in control of the independent regulatory agencies, even though he may popularly be held accountable for their actions. His main power is twofold: (1) he makes the initial nomination of a regulatory commissioner, and (2) he is able to inform the public of his views on general regulatory problems and, where appropriate, to seek corrective legislation. Presidents are well-advised to limit themselves to this public comment role, for any behind-the-scenes attempt to intervene on a specific issue before a regulatory agency is understandably seen as an attempt to exert inappropriate presidential control.

The fact is, however, that Presidents are at present poorly equipped to offer a coherent public response or to play a broad educational role in the regulatory process. Historically, the Executive Office and agency heads have not commented in a systematic manner on the development and issuance of government regulation. However, we believe that the increased scope and changing character of regulatory activities now require this pattern to change, and that a systematic mechanism must be established to respond to major regulatory proposals involving important policy issues. The President, as the principal integrating force in our system of government, must play an important role in this regard.

Some significant steps have already been taken in this direction: the establishment of the Inflation Impact Statement process under President Ford, and the issuance of Executive Order 12044 establishing improved regulatory decision-making processes under President Carter. However, despite these steps the presidential role in regulatory decision-making remains ill-defined and the institutional support for that role poorly developed. As a result, presidential involvement tends to be ad hoc and unsystematic.

To remedy this, we recommend the establishment of a systematic process, modeled on the legislative clearance process conducted by the Office of Management and Budget for many years, to assist in the formulation of administration views on major regulations involving significant policy issues. This process would be coordinated by a special staff within the Office of Management and Budget and would allow the Executive Office and interested agencies to review major proposed regulatory rules. The administration would thus be able to prepare coordinated and informed comments on the proposed rule's effect on other regulatory goals and other government policies. Although OMB would coordinate the preparation of administration views, the affected agencies would have responsibility for analyzing the proposal and preparing the comments.

It is not our intention to suggest that the Executive Office should review all proposed regulations, or that Presidents should assume the rule-making authorities now vested in the agencies. Nor is it our intent to short-circuit the procedural safeguards built into the regulatory process or to encourage the injection of unwarranted considerations into regulatory decision-making. The objective of this recommendation is simply to provide a systematic, manageable structure through which presidential efforts can be made to relate regulatory decision-making to other policies.

We believe that, if implemented, this recommendation could help to avert constitutional confrontations among Presidents, Congress, and regulatory agencies. We also believe that it would provide a suitable response to the substantial pressures that now exist for more detailed White House participation in regulatory policy-making.

CONCLUSION

The five recommendations in this chapter all deal with major managerial processes or problems; all entail a sustained effort; and all pertain in one way or another to OMB.

We believe there are important dividends to be gained from placing all these functions within the Office of Management and Budget, rather than creating additional independent staffs reporting to the President. The five functions we have discussed have much in common with others currently existing in OMB. All would require a high degree of managerial skill and sustained effort, and for these and other reasons could be mutually reinforcing if housed within the same agency. Furthermore, momentum would be given to an agency that has been an invaluable resource to Presidents, and a step would be taken to strengthen the professionalism, continuity, and neutral competence that characterized its activities.

In such a restructuring of the Office of Management and Budget, the question of balance should be carefully considered so that the budget process does not dominate the other functions. The variety of functions within OMB and the high level at which many of them must be performed suggest a more horizontal type of structure than the present one. Major functions should be structured to have an independent identity, yet they must be related to one another so that mutual reinforcement and interchange occur. With regard to this point, it is important to note that the value of OMB as an information source does not derive from any one function, but from them all—indeed, from the interactions among them.

In our recommendation on program evaluation, we noted that it logically falls under the "umbrella" of administrative management. The federal assistance and regulatory review functions we have recommended could also be placed within an Administrative Management Division. Again, the specific organizational structure that might be devised is of less concern than the fact that all three functions are granted sufficient authority, resources, and support to perform effectively.

Chapter V

THE PRESIDENT, DEPARTMENTS, AND EXECUTIVE AGENCIES

Our discussion of a strategy for change has thus far focused on the Executive Office of the President, and the need for improved policy coordination and central managerial processes. To make these recommendations effective and to improve governmental performance generally, related and reciprocal change must occur in the executive departments and agencies.

In seeking an improvement in the performance of line agencies, one encounters a host of difficult problems. To a very considerable extent, the agencies represent the battleground on which many of the struggles between the President and the Congress are waged. In formal terms, the Congress is the source of all executive authority unless the Constitution specifies otherwise, which it does in only a relatively few cases. The power of Congress rests on its power to make basic law—that is, its power to create, change, or terminate programs; to specify the administrative arrangements to be employed; and to provide the funds needed to carry them out.

Against this legislative power are ranged the President's broad and unspecific mandate of executive power, his strong powers of appointment and veto, and his formidable base of informal power that rests on the stature and prestige of his office.

This separation and sharing of power between Congress and the President has made for a turbulent and divisive relationship. One effect is that those political appointees chosen by the President to head the executive agencies frequently find themselves in an ambiguous situation: They are accountable to the Congress for their authority, funds, and performance, but they are also accountable to the President who appointed them, who sets the general policy framework in which they must work, and who is responsible for see-

ing that the laws are faithfully executed.

Another barrier to agency improvement is the difference in the rate of turnover for political appointees as compared with career personnel. Several recent studies have shown that the average tenure of presidential appointees (from the level of assistant secretary on up) is about two years. In contrast, career employees generally have long terms of office, often running into decades, in the same organization. This difference in tenure makes it difficult for the two groups to work together. If agency heads, aware that their term of office will probably be short, press too rapidly for change, they are likely to meet strong resistance; if they move too slowly, they are likely to be regarded as captives of their own bureaucracy.

A further complicating factor is the organizational structure of the executive branch. As government has grown, it has tended to create new agencies rather than to consolidate and broaden the mandate of existing agencies. The result is a confusing array of departments, administrations, agencies, and so on, and such consequent weaknesses as narrow perspectives, overlaps and redundancies, inadequate commitment to collaboration, and disparities in administrative standards and performance. These weaknesses are exacerbated by the lack of strong central administrative management services, as discussed in the preceding chapter.

Some of these factors are not likely to change at all—for instance, the basic division of powers between President and Congress—while others will alter only very slowly. We do not mean to indicate in any way that the situation is hopeless, but only that some boundaries are relatively fixed. Their effects can be diluted, and other improvements can be made, through changed attitudes, relationships, processes, and administrative policies. We are particularly mindful of two of the principles central to this report: (1) to the greatest extent possible, operational responsibilities must be moved away from the Executive Office and given to the line agencies, and (2) the capability of the President to intervene selectively must be recognized and improved. Both of these principles must be acted on in ways that will bring greater coherence to government and improve administrative performance.

These related principles address a practical problem—the impossibility of the Executive Office to concern itself with more than a fraction of executive branch activity. A President who attempts to manage the details of government from the center dooms himself to frustration and an image of ineffectiveness. Such a President will undermine the administrative viability of the federal establishment and the prevailing mechanisms of accountability.

We believe that our recommendations in the previous two chapters for new and realigned staff resources in the Executive Office offer a strong foundation for the resolution of these problems. They are buttressed by the five recommendations contained in this chapter for corresponding changes in the executive departments and agencies.

IMPROVING THE QUALITY OF THE GOVERNMENT'S EXECUTIVES AND MANAGERS

Recommendation 12

The primary orientation of top political and career appointees to executive positions should be to bring the governmentwide perspective of the Presidency to bear on substantive matters within their jurisdiction. To accomplish this, far greater weight should be given in recruitment and promotion to substantive and managerial competence.

Presidential appointees to key executive posts frequently find themselves at the center of a four-way tug-of-war involving the White House, congressional subcommittees, agency personnel, and special-interest groups. At issue is the question of whether the appointee is primarily the President's representative to the agency, or vice versa. Failure to clarify this relationship and resolve the dilemma has in large part caused the erosion in the role of agency executives and the shifting of decision-making to the Executive Office.

We believe that agency heads and key politically appointed subordinates must function pri-

marily as agents of the President. They are appointed and can be removed by him, and they must be responsible for carrying out his policies and his program as broadly conceived. This statement is not meant to suggest that agency heads can ignore the other forces in the tug-of-war, but rather that their basic perspective and orientation must be clarified and communicated to all of the forces involved. Without this common understanding of the agency head's role, the tendency for decision-making responsibilities to gravitate from the agencies to the Executive Office cannot be reversed. And in the long run, this tendency will seriously undermine the President's role as chief executive.

There is wide support for this definition of the agency head's role; the problem is not so much supporting it in theory as affirming it in practice. Many steps can be taken to make such an affirmation; two possible ones relate to practices in the Executive Office. First, agency heads must be an integral part of any presidential decision affecting their agencies and must be at the center of the flow of information and advice from constituent units of their agency to the Executive Office. If an agency head is not in such a position, his authority and effectiveness will be quickly eroded and his or her ability to represent the President's program rapidly destroyed. There may be short-term advantages for Executive Office personnel in bypassing the agency head, but the long-term consequences are almost always destructive.

The second requisite is that the responsibility for selecting key subordinates of the agency head must be shared by the agency head and the President. Agency heads cannot operate as responsible managers if they are surrounded by subordinates who owe their positions—and hence their loyalties—to others. By the same token, however, Presidents are likely to have greater confidence in the management team of an agency if they have participated in the selection of that team.

Even with the most cooperative and mutually supportive relationships between the White House and agency heads, however, all our recommendations will fail unless highly qualified and competent persons are recruited or promoted to top career and political positions throughout government. The complexities of government today require a shift in the criteria by which key personnel are selected. Demonstrated party or personal loyalty and support are not sufficient to warrant appointment. Substantive knowledge and experience in administration and management must also be a part of the selection test for appointment to the top levels of government. Key appointments must reflect greater appreciation of this fundamental truth.

INTERAGENCY COLLABORATION

Recommendation 13

Agency heads should actively support and cooperate with collaborative processes of decision-making involving the Executive Office and one another.

As we have repeatedly stressed in this report, the most important issues confronting government today are interrelated and cut across the conventional boundaries of agencies and functions. If agency heads enter the process of joint decision-making as narrow advocates for their agency's position rather than as promoters of cross-cutting presidential perspectives, then more detailed Executive Office involvement will inevitably occur. We believe it is imperative that exactly the reverse occur—that the President place increasing reliance on agency heads for policy leadership and program implementation. For such to occur, agency heads must participate in collaborative processes of decision-making in an active and cooperative way.

As an aid in this regard, we urge the increased use of "disappearing" task forces composed of agency and Executive Office personnel as a management device to formulate and execute policy in areas that involve cross-cutting concerns. These task forces comprising ad hoc groupings of agency personnel organized to deal with a particular policy problem or to "staff out" a particular presidential decision, can quickly be disbanded at the conclusion of their work. They would thus form a more flexible alternative to statutory interagency committees. The staffing reforms for the Executive Office suggested in Chapter III should facilitate this arrangement.

To the extent that such task forces had clear goals, a definite timetable, and basic consensus on the boundaries of ultimate decisions, they would provide an effective vehicle for the collaborative, interdependent decision-making that current circumstances increasingly require.

EFFECTIVE USE OF THE SENIOR EXECUTIVE SERVICE

Recommendation 14

Agency heads should make effective use of the Senior Executive Service.

In creating the Senior Executive Service, the Civil Service Reform Act of 1978 opened new opportunities for improving the staffing patterns of federal executive agencies. Typically, those in the higher civil service positions have made their careers in individual agencies and bureaus, with little or no mobility between agencies or from the agencies to the Executive Office. This lack of mobility has in many cases bred a tendency toward insularity and a protective attitude which stands in the way of effective decentralization and coordinated decision-making. Many top career officials have come to identify their loyalties with the agency or bureau rather than with the Presidency or the executive branch in general.

The establishment of a corps of Senior Executives who have voluntarily surrendered their rights to a particular job and accepted a performance-based reward system has made changes possible in this parochial staffing pattern and encouraged mobility among agency and Executive Office positions.

The Senior Executive Service clearly has the potential to add a vital and productive alternative to the short tenure of presidential appointees and the long tenure of those protected by civil service rules. Senior Executives can represent new perspectives drawn from previous experience within and outside of government. Yet most Senior Executives are career people, and thus retain a kinship with other career employees. Those in the Senior Executive Service represent both mobility and continuity—mobility from the point of view of the President and his appointees, continuity from the point of view of the government in general and agencies and their personnel in particular.

If effective use is to be made of the Senior Executive Service, it must be constituted as a governmentwide "pool" of talent, as a career service within a larger career service. This can only happen if the Office of Personnel Management creates a mechanism for greater flexibility in interagency assignments. Without such a mechanism, the overwhelming tendency will be for agencies to keep their best people, thus tending to lock Senior Executive Service members into their jobs.

The Senior Executive Service is new and relatively untested. Whether its potential benefits are realized will depend on the facilitative measures taken by the Office of Personnel Management and on the support given to and use made of the Senior Executive Service by the Executive Office and the line agencies. The extent to which younger careerists aspire to the Senior Executive

Service as the pinnacle of their careers will depend on the use made of it in the next few years.

STRENGTHENING AGENCY MANAGEMENT

Recommendation 15

Executive agencies should take concrete steps to improve internal management, particularly in reference to proposed changes in the Executive Office of the President.

Each executive agency should undertake changes in its own policy development and administrative management processes to take full advantage of new capabilities in the Executive Office.

Obviously, an injunction to agencies to improve their performance is hopelessly generalized and can have specific meaning only when individual agency prescriptions are included that are based on a close analysis covering a wide range of possible subjects. What we are suggesting here is that agencies must participate in a broad process of change that involves internal improvements related to the enhanced capabilities of the Executive Office. For example, large agencies should establish their own secretariat function modeled on the White House Secretariat we proposed in Chapter III.

For a wide range of managerial practices and functions, in all executive agencies, the enhanced administrative management capability of the Office of Management and Budget would constitute a major resource in achieving higher standards of performance. Similarly, the existence of a Program Evaluation Staff in the Office of Management and Budget would provide standards and methodologies and assistance in developing this vital managerial function.

The suggestions offered here do not speak to all the changes needed to upgrade and strengthen the executive agencies as policy-making and management units of government. What is important is not a comprehensive list of changes, but the full participation in and commitment to a broad strategy of change by all agencies, with provisions for adequate communication and staff development, training, and linkages to networks of in-

formation and assistance. In the absence of these, the effectiveness of government and the successful operation of the Presidency cannot be ensured.

STRENGTHENING REORGANIZATION POWERS

Recommendation 16

To promote greater coherence and effectiveness in government, the President should be granted permanent reorganization authority by the Congress, subject only to a two-house veto.

Although the value of government reorganization is often exaggerated, there is a clear need for a rational restructuring and reordering of functions in the executive branch as a whole, and for a streamlining of agencies and their programs.

For more than 40 years, the Congress appears to have recognized its own limitations in bringing order to the executive branch, and has granted the President a measure of reorganization authority, subject to a "negative option." That is, Congress does not have the power to take positive action to approve a reorganization, but has the power to take negative action—a veto power—within a specified period after the issuance of a presidential reorganization plan. This authority provides a President with a more efficient way to bring about reorganization than would a requirement for new legislation in each case. Yet this authority has always been limited; it has always been in force for only a temporary, specified period, and it has occasionally lapsed entirely. Several times, the extension deadline has provoked bitter controversy between the two branches.

Given the complexity of the executive branch, we believe the time has come for Congress to strengthen the President's reorganization authority. The autority should be made permanent, with specific reorganization plans being overruled only when *both* houses take negative action. At the same time, it should be made clear that no arbitrary power was being placed in the President's hands. The Congress would retain its prerogatives and protections against an abuse of power and would remain able to reject any unacceptable plan.

Chapter VI

APPROACHES TO PRESIDENTIAL MANAGEMENT

As important as efficient machinery of government is an understanding of how to use the apparatus. Such an understanding is important not only to Presidents and their staffs, but also to an informed public in evaluating White House performance and in distinguishing the use of government machinery from its misuse.

Much attention has been paid to the need to allow flexibility to the President in the running of his office. Equal attention has not, however, been paid to how Presidents must accommodate themselves to the necessities of government. Presidents should, and do, have considerable freedom in how they choose to manage, but they cannot be freed from the consequences of their choices. There are guidelines for effective management that are relevant to any President whatever his approach, and regardless of whether or not our proposed framework for central staffing is accepted.

MANAGEMENT BY INADVERTENCE

Just as there is an informal, unwritten aspect to our Constitution, so too is there an unwritten management system within which Presidents operate. *Whatever the formal machinery, a President by his own actions and by others' anticipations of his actions creates in major part this de facto system.* Such de facto systems tend to arise around all offices of authority, but the powers and visibility of the Presidency heighten this tendency, and the gravity of the office increases its significance. No past experience can ever fully prepare a new President for this phenomenon.

Presidential candidates and their staffs spend the bulk of their time trying to accommodate themselves to a stream of demands and activities created by others—the primary schedule, fund raising, interest-group demands. Although similar pressures continue once the candidate assumes office, as President he is quickly faced with another dynamic: vast numbers of watchful people now try to accommodate themselves to the way in which he works. In this environment it is extraordinarily easy for a President to unintentionally create a management system that suits his immediate convenience but not his or the government's longer term interests.

A President creates his management organization by deciding whom to consult, and whom to be seen consulting; by how he orders his time; by where he bestows trust; and by how he polices those in his confidence. A President may imagine he is acting only on the matter at hand, but he is also shaping the anticipations of others and thereby reaffirming, amending, undercutting, or rendering incomprehensible his management system. Those whose anticipations are so shaped include not only internal White House staff, but also the core units of the Executive Office, department heads, Congressmen, the media, and interest-group representatives—all play a part in presidential management.

One great danger in this situation is that a new President will, without reflection, carry over familiar arrangements into the Presidency simply because they are familiar. Even the most well-tried of the arrangements used by a new President in his past career are likely to need to be adapted to the larger arena of the Presidency. And no one but the President—by his behavior as well as his instructions—can make the necessary adjustments. This responsibility remains the President's even if he chooses a chief of staff, for only the President, it is important to emphasize, is in a position to keep the staff chief in his proper role.

Campaigns and Transitions

The changing nature of the presidential selection process has increased the likelihood that a new president will simply bring to the office those management arrangements he found to work well in the past. Within the last generation, campaigning for the Presidency has become virtually a full-time occupation, and each candidate has his own complicated staffing arrangements. In these circumstances, it is a great temptation for the candidate to continue these arrangements once he is elected. His White House aides are then close at hand, highly dependent on him, and familiar from campaign days. They are also likely to have created a feeling of obligation on the President's part for their past services, and without a deliberate presidential effort to offset this tendency, it is easy for their views and staff work to acquire undue prominence.

The transition into office is a period during which many of the most far-reaching arrangements for presidential management are made—some inadvertently. Procedures for the formal transfer of power—a period encompassing the first month or two of any new administration—have become increasingly regularized and sophisticated, and by and large this formal transition has worked well in the recent past. It is rather the informal, more extended transition that occurs in a President's first year which produces some of the greatest difficulties.

During the short, formal transition the new President, whether or not he realizes it, is engaged in meeting other people's needs. Congress, the media, and others expect a legislative program in the first "hundred days"; budget revisions to carry out campaign promises must be prepared within weeks; hundreds of presidential appointments to the government are expected. In short, a host of substantive decisions are made, both supported by and helping to fashion a de facto management process that has probably been given little forethought. It is after these first few months—in the longer transition process—that Presidents begin to pay the price for not having taken the time to consider the processes of management as well as the substance of policy.

There is little evidence that new Presidents are in general confronted by such pressing policy issues that time is unavailable for a careful review of management arrangements. There is, however, much evidence that acquiescing to a rush for ad hoc decisions has severe costs. Except in grave national emergencies, a new or reelected President would be well advised to resist pressures to do everything at once. Instead, time should be taken to learn about and shape government processes and find a longer term strategy against which to test the pressures of the moment.

The staffing recommendations made in Chapter III of this report could provide some resources to help a President come to grips with government processes during the transition period. In the end, however, one cannot avoid the fact that only the President can manage the Presidency. *A President must try to see the general in the particular, and the effect of each of his actions on the ongoing management processes and relations of government.*

Congressmen and Cabinets

A long range management view is vital in presidential relations with Congress and the Cabinet.

No matter what their party affiliations, Presidents and the elected leadership of Congress share a critical responsibility for making the government work effectively. The fragmentation of Congress and our other political institutions has made it imperative for Presidents to exercise a broad vision in the management of issues. By their day-to-day actions, the President and his staff can undercut or can strengthen congressional leadership. In his relations with Congress, a President can become so preoccupied with immediate needs for decision-making that he is oblivious to the effects of his actions on the larger workings of the Congress. He may also be tempted to adopt a "divide and conquer" strategy with Congress in view of the short-term advantages this might yield. However, in the long run such a strategy may result in an even more chaotic and unreliable Congress with which he must bargain. In the interests of longer term political management, a President is better advised to search out and consult with potential allies in those parts of Congress that are likely to have an integrating, government-wide perspective. In this regard, he should give special attention and serious consideration to the views of the elected leadership of Congress and to ranking members of congressional budget committees and other major committees.

This is not to deny that confrontations between President and Congress will occur, even when the two branches are controlled by the same party. In fact, depending in part on how well a President helps congressional leadership define the issues, confrontations can help to clarify major public choices. Moreover, even in a public confrontation between the White House and Congress, a President who has invested time in supporting congressional leadership will find he has created relations that can help the necessary work of government to proceed quietly.

As with Congress, a President's methods of operation can help to unite, or can further fragment, the Cabinet. Unfortunately, most new administrations raise false expectations by announcing that the new President, unlike his predecessors, is going to govern through his Cabinet.

A more realistic approach recognizes that the Cabinet—a collection of department heads with diverse concerns—is not an instrument for collective decisionmaking. Instead, the President's relationship with his Cabinet members and other agency heads can be extremely valuable as a communication device, in both directions. Personal contact between the President and these top officers of the executive branch can allow the President to convey his overall philosophy of government, and to receive their confidential advice, in a way that no impersonal arrangements can. With or without specific decisions, meetings between the Cabinet and President can help to ensure that each member, in the presence of all, knows the position of the entire administration. Cabinet officers who are known not to have access to the President and his thinking are gravely weakened in all their governmental and legislative relations.

Ultimately, the President must ensure that attention is given both to (1) the substantive issues at hand, and (2) how a given presidential action will enhance or diminish the positions of accountable legislative and departmental leaders and their effectiveness in future bargaining sessions.

MANAGING PRESIDENTIAL STAFFS

The Presidency is a demanding combination of personal and institutional activity. Although the Executive Office must serve the needs of the President of the day, its organization must be equally able to evolve to serve the needs of succeeding Presidents. The White House is not a President's personal property, nor is it simply a prize at the end of an electoral contest, however hard fought. Each President holds office as a national trust. Hence a President must, in viewing changes in central staffing, be mindful not only of his immediate concerns but also of the nature of the office to be handed on to successors.

White House Aides and Department Executives

By the nature of their jobs, personal White House assistants have to speak for the President.

They are close at hand, dependent on him, and ready to serve his every immediate need. They are responsive to the President as is no one else with whom he deals. There is thus an understandable temptation for a President to attempt to administer government affairs through his White House aides. It is a destructive temptation.

As we have noted previously, under our "unwritten" constitution, a President can retain discretion in running his office only if the White House abstains from taking over the work of the executive departments and agencies. If these operating responsibilities are drawn into the White House, Congress will inevitably insist on overseeing the work of the presidential staff so as to hold them accountable. Moreover, no matter how available and responsive White House assistants may seem to a President, he must realize that the experience and detailed knowledge to turn his intentions into administrative realities reside within the departments and agencies, and not with his aides.

The President must therefore ensure that the White House staff does not usurp the duties of the agency and department heads, the men and women who have been entrusted by Congress with carrying out the laws. The most effective way he can do this is not by issuing formal instructions; it is through the management system created by his own behavior. If the President does not share his thinking with departmental executives, power will shift to the White House staff.

It follows that *a President can most effectively keep his own staff functioning legitimately—as staff, and not as executives—if he develops a close, confidential relationship with top appointees in the departments and agencies.* Unfortunately, most departmental appointments occur under the hurried pressures of the first two months of an administration, with little opportunity for testing working relationships. Even more rare are serious, in-depth consultations between the President and departmental and agency executives.

No neat formula can be given to remedy this situation. The point to emphasize is that, one way or another, ongoing relations with these executives are among the most essential of a President's regular duties. This relationship seems undramatic, but it is decisive both in the operation of the government and in maintaining the proper restraint within the White House staff.

Institutional Staff

Institutional offices—the core units in the Executive Office of the President—must be redirected with every change in administration. However, they must also retain their integrity as institutions of the Presidency. Persons appointed to these staff positions must in consequence serve to bridge the personal political interests of the President and the institutional life of the Presidency. *These top Executive Office appointees must be sensitive to the President as an individual, but must also be sensitive to the operation of continuing staff institutions of the Presidency.* It is an extremely difficult combination to sustain, and one that calls for care in making appointments to these positions.

What should a President expect from these institutional units? That is, what should a President try to impose on the system of central staffing through his de facto management process? What is needed is not one fixed, immutable method of operation for all circumstances, but a steady standard of conduct that will put the daily emergencies in perspective.

A President should discipline his core institutional units to provide such information and advice as does not arise through the natural operation of the other pressures around him. Inasmuch as staff members in the White House are extraordinarily sensitive to his immediate interests, the institutional units of the Presidency should act to draw attention to the longer term political and administrative interests of the President. Because almost every other pressure around him encourages the President toward ad hoc, unrelated decisions, the institutional units should provide cautions based on past experience and potential precedents.

To fulfill their role, institutional staff must perform three not entirely compatible functions. First the staff must be, and must be seen to be, facilitators who manage a deliberative process that gives a fair hearing to all sides. Second, they must be presidential representatives, ensuring that consultation and interdepartmental work bring forth proposals with a governmentwide—rather than simply departmental—perspective. Third, they must be sufficiently knowledgeable to offer substantive advice to the President when this seems necessary. Departmental operating duties often produce too narrow a frame of reference to be the only source of advice to Presidents, and institutional staff members therefore have a duty to speak their minds to Presidents.

No person or staff unit can perform all these services in perfect combination. The President, however, must expect the personnel of the Executive Office to try to do so. He must insist that their honest brokerage function does not pas-

sively produce the lowest common denominator of departmental agreement. Hearing their substantive advice, he must be sure that their privileged access has not denied a fair hearing to others. The President must be "unreasonable" enough to demand that they represent his interests, but not entangle him in and commit him to the outcome of interdepartmental or other consultation except when he so chooses.

It is in the President's political interest to have, and by his own behavior to sustain, these institutional services. If a President does not know he needs these services, if he does not use them, if he does not complain when they are not forthcoming, then no one else can.

MAINTAINING PERSPECTIVE

Many people, although they may not like the man, need the President. The inevitable contradictions between what these people need and what the President needs create the basic dilemmas in managing the Presidency.

On the one hand, departments and agencies need the President as a reliable referee in their disagreements, and as a protector and advocate of their position before Congress and the people. The President, on the other hand, needs to be selective and flexible in his involvements, and requires early warnings of agency and departmental problems and access to detail at his own discretion. To the degree that the President does not satisfy departmental needs, he builds resentment, possibly disloyalty, and certainly incentives to bypass him in favor of Congress. In failing to satisfy these needs, the President can erect enormous constraints to his own leadership.

A similar relationship exists between the President and the increasingly powerful news media. The media need newsworthy stories, preferably with a White House backdrop. The media need presidential statements, controversy, favored access to White House aides, or at least a steady stream of handouts in the President's press room. The President needs the media, but he also needs private deliberations, discretion as to when to appear in the news, and an administration that appears to be cohesive. Hence the chain of mutual dependence and mutual disadvantage continues unbroken.

Similar dilemmas face the President in his dealings with Congress. To do its work, the Congress relies on a steady stream of proposals and positions from the President. Although members of

Congress wish to have private advance consultations with the executive, they will also attack advance understandings when it suits their interests. Congressional committees and subcommittees attain influence through an involvement in administrative details and management, yet they also gain notice by criticizing the executive for failing to take charge of the bureaucracy and run it in a businesslike manner. Presidents for their part clearly need Congress, but they also need to protect themselves by not producing the steady stream of proposals and positions on every subject that Congress might desire. Presidents need privacy in their deliberations to obtain a free airing of views, and they need to consult partners who can be counted on to keep secrets and bargains.

There is no way to resolve these and similar dilemmas. The media, departments, and Congress —the President's need of them and their disadvantages to him—are realities which any President must accept.

A President does, however, have choices as to how he integrates these realities with his conduct and decisions. Because he cannot meet every need of Congress, the bureaucracy, or the media, the President must calculate the cost of not meeting a specific need, and then make whatever appropriate compensation he can. In assessing the general implications of his decisions, a President will face choices concerning:

- *Immediate advantage versus longer term relations.* Does a particular action build or cripple ongoing relations with other power centers in Congress, the departments, the media, and elsewhere?

- *Presidential activism versus departmental responsibility.* Which questions to the government will the President answer, and which will he and the White House refer to the appropriate department or others?

- *Secrecy versus consultation.* Which issues will not be discussed because they are still in the decision process, and when do the rewards of wider consultation outweigh the risks of premature disclosure?

If the President is aware of these and other choices, he can at least in some degree weigh the broader effects of his actions and take corrective measures. For example, if a President overrides the needs of departmental bureaucracies, his relations with the bureaucracy may be soured and departmental reliance on congressional subcommittees may increase. Yet he may be able to compensate by providing an explanation of his actions to those who have been overturned, or by demonstrating that his failure to meet their needs was an exceptional circumstance. Likewise, in meeting the media's need for presidential statements, the President should recognize that, given the media's time pressures, he will likely be relying more on his immediate White House aides than on department heads and that he will be attracting new problems into the White House. He may be able to compensate by redoubling efforts to give background briefings to the departments as well as to the media.

As the Presidency now operates, managerial dilemmas appear before the President in an asymmetrical way. All the pressures encourage a presidential preoccupation with short-term power—the immediate power of making decisions. The problem is that *in yielding to the pressures of short-term power, a President is likely to lose long-term influence.* Our recommendations have therefore emphasized the Presidency's need for improved institutional advice.

The media, Congress, interest groups, and the President's own staff all have an intense interest in generating and reworking presidential decisions. Yielding to this tendency leaves the President publicly responsible for everything and with no opportunity for reflection and second thoughts. It is possible for a President to excel in weighing the pros and cons of each policy option, and yet have little continuing influence on the larger processes and working relationships of government. Most of a President's acts of decision are probably of far less importance than the way in which he works through others to meet the nation's needs. That, after all, is the real meaning of presidential management.

Chapter VII

THE UNFINISHED AGENDA

The recommendations and comments we have presented in this report are based on the conviction that a presidency improved to more effectively manage the federal government is an essential step in strengthening the nation's larger capacity for self-government. We need not simply a Presidency, but a complete process of democratic government, that is fit to meet the challenges of the 1980s and beyond. This Panel believes the following major topics deserve further study:

1. Congressional organization and management: Attention should be given to the overlapping and competing jurisdictions of committees, subcommittees, and staffs; the growing tendency of Congress to attend to minor details of administration at the expense of longer range basic problems or policies; the increasing use of annual authorizations and of legislative vetoes; and the means of strengthening leadership and party cohesion within Congress.

2. Judicial administration: In part because of weaknesses in other areas of our political system, the courts have undertaken an active role in the interpretation of public policy and the application of redress through administrative directives. The cumulative effect on public management of these actions—usually taken on a case-by-case basis without a consideration of larger ramifications—deserves careful study.

3. The election and nominating process: Numerous questions have been raised about such matters as the effectiveness of the primary process; the length of the nominating and election campaigns; public and other financing of such campaigns; the merits of altering terms of office for Congress and the Presidency; and the role of

the media in shaping the political selection process.

4. The modern role of political parties and other forms of mass participation: A decline in the political organizing power of parties and a concomitant increase in both the number and the strengh of special-interest and "non partisan" groups have aroused concern. These shifts have apparently weakened the centripetal influence of the President, the Congress, and state and local government leaders.

5. Public access to and communication with the government: At issue here are the uses, abuses, freedoms, and responsibilities of the media and of the President in relation to the media; devices for citizen participation in the making and administration of public policy; freedom of information; the protection of personal privacy and secrecy, particularly in national security affairs; and executive privilege.

6. The role of the Vice President: The selection of the Vice President and the delineation of his responsibilities have largely been left a matter of presidential choice. Whether this situation should continue, whether the Vice President's responsibilities should be prescribed, or whether the office should in fact be substantially changed are questions of legitimate concern.

7. The management of federalism: Attention should be given to restructuring the entire grant system; and to better defining the relations and the division of functions among federal, state and local governments.

This Panel believes these subjects deserve serious, objective study by responsible groups. A federal commission on the processes of government, as proposed in Congress, could be one such group.

The basic goal in reviewing our democratic institutions should be to bring greater coherence and integration to the workings of government. By assigning powers among the three branches, the Constitution ensured that this nation would *not* have a single political center in a structural sense. This sharing of power was designed to protect citizens from arbitrary power and from the tyranny of the majority, and thus special safeguards were provided for individual rights and for the views of minorities and special interests.

The challenge facing Americans in the 1980s is whether we can preserve those values and at the same time realize our collective national interests. Formal legal changes, as expressed in statutes and congressional resolutions or in executive orders and reorganization plans, can help us attain this goal. But ultimately, we can reconcile our individual and collective interests only if all concerned—not only responsible members of the three branches of government, but also the media and the public—reach a better understanding of the proper roles and responsibilities of our political institutions in making such a reconciliation.

As a first step in this direction, we must reduce the over-emphasis on the constitutional separation of powers, and acknowledge that in all major issues of policy and management the President and the Congress are *jointly* involved in the direction and control of departments and agencies. If coordination were increased both within and between the branches, neither would lose, but rather would gain in control over divisive forces.

We do not feel our attitude is an overly optimistic one. We recognize that political confrontations in a democracy are inevitable. But they must not be so pervasive and continuous as to paralyze government action. There *is* a commonality of purpose among our people: What unites us is greater than what divides us. If our political institutions operate so as to reflect that fact, then both our individual liberties and our collective strength will prosper.

BIOGRAPHICAL SKETCHES OF PANEL MEMBERS

(Appendix A)

Co-Chairmen:

Don K. Price, professor emeritus at Harvard University, was dean of the Kennedy School of Government for 19 years. Previously he headed the government organization branch of the Bureau of the Budget; served as deputy chairman of the research and development board at the Department of Defense; and served as assistant to the chairman of the first Hoover Commission.

Rocco C. Siciliano is chairman and chief executive of TICOR, a Los Angeles-based financial services company. He has had a legal career as well as experience in the federal government, including the position of assistant secretary of the Department of Labor, special assistant to President Eisenhower for personnel management, and later as Under Secretary of Commerce. He served on the Federal Pay Board, the California Commission on Government Reform, and other advisory bodies.

Panel:

David E. Bell is vice president of the Ford Foundation for international activities. He has served as director of the Bureau of the Budget; administrator of the Agency for International Development; and administrative assistant to the President.

Fletcher L. Byrom is chairman and chief executive officer of Koppers Co., Inc. In addition to his work on corporate and philanthropic boards, Byrom serves as chairman of the Committee for Economic Development.

Lisle C. Carter is president of the University of the District of Columbia. He previously served in a number of academic positions, including that of chancellor of the Atlanta University Center, and in several high-level government positions.

William T. Coleman, Jr. is an attorney in Washington, D.C., with significant experience at federal and local levels of government. He serves on a variety of corporate boards and has served as Secretary of Transportation and as a staff member of the Warren Commission.

Alan L. Dean is chairman of the board of trustees of the National Academy of Public Administration and a part-time consultant and lecturer. He has held a number of high federal posts, including assistant secretary of the Department of Transportation, deputy assistant director of the Office of Management and Budget, and vice president of the United States Railway Association.

Thomas R. Donahue is secretary-treasurer of the AFL-CIO. Along with his prior positions with the Service Employees International Union, Donahue has served as assistant secretary of the Department of Labor.

Daniel J. Evans is president of Evergreen State College in Washington. Following his education as a civil engineer, Evans served in a variety of elected positions in Washington, including twelve years as State Governor.

Andrew J. Goodpaster serves as superintendent of the U.S. Military Academy at West Point. His military career included assignments as assistant to the chairman of the Joint Chiefs of Staff and as supreme allied commander of NATO. He has served as presidential representative on numerous advisory groups on strategy, security, international affairs, and management.

James D. Hodgson is a corporate director in Los Angeles. In addition to a long career in business, Hodgson has served as Secretary of Labor and as Ambassador to Japan.

Dwight A. Ink is vice president of the National Consumer Cooperative Bank. During his government career, Ink held top management positions with the Atomic Energy Commission, the Office of Management and Budget, and the Department of Housing and Urban Development, and was deputy administrator of the General Services Administration.

Carol C. Laise served as director general of the U.S. Foreign Service. She was Ambassador to Nepal, assistant secretary of the State Department, and also serves on numerous educational and corporate boards.

Arjay Miller is dean emeritus of the Stanford Graduate School of Business and was president of Ford Motor Co. He is a director of several major corporations and nonprofit organizations and has served on a variety of presidential commissions.

Frank Pace, Jr. is president of the International Executive Service Corps and a director of several major corporations. He has served in a variety of top-level positions both in the federal government, including director of the Bureau of the Budget, and in major corporations.

James H. Rowe, Jr. is an attorney in Washington, D.C. In addition to his legal career, Rowe has served as administrative assistant to the President; in a wide variety of government positions; and on most major government reorganization commissions.

Abraham A. Ribicoff is senior U.S. Senator from Connecticut. He has served extensively in public positions as an elected official (U.S. Congressman, Governor of Connecticut) and as an appointed official (Secretary of Health, Education and Welfare).

Donald Rumsfeld is president of G.D. Searle & Co. He served as director of the Office of Economic Opportunity, director of the Cost of Living Council, Ambassador to NATO, chief of the staff of the White House, Secretary of Defense, and was a member of Congress.

Irving S. Shapiro is chief executive officer and chairman of E.I. duPont de Nemours & Co., Inc. He serves on a variety of corporate boards as well as on the boards of the Conference Board and the Business Roundtable.

Charles B. Stauffacher is a corporate director and was formerly chief executive officer of Field Enterprises. In addition to his business career, he was deputy executive director of the Bureau of the Budget and was deputy director of the Office of Defense Mobilization.

Sydney Stein, Jr. has been an investment counsellor in Chicago, with extensive federal government experience. During World War II, he served as a consultant to the Bureau of the Budget on problems associated with military supplies and international relations. He serves on several educational and advisory boards.

Donald C. Stone is adjunct professor at the School of Urban and Public Affairs, Carnegie Mellon University and dean emeritus of the University of Pittsburgh's Graduate School of Public and International Affairs. He has served in top federal and international administrative positions as well as college and association presidencies.

James L. Sundquist is a senior research fellow at the Brookings Institution. He has served in a variety of government positions, and has written extensively on post-World War II politics and policy-making.

Glenn E. Watts is president of the Communications Workers of America. He serves in a variety of union leadership positions, as well as on a number of government advisory bodies and philanthropic boards.

James E. Webb is an attorney in Washington, D.C. He has served as administrator of the National Aeronautics and Space Administration; director of the Bureau of the Budget; and Under Secretary of State and Treasury.

Arnold Weber is an economist, currently president of the University of Colorado. He was provost of Carnegie Mellon University and professor of economics and public policy. He has served as assistant secretary of the Department of Labor; associate director of the Office of Management and Budget; executive director of the Cost of Living Council; and as special assistant to the President.

LIST OF STAFF MEMBERS

(Appendix B)

Alan Abramson	*Research Assistant*
Richard Barrett	*Consultant*
Elise Butler	*Project Secretary*
I.M. Destler	*Research Contributor*
Scott Ellsworth	*Editorial Consultant*
Louis Fisher	*Research Contributor*
James Galbraith	*Consultant*
John Harr	*Deputy Project Director*
Hugh Heclo	*Research Director*
John Helmer	*Research Contributor*
Phillip Hughes	*Project Director*
Jeffrey Jacobs	*Administrator*
Aileen Laughlin	*Editorial Consultant*
Calvin Mackenzie	*Research Contributor*
Michael McGeary	*Research Assistant*
Frederick Mosher	*Senior Consultant*
Anna Nelson	*Historical Consultant*
Richard Neustadt	*Senior Consultant*
Roger Porter	*Research Contributor*
Lester Salamon	*Scholar-in-Residence*
Allen Schick	*Research Contributor*
Peter Szanton	*Research Contributor*
Elmer Staats	*Adviser*

SUPPORTING ORGANIZATIONS

(Appendix C)

This report was made possible with support from the
following organizations and several anonymous donors:

The Chubb Corporation*	IBM Corporation
Congressional Quarterly, Inc.	Koppers Company, Inc.
Conoco Inc.	L T V Corporation
Dayton Hudson Corporation*	Rockefeller Brothers Fund
Exxon Corporation	Rockefeller Foundation
Field Enterprises Charitable Corporation	Alfred P. Sloan Foundation
Ford Foundation	Sydney Stein, Jr.
General Motors Corporation	TICOR
George Gund Foundation	Union Pacific Corporation

*These corporations provided general support to
the National Academy of Public Administration.

Bernard L. Gladieux and Robert R. Nathan, co-chairmen,
Academy Committee on Financial Development.

Index

About the Book and Editors

The Illusion of Presidential Government
edited by Hugh Heclo and Lester M. Salamon

"Presidential government is an illusion. It is an image that misleads presidents no less than the media and the American public." Thus begins this realistic look at the presidency, in which nine leading presidential scholars examine how and why we are under the illusion of presidential government and ask such questions as: What is the president's actual role? What has happened to his traditional tools of executive leadership? How is the office of the president organized to deal with domestic, economic, and national security affairs? Is federal regulation an area of potential power for the president? And, if "presidential government" is indeed a myth, what can be done to help the presidency play a more effective part in constitutional government?

Each chapter probes a different facet of the image of presidential government by looking at the major operations of the modern presidency—from struggles with Congress for control of administrative detail to problems of managing the economy and national security. The book closes with the final report of the National Academy of Public Administration's Panel on Presidential Management. Not surprisingly, the authors do not always agree; nevertheless, they are united in the view that the managerial role of the president must be seen as a whole—and without illusions.

Hugh Heclo is a professor of government at Harvard University and a former senior fellow at the Brookings Institution. He is author of *A Government of Strangers: Executive Politics in Washington* (1977). **Lester M. Salamon** directs the public management and government studies program at The Urban Institute in Washington, D.C. From 1977 to 1979 he served as deputy associate director of the Office of Management and Budget and before that was an associate professor at Duke University.